Professionalising English Language Teaching

The issue of the professionalisation of English Language Teaching (ELT) remains underexplored in academic discourse. Written by experienced teacher educators, this book presents a timely guide to professional teacher development in ELT, showing how teacher educators and classroom practitioners can develop their practice. It scrutinises key topic areas for teacher education, detailing the specific competences that professional teachers need to demonstrate in the twenty-first century, including transforming English language classrooms, engaging in ongoing debates that examine theory, research, and practice, responding to managerial and policy discourses on English language instruction, and playing a leading role in regulating the entire teaching profession. It highlights how meaningful, impactful, transformative, and sustainable language education requires high-quality teachers who are lifelong learners, classroom ethnographers, and educational leaders. It is essential reading for pre- and in-service teachers, teacher educators, professional development providers, educational researchers, and policymakers in the field of ELT.

ANDRZEJ CIROCKI is Associate Professor in English Language Education at the University of York in the UK and Adjunct Professor in English Language Teaching at Universitas Negeri Surabaya in Indonesia. His recent publications include *Current Perspectives on the TESOL Practicum* (with Madyarov and Baecher, 2019) and *Continuing Professional Development of TESOL Practitioners* (with Farrelly and Buchanan, 2023).

WOLFGANG HALLET is Professor at Bonn University in Germany. His research focuses on complex tasks, the genre approach, content and language integrated learning, teaching literature and culture, and the multimodal novel in literary studies. His recent publications include *Teaching Cultures in the English Language Classroom* (2024).

Professionalising English Language Teaching

Concepts and Reflections for Action in Teacher Education

Andrzej Cirocki
University of York

Wolfgang Hallet
University of Bonn

Shaftesbury Road, Cambridge CB2 8EA, United Kingdom

One Liberty Plaza, 20th Floor, New York, NY 10006, USA

477 Williamstown Road, Port Melbourne, VIC 3207, Australia

314–321, 3rd Floor, Plot 3, Splendor Forum, Jasola District Centre, New Delhi – 110025, India

103 Penang Road, #05–06/07, Visioncrest Commercial, Singapore 238467

Cambridge University Press is part of Cambridge University Press & Assessment, a department of the University of Cambridge.

We share the University's mission to contribute to society through the pursuit of education, learning and research at the highest international levels of excellence.

www.cambridge.org
Information on this title: www.cambridge.org/9781009350242

DOI: 10.1017/9781009350235

© Andrzej Cirocki and Wolfgang Hallet 2024

This publication is in copyright. Subject to statutory exception and to the provisions of relevant collective licensing agreements, no reproduction of any part may take place without the written permission of Cambridge University Press & Assessment.

When citing this work, please include a reference to the DOI 10.1017/9781009350235

First published 2024

A catalogue record for this publication is available from the British Library

A Cataloging-in-Publication data record for this book is available from the Library of Congress

ISBN 978-1-009-35024-2 Hardback
ISBN 978-1-009-35019-8 Paperback

Cambridge University Press & Assessment has no responsibility for the persistence or accuracy of URLs for external or third-party internet websites referred to in this publication and does not guarantee that any content on such websites is, or will remain, accurate or appropriate.

We dedicate this book to all the teachers and colleagues who inspire us in our professional practice.

Contents

List of Figures		*page* xi
List of Tables		xii
Acknowledgements		xiii

1 English Language Teaching in the Twenty-First Century:
   A Systematic Approach to the Profession 1
   1.1 Professionalising English Language Teaching 1
   1.2 The Purpose of This Book: A Guide to English Language Teacher Education 5
   1.3 *Bildung*, Communication, and English Language Learning 9
   1.4 Frameworks of Language Learning and Teacher Education 13
      1.4.1 The Common European Framework of Reference for Languages 14
      1.4.2 Standards of Teacher Education 16
   1.5 Outlining the Disciplinary Realm of English Language Teaching 17
      1.5.1 Areas Related to the Classroom and the Teaching–Learning Process 18
      1.5.2 Institutional and General Pedagogical Areas 20
   1.6 Readership and Structure of This Book 22

2 Conceptualising Teacher Professionalism in English
   Language Teaching 26
   2.1 Particularising Teacher Professionalism 28
   2.2 Professional Standards for English Language Teachers 31
      2.2.1 Professional Knowledge 32
      2.2.2 Professional Practice 33
      2.2.3 Professional Engagement 34
   2.3 Teacher Professional Identity 36
   2.4 Professionalism and Ethics in English Language Teaching 38
      2.4.1 Beliefs and Attitudes 38
      2.4.2 Relationships 38
      2.4.3 Classroom Practices 39
      2.4.4 Professional Conduct 39
   2.5 Supporting Teacher Professionalism 40
   2.6 Conclusion 41

3 Teacher Education and Professional Competences 43
   3.1 Discourse Competence as a Core Concept of Language Learning 44
   3.2 The Concept of Competence 47
   3.3 Modelling Discourse Competence as a Professional Meta-Competence 48

		Contents	
	3.4	Competence Models and Outcome Orientation in Teacher Education	49
	3.5	Professional Knowledge and Competences for the Language Classroom	54
		3.5.1 Professional Discourse Competence	55
		3.5.2 Language Proficiency	56
		3.5.3 Subject Matter Knowledge	57
	3.6	Evaluation and Assessment Competence	62
		3.6.1 Types of Assessment	63
		3.6.2 Criterion-Based Assessment	65
	3.7	Syllabus and Lesson Design Competence	66
	3.8	Teacher Education Curricula and Programmes	67
	3.9	Conclusion	70

4 Reflective Practice and Teacher-Led Research: The Path to Teacher Professionalism — 72
  4.1 Defining Reflective Practice — 72
  4.2 Reflection, Critical Reflection, and Reflexivity — 74
  4.3 Types of Reflective Practice — 76
  4.4 Farrell's Framework for Reflecting on Teaching Experience — 78
  4.5 Instruments for Reflective Practice — 81
    4.5.1 Teacher Journals — 81
    4.5.2 Collaborative Blogging — 82
    4.5.3 Critical Incident Focus Groups — 83
    4.5.4 Peer Coaching — 86
    4.5.5 Post-Observation Conferences — 88
    4.5.6 Lesson Study Projects — 89
  4.6 Teachers as Researchers — 91
  4.7 Conclusion — 96

5 Teacher Autonomy: The Professional Independence of Teachers — 99
  5.1 Defining Teacher Autonomy and Teacher Agency — 100
  5.2 Research Findings on Teacher Autonomy — 106
  5.3 Strategies for Developing Teacher Autonomy — 110
  5.4 Conclusion — 114

6 Materials Development and Task Design: A Professional Challenge — 117
  6.1 Coursebooks and Ready-Made Materials — 118
    6.1.1 Common Practice — 118
    6.1.2 Evaluating Coursebooks and Published Materials — 120
  6.2 Materials Development and Task Design by Teachers — 123
    6.2.1 Advantages — 123
    6.2.2 Challenges — 124
    6.2.3 The Interdependence between Materials and Tasks — 126
    6.2.4 Collaborative Design of Materials and Tasks — 127
    6.2.5 Materials and Task Design as Stepping Stones to Teacher Autonomy and Agency — 128
  6.3 The Selection of Texts and Compilation of Materials — 130
    6.3.1 Criteria and Principles for Selecting and Combining Texts and Materials — 130
    6.3.2 The Representation of Cultures through Texts and Materials — 136
    6.3.3 Texts and Materials in the Digital Age — 137

	6.4	Approaches to Tasks	139
		6.4.1 Purposes and Functions of Tasks in the English Language Teaching Classroom	139
		6.4.2 Types of Tasks	140
		6.4.3 Task-Based Language Learning	144
		6.4.4 A Model for the Procedure of Task Design	146
	6.5	The Complex Task: A Model and Planning Tool	148
		6.5.1 The Purpose of Task Complexity	149
		6.5.2 The Model of the Complex Task	150
		6.5.3 The Model as a Tool for Task Design	152
	6.6	Assessing the Outcomes of Complex Tasks	153
	6.7	Conclusion	155
7	Teaching English in the Digital Age: Professional and Cultural Intricacies		157
	7.1	Cultural Transformations: The Digitality of Culture and Digital Deep Structures	159
		7.1.1 Referentiality	160
		7.1.2 Communality	160
		7.1.3 Algorithmicity	161
		7.1.4 Communication	162
	7.2	Levels of Digitisation	165
		7.2.1 The Digitisation of Information, Representation, and Communication in the Lifeworld	165
		7.2.2 From the Traditional Four Language Skills to Multiple Literacies	166
		7.2.3 The Digitisation of Classroom Technologies	167
		7.2.4 The Digitisation of Language Learning	168
		7.2.5 The Digitisation of Classroom Communication and Discourse	169
		7.2.6 Reflections and Discourses on Digitisation	170
	7.3	Teacher Digital Literacy	170
		7.3.1 Competence 1: Digital Information, Resources, and Data Literacy	174
		7.3.2 Competence 2: Digital Communication	174
		7.3.3 Competence 3: Digital Content Creation	175
		7.3.4 Competence 4: Digital Collaboration	176
		7.3.5 Competence 5: Safety and Protection in Digital Environments	176
		7.3.6 Competence 6: Digital Technological Troubleshooting and Problem-Solving	177
		7.3.7 Competence 7: Cultural Empowerment – Participation, Critical Reflection, and Content Evaluation	177
	7.4	Teaching Digital Literacy: The Languages of Digital Communication	178
	7.5	Conclusion	182
8	Teacher Leadership: Reinforcing Professional Practice in Schools		184
	8.1	Teacher Leadership and Teacher Leaders	185
	8.2	Fostering Teacher Leadership in Schools	190
		8.2.1 Types of Leadership	191
		8.2.2 Types of Power	192
		8.2.3 Helping Teachers to Develop as Leaders	193
		8.2.4 Five Principles of Successful Teacher Leadership	200
	8.3	Leadership through Mentoring	204
	8.4	Conclusion	206

9 Building Professional English Language Teaching Development Communities — 208

- 9.1 English Language Teacher Professional Learning: A Sociocultural Perspective — 208
- 9.2 The Value of Teacher Collaboration for Professional Development — 210
- 9.3 Professional Communities of English Language Teaching Practitioners — 212
  - 9.3.1 Professional Learning Communities — 213
  - 9.3.2 Professional Communities of Practice — 215
  - 9.3.3 Professional Communities of Inquiry — 217
- 9.4 Creating Professional English Language Teaching Development Communities: A Principled Approach — 218
- 9.5 Professional Development as Lived Experience: Professional Development Communities in Action — 225
- 9.6 Conclusion and Future Directions — 232
  - 9.6.1 Professional Teachers as Lifelong Learners — 233
  - 9.6.2 Professional Teachers as Classroom Ethnographers — 233
  - 9.6.3 Professional Teachers as Educational Leaders — 234

References — 237
Index — 276

Figures

1.1	Outline of the ELT profession	*page* 17
3.1	Stages and components of planning language learning: an example from the *Cambridge English Teaching Framework*	53
4.1	Five discrete stages of reflection: Farrell's framework	79
4.2	Five elements of peer coaching	86
4.3	Six stages of a lesson study project	90
4.4	Action research steps	93
5.1	Types of teachers' decisions	101
5.2	Attributes of autonomous teachers	105
6.1	A framework of materials analysis, evaluation, and action	122
6.2	Three discourse spheres constituting the ELT classroom as a transcultural space	135
6.3	Classroom discourse and cultural discourses intertwined through tasks	146
6.4	Stages of task development	147
6.5	The model of the complex competence task	150
7.1	DigCompEdu – digital competences and their connections	172
8.1	Teacher leadership competences	186
8.2	The power of teacher leaders	193
9.1	Potential members of a professional ELT development community consisting of selected members of the actual institutional community and the community's network	221
9.2	The PDC cycle: standard stages of the working process	223

Tables

1.1	Overall oral production: an excerpt from the CEFR	*page* 15
3.1	Professional teaching standards	51
3.2	Example structure of a two-year Master of Education programme in TEFL at the University of Bonn, Germany	68
5.1	Strategies for developing teacher autonomy	112
6.1	Correspondences between materials and tasks	127
6.2	Task types for the intercultural and transcultural literature classroom	142
7.1	Conventional and digital modes and genres of communication	181
8.1	Designing a welcome newsletter for prospective students: a collaborative project	195
9.1	Key principles underpinning twenty-first-century PDCs	219

Acknowledgements

Our thanks go to all the teachers and colleagues who inspire our work. Specifically, we would like to thank four colleagues: Bill Soden, for listening to our ideas and providing valuable suggestions for the scope and content of some of the chapters; David Almeida, for designing some of the tables and figures; James Lamont, for proofreading our manuscript; and Katharina Roth, for helping us to prepare the final version of the list of references.

This book would not have been possible had it not been for the support and guidance provided by the Cambridge University Press team. We are particularly grateful to Rebecca Taylor, our commissioning editor, for her continued support during the manuscript writing and publication stages. We also wish to thank the external reviewers whose expertise and constructive feedback helped us to improve this book's first draft.

Finally, we would like to acknowledge other publishers who granted us the necessary permissions to reproduce material in the form of tables and figures in the book.

1 English Language Teaching in the Twenty-First Century

A Systematic Approach to the Profession

In the contemporary post-industrial knowledge society, education systems and learning and teaching practices rapidly develop and face novel challenges. These developments apply to all cultural domains, primarily language and communication, where digital environments and social media continue to evolve. New communication formats, practices, and forms of social interaction constantly emerge within this online environment. Therefore, educational institutions and English language teachers need to respond by engaging in ongoing learning and enhancing their knowledge and qualifications (London, 2011). Individual flexibility needs to be supplemented by a willingness to innovate and learn at a systemic level. Therefore, education systems that provide insufficient support for individuals must be viewed as dysfunctional (Gill, 2005). It is thus essential that all individuals preparing for or working in educational and training institutions are cognisant of the ongoing transformations taking place and nurture their teaching and learning competences and methods of knowledge transfer in accordance with the needs of their respective societies.

Within this frame of reference, this chapter begins by clarifying the concepts of *teacher professionalism* and *professionalisation of teaching* in the field of English language teaching (ELT). The purpose of this book – a conceptual and reflective guide to English language teacher education – is rationalised and the concept of *Bildung* is briefly introduced. The latter, being an essential dimension of the formation of the professional self, refers to the lifelong process of personal development and cultural maturation and to the final result of this process: namely, the state of being educated. Standards of teacher education, as well as teacher competences, are also included. Finally, the target audience and the structure of the book are outlined.

1.1 Professionalising English Language Teaching

Since the 1970s, the topic of teacher professionalism has been the focus of a series of intense scholarly debates in the fields of education and sociology. Some scholars have argued that teaching meets the requirements to be labelled a profession, while others have disputed this. In recent times, however, the theoretical and empirical literature has focused on the professional practice of English language teachers and resolutely considers teaching a profession (e.g., Burns & Richards, 2009; Caspari & Grünewald, 2022; Crandall & Christison, 2016; Elsheikh et al., 2018; England, 2020; Farrell, 2015; Liu & Berger, 2015; Mann & Walsh, 2017; Richards, 2012; Seery, 2008). Professionalising teacher education, however, requires institutional settings that are geared to the needs of the profession and, certainly, to the needs of all those that are taught (Gutierrez et al., 2019; Luke & Gourd, 2018). Therefore, teacher education cannot be regarded as merely transforming academically trained experts in various disciplines into classroom practitioners in different subjects, including language teaching. The most substantial implication of language teaching as a profession is that it is also regarded as an academic discipline in its own right, one engaged in researching the entire field, developing concepts and theories of language learning and teaching, devising academic curricula for teacher education, and equipping future teachers not only with the available disciplinary knowledge but also with appropriate attitudes and pedagogical and ethical values.

The research literature thus renounces the *attributes approach*, whereby occupations are compared against features of the professional model (Ingersoll & Perda, 2008). By the same token, it contends that the uniqueness of the teaching profession lies in the fact that it is an epistemic community or a network of experts that exhibits and employs advanced knowledge (both theoretical and practical), possesses shared values, provides an essential public service, and adheres to ethical precepts. Moreover, teaching is a profession that feels sufficiently able to convey itself to the public in a highly valued manner and elicits respect and trust. It is therefore crucial that its uniqueness be emphasised whenever possible and its differences cultivated where appropriate.

However, recent works reveal that the teaching profession is not deemed particularly prestigious (Reis Monteiro, 2015). It is frequently seen as easy to enter, poorly remunerated, subject to a centralised management system, and offering few exciting avenues for the future enhancement of careers. Teachers are often equated with public servants or treated as 'craft' workers (Reis Monteiro, 2015). To free teachers from this paradoxical situation, it is important to stress that they represent a profession that lays the foundation for all others and teaches people 'to be human and to live humanly with other human beings' (Reis Monteiro, 2015, p. 67). Thus, it merits special recognition, respect, and appreciation on these grounds alone. Furthermore, applying the socioeconomic connotations of 'craft' workers to teachers is inappropriate. This reduces their standing to a profession that can be pursued by anyone (Jarvis, 2005). It is essential that teacher professionalism be understood as the result of academic research and the development of concepts and theories of learning and teaching. Moreover, like any other profession, it must be seen as a blend of qualifications and competences (Chapters 2 and 3), values and beliefs, and behaviours – all of which are required of teachers. These are explicitly specified in government-approved standards regulating their pedagogical practice and professional conduct, mirrored in the corresponding school curricula, and practised in institutionalised settings such as secondary schools and colleges.

In addition, teachers – both during teacher education at universities/teacher training colleges and on the job – need to develop a self-conception and attitude commensurate with those of academically educated professionals who have acquired the disciplinary knowledge and competences required to be experts who reflect continuously upon their classroom practices and experiences (Cirocki & Farrell, 2017a; Cirocki & Widodo, 2019; Farrell, 2015; Klippel, 2016; Legutke & Schart, 2016; Mann & Walsh, 2017). To facilitate this, they must develop a profound knowledge and awareness of their students' living and learning conditions and of the social, media, and communicative changes that affect students' lives. Moreover, the willingness to keep learning also requires the constant innovation of the disciplines that inform educators' professional knowledge and competence with respect to language teaching. Theoretical, pedagogical, and methodological developments necessitate regularly updating the academic and pedagogical knowledge base of teaching English (Kowalczuk-Walędziak et al., 2019; Kumar et al., 2019).

This blend of qualifications, competences, values, beliefs, and behaviours necessitates a distinction between *institutional* (in some contexts referred to as *sponsored*) and *independent* professionalism (Eckerth & Leung, 2009; Evans & Esch, 2013; Liu & Berger, 2015). The former is related to externally endorsed standards and qualification frameworks as well as disciplinary knowledge and pedagogical practice, as defined by regulatory bodies, educational institutions, or professional associations (Chapter 3). The latter, by contrast, is more personal in nature. Developing over time, independent professionalism, also defined as professional autonomy, denotes teachers' engagement in a reflective analysis of their behaviours and pedagogical practices with reference to professional knowledge. It also refers to the principled and conceptualised decision-making that mirrors their 'individual values and the social, political and pedagogical impact of their actions' (Liu & Berger, 2015, p. 38). This volume, however, does not strictly follow this differentiation. Instead, institutional and independent types of professionalism are combined under the label of teacher professionalism. This is because professional teachers are expected to exhibit elements of both in order to deliver high-quality, evidence-based, learner-centred, and individualised teaching. In this way, teachers can expertly represent the present-day profession of language teaching in teaching English to speakers of other languages (TESOL), teaching English as a second language (TESL), teaching English as a foreign language (TEFL), or teaching

English as an additional language (TEAL) contexts; within this book, all four of these terms are subsumed under one umbrella term – ELT.

Notably, the twenty-first century holds high expectations regarding the professionalism of teachers. The contemporary knowledge society is one in which all knowledge acquired at different stages of education and training should be prevented from becoming obsolete. For example, recent literature (e.g., Cirocki & Burns, 2019; Cirocki & Farrell, 2017a; Cirocki & Levy, 2018; Crandall & Christison, 2016; Dudeney & Hockly, 2007; Richards, 2015) within the field of ELT suggests that teachers are expected to be lifelong learners who are adventurous, innovative, imaginative, reflective (Chapters 4 and 9), autonomous (Chapter 5), technology/media-savvy (Chapter 7), and adaptable. Chapter 9 further shows how beneficial all these characteristics are within teacher communities and how they contribute to teachers' collaborative, innovative, and sustainable development if promoted in a systematic manner. The ability to innovate and constantly develop one's qualifications and competences is a professional skill to be acquired and learnt. The willingness and ability to constantly innovate concepts and methods of teaching and learning are therefore central competences of functional teacher education in post-industrial society (Kennedy et al., 2016; Kowalczuk-Walędziak et al., 2019). In general, this willingness to innovate and accomplish a higher degree of reflection on one's professional actions must be understood as the necessary professionalisation of any teaching activity. True professionalism includes constant reflection on one's own classroom activities and their conditions (i.e., reflective practice), as well as lifelong learning in response to the changing conditions of language use and communication and teaching and learning processes (Bauer, 2002; Cirocki & Farrell, 2017a; London, 2011). Teachers are also required to respond promptly to changes induced by new educational reforms, typically established and controlled by political leaders, with practitioners often excluded from the process. Central control of the education sector also increases the liability of other stakeholders in education, which contributes to the ongoing enrichment or alteration of current definitions of teacher professionalism.

Taking all these factors into account, the topic of teacher professionalism requires further exploration within the field of ELT. It is vital that a clear and comprehensive understanding of the concept of professionalism is obtained, especially with regard to the standards that English language practitioners must adhere to in their daily pedagogical practice. Clear guidelines are required to direct teachers along their journeys towards professional excellence. In a similar vein, the concept of professionalisation – the procedure that entails nurturing the knowledge, skills, norms, identities, and values required to become a member of a professional organisation – needs to be examined. Through this process, English language teachers acquire target language awareness, disciplinary knowledge, and pedagogical content knowledge (Chapter 2) and develop an understanding of their roles that permits them to perform as professionals in their field. Though the process is necessary in the ELT field, it is not an easy undertaking. Its complexity is contingent on embracing cultural and social changes; administrative regulations and guidelines; curricular reforms; diverse education systems; and the established routines, practices, and identities of the institutions involved in teacher education and the schools in which teachers work across the globe. All these challenges bring new perspectives and outlooks to the table, guiding professional practice, determining professionalism within the field of ELT, and shaping the entire profession.

1.2   The Purpose of This Book: A Guide to English Language Teacher Education

The purpose of this book is to develop and provide a conceptual and reflective guide to English language teacher education that is useful for teacher educators, classroom practitioners, students pursuing teaching degrees, school administrators and management teams, and policymakers. This means its focus must extend to issues beyond the English language classroom. For instance, schools and professional teacher education bodies need to respond to the increasing social and cultural diversity of classrooms and learning groups. This requires a broader perspective on the complex process of educating English language teachers, considering the domain of ELT as a whole and including the extensive body of research generated. Thus, approaches to teacher education, especially English language teacher education, need to be grounded in contemporary pedagogical theories and contingent on high-quality teacher education programmes.

The spectrum encompassing what is researched, described, and designed in such a meta-pedagogical theory ranges from general theories of education and *Bildung* (Section 1.3), defined as self-cultivation and self-realisation, through conceptual descriptions of the connections between teaching and learning, to empirical research on processes of instruction and language learning (Hu, 2015; Siljander et al., 2012; Varkøy, 2010). In addition, theories around content construction (selection of texts, materials, and resources; see Chapter 6 for details) and the description of language competences and skills constitute part of English language teachers' professional expertise. Since the early 2000s, there has also been a pronounced interest in a more precise framing of the competences that form part of the teaching profession and language learning (Section 1.4).

However, a conceptual approach to professionalising English language teacher education must also account for the culture-specific contexts of education systems, the various histories and traditions of different systems of teacher training and education, and established classroom practices

(Kumaravadivelu, 2006; Vinogradova & Shin, 2020). This is why a systematic description of teacher qualifications and competences is all the more desirable; it makes it possible to compare and share concepts and experiences across cultures and societies and define standards and goals that synthesise different educational and disciplinary accomplishments. This helps create a culturally and systemically coherent concept of teacher education for a specific school system in accordance with the established traditions and norms of teacher education.

Such a systematic approach will help justify why ELT, derived from pedagogy and applied linguistics, should be regarded as a discipline in its own right, as the purpose and goals of the school of ELT and English language (teacher) education need to be researched, conceptualised, and theorised. The following four functions can be attributed to ELT as a discipline:

1. *A pedagogy of ELT for learning describes and investigates teaching and learning processes in institutions.* Such a pedagogy researches and explores strategies for teaching English in which learning is a planned, guided, and goal-oriented process, as opposed to the intuitive, natural, non-guided process taking place during early childhood. ELT as a discipline seeks to examine and describe teaching and learning constellations as well as the factors that determine them and offers teachers concepts for optimising the conditions of teaching (e.g., for designing optimal learning environments) or criteria for making individual decisions for their classrooms (the use of media, learning and teaching methods, etc.).
2. *A pedagogy of ELT for learning is an educational theory.* Beyond teaching and learning processes, a pedagogy of language teaching for learning concerns itself with more general questions about the social conditions, frameworks, and objectives of all teaching and learning and of institutional education. In particular, it strives to learn more about the impact and effects of sociocultural changes on teaching and learning as they occur, for instance, in the wake of migration and the movement of refugees (Cirocki & Farrelly, 2019; Shapiro et al., 2018). Since the 2000s, educational standards and curricular frameworks of reference have emphasised these close interconnections between more general political conditions, the objectives of language learning and instructional methods, and approaches at the classroom level.
3. *A pedagogy of ELT for learning is a theory for the classroom.* Such a pedagogy develops theories or concepts for the content and design of lessons and teaching units. This is also how recent developments in the social sciences and in the pedagogy of teaching English, applied linguistics, media studies, and cultural studies have been taken up and integrated into new concepts and proposals for learning and teaching.

4. *A pedagogy of ELT for learning is a theory of the ELT profession.* Research on and questions surrounding the conceptualisation of teaching as a profession are paramount for teacher education and educational processes at all levels, ranging from school and classroom organisation to the design of lessons and materials. This pedagogical theory investigates teachers' subjective theories of teaching and learning, their professional self-image and self-conceptions, and their roles as learning facilitators, classroom managers, or mediators. As a theory of the competences required for designing and delivering teaching and learning processes, it theorises the way teachers must be educated to teach students and organise processes of language learning or, more specifically, of teaching and learning English.

The preceding discussion on the functions and purposes of the pedagogical theory of teaching for learning applies to all forms of language teaching at all stages, from teaching English as a second or foreign language in kindergartens and primary schools to upper secondary classrooms and adult language courses. However, if language teaching in general, and English language teaching more specifically, is a profession reliant on academic disciplines and professional training, the critical question that arises is as follows: How can the field of ELT be systematised and described so that all the different types of knowledge and professional competences required are institutionalised, including standards of teacher education (Chapter 3) and curricular definitions? Regarding ELT, teacher educators require a clear idea of the its disciplinary structure and its various components, including language learning itself, but also more general pedagogical concepts such as learning as social interaction or classroom management. Only then will it be possible to define English language teachers' essential and desirable skills and competences (Chapter 3).

The primary aim of this book is to systematise the areas of English language teacher education and define the basic set of core pedagogical competences required to teach English successfully and professionally in institutions such as schools and universities but also in vocational language training and adult language learning. There is also a growing awareness of the need to professionalise the early stages of ELT in kindergartens and primary schools; as in secondary schools, learning English at these levels must become increasingly oriented towards professional concepts of teaching for learning and towards the systematic transfer of knowledge and the training of language skills. Although the focus of this book is on the ELT context, its contribution to the education of language teachers is much broader. The various concepts included in this book are transferable and apply to teachers of other languages. It is therefore hoped that this volume will also guide teacher education programmes focusing on languages other than English.

Prior to setting out the core areas of professional teaching and the concepts relevant to teacher education, ELT needs to be situated within the broader context of societies that require competent users of the target language. In the twenty-first century, these societies are characterised by high degrees of globalisation; by social, ethnic, cultural, and linguistic diversity; by digitised communication and representation; and, in Western societies at least, by individualised ethical and religious orientations (Eunson, 2015; Healey, 2020; Jarvis, 2007). All these aspects inform the current theories and practices that underpin ELT and stimulate original research in this domain. Regrettably, existing knowledge on these aspects is rather abstract and vague. Another essential point to emphasise is that language learning is inevitably connected to the reception, comprehension, and production of texts in diverse media formats (Chapter 7). The English language classroom must therefore account for the cultural knowledge communicated by texts, the range of communicative practices that prevail in societies or communities, and the diverse needs – both objective and subjective – of language learners. For instance, refugees bring cultural backgrounds and beliefs to classrooms in a cultural context that is often substantially different to their own (Cirocki & Farrelly, 2019; Shapiro et al., 2018). Their objective in learning English may therefore differ substantially from that of a learner in a secondary classroom, where the principal aim is to prepare students for vocational training or university studies in their own country.

Every teacher has more or less precise ideas about the kind of education learners should undergo, their background and predispositions, and the educational goals for which instruction in their classroom is designed. However, such theories and reflections are rarely made explicit; they often remain implicit and subjective, shared through informal conversations in the staff room with colleagues or friends. This is not especially surprising because, socially and academically, ideas about the goals and purposes of education are often inconsistent, fuzzy, and controversial. One of the implications of the professionalisation of English language teacher education is that concepts of education require closer inspection, reflection, and re-definition – hence the current book.

One of the underlying assumptions of this volume is that defining and describing the goals of professional English language teacher education is impossible without recourse to a more general theory of education (Section 1.4). If no such pedagogical framework of reference is available, pedagogical decision-making becomes arbitrary as there are no criteria for deciding on the type and number of competences that are to be taught and acquired both in a school subject and in teacher education. In fact, as Klafki (2007, p. 44) observes in relation to school education, there is a 'necessity for overarching pedagogical goals and categories'. If, however, overarching, foundational notions of education and definitions that broadly specify the purposes of learning English and the societal goals of language education are not available, pedagogical efforts are reduced to a collection of incoherent and inconsistent individual activities and dysfunctional teaching practices.

1.3   *Bildung*, Communication, and English Language Learning

Language learning is often conceptualised as the process of learning grammatical structures and words. Such a narrow idea of what it means to learn a language, particularly English, ignores the cultural and individual role of language and communication. Once the latter is considered, it becomes evident that whole societies are built on languages – their own and others – and that every individual who learns a new language undergoes a personal transformation and personality development. Therefore, in the European context and as a critical response to both the *Common European Framework of Reference for Languages* (hereafter CEFR; Council of Europe, 2001, 2020) and educational standards in Germany, the concept of *Bildung* in the Humboldtian sense has been revived and re-introduced into the realm of (English) language education (Bausch et al., 2005; Heidt, 2015). Consequently, it is given a prominent place in this volume. As Hu (2015, p. 17) contends, *Bildung* is a neo-humanistic concept that emphasises 'a process of holistic growth, self-realization of the individual as an entirety, freedom, and self-understanding as well as a sense of social responsibility, and which puts the development of the individual's unique potential and self at the center of educational processes'.

The consequences of this vision of an individual's self-reflexive positioning vis-à-vis the world and the individual's role in a society are far-reaching (Breidbach, 2007; Koller, 2018; Kramsch, 2009). The precondition for an individual's freedom and autonomy in a society is determined by this vision of their position, which offers and warrants the individual sociocultural agency and spaces for independence. At the same time, individuals engage in building and sustaining precisely the kind of civil and democratic society that is able to offer its members spaces for citizenship and active participation (The New London Group, 2000).

Therefore, in its broadest sense, education must be regarded as a process of empowerment and as providing a time and space in which individuals can develop their intellectual potential, talents, and personalities (Chowdhury, 2018; Mawani & Mukadam, 2020). At the same time, schools and teachers need to ensure that each individual develops in a socially and culturally responsible manner, one that serves the interests and needs of both society and its citizens. This process of sociocultural development couples *Bildung* with Vygotsky's sociocultural theory, which regards human development as a socially mediated process influenced by various semiotic modes and tools, the most important of which is the human language (Vygotsky, 1978). According to Vygotsky (1978), learning within institutional contexts or professional communities (Section 9.3) is a collaborative process whereby individuals acquire culturally valuable skills and capabilities through social interactions with peers and more knowledgeable others.

Language and communication, including English as a second or a foreign language, are thus of paramount importance in an approach informed by the Humboldtian idea of *Bildung* and education. There can be no true formation and empowerment of the learning subject without language, and all additional languages enhance an individual's symbolic empowerment (Kramsch, 2009). This insight significantly informs all English language teaching and learning processes. From this standpoint, English language education reaches far beyond teaching language structures and linguistic repertoires. These are merely different means to an end, albeit crucial ones, and English language instruction must be embedded in the complex, holistic process of developing personalities, with individuals as subjects and citizens seeking to find their place in a society and the world.

As brief and incomplete as any discussion of the concept of *Bildung* must be within this introductory chapter, it is of fundamental importance to clarify the functions and purposes of school education and language learning that provide English language teachers and teacher educators with clear guidance. As mentioned previously, a central concept is the notion of the individual as the reference point of all democratic and humane thinking. However, a certain degree of commonality and cultural consensus is also required upon which societies – democratic societies in particular – can be built. This constant act of striking a balance in education between the needs of the individual and those of the society ultimately remains an irreconcilable dichotomy. Nevertheless, it is important to ensure that education equips individuals with all the abilities, competences, and skills required to enable them to participate actively in societies and cultures in every respect, including political discourses and cultural controversies. At the same time, to facilitate the socialisation of individuals, it is necessary to ensure a 'minimum standard of cultural commonality, the "basic skills", on which all societies depend' (Klieme et al., 2003, p. 59).

Therefore, the two critical concepts through which the roles of individuals and the needs of societies are defined are *participation* and *self-determination* or *autonomy*. These rely on the basic assumption that societies – democratic ones in particular – are constituted through the active participation of individuals and that these individuals determine both the nature and form of this society and how they are able and prepared to participate and live in it. As Klieme et al. (2003, p. 63) observe:

For modern societies committed to the tradition of the Enlightenment and democratically organized, an image of individuality is considered as guiding in which...human dignity and the free development of the personality are supreme maxims. These premises become general educational goals because it is only in the process of growing up that it can be ensured that all adolescents of a generation, regardless of origin and gender, are enabled to live in accordance with this claim in their independent participation in politics, society and culture and in the shaping of their own lifeworld, and to act in a self-determined manner as responsible citizens.

The competences taught during an educational process and acquired by students serve precisely this purpose; education and English language learning enable and prepare learners to participate fully and maturely both in the society in which they live and in shaping their own lives and their more immediate lifeworld. It is evident that the concept of education as *Bildung* affects language teaching and learning, particularly in communication and language where cultural and social participation materialises. This is also why the role of English cannot be overestimated. In an age of globalised economies, worldwide electronic communication, and the global circulation of knowledge and cultural artefacts, being proficient in English as a global language in multiple institutions and contexts is one of the preconditions of cultural participation and an individual's discursive competence.

From these general educational goals at all levels and the learners' *Bildung*, the goals of English language teacher education and English language teachers' competences can be derived. Teachers should be equipped with the knowledge, skills, abilities, and competences that enable them to pursue school education goals and all institutional language learning in democratic societies. This is the only way they can account for ongoing social, cultural, and media changes. In the twenty-first century, ways of life and thinking are characterised by the constantly diminishing power of cultural, political, ethical, or religious meta-narratives. These have been replaced by a large number of diverse, often highly individualised, approaches that re-define the social position of the individual and place upon them the burden of self-realisation. Ongoing and fundamental changes also concern the interconnectedness between nation states and individual societies and cultures to the world society (globalisation), not least in terms of migration and economic, cultural, academic, and professional exchange.

Another fundamental change, and ongoing transformation, is that of the technological revolution; digitisation affects all fields of technical, economic, and cultural development, particularly communicative and media practices. In the digitised and globally networked world, any text can, in principle, be linked to any other text; the number of possible links is infinite. In the electronic age, digital hypertext has therefore become the most frequent kind of text (Section 7.3). Even formerly conventional print texts are now converted into digital texts. As a result, an author's authority over any text and its subsequent outreach, whether a blog post, a video clip, or a tweet, is enormous and incalculable, and the definition of a text's sense (or non-sense) lies with the user. Because the English language classroom is continually concerned with the reception and production of all kinds of texts, it is essential to teach orientation strategies within the digital universe of texts, text selection strategies, and information processing among teachers and learners alike.

It is vital that the field of ELT constantly reflects upon and conceptualises its notions of communication and communicative practices. English language instruction and teacher education programmes must account for all these fundamental transformations as they directly affect communicative practices and standards. New genres and new modes of communication continually emerge (Chapter 7). The role of verbal language is changing to the point that it has become just one mode of communication among a range of others, visual images in particular (The New London Group, 2000). Therefore, English language learners and teachers need to be able to cope with enormous numbers of texts, instead of dealing with a single or very limited number of texts, as is usually the case in coursebooks. Also, the selection of texts is no longer a privilege of teachers or textbook makers, and canonisations of the conventional kind, such as prescriptive reading lists, are now barely enforceable. This abundance of accessible texts and information presents the individual with various perspectives, orientations, and meanings. The uniformity and clarity of orientations, life plans, and values are fading, completely different cultural contexts are now easily accessible, and remixes and combinations of hitherto unknown orientations, non-uniform designs, identities, and cultures have become standard practice. The resulting concepts are hybrid or patchwork-like and often temporary or tentative.

In terms of significance and interpretation, the meanings into which readers of texts are initiated in their own and other languages are no longer socially and culturally given; rather, the individual must be able to construct meanings in a more autonomous fashion. Consequently, in every encounter with a text, many individual constructions of meaning and readings are possible (Roe et al., 2019; Yandell, 2013). This means that 'subjective abilities that enable the individual to create valid orientations for themselves' (Brater, 1997, p. 155) are required. Training and fostering the language learners' ability to construct meaning and significance must therefore be one of the primary goals of teaching English, such that comprehension and active communication are understood as active, meaning-generating activities in all interactional and cultural contexts. Because discourses in a globalised world do not or cannot take place monolingually, the necessity and importance of communicating in a second or a foreign language, particularly in English as a lingua franca, is constantly increasing. As the following section will demonstrate, this philosophy underpins recent frameworks of (English) language learning and teacher education programmes.

1.4 Frameworks of Language Learning and Teacher Education

Curricular frameworks, both of language learning and of teacher education, seem to be the most impactful instruments of professionalisation as they are the result of educational and language policies and political decision-making. Since, in many countries, teacher education is in the hands of state authorities, it is evident that frameworks providing standards and curricular objectives will be implemented and become highly influential in classrooms and teacher education institutions. In most countries, professional teacher education is therefore not only concerned with classroom practices and pedagogical methods and approaches but also with describing the abilities and competences of learners of foreign and second languages, including English, and with defining the curricular objectives of foreign language learning at certain stages and/or at the end of the learning process.

Such structured forms of systematisation can be regarded as first-order frameworks of the goals and outcomes of institutional language learning, as opposed to individual methods of language learning that require the help of language learning software or online courses. Given that teacher education's contents, concepts, and goals are more or less directly derived from these first-order frameworks, they are highly relevant to teacher education. Moreover, drawing and depending upon the latter leads to the formation of second-order teacher education frameworks and theories. These must be able to specify the professional knowledge and competence that both prospective and in-service teachers must acquire to accomplish the language learning goals defined for their classrooms within first-order frameworks.

It is therefore recommended that current educational literature, policies, and teacher education programmes promote such an approach. This would also align with influential and powerful EU documents such as the *Common European Framework of Reference for Languages: Learning, Teaching, Assessment* (Council of Europe, 2001; and the *Companion Volume*, 2020, in its most recent version: Council of Europe, 2020), where *learning* and *teaching* are emphasised in the subtitle. As the plural of *languages* in the title also suggests, this European framework conceptualises learning for all languages, not just English. Nevertheless, all these proposed documents apply directly to the teaching and learning of English.

The purpose of the following two sub-sections is to illustrate the philosophy of such frameworks using examples from Europe and the United Kingdom, as the frameworks developed there not only have a lot to offer but have also proven to be highly influential regarding school and language education.

1.4.1 The Common European Framework of Reference for Languages

The notion of standardised can-do descriptors and competence scales emerged at the beginning of the twenty-first century, primarily in Europe and the United States. This can be regarded as an attempt to respond to the high degree of diversity, heterogeneity, and differences of learning foreign languages and teacher education across Europe and worldwide (Cirocki et al., 2019a). As the CEFR demonstrates, one of the underlying assumptions is that no matter in what context and for what purposes a language is learnt, the levels and skills defined in the CEFR make it possible to assess a person's language skills and abilities reliably and objectively; by scaling these skills, they are rendered comparable to the abilities of those who have acquired and/or learnt a language in different and distant contexts. A second assumption, widely regarded as a pedagogical paradigm shift, is that defining the outcomes of a language learning process through can-do descriptors leads to greater efficiency and more freedom for learners, teachers, and institutions with regard to how these goals are accomplished. It is left to them to create the curricula, time frames, or methodologies that are deemed most efficient and productive. A third assumption is that such frameworks do not define language course content in terms of the topics and tasks that are negotiated in foreign or second language classrooms. Finally, as stated previously and with regard to the substance of this book, in most cases, language learning or teacher education frameworks are not language-specific but generic, thereby applying to all second or foreign languages and their teachers (Section 1.2).

Most importantly, the CEFR (Council of Europe, 2001, 2020) is a result of the declared will of several European countries to promote multilingualism among their citizens and to make language skills comparable not only within one language but also across languages by setting rigorous educational standards. European citizenship, which is one of the primary goals of the European Union, needs to rely on the mobility of citizens across Europe, a shared economy, and a European job market. These make it necessary to define standards for comparing skills and professional qualifications across Europe, including an applicant's or employee's proficiency in different languages. Table 1.1 is a small example from the CEFR (Council of Europe, 2020, p. 62), which illustrates the principle of using descriptors to define learning outcomes and learners' speaking abilities on six levels from A1 to C2, plus a Pre-A1 stage that was added in the 2020 version.

The purpose of the CEFR is to enable teachers, as well as educational institutions and employers, to reliably assess the language skills of students, trainees, and employees. More specifically, their language proficiency is classified and perhaps certified in school and university reports or language certificates in accordance with the receptive and productive skills as defined by the Council of Europe.

Table 1.1 *Overall oral production: an excerpt from the CEFR*

	Overall oral production
C2	Can produce clear, smoothly flowing, well-structured discourse with an effective logical structure which helps the recipient to notice and remember significant points.
C1	Can give clear, detailed descriptions and presentations on complex subjects, integrating sub-themes, developing particular points and rounding off with an appropriate conclusion.
B2	Can give clear, systematically developed descriptions and presentations, with appropriate highlighting of significant points, and relevant supporting detail. Can give clear, detailed descriptions and presentations on a wide range of subjects related to their field of interest, expanding and supporting ideas with subsidiary points and relevant examples.
B1	Can reasonably fluently sustain a straightforward description of one of a variety of subjects within their field of interest, presenting it as a linear sequence of points.
A2	Can give a simple description or presentation of people, living or working conditions, daily routines. likes/ dislikes, etc. as a short series of simple phrases and sentences linked into a list.
A1	Can produce simple, mainly isolated phrases about people and places.
Pre-A1	Can produce short phrases about themselves, giving basic personal information (e.g., name, address, family, nationality).

Note: Reprinted with permission from Council of Europe, (2020, p. 62). Copyright 2020 by the Council of Europe.

Now that the CEFR has become a successful framework, many countries, including those outside Europe, have implemented it in their education systems. As such, the CEFR model determines their curricula and classroom practices, guiding the design of English language coursebooks in which the language levels of tasks and types of assessments are clearly defined. In addition, influential language certificate examinations such as *B2 First for Schools* or *C1 Advanced* are based on the CEFR. In numerous countries, both in Europe and beyond, the framework has dominated the area of language testing, including language examination requirements.

What contributes to the success of the CEFR is undoubtedly its multifunctionality (Nagai et al., 2020; Piccardo et al., 2011). For instance, it promotes intuitive assessments that teachers can operate effectively while planning and evaluating lessons without the need for validated test procedures. Texts and teaching materials can also be classified according to the CEFR descriptors to determine their appropriateness for specific levels of education. Similarly, the level of learners' oral or written utterances can be quickly determined using the CEFR descriptors. Given this evidence, the CEFR seems instrumental in developing language education policies worldwide.

However, despite its widespread implementation in foreign language education, the CEFR has limitations (Nagai et al., 2020). For instance, it has been criticised for its use of everyday language, conceptual vagueness, terminological inconsistency, and a lack of empirical evidence and scientific unreliability (Quetz & Vogt, 2009). Additionally, the reliability of the scales for empirically validating proficiency levels has been called into question (Quetz & Vogt, 2009; Vogt, 2011). The CEFR has also been criticised for a rigid reliance on standards and a standardised concept and model of language learning that leads to global uniformity, lacking individuality and cultural specificities. Also, despite the European commitment to strengthen the cultural position of minority languages, it is regarded as enhancing the ever-growing dominant position of English as a European and a global language.

1.4.2 Standards of Teacher Education

In addition to the aforementioned frameworks for learning languages, similarly structured frameworks of professional standards for teachers have also been developed by states and/or teacher education institutions. For example, such professional benchmarks have been established by the National Board in the United States (*National Board for Professional Teaching Standards*; see Section 3.4 for details), the Education Council in New Zealand (*Standards for the Teaching Profession*), and President Joko Widodo in Indonesia (*National Standards of Education*). In the field of ELT, the most recent and pertinent example is the *Cambridge English Teaching Framework* (UCLES, 2018), developed and disseminated by Cambridge Assessment English. The four career stage descriptors presented in this framework (i.e., Foundation, Developing, Proficient, Expert) are intended to summarise 'the notion that gradual development of teachers' expertise over time involves growing understanding of teaching and learning, growing awareness of their own strengths, weaknesses and potential as a teacher, increasing sophistication in their planning, decision-making, teaching skills and reflection, as well as the ability to respond to a more complex range of classroom situations' (UCLES, 2018, p. 2). The skills descriptors for teachers of English are structured in accordance with the following five areas of ability: (1) learning and the learner; (2) teaching, learning, and assessment; (3) language ability; (4) language knowledge and awareness; and (5) professional development and values, which are then detailed in sub-categories so that various practices can be reflected upon and also assessed (see Section 3.4 for details). One of the advantages of such a framework is that it provides teachers and teacher educators with a concrete summary of a wide range of professional competences. Teachers can use it to assess their own teaching skills and competences, or teacher educators can use it as an evaluation instrument to appraise teachers at four different career stages. Also, such frameworks present professional teaching as a developmental process and can therefore be regarded as a guideline for the professionalisation of ELT teachers. For more details on the *Cambridge English Teaching Framework*, see Section 3.4.

1.5 Outlining the Disciplinary Realm of English Language Teaching

One of the implications of professionalisation is that classroom practitioners will have a complete understanding of how the various dimensions of teaching and learning English are defined and conceptualised. In this introductory chapter, it may suffice to provide a brief sketch – or an outline – of these critical areas to standardise and systematise the field of ELT (Figure 1.1). Later, in Chapter 3, the various pedagogical areas, teacher actions, and classroom interactions for which teachers need to be professionally prepared are considered in more detail.

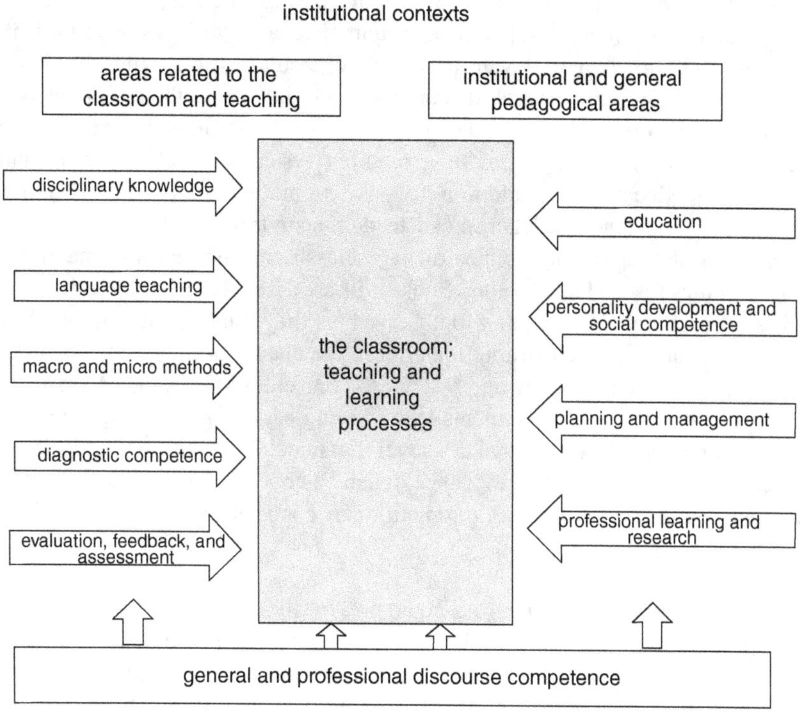

Figure 1.1 Outline of the ELT profession
Note: Adapted from Hallet (2006a, p. 36). Copyright 2023 by Wolfgang Hallet.

Regarding specification and teacher competences, it is important to distinguish two major areas that define an English language teacher's actions and interactions. On the one hand, these areas are more or less directly related to the classroom and all the teaching and learning processes within it (Section 1.5.1). On the other hand, there are more general areas that are not language-oriented, that is, institutional and pedagogical areas in which every teacher is continuously and inevitably involved (Section 1.5.2). These two areas are briefly discussed next.

1.5.1 Areas Related to the Classroom and the Teaching–Learning Process

1.5.1.1 Disciplinary Knowledge   English language teachers must acquire and bring to the classroom a profound professional knowledge base that is usually acquired at university or in academic institutions (Banegas, 2020; Freeman, 2016). It includes a very high level of proficiency in English (ideally C2), a detailed familiarity with the linguistic aspects of the English language (extremely broad in itself, encompassing, for example, phonetics and phonology, syntax, semantics, pragmatics, and varieties of English), and cultural knowledge relevant to anglophone cultures, including the living conditions, ongoing political discourses, and literary-aesthetic knowledge of literary history, film, and other popular genres. Because this knowledge rapidly becomes obsolete, this area requires systematic (self-)learning and continuing education. In addition to an extremely high level of English language competence, teachers need to demonstrate other discursive skills, such as those that enable them to manage classroom discourses to maximise opportunities for student learning. Such skills are associated with the following areas of teaching: (1) the ability to observe how they use language so that they can deliver appropriate learning material in the classroom, (2) eschewing the use of informal expressions and jargon, (3) presenting a model for speaking English that is suitable for students learning English as a global language, and (4) teaching the target language at a level that matches the abilities of learners (Richards, 2010). Given this evidence, it can be concluded that solid language awareness and high proficiency of practitioners contribute substantially to their professional profile.

1.5.1.2 Language Teaching   As noted previously, language teaching cannot be defined as a mere practical dimension added to disciplinary knowledge in linguistics or theories of anglophone cultures. Instead, as mentioned earlier in this chapter, ELT must be regarded as an academic discipline in its own right, which involves research into all aspects and processes of the acquisition and learning of the target language, empirical studies on language classrooms, language teaching methodologies, and a large number of other theories pertinent in the field. It is essential that the entire discipline be highly developed and specialised so that theoretical foundations and concepts are available for (future) teachers and guide both their classroom practices and reflections on their own teaching (Chapter 3).

1.5.1.3 Macro- and Micro-Level Approaches in English Language Classrooms Teaching and learning processes can be initiated and designed in several different ways. English language teachers must therefore be familiar with a rich repertoire of approaches to teaching the target language that are varied and holistic as well as appropriate for diverse classrooms, different preconditions, and the range of learning styles presented by learners (Freeman, 2016; Gebhard, 2017; Richards, 2015; Rose et al., 2020; Vinogradova & Shin, 2020). Various teaching and learning formats are available, some of which define macro-level approaches to teaching English, such as task-based language learning and teaching. At a micro level, classroom procedures and teaching techniques define types of classroom interaction. Also, a combination of macro and micro approaches within one teaching unit is desirable, whereby more traditional language instruction in one lesson may alternate with project-like phases in other parts. Accordingly, the roles of English language teachers and learners need to be re-defined in each case.

1.5.1.4 Diagnosis In learner-oriented classrooms and at the beginning of every teaching–learning process, English language teachers are required to assess the skills and prior knowledge that learners bring to the classroom so that they can make a good assessment as to what they already have, to what extent and with what certainty this is the case, and on what areas the teaching can build. Above all, it is important to know the different learning levels and prerequisites in a learning group to teach in an appropriately differentiated manner. Diagnosis is indispensable in diverse classrooms as a means of accounting for the different abilities, talents, experiences, prior knowledge, and multiple predispositions of learners. If teaching English is to be adapted to the individual classroom and its members, diagnosis is the tool that makes it possible to plan and teach lessons by considering learners' needs and talents.

1.5.1.5 Assessment, Feedback, and Evaluation Language learning and teaching are two processes requiring systematic assessment and evaluation to determine and plan a course of action (Cirocki & Brown, 2021; Gitsaki & Coombe, 2016). Therefore, designing different types of assessment (e.g., essays, presentations, posters, and portfolios) and promoting different types of feedback (e.g., formative, summative, peer, audio, and video) constitute an essential element of a teacher's professional competence and pedagogical practice. Assessing and regularly monitoring students' work enable teachers to not only identify strengths and weaknesses in students' learning journeys but also help them to ensure improvements are observed and successful progression from one level of language proficiency to another is made possible. Because summative assessments often affect language learners' future chances and options, teachers are expected to promote both assessment for and assessment of learning in the teaching–learning process.

The process of implementing diverse assessments, their objectives, and various formats must be regularly reflected upon and evaluated so that high-quality assessment takes place in the classroom. The evaluation process ideally entails the collaborative formation of judgements made by classroom practitioners regarding the importance, quality, and value of assessment practices. The critical discussions that form part of the evaluation process also enhance teachers' assessment literacy.

With this in mind, and considering the readership of this book, three concepts are examined from a practical perspective in this volume: the skills, the strategies, and the actions teachers need to employ to measure and then evaluate student learning effectively. Specifically, it is vital that teachers be competent in the following: (1) selecting and refining tools for assessment and grading strategies that are suitable and fair for all students; (2) delivering, marking, and drawing appropriate conclusions from the results of assessment strategies developed by teachers and generated by external bodies; (3) utilising the results of assessments to make decisions about individual students, plan teaching, devise the curriculum, and enhance the school; (4) conveying the results of assessments to students and all other relevant parties; and (5) reviewing assessment strategies and instruments to determine their effectiveness and the conditions under which they work – this is essential both for approving existing approaches and validating future strategies (Pastore & Andrade, 2019).

1.5.2 Institutional and General Pedagogical Areas

1.5.2.1 Education Teaching English successfully and effectively requires teachers to have a deep awareness and understanding of the contexts in which they teach (Illes, 2020; Wedell & Malderez, 2013). This includes in-depth knowledge of the respective conditions and purposes of English language learning as well as paying attention to learners' needs. For instance, the vast majority of language learners are adolescents in lower and upper secondary classrooms. Therefore, teachers should be aware of the interrelatedness of adolescence and language learning (e.g., age-specific and age-appropriate materials and teaching methods) as well as of the more general anthropological conditions governing language learning at a certain age, from teaching English in primary schools to adult language learning and education for vocational purposes. However, English is also learnt by adults and at a tertiary level of education, not only at university but also in vocational contexts, including language schools run by big private companies that operate internationally.

1.5.2.2 Personality Development and Social Competence Learning an additional language adds a new dimension to a learner's personality. It offers them alternative ways of looking at the world, enabling them to connect to other cultural and linguistic communities and develop new modes of self-expression (termed *symbolic empowerment* by Kramsch, 2009). This is linked to a person's repertoire of social and cultural interactions and behaviours. In the digital age, in particular, proficiency in English makes it possible to engage in new communicative and social practices and join new online and offline communities. Accordingly, language learning and teaching require holistic approaches that account for the personal and social dimensions of communication and discourse in English, whether as a second, foreign, or additional language. Teachers must therefore develop interpersonal and social competences to be aware of and teach the social dimensions of all forms of communication. To achieve this, as mentioned previously, teachers need to have high proficiency levels in the target language.

1.5.2.3 Planning and Management In connection with the dynamics of cultural and communicative changes in the twenty-first century, English language teachers are expected to be good planners, effective managers, and innovative leaders (Benegas & Stolpestad, 2020; Christison & Murray, 2009; Coombe et al., 2020; for details, see also Chapter 8 in this volume). In institutional contexts and school education, teachers must be able to plan, structure, organise, and manage all processes connected to the teaching of the target language, from curricula to materials design and from lesson plans to initiating and organising the classroom discourse, classroom management, and school education in a more general sense, such as through collaborative work with colleagues in the language department or in matters pertaining to school administration.

1.5.2.4 Professional Learning and Teacher-Led Research The insights, concepts, theories, and methodologies of language learning and teaching are continuously changing and developing, which makes ongoing professional learning a requisite (Cirocki & Coombe, 2023; Cirocki & Farrell, 2019; Crandall & Christison, 2016). In the digital age – in particular, learners' lifeworlds – their social and cultural living conditions and their communicative and social practices are simultaneously and constantly developing. Successful ELT requires professional tools and strategies to acquire reliable research-based insight and knowledge of the social–cultural conditions of language teaching and learning. In the same vein, anglophone cultures and societies constantly change and evolve; such processes must be observed and researched continuously to be integrated into and discussed in the English language classroom. Thus, professional teachers are expected to research their classrooms to improve their own pedagogical practice (Borg, 2013; Cirocki & Burns, 2019) and, additionally, the cultural developments in the anglophone world (Section 4.6).

1.5.2.5 General and Professional Discourse Competence English language teachers must be able to participate in, contribute to, and initiate discourses at various levels. In the language of schooling, which is typically the national language (e.g., Polish in Poland), and often, as is the case in some Asian or African countries, English as an additional or second language, a teacher must be able to participate in more general and public discourses of education in the respective language of schooling. These may centre around general questions pertaining to school education, the role of English in a given society, or the language policy. However, conducting the classroom discourse in English so that the language of instruction is also the target language has now become a pedagogical standard. Finally, teachers should be able to fully participate in ongoing social, cultural, and political discourses in (anglophone) societies, introducing them into the language classroom while simultaneously promoting them within the broader context of their profession. Nevertheless, teachers' extensive disciplinary knowledge and high target language proficiency principally guarantee active participation in such discourses.

1.6 Readership and Structure of This Book

The themes in this conceptual and reflective guide to English language teacher education have been chosen to appeal to a wide readership. The primary audience includes English language teacher educators and classroom practitioners, undergraduate and postgraduate students pursuing English language teacher education programmes, and school administrators, management teams, and policymakers. Additionally, this volume is a valuable resource for pre-/in-service English language teacher professional development providers, teacher trainers delivering certificate courses (e.g., Cambridge CELTA and DELTA, London Trinity College CertTESOL and DipTESOL or the US TESOL certificate), and educational and applied linguistics researchers whose research interests lie within the area of English language teacher education and professional development. Because the various concepts included in this book are universal, it is hoped that this volume will also be of value to teachers and teacher educators of other languages.

This volume is divided into nine chapters. They offer an in-depth discussion of key topics and concepts in the field under consideration and explain how these contribute to the professionalisation of ELT. As clarified earlier,

Chapter 1 prepares the ground so that the whole field of ELT can be systematised. It identifies the various areas that must be covered in the education of teachers and presents a rationale that regards teaching and learning English as part of the broader process of *Bildung*. It also argues why teaching the English language must be defined as a profession that requires academic education and practical training in the classroom context.

Chapter 2 focuses on teacher professionalism. This discussion is supported by briefly examining the professional standards obligatory for the teaching occupation. These are discussed in relation to three dimensions: professional knowledge, professional practice, and professional engagement. The chapter then analyses the construct of teacher professional identity, followed by a concise consideration of the relationship between professionalism and ethics. It concludes with constructive suggestions for sustaining teacher professionalism.

Chapter 3 examines more closely the various professional areas mapped out and sketched in Chapter 1. Such mapping is expanded and developed into a more detailed description of the competences teachers must acquire and develop as lifelong learners. This chapter is designed to provide teachers and their professional educators with a clear idea of what must be taught and learnt on teacher education programmes and in educational institutions such as schools.

Chapter 4 focuses on reflective practice, which aims to increase teachers' comprehension of the teaching–learning process, enhance their experiences of teaching and learning, engage with daily work operations at a deeper level, and increase their personal and professional efficacy. The chapter first explains what reflective practice means and what this involves. This includes elucidating concepts such as reflection, critical reflection, and reflexivity. This is followed by a summary and endorsement of Farrell's theoretical framework for reflective practice. The chapter outlines the tools teachers are advised to adopt to examine and enhance their teaching reflexively and concludes with the importance of teacher-led research.

Chapter 5 revolves around the concept of teacher autonomy, which is a key component of teacher professionalism. The chapter defines what teacher autonomy means and presents an autonomous teacher's profile. This is followed by an overview of empirical projects investigating teacher autonomy. The aim is not only to show what has been done and what the findings reveal but also to identify possible gaps practitioners and educational researchers could fill in future research. The focus then shifts to pedagogical strategies for promoting teacher autonomy in teacher education programmes or professional development events.

Chapter 6 discusses designing language learning tasks and materials as one of the outstanding professional activities teachers should systematically engage in. The chapter addresses this aspect of the profession and describes in detail the various options and considerations available to teachers. In particular, it is argued that materials design and task development define the types of learning processes in which target language learners engage. This is also why designing tasks and materials always go hand in hand.

For a long time, media have been an established part of the language classroom. However, teaching and learning English in the twenty-first century also need to account for the rapid changes in media and the emergence of digital communication. The latter, in particular, has created a large number of new communication environments and communicative practices. Chapter 7 examines these developments and proposes how the English language classroom can adapt to these changes and how teachers can prepare to meet this challenge.

Chapter 8 focuses on the notion of teacher leadership. Contemporary English language education requires teachers who can passionately implement effective and innovative practices in the classroom, develop and take ownership of new pedagogical strategies, utilise professional knowledge to contribute to school improvement plans, and establish close relationships with other school stakeholders to enhance the student learning experience as well as overall school functioning. With this in mind, the chapter defines the concept of teacher leadership and presents a profile of a teacher leader who can exert their influence, both in the classroom and in the wider school, through a variety of formal and informal channels. This is followed by a discussion of the process of developing teacher leadership.

Chapter 9 scrutinises the general assumptions underlying the previous chapters. The constant cultural transformations we observe and the challenges learners encounter in their lifeworld can be successfully addressed in the classroom only if teachers are willing to develop their knowledge and professional competences further. The chapter argues that this is best achieved if teachers regard and establish themselves as a community of professional learners and practitioners. It therefore proposes creating professional development communities for ELT practitioners in a principled fashion and provides examples of such communities in action. The chapter concludes with a brief discussion of future directions and recommends that professional ELT be viewed in three meta-dimensions: lifelong learning, classroom ethnography, and educational leadership.

Taken as a whole, this conceptual and reflective guide contributes to the existing body of literature on professionalism in and professionalisation of ELT. It broadens and deepens the concept of teacher professionalism by detailing the dispositions, knowledge, and skills professional teachers must learn and be able to demonstrate to thrive in twenty-first-century schools. This book will therefore be helpful for English language teacher educators, school administrators, management teams, and policymakers. Needless to say, the book also seeks to empower current and future teachers, because we believe that every teacher ought to be a professional.

REFLECTION FOR ACTION

Future Teachers

- Think about the content of this chapter and discuss with your classmates what you feel makes a good teacher.
- To what extent does the content of this chapter give you a clear idea of what your future job will entail?
- Think about the various types of knowledge and competences in the chapter and identify one that you think will be the most challenging.
- Reflect on your own learning experiences at the secondary school level. Would you say that ethical professionalism was evident in these contexts?

Novice Teachers

- Reflect on the CEFR and how it guides your teaching. What advantages or disadvantages do you notice?
- What do you think about defining teacher education standards as presented in the *Cambridge English Teaching Framework*?
- How has your teacher education programme prepared you for your teaching career in terms of disciplinary knowledge and language teaching methodology? What message would you send to your former tutors?
- Is teaching a vocation or a profession? Answer this question reflecting on your school work as well as the content of this chapter.

Experienced Teachers

- Reflect on your pedagogical practice and explain what makes you a professional teacher.
- Think about the concept of *Bildung*. To what degree is it present in your pedagogical practice? How important is it for *Bildung* to guide teaching and underpin teacher education programmes?
- Discuss the available teacher standards in your context and explain their significance. Is there a need to update them?
- Reflect on the concept of discourse competence and evaluate your own participation in general and professional discourses in the workplace.

2 Conceptualising Teacher Professionalism in English Language Teaching

The topic of teacher professionalism has initiated a series of debates in the disciplinary fields of general education and sociology over the past five decades. Although their scope has varied, a recurring theme has been whether teaching should be considered a profession. In recent times, as Chapter 1 has demonstrated, the theoretical and empirical literature in the field of ELT has focused on the professional practice of ELT; thus, it is now clearly deemed a profession.

The level of skill and sophistication required to undertake such work distinguishes teaching from other types of occupations (Ingersoll & Collins, 2018). According to this sociological perspective, work defined as professional is characterised by possessing difficult-to-acquire knowledge, an elevated level of intellectual ability, and an extremely sophisticated skillset. Those striving to become teachers also need an additional qualification, more often than not a certificate, which is obtained only after the successful completion of officially approved teacher education programmes or training (Clark et al., 2012; Ellis, 2016; Salisbury & Lartigue, 2004; Tedick, 2005). Such credentials serve as screening instruments which protect the interests of educational institutions by ensuring that English language practitioners hold the required level of teaching competences and expertise and that those with insufficient degrees of skill and knowledge are not employed as teachers.

There has been an ongoing debate among teacher educators, practitioners, and school administrators about what defines someone as a 'professional'. In ELT, a methodological and theoretical consensus has not yet been reached regarding what constitutes the absolute characteristics of teacher professionalism. Although final agreement and precise descriptors are lacking, it is important that a set of characteristic features be established to clarify what teacher professionalism means and entails in the case of English language practitioners – hence the current chapter. For instance, multiple scholars (e.g., Al-Issa, 2017; Bukhatir, 2018; Coombe et al., 2020; Gerlach, 2020; Sehlaoui, 2018; Stronge, 2018) suggest that teacher professionalism requires generalised and systematic knowledge, a full-time occupation, a deep commitment, a high degree of standardisation, ethical behaviour, and a high degree of confidence in the services performed. Other scholars (e.g., Evans, 2011) identify *behavioural*, *attitudinal*, and *intellectual* components of teacher professionalism. The behavioural component refers to what professionals actually do at work (e.g., skills and competences; productivity, outputs, and achievements; and the strategies teachers employ in their work). The attitudinal component refers to the perceptions, beliefs, and views teachers possess. Finally, the intellectual component denotes the understanding and knowledge held by teachers, the framework of such knowledge, and the extent and type of reasoning and analytical ability displayed.

As this volume reiterates, shaping teacher professionalism is a multi-agentic and constantly evolving process (Akkerman & Meijer, 2011; Kayi-Aydar et al., 2019). A key determinant of teachers' agency in this process (Chapters 5 and 9), which is relational, social, and contextual in nature, is the degree to which teachers adhere to a specific strand of professionalism they perceive as offering 'a better way' for their students, wider society, and themselves as people for whom teaching constitutes just one element of an extremely busy and complicated life.

Recent debates additionally stress that classroom practitioners – through their professional agency, that is, their active participation in shaping their work and its conditions by adhering to *a specific set of* knowledge, beliefs, values, and objectives – create a professional community within their schools (Chapter 9) by enhancing teaching standards and learning outcomes (Bonnet & Hericks, 2022; Priestley et al., 2015; Teng, 2019, 2020; Toom et al., 2015). It is important to remember that the key to improving the quality of schools is to pursue and advance the professionalisation of teaching by enhancing teachers' training, status, and working conditions. This will boost their commitment and motivation; consequently, their performance will improve, leading to better student learning outcomes.

Taking all these aspects into account, the topic of teacher professionalism requires further exploration in the field of ELT. It is vital that a proper understanding of the concept is acquired, especially with regard to the competences and standards that English language practitioners must adhere to in their daily pedagogical practice, as described in Chapters 1 and 3. Clear guidelines are required to direct teachers along their journeys to professional excellence. This chapter therefore explores essential components of the notion of teacher professionalism. It begins by examining various definitions of teacher professionalism. This is followed by a discussion of the professional standards required for the teaching occupation. The chapter then analyses the complexity of teachers' professional identity. A brief discussion of the relationship between professionalism and ethics supplements this. Finally, suggestions are made regarding ways to sustain teacher professionalism.

2.1 Particularising Teacher Professionalism

Teacher professionalism has frequently been the focus of wide-ranging discussions in the fields of sociology and education. However, only the latter will be focused on in this section. It is important to clarify from the outset that the concept is not easy to define as it is socially constructed and subject to constant review due to ever-changing educational theories, policies, and practices. It is also shaped by several important factors, including performance cultures, increased accountability, standards, and parent expectations (Sachs, 2016). It is thus subject to shifting, diverse, and frequently competing interpretations (Hargreaves, 2000; Helsby, 2000; Tateo, 2012).

The field of ELT, for instance, does not have its own widely accepted definition of teacher professionalism and has borrowed definitions from the field of education. Some of the earlier definitions describe professional teachers as individuals who possess a thorough knowledge of the subjects they teach, are familiar with the standards of practice relevant to their profession, and can analyse the needs of the students to whom they are accountable (Wise, 1989). Similarly, Talbert and McLaughlin (1994) suggest that teacher professionalism includes a technical culture, service ethics, professional commitment, and professional autonomy (Chapter 5). Consequently, teachers are required to exhibit a sound foundation of knowledge and a firm commitment to ensuring that the varying requirements of students are met. They are also required to display sound cognisance of ethical precepts, adopt robust identities of both an individual and a collective nature, and demonstrate a capacity to utilise their knowledge to make vitally important decisions that benefit students.

Although many of these characteristics apply, the twenty-first century has brought new perspectives to ELT. The educational demands of the twenty-first century have expanded the view of what professionals require and have moved beyond the commonly accepted model of knowledgeable and technically skilled practitioners (Goldhaber & Hannaway, 2009). Contemporary educational professionals are required to be reflective thinkers (Chapter 4); effective communicators, decision-makers, and problem-solvers (Chapter 5); classroom researchers (Chapter 4); inspiring leaders (Chapter 8); and ethical practitioners (Section 2.4) who not only use but also construct new knowledge (Bonnet & Hericks, 2022; Borg, 2013; Christison & Murray, 2009; Cirocki & Burns, 2019; Farrell, 2015; Hegarty, 2000; Low et al., 2014). Consequently, teacher professionalism is now discussed in relation to three broad areas: *attitudes*, *behaviours*, and *communication* (Kramer, 2003). These encompass a wide range of beliefs, practices, and characteristics, all of which classroom practitioners are expected to demonstrate professionally. Examples include the following: risk-taking, confidence, integrity, punctuality, enthusiasm, observing dress code policy, and clear communication with students, colleagues, and parents. The latter can be verbal, non-verbal, written, face-to-face, online, synchronous, or asynchronous.

An alternative definition conceptualises teacher professionalism as consisting of the following four components: *teacher efficacy*, *teacher practice*, *teacher leadership*, and *teacher collaboration* (Rizvi & Elliot, 2005). Teacher efficacy relates to the utilisation of novel approaches in the classroom. Teacher practice refers to the hands-on experience of being a teacher. Teacher leadership (Chapter 8) denotes the extent to which teachers become involved in shaping innovative policies and making decisions in relation to resources, curricula, and assessment. The final element, teacher collaboration (Chapter 9), refers to whether teachers are proactive in undertaking activities relevant to the profession to initiate change, improvement, or innovation (van Maele & van Houtte, 2011).

Some definitions also allude to the moral aspects of teacher work. For instance, teacher professionalism can refer either to the way in which teachers behave as professionals and integrate their duties with their expertise and abilities or to the impact professional contracts and associated ethical standards have on teaching and engagement with students in the classroom (Crookes, 2003, 2009; Sockett, 2012). Professional teachers also need to fulfil obligations outside the classroom, such as educational visits, school outings, and field trips. For both in- and out-of-school obligations, professional teachers are expected to systematically exhibit dispositions of character (e.g., self-knowledge, integrity, perseverance), intellect (e.g., fairness, thoughtfulness, open-mindedness), and care (e.g., tolerance, respect, compassion). This is because teaching is fundamentally involved in assisting with the development of students as people (Sockett, 2012).

An overview of the definitions of teacher professionalism would not be complete without mentioning the concept of empowerment, which is a valid objective with respect to teachers' practice as professionals (Steinberg, 2015). Teacher empowerment is defined as a process whereby practitioners (1) confidently exercise their professional judgement about what and how to teach, (2) competently and successfully deliver classes, maximising their impact on students, (3) engage in school decision-making (e.g., school goals, policies), (4) ensure that their decisions are linked to their values and beliefs, and (5) take responsibility for their own development to become better teachers and make a difference in their classrooms (Amzat & Valdez, 2017; Carl, 2009; Christodoulou, 2016; Sachs, 2016). There are four ways in which teachers can be empowered: (1) *meaning*, which refers to the alignment between a teacher's professional duties and their behaviours, values, and beliefs; (2) *competence*, which refers to the confidence a teacher has in being able to fulfil the requirements of their role to a high standard; (3) *self-determination*, which refers to the extent to which teachers feel they have autonomy in how they perform their duties; and (4) *impact*, which refers to a teacher's belief that they can have a practical impact on processes relating to administration or strategy (Spreitzer, 1995). These aspects render teachers professionals in their own right as they endow them with the power to enact changes in schools in general or classrooms more specifically.

A more recent development is that teacher professionalism requires teachers to become reflective practitioners (Chapter 4). This has been widely discussed in the field of ELT (e.g., Cirocki & Farrell, 2017a; Farrell, 2015; Mann & Walsh, 2017), which calls for practitioners to be reflective educators who regularly work together, both in their everyday teaching duties and in broader issues pertaining to teaching the English language. Importantly, reflective practitioners also need to:

- demonstrate awareness of the beliefs, attitudes, and values they bring to the teaching–learning process;
- promote learning-oriented, needs-based, and dialogic education;
- devote considerable attention to developing autonomy in both themselves and their students;
- solve classroom problems effectively and creatively;
- integrate open-mindedness, responsibility, and wholeheartedness into their teaching;
- participate in curriculum development;
- become involved in efforts to change schools;
- monitor and evaluate their own practice to plan potential improvements;
- engage in classroom inquiry; and
- take responsibility for their professional development.

The various definitions presented thus far constitute a transformative view of teacher professionalism (Chapter 9). According to this view, teachers can devise original and imaginative approaches to teaching and the formulation of curricula; engage in in-depth work with students, fellow teaching staff, and other important stakeholders; and cultivate the expertise required 'to conduct their own research, individually and collectively, to investigate the impact of particular interventions or to explore the positive and negative effects of educational practice' (BERA-RSA, 2014, p. 5).

These definitions align with those of Liu and Berger (2015, p. 39), who specify that professionalism in ELT is 'ongoing; multidimensional in nature (i.e., it involves knowledge, proficiency, personality, environment, materials, and hands-on experience); includes a combination of discipline-based knowledge and ethical awareness; and requires reflective, responsive and context-specific practice'.

Closer scrutiny suggests that these definitions additionally refer to two competing discourses of professionalism – *occupational* and *organisational* (Evetts, 2008, 2011). The former denotes the authority afforded to being a teacher and concerns the development of relationships based on trust with students, their parents, and employers. It is predicated on having the freedom to make informed judgements and evaluations in cases where many factors need to be considered. By contrast, organisational professionalism refers to the integration of authority into stratified layers of management to facilitate effective decision-making. It places an emphasis on the importance of efficacy, good organisation, and adherence to relevant rules and regulations. It is dependent on the use of external measures to assess and ensure professional responsibility and effective performance.

Having synthesised the various aspects of teacher professionalism, an exhaustive definition needs to be proposed to guide English language professionals. Combining the tenets of transformative, sponsored, independent, occupational, and organisational types of professionalism with the construal of teachers as lifelong learners driven to pursue a never-ending quest for knowledge for both personal and professional reasons, the proposed definition of teacher professionalism is as follows:

In general, teacher professionalism denotes an ongoing concern with the calibre of teaching within institutions, which is encapsulated in a set of standards deemed appropriate to the profession. More specifically, it is a dynamic exercise that involves teachers shaping their professional careers through systematic interactions with others. This entails (1) acting as English language experts, innovative problem-solvers, effective communicators, critical thinkers, active collaborators, and lifelong learners; (2) demonstrating creativity, autonomy, agency, leadership, and dispositions of character, intellect, and care; and (3) engaging in broadly defined reflective practice in order to deliver effective and research-informed teaching and make a difference in the classroom.

2.2 Professional Standards for English Language Teachers

The various definitions of teacher professionalism presented in the previous section touch upon the issue of professional standards for teachers. A core component of teacher professionalism, professional standards are statements of a teacher's professional attributes (e.g., communicating and working with others), knowledge and understanding (e.g., teaching and learning, assessing and monitoring progress, educational technology), and professional skills (e.g., planning, team working).

Professional standards play an essential role in the education sector as they enhance teachers' performance, which directly impacts student outcomes (AITSL, 2022; Education and Training Foundation, 2014; Kuhlman & Knežević, n.d.). They are also useful in determining whether teachers or schools meet the governmental requirements with respect to English language education. Such standards are important in the assessment of teacher performance and are used in the evaluation and accreditation of teacher training institutions.

Although professional standards vary across teaching contexts, they can be arranged into three generic domains: *professional knowledge*, *professional practice*, and *professional engagement*. The scope of these domains is briefly described in the following sub-sections.

2.2.1 Professional Knowledge

Professional language teachers demonstrate three types of specialised knowledge: *target language awareness*, *disciplinary knowledge*, and *pedagogical content knowledge*.

Target language awareness refers to teachers' cognitions (knowledge and beliefs) about language in general and their ability to use, analyse, and teach the target language competently (Chapter 1). The concept consists of three dimensions: *linguistic-systematic*, *cultural-political*, and *sociocultural* (Breidbach et al., 2011). The linguistic-systematic dimension concerns the language, its structure, and its consistencies and disparities. The cultural-political dimension is concerned with how power and control function via language and the deployment of this in everyday discussion. Finally, the sociocultural dimension is concerned with the beliefs, opinions, and attitudes expressed by both teachers and students with regard to teaching and learning language (Breidbach et al., 2011). Target language awareness therefore functions as a filter that moulds the language input teachers select and present to students in the classroom (Andrews, 2007).

Additionally, teachers' deep awareness of the target language is intertwined with the notion of English-for-teaching (Section 3.5.3), conceptualised as the vital skill that English language teachers must possess in order to devise and implement lessons in a standard English curriculum so that they can be easily recognised and understood by everyone who speaks the language and to effectively manage the complex and situated culture of a language classroom (Freeman, 2017; Young et al., 2014). The latter includes comprehending and conveying the content of lessons to students and then assessing their work and providing feedback. According to Young et al. (2014), in using this professional language, teachers have the following aims:

- to use English either partly or wholly as the medium of teaching;
- to deliver a curriculum established at a national level along with the relevant policies;
- to implement strategies in the classroom that will help to forge expectations, create norms, construct productive *classroom* relationships, and facilitate seamless changes between tasks, thereby minimising the potential for disruption; and
- to engage with students in a straightforward and consistent manner.

Disciplinary knowledge concerns 'the body of knowledge that is considered by the language teaching profession to be essential to gaining membership of the profession...and leads to professional recognition and status' (Richards & Farrell, 2011, p. 19). It is acquired through professional education (Chapter 3). By way of illustration, courses such as psycholinguistics, pragmatics, and theories of second language learning are all included in the domain of disciplinary knowledge.

Pedagogical content knowledge, which lays the foundations for language teaching, is derived from 'the study of language teaching and language learning itself' (Richards & Farrell, 2011, p. 19). It constitutes a blend of 'content and pedagogy that is uniquely the province of teachers, their own special form of professional [knowing and] understanding' (Shulman, 1987, p. 8). It therefore covers areas such as curriculum design, teaching methods and approaches, educational technology, and teaching receptive and productive skills.

Professional knowledge has therefore been shown to combine language and subject expertise with skilled teaching. It is dynamic in nature as it evolves with experience and is validated through the work shared with other teachers. Professional teachers are expected to combine professional knowledge with a deep comprehension of the cognitive, social, and bodily attributes of those they teach. Knowledge of student characteristics and individual differences enables teachers to maximise student learning by using appropriate teaching methods and selecting meaningful and appropriate feedback formats.

2.2.2 Professional Practice

In education, the concept of professional practice refers to the conduct of and work undertaken by teachers. To engage in such practice, teachers are obliged to develop and maintain professional relationships with a diverse range of students, teaching staff, and administrative colleagues; effectively communicate with parents; act ethically; promote positive values; and deliver high-quality inclusive student-centred instruction.

In their pedagogical practice, teachers are expected to be instructive, considerate, and fully immersed in the joy of being a teacher while remaining mindful of the fact that they have one of the strongest and most salient impacts on the way in which their students learn. Thus, it is vital that teachers be cognisant of learning aims and benchmarks for success in advance of their lessons, plan lessons carefully, have a clear sense of where to go next, and keep students actively engaged in the teaching–learning process.

Another vital element of teacher professional practice is constructing an atmosphere in the classroom that is both congenial and focused on the learner (McGee & Fraser, 2012). Such environments are crucial as they consider the knowledge, skills, attitudes, and beliefs learners bring to the educational setting, thus ensuring that teaching is culturally responsive, appropriate, and relevant (Crookes, 2003; Herrera, 2016; Ladson-Billings, 1995; McGee & Fraser, 2012). Additionally, learners must feel physically, emotionally, and socially comfortable in the classroom to ensure that effective language learning is achieved. Students expect their needs to be cared for and the entire classroom community to be protected by a caring teacher. Language learners, in particular, need to feel that it is a comfortable environment in which to learn, re-learn, and examine what they know and comprehend of the target language; mistakes therefore need to be construed as a valuable opportunity for learning (Newton & Nation, 2020; Spiro, 2013; Ur, 2012). It is also vital that opportunities for feedback and revision are systematically provided, and both formative (i.e., assessment for learning) and summative (i.e., assessment of learning) types of assessment are strongly promoted (Al-Mahrooqi et al., 2017; Cheng & Fox, 2017; Cirocki & Brown, 2021). For such professional practice to occur, as pointed out in the previous section, teachers must demonstrate a high level of English-for-teaching competence.

2.2.3 *Professional Engagement*

Professional engagement is the third domain of teacher professionalism. This refers to the wide range of educational activities teachers participate in, both inside and outside school. It also deals with professional development, as teachers are lifelong learners.

Although school principals and administrators have their tasks and responsibilities, it would not be sensible to expect them to respond alone to all the possible challenges faced by modern-day schools. For example, in some schools, urgent calls are increasingly being made to update pedagogical systems using cloud, mobile, and digital technologies. This will enhance the efficiency with which education is delivered and ensure that schools are successfully run. Some schools may find it problematic to manage students who are consistently late and to remedy problems arising from poor behaviour and a lack of discipline. Although the list of school problems is long, they will vary from one place to another. However, constructing a cooperative climate that strives to be inclusive enables management personnel and teachers to work together on such matters. This type of collaboration is uniquely effective because it is embedded within the systems and processes of the school. Moreover, it fosters a common approach towards cooperative responsibility, planning, and decision-making founded on high levels of dedication, regard for one's colleagues, and mutual trust.

Professional teachers are also expected to be involved in school committees (e.g., policy and strategy, finance, health and safety, special educational needs and disabilities), organise open days with demonstration classes for parents, and hold interschool English language competitions. Another task they undertake is to organise field trips. These may take different formats depending on the schools involved and the needs of English language learners. For example, teachers could take students to a shopping mall to practise productive skills in the target language (e.g., describing the place in writing, buying various objects, or ordering food in the food court) or to a local museum where the teacher, using specially designed activities, engages students in practising receptive skills and teamwork and in revising recently learnt vocabulary. Arranging informal chats with native speakers in local cafes is another option that can be employed to help students to practise English or explore the target language culture. The subsidiary aims of such trips include developing students' social, personal, observation, and perception skills, bringing relevance and meaning to learning, offering authentic and experiential learning, and stimulating interest in the target language (Behrendt & Franklin, 2014; Larsen et al., 2017).

In addition to the various educational activities, teachers also engage in professional learning and development as calls are increasing for educational opportunities relating to English language education to be more diverse in terms of what they offer. Additionally, educational technology, ministry guidelines for schools, and curriculum standards are continually being transformed, creating difficulties for teachers in keeping pace with new requirements and modifications. Teachers are therefore encouraged to engage in professional communities (Chapter 9) in which groups of practitioners meet regularly to reflect on and share expertise and best practices, identify and analyse their own learning needs, evaluate and expand their professional learning, and work collaboratively to improve English language instruction in general and the academic performance of their students in particular (Abatayo, 2018; Cirocki & Farrell, 2019).

Continuing professional development may take different forms (Cirocki et al., 2023), and professional teachers, as autonomous practitioners (Chapters 5 and 9), decide for themselves how they want to develop professionally and what activities they want to engage in. Some may opt for action research projects, which enable teachers to explore issues and areas of uncertainty pertaining to teaching and how their students learn. It also offers them the chance to enhance further the way they teach and increase the efficacy of the teaching–learning process (Burns, 2005, 2010; Farr, 2015; Richards & Farrell, 2005). Others may choose to teach classes with more experienced colleagues. Co-teaching allows teachers to share the responsibilities of planning, teaching, and assessing students. This provides opportunities not only for collective learning but also for collective responsibility and accountability for the classes taught. Further examples of how English language teachers can engage in reflective practice are included in Chapter 4.

2.3 Teacher Professional Identity

As the previous discussion reveals, teacher professionalism is about creating and maintaining a professional identity. A professional identity offers teachers a structure within which they can formulate their intentions with respect to how they feel they should behave and their ideas on how to comprehend the nature of what they do and their position within both the teaching profession and society at large (Sachs, 2005). It is therefore important to recognise that it comprises several types of identities.

Indeed, recent literature reveals that teachers create multiple identities (Barkhuizen, 2017; de Dios Martinez Agudo, 2018; Golombek & Doran, 2014; Meyer, 2009). These constitute an ever-changing mixture of personal details, the broader culture, significant others (e.g., colleagues, students, parents), and values embedded within the institution that constantly alter depending on the situation and the role they occupy (Day et al., 2006). This means that teacher identities are co-constructed through interactions with others (teacher colleagues, students, administrators, policymakers), the context of their experiences, and the activities in which they are engaged (Barkhuizen, 2017; Pennington & Richards, 2016). As teachers extend their networks of professional and social contacts, and thus the environment within which they operate as teachers, they will be involved in an ongoing process of building and transforming their identities to align with the different roles they assume and the varying range of personnel with whom they engage and cooperate. Thus, a teacher's professional identity, a blend of sub-identities, is continually refined through a never-ending exercise that elucidates and re-elucidates their teaching and learning experiences (Cheung et al., 2015; Crandall & Christison, 2016).

Apart from being social and negotiated, and thus ideological in nature, such multiple identities are cognitive and, as mentioned earlier, exist both inside teachers and externally in the context in which they work while undertaking their work (Barkhuizen, 2017). To expand further, because identities are essentially a mental phenomenon, they are strongly associated with teachers' feelings, professional knowledge, convictions, and principles. At the same time, they reside in the teaching environment and can be externally forced upon teachers, particularly when engaging with specific locations (such as the classroom) or physical entities (such as educational technology).

In the context of the ELT classroom, the professional identity teachers assume and enact reflects their perception of the particular role they should play within the school and their unique sense of themselves as human beings (Pennington & Richards, 2016). Both are additionally influenced by such factors as teachers' professional knowledge (i.e., disciplinary identity), their language background and language proficiency (i.e., language-related identity), the characteristics of their students (i.e., student-related identity), and, of course, the context in which teachers perform their pedagogical practice (i.e., context-related identity).

The concept of teacher professional identity has been widely researched in the fields of sociology, psychology, and education (e.g., Cheung et al., 2015; Gray & Morton, 2018; Hannula et al., 2019; Yazan & Lindahl, 2020). Several psychological concepts have subsequently emerged as dimensions of this identity. For instance, Kelchtermans (2009) identified five interconnected facets of teacher professional identity: *self-image* (i.e., the teacher's view of how they represent themselves as a teacher), *self-esteem* (i.e., a broad evaluation of how they are performing in their role), *job motivation* (i.e., the factors that impel them to behave in certain ways while in their role), *task perception* (i.e., how the teacher views their job and the particular duties they believe they have to carry out), and *future perspective* (i.e., the teacher's perceptions with regard to their anticipated future in this career). Similar findings were reported by Day (2002) and Karaolis and Philippou (2019).

Regarding the field of ELT, various dimensions of teacher identity have been both quantitatively and qualitatively investigated (Barkhuizen, 2017; Cheung et al., 2015; Yazan & Lindahl, 2020). However, it is Pennington and Richards (2016) who, by adopting an extremely pragmatic approach in their research-based discussion, best explain the concept of teacher identity in relation to language teaching. More specifically, their analysis connects teacher identity to Richards's (2012, p. 46) dimensions of teachers' knowledge and skills regarded as 'the core of expert teaching competence and performance in language teaching'. Their discussion is divided into two stages. First, they examine the foundational competences of language teacher identity that subsume language-related identity, disciplinary identity, context-related identity, self-knowledge and awareness, and student-related identity. They then examine the advanced competences of language teacher identity – the coveted outcome of continuous professional learning and experience. These competences encompass practised and responsive teaching skills, theorising from practice, and membership in communities of practice and profession. Pennington and Richards (2016, p. 20) conclude that language teacher identity 'includes a sense of having specialized knowledge and expertise and of being part of a larger profession and what this represents, such as certain standards, ethics, and accountability for performance in teaching'.

Overall, it is reasonable to extrapolate that the professional identity of an English language teacher is about being or doing, as opposed to possessing, as teachers perform being teachers. In particular, being a language teacher is a continuous personal and professional development process shaped by teachers' diverse beliefs, values, experiences, and emotions. The latter form the landscape of teachers' professional lives by significantly impacting on their pedagogical decisions and actions, creativity, teamwork, and overall job performance.

2.4 Professionalism and Ethics in English Language Teaching

Teaching is both an independent profession and a challenging task that intrinsically necessitates the application of professional ethics (Crookes, 2009). It requires teachers to be moral exemplars both inside and outside school. Notably, teachers of English not only teach language knowledge and skills to their students, they also focus on such issues as race, religion, gender, sexual orientation, and disability while mentoring their students by instilling invaluable life lessons into them through the medium of English (Carr, 2000; López-Gopar, 2019; Maxwell & Schwimmer, 2016; Motha, 2014; Richards & Armstrong, 2016; Tirri & Kuusisto, 2022). For this reason, teachers are expected to develop, maintain, and exhibit strong personality traits such as honesty, respect, integrity, fairness, and perseverance, all of which exert a powerful impact on students' characters.

As a sign of professionalism, it is therefore vital that teachers follow a code of ethics to demonstrate such qualities as integrity, confidentiality, and impartiality and forge healthy relationships among colleague teachers, students, parents, administrators, and the wider community (Atjonen, 2012; The Teaching Council, 2012). The purpose of the code of ethics is fourfold: (1) to provide a moral foundation that guides teachers in their careers, (2) to inform the broader public's understanding and expectations of teachers and the teaching profession, (3) to serve as a reference point in exercising investigative and disciplinary functions, and (4) to promote the reputation and standing of the teaching profession (The Teaching Council, 2016).

To be regarded as ethical professionals, it is essential that English language teachers hold rational beliefs and attitudes, engage in friendly and collegial relationships, and promote good practices and conduct. Several examples of these are listed in the following sub-sections.

2.4.1 Beliefs and Attitudes

Teachers should:

- be caring and compassionate;
- hold sincere and unbiased beliefs;
- be forgiving and reconciling; and
- hold democratic values.

2.4.2 Relationships

Teachers should:

- create and sustain a culture of shared trust and respect in the classroom/school;

- engage in professional and supportive communication based on respect, trust, and fairness; and
- create a student-friendly learning environment where students act as agents in the teaching–learning process and develop transferable skills.

2.4.3 Classroom Practices

Teachers should:

- promote high standards of practice with regard to planning, monitoring, assessing, and providing detailed and constructive feedback on students' progress;
- promote the holistic development of students, appreciating their individuality, differences, and specific educational needs;
- integrate democratic values and practices in classrooms to foster or modify students' democratic beliefs and/or thinking to satisfy the social demands of democracy; and
- embed inclusive practices into the design, preparation, delivery, and evaluation of classes to account for diversity and ensure that all students receive equal opportunities and treatment.

2.4.4 Professional Conduct

Teachers should:

- consider the privacy of others and the confidentiality of information throughout their professional practice;
- avoid clashes between professional duties and private interests that could negatively affect students;
- make morally justifiable decisions based on rational criteria that serve the best interests of students;
- conform to policies and procedures which promote student-centred high-quality education and ensure student safety and well-being;
- share best practices with teacher colleagues to ensure the highest quality of educational experiences for students;
- seek learning opportunities and assume responsibility for improving the quality of own professional practice; and
- engage in critical reflection and research on own practice and disseminate own findings to maximise the impact on improving the teaching and/or learning of the English language.

Although this list is not exhaustive, it does provide a number of specific attributes which bridge the abstract concept of professional ethics with ethical practices in the classrooms and schools more broadly. It is vital, however, that these features are implemented with contextual differences and variations in mind.

2.5 Supporting Teacher Professionalism

The discussion thus far reveals that English language teachers working at a professional level contribute to sustainable education. Through their engagement in professional practice, they enable others to acquire the knowledge, skills, and values required for creating a sustainable future. It is therefore important that teacher professionalism is strongly supported and that the correct type of infrastructure is available to sustain it (Coleman et al., 2012). This infrastructure includes:

- *introducing policies* that focus on (1) shaping professional practice on a large scale, (2) formulating expectations for professional practice, (3) establishing the criteria under which professionals operate, (4) introducing compulsory continuing professional development (CPD) to enable teachers to further their professional learning and development, and (5) improving equity of access to available support so that teachers from high-needs and low-needs schools or urban and rural areas are afforded equal chances. Such policies are crucial as they seek to define and standardise professional practice to promote wide-ranging consistency and parity, as well as enhanced quality assurance.
- *providing systems of support*, both monetary and non-monetary, for teachers to promote professional development (Cirocki & Farrell, 2019). For example, schools or regional offices could offer salary supplements or non-monetary support, including transportation to and from CPD training, or offer teachers additional time to pursue professional development.
- *enabling teachers to apply their learning to classroom practice.* There is a need for innovative models that not only successfully connect the field of ELT with the classroom but also take the English language classroom out into the field. This concurs with Dewey (1929), who argued that theory and practice should be integral to each other, emphasising that the practical knowledge of instructors serves as an indispensable resource for advancing pedagogical theory. For example, to apply their learning to classroom practice, teachers can conduct, individually or collaboratively, classroom-based research and explore how to convert the theoretical knowledge gained through CPD into practical teaching. Another opportunity for teachers to combine theory and practice in the classroom is by engaging students in experiential learning, where students learn as a result of completing complex tasks (Cirocki, 2016) and then reflecting on the process of accomplishing them. In both cases, teachers develop decision-making skills critical for

successful teaching and enhance their awareness of the relevance of particular theories and their necessity and usefulness in understanding or solving problematic issues in the classroom.
- *focusing teacher professionalism on teachers' needs.* Teachers learn best when they engage in professional development that responds to their needs (Díaz Maggioli, 2004; Meissel et al., 2016). Such needs relate to several areas, ranging from technology usage through special educational needs to action research. Although they are sometimes universal, they also vary across contexts. It is therefore important for teachers' needs to be considered on a case-by-case basis. For instance, research conducted in several countries has revealed that upper secondary school teachers begin their teaching careers having less exposure to pedagogy principles and less experience with pre-service teaching practice than teachers from primary and lower secondary schools (OECD, 2016). To remedy this situation, it is important that upper secondary school teachers be offered training explicitly aimed at pedagogy and teaching practice.
- *encouraging teachers to join professional communities.* In such communities, teachers work with other professionals to share interests, best practices, or classroom issues; improve teaching skills; and learn from one another's experiences (Hadar & Brody, 2010; McDonald & Cater-Steel, 2017; McLaughlin & Talbert, 2006). In this way, such communities encourage collaboration and knowledge construction. They also have significant potential for improving teachers, their pedagogical practice, their professional learning, and the learning of their students. For more information on professional communities for English language professionals, see Chapter 9.

2.6   Conclusion

The purpose of this chapter has been to define the concept of teacher professionalism and discuss its various component parts. The discussion has shown that teacher professionalism is an intricate and evolving construct; this is because a teacher's professional identity continues to grow from the beginning to the end of their careers. In other words, the longer teachers practise teaching and the more they learn about it, the more they develop professionally. Competent teachers demonstrate professional knowledge, engage in professional practice, undertake professional engagement, and act ethically; they also develop a professional identity – the valued professional self – through which they define themselves as teachers and their teaching journey. In order for practitioners to engage in high-quality pedagogical practice and commit themselves to lifelong learning, teacher professionalism must be supported with a well-developed infrastructure. The latter should be context-dependent and needs-based.

The next chapter focuses on teacher education, competences, and roles.

REFLECTION FOR ACTION

Future Teachers

- Reflect on the content of this chapter. To what extent is it reflected in your current curriculum?
- To what degree is the content of this chapter relevant to your future classroom teaching?
- Does your teacher education programme help you to develop your professional identity as a teacher?
- Reflect on the profile of an ethical teacher in Section 2.4 and discuss with your classmates the importance of codes of conduct in schools.

Novice Teachers

- Choose your favourite definition of teacher professionalism and explain why it is important to you. Why do you think other teachers should consider integrating it into their professional lives?
- Reflect on the different aspects of professional knowledge; identify areas you are good at and those you need to work on. Explain why these areas need to be given attention and how you plan to go about this.
- Reflect on the issue of ethics and describe the extent to which it is embedded in your teaching and professional conduct.
- Think about the content of this chapter and explain which aspects are promoted well in your current context and which should be explored further in teacher education programmes.

Experienced Teachers

- Reflect on your professional practice and engagement; identify areas where you excel and those you could improve. What precisely could you improve, and how do you plan to go about this?
- Think about the factors that are currently shaping your professional identity. Arrange a meeting with a colleague and discuss whether there are any similarities/differences in your experiences.
- Reflect on your teaching journey and think about the way(s) in which you could help your school, or your school could help you, to maintain your professionalism.
- Which aspects of teacher professionalism discussed in this chapter would you like to explore further as part of your continuing professional development?

3 Teacher Education and Professional Competences

In recent decades, intense debates on language education have brought substantial changes and developments to the nature of the teaching profession. Similarly, recent improvements and innovations in people's social lives, the economy, and educational environments have exerted a strong and enduring impact on the makeup and substance of teacher education and training – which vary in different contexts – as well as being compelling reasons for the qualifications language teachers must obtain and the competences and skills they should demonstrate in the workplace. Consequently, universities have responded to these advances, more or less successfully, by offering programmes that ensure future teachers have detailed knowledge and a clear understanding of teaching, learning, social, and cultural contexts and can enact these within the complex realities of twenty-first-century classrooms and schools which serve highly diverse communities of students. Ideally, for the latter to occur, which is already in place in some countries, universities need to establish close links with schools where student teachers can learn to teach. This implies that universities must inform both policymakers and the public about the knowledge and skills that need to be developed in order for teachers to be effective in this modern era and the types of environments that need to be established in schools so that teachers can nurture and apply their knowledge to achieve this goal.

It is essential to clarify, however, that this chapter does not aim to present a comprehensive framework of professional language teacher competences. Instead, the following sections focus on some of the most important competences that English language teachers need to develop and demonstrate as part of their daily routine, explicitly focusing on discourse competence as an overarching goal (Section 3.1). There are two key arguments presented in this chapter. The first is that discourse competence in English is the principal objective of language teaching and learning in all schools. The second, which follows from this, is that discourse competence must be fully developed in student teachers so that they, in turn, can foster the discursive and linguistic competences in their classrooms. The chapter first provides a detailed explanation of competence before explaining the meta-concept of discourse competence.

Examples are then provided of how competence orientation can be made concrete in the form of can-do descriptors for student teachers prior to their developing a wide array of ELT competences. The final part of the chapter clarifies and demonstrates how competence orientation can be transformed into the structured curricula of teacher education programmes.

It is also important to explain that, for consistency and clarity, pre- and in-service teachers who pursue teacher education programmes at undergraduate and postgraduate levels in different contexts are referred to throughout this chapter as student teachers.

3.1 Discourse Competence as a Core Concept of Language Learning

As elaborated in this section and Section 3.2, it is the global objective of all language learning to enable learners to utilise the additional language appropriately in all sorts of situations and in accordance with cultural conventions and linguistic rules. This reflection on language learning is crucial in the context of language teacher education, as the teacher's orientations and competences primarily need to be derived from the goals and content of language learning and the curricular content of the language learning classroom. One of the aims of teacher education programmes is to raise and develop this awareness along with corresponding knowledge about language learning goals. In short, a language teacher needs to be able to understand and define the competences of language learning, which are reflected in the learner's discourse competence. This is what is defined and explained in detail as a meta-competence in Section 3.3.

It is in the nature of all learning that it is always directed towards managing situations, demands, and problems. This applies to natural learning in the lifeworld as much as to institutional learning in schools and universities. However, as public discourses on issues of education demonstrate for India (e.g., Rai, 2021) or for Europe (Council of Europe, 2018), learning processes and pedagogical goals of school education are socially and politically framed and determined through educational policies and by state institutions. According to this general principle, all learning must align with the overarching goals, which, in Western-oriented democracies, reconcile the needs and rights of the individual with the needs and demands of the respective society. It can thus be said that:

pedagogical objectives standardise the relations between individuals and societies. They determine the demands and forms of socialisation and the role of the subjects. For modern societies committed to the tradition of the Enlightenment and organised as democracies, a concept of individuality is therefore regarded as guiding, in which as a basic principle, human dignity and the free development of the individual's personality are the prime maxims. (Klieme et al., 2003, p. 63)

According to this guiding principle, all education and the teaching–learning process must enable language learners to participate in political, social, and cultural processes and know how to shape their own lifeworld, acting self-determinedly and as responsible citizens. All competences taught and developed in various school subjects serve this purpose. In light of this general principle of school education, language learning involves much more than training in language structures and devices. Instead, all competences that are developed in the language classroom must be derived from the two core goals, namely self-determination and participation, as defined later.

This is where the concept of discourse comes into play. Discourse can be understood as a more significant, thematically coherent, social, and cultural, possibly also transcultural, body of utterances, a set of culturally circulating and thematically interrelated texts (Section 6.3), and other communicative artefacts of all kinds, such as pictures or diagrams (Bibri, 2018; Foucault, 1972). Discourses are usually organised thematically along cultural domains and social spheres or in discourse communities and in relation to relevant issues and topics so that one can speak of, for instance, the climate discourse, a professional football discourse, and the like. As Kramsch (1998, p. 61) notes:

In order to understand a text, one has to understand what the text is responding to or against. This existing prior language, accumulated over the life of a discourse community, has been called Discourse with a capital D. Discourses, in this sense, are more than just language; they are ways of being in the world, or forms of life that integrate words, acts, values, beliefs, attitudes, and social identities.

Such discourses are circulated and developed transmedially, that is, they are negotiated and communicated on television, in print media, in face-to-face conversations at the pub, in literature, and in a large number of other contexts (Kress & van Leeuwen, 2001). Moreover, individual texts, voices, and utterances are produced in different modes, from the documentary photo to the satirical caricature, the medial format of the talk show, and the newspaper article.

Terminologically, discourse may also denote the single utterance or text individuals produce (discourse with a small 'd'). Verdonk (2002) defines a discourse as a communicative act articulated within a text bound within a particular context, which the reader then infers. However, only when it is actively used within a given context can the meaning of a text emerge. This process of relating a text to the particular context in which it is used is known as discourse (Verdonk, 2002). These two different meanings of discourse may serve to define discourse competence as the overarching goal of all language teaching and learning, as they correspond with the two global educational goals of self-determination and participation. Thus, there are two ways in which to construe discourse competence:

1. The goal of self-determination implies that language learners need to become proficient in the language they learn to produce meaningful and relevant utterances, such that they are able to articulate what they want to express (discourses with a small 'd') and communicate with others in the appropriate mode (e.g., oral or written) and medium (e.g., face-to-face or digital distance communication).
2. Language learners must be able to participate in and contribute to ongoing Discourses (with a capital 'D'), producing statements and uttering opinions on the respective issues. Because the issues are thematically organised, learners also need to acquire cultural, political, or other kinds of knowledge as a pre-condition for making pertinent contributions in the respective field.

Discourse competence thus becomes a critical concept which entails the connection between linguistic-discursive abilities and content-thematic negotiations about the world (Hallet, 2020a; Legutke & Thomas, 1991). As such, it concretises the notion of school education and teacher education as *Bildung* delineated in Chapter 1; both teachers and learners need to develop the abilities required to actively participate in and contribute to social, cultural, and political discourses and processes in their respective societies. The implications are far-reaching, connecting teaching and learning to the world beyond the narrow context of the classroom or simply preparing learners for tests and examinations only. The New London Group (2000, p. 18) elaborates further:

Schools regulate access to orders of discourse – that is, the relationship of discourses in a particular social space and to symbolic capital; symbolic meanings that have currency in access to employment, political power and cultural recognition. They provide access to a hierarchically ordered world of work; they shape citizenries; they provide a supplement to the discourses and activities of communities and private life worlds.

This is why weak or insufficiently developed discourse competence leads to exclusion from socially relevant discourses and social or cultural marginalisation. Therefore, discourse competence as the outcome of language learning is decisive in determining learners' individual career paths and their place in society.

There are several implications of this for language teacher education. For the teacher, the concept of discourse competence implies the need to design language practices and model discursive participation according to the characteristics and nature of real-life discourses. The types of utterances or texts and the kinds of interaction practised in the language classroom must simulate or imitate those in real-life communication, the so-called communicative tasks in the communicative approach (Legutke & Thomas, 1991). Much like classroom practices, the topics and contents of language learning need to be oriented towards real-world negotiations. Moreover, texts and materials, as well as tasks and a sustainable learning environment, must be designed to more or less represent real-world topics and issues, including the plurality and diversity of voices in a discourse (Chapter 6). In their most advanced form, classroom discourses and the texts produced by the learners may contribute to real discourses, as is the case in direct email exchanges with English-speaking partners or in the extramural presentation or communication of classroom-based project results. In such contexts, language learners are not simply learners engaged in producing learning outcomes; they are cultural agents producing culturally relevant utterances, positioning themselves in ongoing discourses, and interacting with other cultural agents (Hallet, 2020a; Kaliampos, 2022). Accordingly, teachers also assume the roles of cultural agents, acting and interacting in contexts beyond their narrower roles of instructors and facilitators. This particularly applies to the active development of curricula and teacher education programmes; teachers have to perform as professional agents in such developmental processes and collaborate with colleagues and experts in these professional enterprises (Section 3.7, Chapter 9).

3.2   The Concept of Competence

As explained in the previous section, any definition of a teacher's professional abilities and skills must resort to those abilities their learners are supposed to develop and demonstrate in the language classroom. Therefore, a more general definition of competence is needed to determine what is meant when defining professional competences (Section 3.5).

If language education aims to enable learners to participate in social and cultural processes and shape their own lives in a self-determined way, the competences that are taught and developed must enable them to manage the challenges of all kinds of situations and problems, as well as the associated discursive and communicative demands. According to such a functional concept of competence, Weinert (2001) and the educational study based on his concept define competences as:

the cognitive abilities and skills available to or learnable by individuals to solve specific problems, as well as the associated motivational, volitional, and social readiness and ability to engage in problem solving successfully and in a responsible manner in variable situations. According to such an understanding of skills and abilities, competence is a disposition that enables persons to successfully solve certain types of problems, i.e., to cope with the demands of situations of a certain type. (Klieme et al., 2003, p. 72).

Regarding the contexts of both language learning and teacher education, it follows that competences are complex and multidimensional and should by no means be reduced to basic abilities or skills, as is often the case in language learning contexts – for example, the skills descriptors provided by the CEFR (Council of Europe, 2020). This is significant not only because language learning standards often succumb to such reductionism but also because in all contexts of language education, including teacher education, it is important to be aware that the willingness to communicate or the motivation to use one's communicative competence is often more necessary for successful communication in the target language than the ability to use language structures correctly. It is therefore essential to adhere to a concept of competence that is open and complex. According to Weinert's (2001, pp. 27–28) definition, the individual shape of competence must be understood as a complex bundle of abilities and skills, experience, knowledge, understanding, problem-solving, actions, attitudes (e.g., social, ethical), willingness, and motivation.

All these dispositions are challenged and activated in concrete situations. Therefore, they have to be developed and demonstrated in the language classroom whenever discourse competence is the overarching goal but also and even more so for the purposes of teacher education, as teaching and interacting in classrooms can be regarded as a series of complex social, interactive, and discursive situations.

3.3 Modelling Discourse Competence as a Professional Meta-Competence

In light of the definitions of discourse competence in Section 3.1 and the general concept of competence in Section 3.2, it is self-evident that teachers need to be familiar with the general concept of competence in all teaching and learning processes and the language-learning-specific concept of discourse competence. If all tasks and activities in the language classroom serve the purpose of developing discourse competence, designing lessons, activities, materials, and tasks is a professional competence that needs to be developed and trained at all stages of teacher education and in teachers' later professional careers. Correspondingly, developing and enhancing learners' discourse competence are complex undertakings (Thomson, 2022; Walsh, 2013; Wedell & Malderez, 2013). It encompasses the teacher's:

- well-developed proficiency in the target language so that they can decide which generic forms and types of utterances, linguistic structures, and devices to focus upon or select when teaching the students to participate in a discourse;
- ability to identify emerging or ongoing discourses and to decide whether they are culturally, socially, or politically relevant and whether or in what manner the learners can relate to them;
- broad cultural or domain-specific knowledge concerning issues and negotiations in the societies in question – for instance, social relations and institutions, pop-cultural phenomena, or crucial political issues such as racism or climate change;

- ability to research and find materials and texts (in the broad sense, including videos and social media posts) that may be introduced into the classroom to connect learners' language activities to real-world discourses; and
- ability to initiate cognitive, linguistic-discursive, and social actions and interactions that lead to pertinent language production in the respective discourse.

Given this evidence, it can be concluded that all the choices that teachers make, the way learning processes are designed, and all components of the lesson or project design must serve the purpose of enhancing learners' discourse competence. Thus, the teacher's competence to develop discourse competence in the language classroom establishes a meta-level, on which the goals and contents of language learning can be determined and reflected upon. This meta-competence is therefore the most essential professional competence that teachers need to gain and constantly develop as it connects all learning processes in the classroom with the more general goals of school education (i.e., self-determination and participation) and the broader cultural environment in which the learners act and interact, socially and discursively.

3.4 Competence Models and Outcome Orientation in Teacher Education

Not surprisingly, a general shift to competence orientation in school education also applies to teacher education. As the description of teachers' professional abilities in designing competence-oriented classroom processes in Section 3.3 demonstrates, a teacher's professional qualifications and abilities may take the form of can-do descriptors (see also Rein, 2017). This competence and outcome paradigm mainly emerged during the first decade of the twenty-first century in Europe and numerous other countries and did so simultaneously in both school education and teacher education. First and foremost, the new paradigm is due to a growing awareness – as presented in several international education studies, *Programme for International Student Assessment* studies in particular (e.g., Schleicher, 2019) – that the mere definition of learning objectives says little or nothing about the skills and abilities that are available at the end of a teaching unit or a curricular period (outcome).

By contrast, in outcome-oriented approaches pertaining to school education, the abilities and competences that are available at the end of a curricular unit (a teaching unit, a training programme, a complex task) need to be performed, presented, and made visible. The principle which such a design follows is the strategy of backward planning; the pre-defined outcome determines the content, processes, and strategies of the working and learning process. Above all, defining the expected outcome makes it possible to evaluate and verify whether and to what extent competences, abilities, and skills have been developed. For this purpose, competence-oriented educational models often work with the description of standards or can-do descriptors, as in the well-established CEFR (Council of Europe, 2020).

The shift to competence and outcome orientation in teacher education occurred concomitantly with the general paradigm shift in school education and resulted in approaches that sought to define and describe teachers' abilities and competences in teacher education processes. One of the first attempts to enshrine professional teaching competences in can-do descriptors was professional teaching standards developed and presented by the National Board of Professional Teaching Standards (2012), in the United States at the turn of the millennium. These standards aimed to improve and certify the training of teachers nationwide. They reflected professional agreement regarding the elements of practice that demonstrate an effective teacher. Framed with respect to the activities teachers engage in to enhance their students' performance, such standards encompass the core knowledge, skills, attitudes, and commitments teachers must exhibit to be considered high-quality instructors. The standards, which in 2001 numbered eleven but reduced to nine in the modified 2012 edition, denote essential components of effective teaching and are categorised in Table 3.1.

These standards were the result of consensual negotiations of professionals in the field (teachers, teacher trainers, professors), and, in terms of outcome orientation, they are for use in assessment centres to determine whether candidates meet the professional standards of teaching and can be certified.

As questionable and contingent as some of these standards may seem, they paved the way for a concept of teacher education that was not based solely on ideas, best practice experiences, or master knowledge handed down from teacher generation to teacher generation. Instead, such standardised descriptions of teachers' abilities were created to establish frameworks of teacher education and training that led to a more professional, intersubjective, and evaluable understanding of classroom and pedagogical practices.

In the wake of such early standard descriptions, numerous standards for teacher education were developed at the national, European, and international levels. For example, *A Global Framework of Professional Teaching Standards*, jointly developed by Education International and the United Nations Educational, Scientific and Cultural Organization (UNESCO) (2019), defined ten standards in three domains: *teaching knowledge and understanding*, *teaching practice*, and *teaching relations*. However, such standards address the teaching profession as a whole and do not account for the specificities of domains (e.g., the sciences, languages) or certain school subjects.

A framework that was specifically developed for ELT is the *Cambridge English Teaching Framework: Competency Standards*, published by Cambridge

Table 3.1 *Professional teaching standards*

Competence area	Description Accomplished teachers …
I Knowledge of students	use their knowledge of child development, students as individuals, and students as learners to develop and strengthen relationships that enhance learning.
II Respect for diversity	respect and comprehend the complex nature of diversity. They provide opportunities for all students to access the knowledge, skills, and understanding they need to become caring and thoughtful participants in a global citizenry.
III Establishing an environment for learning	establish and maintain safe and respectful learning communities that nurture relationships and create climates that promote student engagement in learning.
IV Knowledge of content and curriculum	draw on and expand their knowledge of content and curriculum to determine what is important for students to learn and experience within and across the subject areas of the middle childhood years.
V Instructional decision-making	are effective instructional decision-makers. They use a process of assessing, planning, implementing, and reflecting to guide teaching and learning.
VI Partnership and outreach	establish and maintain partnerships with families and the greater community to enhance teaching and support student learning.
VII Professionalism, leadership, and advocacy	are leaders who advocate for the teaching profession and student learning.
VIII Responsiveness to change	are cognisant of the changes that occur in society and in education. They thoughtfully and proactively analyse and respond to change as it affects their students and their profession.
IX Reflective practice	reflect on their practice continually to improve the quality and effectiveness of teaching and learning.

Note: Adapted with permission from National Board of Professional Teaching Standards (2012, pp. 17–18). Copyright 2012 by National Board of Professional Teaching Standards.

Assessment English in 2018. This framework defines competence areas on the one hand and teacher development stages on the other. The descriptions of competences for teachers of English are structured in accordance with the following five areas of ability: (1) *learning and the learner*; (2) *teaching, learning, and assessment*; (3) *language ability*; (4) *language knowledge and awareness*; and (5) *professional development and values*. These global categories are then further divided into sub-categories that specify each area. For instance, the area of *learning and the learner* is sub-divided into *learning theories, first language acquisition and second language acquisition, language-teaching methodologies*, and *understanding learners*. Likewise, *teaching, learning, and assessment* is sub-divided into *planning language learning, using language-learning resources and materials, managing language learning, teaching language systems, teaching language skills*, and *assessing language learning*. Each of these sub-categories is then further divided into professional activities and skills. For instance, the *using language-learning resources and materials* sub-category is divided into *selecting, adapting, supplementing, and using learning materials*; *using teaching aids*; and *using digital resources*.

One of the advantages of such a framework is that it provides teachers and teacher educators with a concrete description and summary of a wide range of professional competences. Teachers can use this framework to assess their own teaching skills and competences. In contrast, teacher educators can utilise it as an evaluation instrument to appraise teachers' abilities and progress.

The latter is possible because this framework conceptualises professional teaching as a developmental process, suggesting that the professional qualifications and competences of teachers need to be systematically honed and refined to be sustainable. Therefore, the framework defines four stages of professional development: *foundation, developing, proficient*, and *expert*. Accordingly, foundation standards are represented by statements such as *Has started to develop...*, developing is defined as *Has a reasonable understanding of...*, proficient as *Has a good understanding of...*, and expert as *Has a sophisticated understanding of...* (Cambridge Assessment English, 2018, pp. 3–11).

These staged descriptors are intended to capture the notion that the gradual development of teachers' expertise involves a growing understanding of teaching and learning; better awareness of their own strengths, weaknesses, and potential as a teacher; increasing sophistication in their planning, decision-making, teaching skills, and reflection; and the ability to respond to a more complex range of classroom situations (Cambridge Assessment English, 2018). For instance, in the area of lesson planning (Figure 3.1), the four stages are defined through a number of statements such as *Has a basic understanding of some key principles ..., Has a reasonable understanding of many key principles ..., Has a good understanding of many key principles ...*, and *Has a sophisticated understanding of key principles of lesson planning...* (Cambridge Assessment English, 2018, p. 4).

What is appealing about the Cambridge framework is that although it has been designed for teachers of English, it covers a wide range of pedagogical skills and competences not specific to language teaching. Lesson planning and classroom observations are pedagogical activities required in all other subjects and classrooms. It can therefore be concluded that this framework combines elements of both language and general education. This aligns with the map of areas of the profession of teaching English presented in Section 3.5, the purpose of which is to structure and systematise the field of ELT by acknowledging

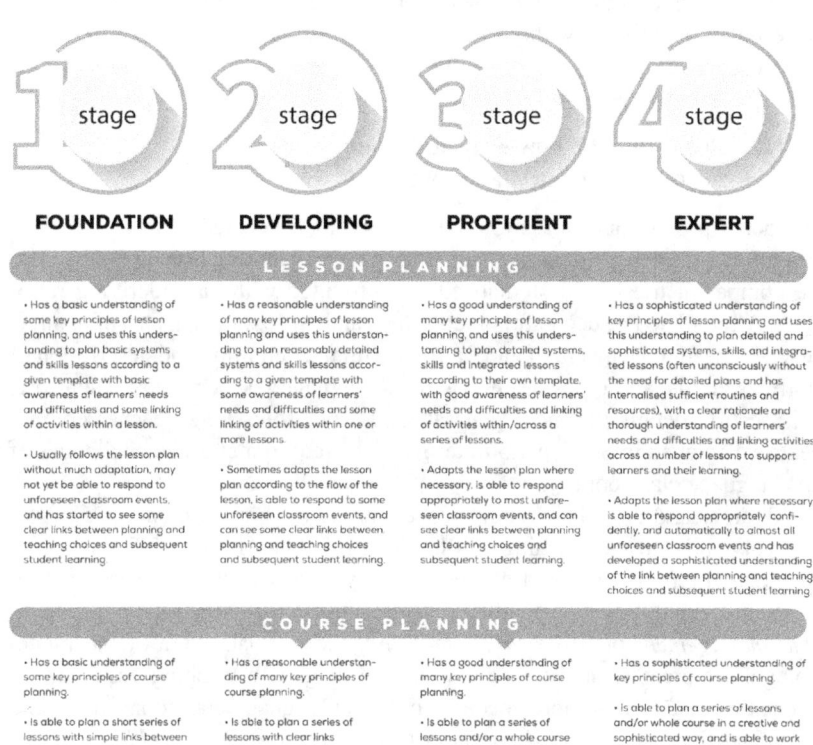

Figure 3.1 Stages and components of planning language learning: an example from the *Cambridge English Teaching Framework*
Reprinted with permission from Cambridge Assessment English (2018, p. 4). Copyright 2018 by Cambridge Assessment English.

the importance of the specific demands of language instruction, as well as the holistic pedagogical quality of all teaching and learning processes.

On the other hand, regarding the stages of development in the Cambridge framework, it is difficult to imagine that students could be taught by teachers with basic pedagogical skills (the Foundation stage) and a rudimentary understanding of course planning. The overall objective of teacher education must always be to equip teachers with pedagogical expertise that serves the needs of school education and language learning at the highest level of knowledge and pedagogical competences. In other words, schools require professional experts 'with a clear rationale and thorough understanding of learners' needs and difficulties and linking activities across a number of lessons to support learners and their learning' (UCLES, 2018, p. 4). It follows that a decision must be made at which stage of their development a teacher is allowed or supposed to teach autonomously without further support or assistance from a tutor or a peer teacher (Chapter 5).

3.5 Professional Knowledge and Competences for the Language Classroom

If teacher professionalism is to be developed and included in structured programmes of teacher education, the various areas in which teachers need to be competent must be systematised and provided with an underlying rationale. After all, to be successful practitioners and professional agents of change, teachers need to be aware of and familiar with the definition and description of abilities, skills, and types of knowledge a language teacher needs. Therefore, this section details the more general model of professional teacher competences displayed in Section 1.5 in terms of the requirements and challenges of the language classroom.

All areas and the related competences represented in the model in Chapter 1 revolve around the teaching and learning processes in the ELT classroom. Whereas the right-hand part of the model systematises more general institutional areas and the corresponding pedagogical competences such as *planning and management* or *professional learning*, the left-hand side of the model categorises areas related to the classroom along with teaching and learning processes that pertain more specifically to the language classroom, including competence areas such as *disciplinary knowledge*, *language teaching*, or *evaluation, assessment, and feedback*. In this section, these areas are described, specified, and geared to the needs of the ELT classroom. Such a specification also requires sub-categories that are derived from the goals of the language classroom and its learning processes. It transpires that seemingly simple categories such as disciplinary knowledge are highly complex areas of competence that need to be sub-divided when concretised in terms of the teaching and learning processes in the language classroom.

Specifically, this section focuses on the following types of knowledge and competences: professional discourse competence, language proficiency, subject matter knowledge, evaluation and assessment competence, and, finally, syllabus and lesson design competence. Although consideration of a teacher's competence and abilities should also include pedagogical knowledge (Section 1.5.2), reflective competence (Chapter 4), and technological competence (Chapter 7), these are discussed in other chapters of this volume. Thus, they have been excluded to avoid overlaps and unnecessary redundancies.

3.5.1 Professional Discourse Competence

Before describing single areas of competence and knowledge, it is necessary to return to the discourse competence of teachers, which is represented as a transversal competence in the model in Chapter 1, as it concerns and affects all other areas. Earlier in this chapter (Section 3.3), discourse competence was described as a professional meta-competence needed to model language practices and tasks that enable learners to develop discourse competence in the English language. Hence, it is a meta-competence. However, this ability is only part of the broader area of professional discourse competence. The latter pertains not only to the ability to initiate learner communication and discourse in the English language but also to a large number of other discourses and communicative requirements in the language classroom and, more generally, in the language teaching profession.

In contexts of learning and teaching languages, communication is so commonplace and taken for granted in the teaching profession that often it hardly seems worth mentioning. However, it is evident that a whole range of discourses and communicative interactions exist beyond the language learning processes in which the teacher needs to engage. Furthermore, a teacher's discourse competence also encompasses discourses and situations not conducted in English but in the language of schooling and/or the national language. This dimension of discourse competence may concern institutional issues, communication with parents, and all kinds of institutional situations, including the head of a school and other levels of school administration. These discourses cannot be elaborated on here. However, if a school's language of schooling is English, as may be the case for international schools, the teacher's discourse competence would also refer to all of these.

The teaching-and-learning-related discourses and the teacher's respective competences in the English language can be categorised as follows:

- *Classroom discourse and its initiation, development, and sustainability*: Beyond all utterances that are part of the language learning process itself, classroom discourse may concern all issues that are potentially raised in the classroom, from instructions and statements to organising the classroom or responding to students' questions (Walsh, 2011, 2013). Following Jenks (2020, p. 5), classroom discourse may be defined 'as the language … communication … practices … texts …, and social structures … that make up, as well as influence, teaching and learning'. The teacher may have to explain curricular content and stages in the learning process, provide rationales for the choice of topics or materials, and motivate students in various ways. The classroom needs to be managed and organised, including classroom rules; working processes and strategies must be addressed or supported; students' achievements need to be classified and assessed; and their behaviour may

have to be thematised – all of this in the English language as it is one of the principles of the language classroom that, whenever possible, issues are communicated or negotiated in the target language.
- *Content-relevant discourses within anglophone societies*: Language teachers need to observe, study, and potentially participate in all kinds of current developments and affairs in anglophone societies to stay up to date and integrate relevant changes into the teaching–learning process. As explained with respect to cultural knowledge (Section 3.5.3), this is a prerequisite for the acquisition of respective cultural knowledge and an appropriate selection of topics and materials for the classroom.
- *Professional discourses on classroom/school development and teacher education*: This book is just one example of a contribution to professional discourses in which teachers of English need to be able to participate, as large parts of them are conducted in English as an international language of teacher education. In order to enable teachers to communicate in such international professional communities, discourse competence also encompasses the teacher's own profession. This kind of professional discourse competence may also be required for professional communication and collaborative work with colleagues in and across schools (Thomson, 2022).

Professional discourse competence, including the pedagogical meta-competence required to model and initiate learners' discourse competence in the English language, is thus the most fundamental and overarching competence of teachers of English as it constitutes a prerequisite for almost all other professional competences.

3.5.2 Language Proficiency

A teacher's proficiency in the English language is directly related to the discourse competence outlined in the previous section. It is yet another complex professional competence, as a teacher's ability to speak the language they teach needs to be fully developed and comprehensive (Faez et al., 2021; Le & Renandya, 2017; Richards, 2010). It encompasses their general competence pertaining to discourses in anglophone societies and potential participation in all kinds of discourses in these language communities. This is because a language teacher must be able to introduce and teach in the classroom cultural, social, or political issues negotiated in the anglophone world. Furthermore, a fully developed proficiency is also needed inside the classroom, given that one of the principles of teaching a language is its constant and, if possible, exclusive use in the classroom. This applies to all processes of teaching and learning and all classroom discourses, as well as to classroom routines and the more personal and individual exchanges with students on any issue that arises.

Freeman et al. (2015, p. 129) also indicate that teaching a language requires a specific proficiency beyond the everyday use of the language, as it must be considered 'a specialised subset of language skills required to prepare and teach lessons'.

The full range of language use and language teaching requires a fully developed proficiency close to that of a native speaker. This is because the teacher needs to be able to negotiate everything in the English language, from political issues in anglophone societies to actions and interactions in the classroom, as well as those related to fictional texts and films. Hence, teachers must be fully fluent in the English language.

Regrettably, the literature does not place enough emphasis on the significance and impact of the teacher's proficiency on classroom assessment. Hence, it is imperative that teacher language proficiency be re-defined as a particular subset of the language skills needed to effectively assess student performance and progress rather than as a general level of proficiency in a language (Freeman et al., 2015). The literature does, however, discuss the importance of a teacher's language proficiency for teaching purposes; specifically, teachers with high language proficiency must provide students with purposeful explanations and repeat instructions in the target language so that learners are given sufficient time to understand what is being asked and respond, provide learners with detailed language input, and offer quick responses to the questions learners ask in relation to the target language and culture (Le & Renandya, 2017; Richards, 2015; Richards et al., 2013).

It is essential to distinguish language proficiency (i.e., knowledge of language) from language knowledge (i.e., knowledge about language), as described and explained in the following sub-sections. Language knowledge is part of a teacher's subject matter knowledge and refers to all kinds of linguistic phenomena, structures, and rules that apply in a given language. However, such declarative knowledge about a language does not necessarily imply that one can speak the language.

3.5.3 Subject Matter Knowledge

As already outlined in Chapter 1 and represented in the model (Figure 1.1), in all school subjects, a teacher's profound and reliable disciplinary knowledge can generally be regarded as indispensable (Section 2.2). For the purpose and context of the language classroom, it is advisable to translate this disciplinary competence into the required subject matter knowledge. This accounts for the fact that in Weinert's concept of competence, knowledge is one of the defining elements (Section 3.2), making it possible to sub-categorise this kind of knowledge. This becomes rather challenging because there is no single knowledge domain that can be more or less easily delimited or defined, unlike, for example, biology or geography. Due to its discursive character, the language classroom needs to draw upon and cover a broad range of cultural topics and discourses in each of the anglophone societies in question (Hallet, 2020a; Kramer & Lenz, 2020). Everything negotiated in a society may be introduced, represented, and negotiated in the language classroom. This applies to all social and political issues with which these societies are currently concerned; of course, there is also a historical dimension to them that may assist in better understanding the present. Because of this complexity and array of potential issues, in the context of the language classroom, it has proved beneficial to categorise subject matter knowledge along the domains of language, culture, and literature.

3.5.3.1 Language Knowledge A well-developed and sophisticated linguistic knowledge of English is a precondition to teaching it (Sections 1.5.1 and 2.2). This aligns with the positions of Thornbury (1997), Myhill (2005), and Andrews (2007), according to whom effective teaching of the target language depends on the knowledge teachers possess regarding the systems that underpin the language. Understandably, the importance of linguistic theory in teacher education has been highlighted in several works (Halliday, 1981; Park-Johnson & Shin, 2020; Russell, 2018) which clarified that to understand what facilitates the teaching–learning process and account for what is happening when it is not occurring, teachers must possess sufficient knowledge of linguistic theories. A second motive for examining teachers' understanding of linguistics is that theories of linguistics and language teaching are continually evolving, as indeed are languages (Meng, 2009). Consequently, teachers need to keep up to date with these developments and changes to understand explicitly how language works and then translate this into classroom instruction (Hudson, 2008; Jones & Chen, 2012).

This complex knowledge pertains to all areas described in linguistics, ranging from lexis, morphology, and phonology over grammatical structures and syntax to textual and generic knowledge, as well as medial forms of discourse in the target language (e.g., a video or a social media post). It is vital that a teacher's linguistic knowledge be broader, more profound, and better developed than the language knowledge possessed by students. For instance, whereas students may be merely expected to learn words and vocabulary, the teacher may support them by explaining word formation rules that make it easy to derive a number of words from one word, such as adding a morpheme (e.g., a prefix, a suffix) and thus also teach the students a language learning strategy. Typically, this knowledge domain is almost entirely introduced in the coursebook, either in a separate part of the book or in the exercises section of a teaching unit. As in many other cases, the coursebook thus becomes a valuable teaching and learning resource that facilitates the teacher's knowledge instruction.

Nevertheless, the teacher must have a fully developed knowledge of the terminology needed to describe the language when teaching it to students or to develop their language awareness. In order to teach the target language effectively and prepare students for successful participation in communication in English in the classroom and beyond, teachers are expected to demonstrate professional language awareness (Chapter 1). Such awareness manifests itself in profound knowledge and understanding of the grammar, syntax, and phonetics, as well as sociolinguistic, dialectological, and structural nuances of the target language, which are indispensable for its effective use. This professional type of awareness is also crucial from a purely pedagogical perspective; it enables classroom practitioners to make key decisions about selecting and integrating texts and materials, as well as exercises, activities, and tasks (often subsumed under the generalising term 'activities') into the teaching–learning process.

Because classroom practitioners are simultaneously language users, analysts, and teachers of the target language in the classroom context, teacher education programmes are advised to include a compulsory module on linguistics for teachers. The purpose of such a module should be fivefold: (1) to familiarise future teachers with the five core areas of linguistics: phonology, morphology, syntax, semantics, and pragmatics; (2) to discuss the nature of language and how it is acquired and learnt; (3) to clarify the relationships between language and culture, as well as language and communication; (4) to explain how and why language changes and how the English language in particular, has transformed and become a global language; and (5) to extend the linguistic theory to classroom practice by explaining how to teach language through communication.

It is important to emphasise that because English is a global language the teacher needs to be aware of and familiar with some of the important varieties of the target language (Galloway & Rose, 2015), at least to some extent, so that differences between them and World Englishes can be introduced and practised effectively in the classroom. This may be the case when, for example, watching videos, TV channels, or feature films with students in varieties other than British or American English. In other words, globally competent English language teachers must be able to create meaningful lessons and prepare their students for interactions in the target language with people from diverse cultural backgrounds, as well as enabling them to develop the necessary skills, attitudes, and knowledge to ensure these cross-cultural experiences are successful (Byram & Wagner, 2018; Mansilla & Wilson, 2020; Tichnor-Wagner et al., 2019; Yaccob et al., 2022).

In fact, language teaching is not only about intercultural communication; it also involves equipping students to understand and appreciate others' perspectives and worldviews, participate in cross-cultural collaborations (OECD,

2020), and actively engage with diverse ideas and opinions in contemporary global society, the latter being somewhat problematic for current students (Fox, 2019). Another reason teachers' global competence is crucial is that in coursebooks the ratio between global and local information is often unbalanced. Therefore, adaptations of coursebook units need to offer a more proportioned approach in the classroom and better contextualise and personalise classroom activities and tasks. This is hardly ever possible without an extensive knowledge of the target language on the part of the teacher.

3.5.3.2 Cultural Knowledge and Competence Cultural knowledge and competence is one of the most complex and broad areas required in the language classroom as it pertains to all anglophone societies and global discourses conducted in any of the World Englishes (Jackson, 2020; Liddicoat & Scarino, 2013; Sercu & Bandura, 2005). Moreover, discourses in the learners' lifeworld also belong here as language learners and users of the English language in contact with other users often have to share their own stories and experiences. Because cultural processes are highly dynamic, cultural knowledge gained during teacher education, for instance, at university, may quickly become obsolete. This observation leads to two conclusions. The first is that teachers need a stock of cultural standard knowledge that pertains to the primary institutions of a country or society and its most striking features. This knowledge helps students to understand and characterise the countries and societies they focus on, such as, for example, the London multicultural community, the United States as an immigration society, or the Chinese Lantern Festival. However, teachers must exercise caution here because, although cultural references are extensive in coursebooks, they tend to be restricted to the anglophone and European cultures. Other global cultures in which English is not a native language, such as Asian and Middle Eastern cultures (Galante, 2015; Johar & Abdul, 2019), seem to be ignored. The teacher's ability to design meaningful lessons, as mentioned in the previous section, refers to promoting contextual learning, which integrates knowledge of the interconnected world and helps students to better examine and address global issues – for instance, through active learning based on multicultural materials (Fox, 2019; Widodo et al., 2018).

Because of the dynamics of cultural developments and constant cultural innovation (in the digital age in particular), the second conclusion is that teachers and learners alike need to be able to engage in cultural research which may pertain to recent or ongoing cultural domains and social or political developments (Kramer & Lenz, 2020). In many respects, it is highly productive to apply the principles and tools of ethnography as these direct students' attention and awareness towards the need to study current cultural developments in a theoretically grounded manner systematically. In the same vein, teachers need to be aware that teaching cultures requires the ability to research anglophone and world cultures (Section 4.6), as well as attending to current developments in their own and students' lifeworlds (Jackson, 2020; Liddicoat & Scarino, 2013). Therefore, language teachers also need to develop basic knowledge and competence in selecting and using ethnographic tools suitable for creating reliable cultural knowledge. One of the apparent advantages of the research approach is that students are not simply taking in prefabricated knowledge. On the contrary, they construct or co-construct it with their classroom peers. This is why students' engagement in research processes can be regarded as a highly productive form of learner orientation (Hallet, 2020a).

Once again, a teacher's abilities need to relate to the competences they are supposed to teach in their classrooms. In the area of cultural learning, a teacher needs to be able to negotiate cultural differences in encounters with English language speakers from societies and communities around the world. In his theory of communication across cultural boundaries and differences, Byram (2021) developed a theory and model of what he calls intercultural communicative competence. This accounts for the need to identify cultural differences that inhibit successful communication or lead to misunderstandings and breakdowns. The dimensions that Byram (2021, pp. 42–50) defines for the learner's intercultural communicative competence also apply to the teacher's competence. These are defined as (1) cultural knowledge of self and others, (2) the ability to interpret documents from a different culture and relate them to others, including one's own culture, (3) the capacity to realise when no prior knowledge exists in interactional acts and that specific knowledge has to be built in order to communicate successfully, and finally (4) attitudes of openness, curiosity, and tolerance towards representatives of other cultures. All these abilities are also part of a language teacher's professional competence. Notably, in such a model and strategy of intercultural encounters, more general goals of school education and teacher education in terms of *Bildung* come into play (Section 1.3).

3.5.3.3 Literary Knowledge and Competence Literary texts, including plays, video games, comic books, and several other types of literature, are among the most authentic cultural artefacts that can be introduced into the language classroom. They are, therefore, in the same way as any other text and artefact, a part of culture. This cultural dimension of literature, however, also explains its specific value in processes of language and cultural learning (Teranishi et al., 2015). In literature, including films, the learner is allowed and able to encounter entire social and cultural environments in the English language; speakers of English may be observed or experienced in both action and social interaction. Furthermore, literary texts often provide learners with occasions where they can experience language being used across various social situations and interactions.

For teachers, a specific competence is required to open up these dimensions of the literary text to the learner and guide them through texts which, due to their authenticity, are often complex and challenging (Beach et al., 2016; Choo, 2013; Osterwalder, 2017; Wiland, 2016). Regarding materials and lesson design, it is also part of a teacher's literary competence to select literary texts that suit their learner's cognitive and language abilities, including easy or graded readers geared towards less developed language competences.

What makes literary texts even more specific is, of course, their fictionality. Fiction is a specific mode of presenting and representing worlds in an imaginary form that has value in itself. This fictionality also constitutes literature as a specific domain of culture (Zapf, 2016). Literature is permanently embedded in and related to the cultural environment in which it is produced. However, it never simply reproduces or imitates cultural processes. More often than not, it counters the cultural mainstream, re-imagining or emphasising cultural phenomena and processes that are not valued in a culture or bringing to the fore ways of thinking and doing that are oppressed or marginalised in a society (Zapf, 2016). To identify the specific relation between a work of fiction and its non-fictional environment, professional competences are required that make it possible to teach ways of contextualising literary texts and interrelating literature and culture (Hallet, 2020b).

Overall, a broad scope of knowledge and competences is required, ranging from the teacher's familiarity with historical and contemporary works of literature to their authors. The teacher also needs to demonstrate analytical and narratological knowledge (i.e., understanding of narrative structures and how these affect perceptions), including the pertinent terminology that enables them to thematise and discuss the features of a literary text and its composition, its genre, and its relatedness to their non-fictional environment. This is why teaching literature is one of the modules in the teacher education programme presented in Section 3.7.

3.6 Evaluation and Assessment Competence

Evaluation is an extremely broad umbrella term that refers to all kinds of external assessment and self-assessment, judgements, and evaluations of learning and teaching processes as well as language learning outcomes and language products (Dahler-Larsen, 2009). Evaluation may concern every activity, product, or accomplishment, from learners' contributions to classroom discourse and single utterances in the target language (e.g., their accuracy, fluency, or content) to learner behaviour and more complex communicative products or artefacts such as a wall poster or a video.

The teacher's evaluation may be informal and occasional such as encouraging learners with a simple *well done* after a learner has completed their work.

Evaluation tends to be informal when it is holistic, but more often, teacher feedback and evaluation are formal and criterion-based. Peer feedback can also assume a more formal character when it is based on criteria that are either developed by the learners or defined by the teacher. Evaluation also includes class tests with a corresponding assessment of students' performance. However, it may also be the result of more structured feedback processes that are based, for instance, on a list of pre-defined evaluation criteria or on evaluation sheets in which learners give their peers graded feedback on their work and accomplishments by ticking pre-defined boxes (Nassaji & Kartchava, 2021).

Evaluation as a term and concept has become a generic term for all kinds of assessments of students' performance. It is all-encompassing, pertaining to almost all language learning and teaching aspects. It may also pertain to the working processes or all conceivable instructional factors such as input materials, the time available, or peer collaboration.

Assessment, by contrast, refers to learners' performance in the target language, their achievements in learning the language, and the progress they are making (Davis et al., 2018; Gebril, 2021; Hidri, 2018, 2020; Legutke et al., 2009; Tsagari & Banerjee, 2016). In this sense, assessment is always outcome-oriented and graded; the assessor's judgement is reflected in a range of marks that form part of a standardised scale or grading system (as documented, for example, by figures or letters in certificates) so that those external to the learning environment can understand a learner's performance. Because this external addressee orientation of grading practices assigns future education and career opportunities and options to the learner, a particular professional competence and sensitivity are imperative. Therefore, teacher education programmes and student teachers' experiences in teaching practice need to prepare them deeply and carefully to evaluate and assess students' work in their classrooms competently and to do so in different ways. Part of such a professional assessment is an awareness and knowledge of the different purposes and functions of assessment, which is the focus of the next section.

3.6.1 Types of Assessment

Evaluating students' performance in terms of their work or their language production in the narrower sense – that is, of work results, learning and performance levels, or learning and work behaviour – is referred to as assessment (Legutke et al., 2009). In language teaching and learning, it is helpful to distinguish assessment in three ways with regard to its respective functions. The first type of assessment involving the use of diagnostic instruments has a formative function. Hence, it is referred to as assessment for learning; it monitors and supports the learning process and gives the teacher and the learner hints for developing learning further (MacDonald et al., 2015; Vassiliou et al., 2022).

Designing tools for formative assessment is also part of a teacher's diagnostic competence and is needed to capture the broad range of abilities in a class and account for the heterogeneity of cognitive and language dispositions at the beginning of every teaching unit.

A second type of assessment, ipsative assessment, refers to students' use of self-assessment tools and strategies (Hughes, 2017). Although this type of assessment is formative in nature (Hughes, 2014), it deserves a separate place in the discussion. The significance of ipsative assessment lies in the fact that it supports the learner's ability to reflect upon and self-assess their own learning processes and progress based on their earlier work and is thus part of the larger concept of learner autonomy (Yan, 2023). Therefore, from the point of view of learners, viewing progress and development in relation to an earlier achievement may have value in motivating them to progress further (Hughes, 2011, 2014). Conversely, it gives teachers insight into how performance changes and enables them to construct a diagnostic scheme in which specified expectations and/or avenues for individual learners are employed as a framework for learning.

Even though research on ipsative assessment is relatively new, the results so far have highlighted three benefits: (1) it facilitates the growth of sophisticated higher-order cognitive processes, an example being the ability to make evaluations (Hughes, 2017; Malecka & Boud, 2021; Sadler, 2010); (2) it helps in constructing a safe space in which learners have evident regard for each other's identities and foster positive, social emotions such as curiosity and resilience (Rattray, 2018); and (3) various learning resources enable comparisons to be made between past and present learning (Malecka et al., 2021; Penn & Wells, 2018). Thus, whereas political and authoritative control underpins criterion-referenced assessments in which teachers impose task performances, ipsative assessments eschew the use of summative tests focused on learning targets in favour of nurturing a broader learning experience. This ensures that students are more aware of the value of learning and have a clearer idea of their future trajectories (Hughes, 2017; Nishizuka, 2022).

By contrast, the third type of assessment, summative assessment, or assessment of learning, is intended to assess the learner's language proficiency and achievement at specific intersections of the educational process and is often associated with grading or awarding certificates (Harlen, 2007). Summative assessments of students' performance can be external, such as all types of centralised or national examinations and tests. They can also be learner-group related, such as class tests or oral examinations designed by the teacher or the Ministry of Education.

Creating assessment tasks is a frequent and regular teacher activity and practice, often supported or offered by coursebooks or in teaching materials. Designing oral and written tests is part of the daily routine of all English language teachers. Summative assessment, by contrast, places high demands on teachers' task and assessment skills as quality standards apply that require a high degree of reliability and objectivity. The same tests must generate comparable results whenever they are conducted in other classes and contexts. Also, relying on prefigured standard descriptors, such as those in the CEFR (Council of Europe, 2020), offers more complex and professionally validated types of assessment that test different levels of language proficiency in large-scale language testing.

When creating assessment tasks, it is essential to decide what the subject of assessment is and which aspects of learning and competence acquisition are to be measured. Assessment tasks may refer to highly complex competences, such as conducting a conversation or creating a video, but also to individual components or sub-competences, such as specific knowledge or content, limited skills or abilities, such as lexical knowledge, the use of generic forms or linguistic structures, and several other features of language proficiency.

A variety of task forms can therefore be employed for assessing learners' language proficiency and knowledge, ranging from very open and complex tasks to closed ones such as those used in multiple-choice tests. The latter are suited to testing declarative knowledge but are not necessarily suited to capturing the ability to perform complex language actions and interactions. For complex tasks, more open and holistic types of assessment must be designed (Section 6.5.2). When choosing the type of assessment task, it is vital to ensure learners become familiar with it in advance and do not encounter a task type during the assessment process for the first time. Teachers need to be aware that task routines are among the factors that determine the learner's chances of success and the degree to which this is achieved.

3.6.2 *Criterion-Based Assessment*

To evaluate a task's validity, the teacher must outline the expected outcome in advance, representing the expected student responses in the form of criteria or key notions. This is the only way to ensure that the subject of the assessment aligns with students' level of knowledge and language proficiency. At the same time, the performance criteria used to define the expected outcome are also used as the basis of the actual assessment and, more often than not, translated into a school grade assigned to a student's work.

Grading judgements or scales must be designed to reflect the degree of competence or proficiency to which the performance corresponds. The grading can follow the official scale of grades in an institution or even in a nation. However, proficiency and competence levels may also be graded along self-defined levels, for example, three-level grades (e.g., +, 0, –; or above average, within expectations, with reservations, and the like). It is also advisable, particularly when teachers plan and develop assessments in collaboration, to create a criteria grid or a rubric by means of which the student's language production or performance can be classified according to an assessment scale. Specifically, assessment rubrics serve as scoring guides that assess and articulate specific components and expectations for both oral and written assignments. Rubrics are helpful for both learners and teachers (Brookhart, 2013; de Boer et al., 2021). Regarding the former, rubrics provide information about their progress and the learning process, enabling them to comprehend the various components of tasks and the corresponding expectations and provide comprehensive and timely feedback to help learners improve their work (Stevens & Levi, 2013). Rubrics enable teachers to consistently assess students' work and enhance their classroom teaching through reflection on the results (Stevens & Levi, 2013).

Self-defined scales can also be used to put task parts or entire tasks into a weighting relationship with each other; these are then included in the overall judgement in different proportions. A purely reproductive task could, for example, constitute smaller percentages of the overall result than a task that requires more complex skills or greater independence. In English lessons, the weighting can also be used to position the assessment of linguistic accuracy and fluency in relation to the content-related or problem-solving components. It should be considered that the more complex the content-related task requirements, the lower the weight of the linguistic performance in the narrower sense. However, the weighting may also be used to determine the focus of an assessment or evaluation. For instance, if a task tests the context-adequate use of new vocabulary, the number of correctly used lexical items is highly important. In contrast, in a content-oriented task, a small number of incorrectly or inadequately used words are given a lower weight.

3.7 Syllabus and Lesson Design Competence

Designing whole teaching sequences and smaller teaching units, such as single lessons, is one of the most fundamental professional routines teachers have to engage in (Scrivener, 2017; Ur, 2012). First and foremost, the competence that is required refers to the ability to structure the learning process and content in a chronological and also progressive form (Harrington & Thomas, 2018; Sammons & Smith, 2017). This requires a clear idea of the objectives and the various stages of the teaching unit as stipulated in a syllabus and to define the position of the single lesson within a more extensive sequence.

Above all, transparency is a core principle; the learners must be able to understand why and in what ways the lessons of a larger unit are intertwined and why they are sequenced in a particular way. Therefore, in terms of advance organisation, students should be introduced to the stages of a teaching sequence by giving them an idea of the various steps and stages they will pass, which will motivate them.

Lessons are traditionally drafted in staged lesson plans (often in tabular form), which provide the teacher with a clear lesson structure and an understanding of how they proceed from one stage to the next. However, this traditional practice of designing lessons has recently been questioned and critiqued in light of contemporary developments such as learner-centred education or the inclusion of new (digital) learning technologies in the teaching–learning process. As a matter of fact, more open and diverse or individualised ways of learning may require more open forms of structuring teaching units. Twadell et al. (2019, p. 8) clarify this issue: 'A critical look at how we instruct students is an important step toward rethinking and redesigning approaches to teaching and learning. A new and better model for instruction and lesson planning can help teachers integrate stronger, more informed, and current research practices that increase student engagement and achievement'. Such an innovation in lesson and syllabus design needs to account for more learner-oriented approaches and more open forms of teaching and learning, such as the research approach or task approach (Chapter 6). In such learner-centred designs, learners are given more autonomy to structure the working and learning process according to their abilities, preferences, and needs. However, teachers still need to provide an overall structure and framework for learner-oriented units because open forms, in particular, need reliable structures and effective organisation.

3.8 Teacher Education Curricula and Programmes

Given all the areas and competences of professional teachers of English described in this and other chapters of this book, the inevitable conclusion is that all of the abilities and competences must be systematised and that teacher education must be organised as a long-term institutional academic process and curriculum. There is no other way of offering and developing all the necessary qualifications and the large number of required competences for student teachers of English. The other far-reaching consequence underlying every single chapter in this book is the need to establish ELT as an academic discipline, including academic research (Section 4.6), by offering certified higher education courses and curricular teacher education programmes that are suited to gradually building the knowledge and competences that student teachers need, whether they be certified programmes or BA or MA programmes for a Bachelor/Master of Education in TESOL or ELT (Liu & Berger, 2015).

Worldwide, an enormous number of disparate teacher education programmes in ELT or TESOL are available. However, what all these need to achieve is:

- a competence-based concept of teacher education, as presented in this book;
- a transparent programme structure that translates the required competence into a sequence of modules or courses; and
- an official certification (university, state) that ensures graduates are employable and successful in the competitive job market.

Inevitably, given the vast number of competences, abilities, and skills required, teacher education programmes are highly selective and therefore follow a paradigmatic principle which equips student teachers with basic competences while enabling them to continually learn after they have completed their curricular teacher education programme (Hoinkes & Weigand, 2016).

The ELT Master of Education programme (Table 3.2) is an example from a German university (University of Bonn). It is essential to point out that in Germany teachers are educated in two different subjects (e.g., English and history), plus a supporting programme in general education that covers issues such as heterogeneity or classroom management. Here, the Master of Education is followed by a twelve- or eighteen-month second stage of teacher education in

Table 3.2 *Example structure of a two-year Master of Education programme in TEFL at the University of Bonn, Germany*

Semester (six months, with a three-month teaching period/ practicum	Components (courses, modules)		
1 (winter)		Linguistics	North American and Postcolonial Literature and Cultures
2 (summer)	Teaching English as a Foreign Language I: Theories, Models, and Methods (two courses)	British Literature and Cultures	
3 (winter)	Teaching English as a Foreign Language II: Practicum tutorial	Practicum (school internship, a whole semester module)	
4 (summer)	Teaching English as a Foreign Language III: Current Issues in the Teaching of English		Master's thesis

Note: Adapted with permission from the University of Bonn, 2023, www.bzl.uni-bonn.de/studium/modulhandbuecher-studienverlaufsplaene/studienverlaufsplaene-ma/2022_ma_englisch_wise.pdf. Copyright 2023 by the University of Bonn.

teacher colleges that further educates and tutors the novices in their schools and leads to a second state teacher education certificate.

This example of a Master of Education programme illustrates how the competence and knowledge areas described in this chapter and in this book can be translated into a curricular structure. Because teachers of English have to teach their students anglophone languages, literature, and cultures, three of the modules or courses (in the grey boxes) are disciplinary components that are not necessarily oriented towards teaching competences; instead, they are designed to equip student teachers with disciplinary knowledge and competences in these areas.

The *Teaching English* components are chronologically structured in terms of a curriculum, starting with two courses in the second semester. One course provides student teachers with an overview of the areas of language teaching, including media and technology, the other with an introductory and paradigmatic overview of teaching anglophone literature and cultures. The entire third semester is covered by a practicum and an associated tutorial that supervises this stage of education and ensures trainee teachers critically and systematically reflect upon students' experiences (Cirocki et al., 2019b).

As large as the number of practicum models and concepts may be on a global scale (Cirocki et al., 2019a), all share the underlying philosophy that knowledge and competences can be developed in academic courses but, in addition, these need to be tested and further developed through practical classroom work and observation (Cirocki et al., 2019b; Pu & Wright, 2022). It is also important to stress that the tutorial serves to introduce student teachers to empirical (ethnographic) classroom research so that they are trained to be creators of knowledge and practitioners who can reflect on classroom and teaching experiences from the perspective of research and disciplinary knowledge (Chapter 4). The fourth-semester module on current issues serves to specify and further develop the field of language teaching through a focus on innovative concepts and new orientations. The Master of Education programme is completed with a master's dissertation in ELT in the same semester.

The foregoing example provides sufficient evidence that a two-year teacher education programme and curriculum is suitable for educating student teachers in a wide range of competences and types of knowledge, thereby enabling them to perform successfully in their future jobs. However, such a master's programme should place more emphasis on classroom research and professional reflection beyond occasional integration into the teaching practicum. It is therefore advisable that a more specific research module be created, similar to that offered by the University of York on its Master of Arts in TESOL (MA TESOL) programme. As research skills are important in enabling teachers to investigate various aspects of the teaching–learning process, thereby improving classrooms and schools, student teachers enrolled on the MA TESOL programme at York attend two core research methods modules. In the first of these, Research Methods for Language Education I: Researching Questions, they develop in-depth knowledge and understanding of research methods, designs, processes, and techniques; learn to assess the degree to which analytical strategies are suitable for disparate research subjects and questions; critically evaluate the strengths and weaknesses of a range of methods for collecting and analysing data; and comprehend the features of educational research studies that exhibit scientific rigour. In the second module, Research Methods for Language Education II: Answering Questions, they accumulate the knowledge and skills required to write a research proposal and ethics application, extend their understanding and knowledge of a broad array of methods for collecting data and undertaking both quantitative and qualitative analyses, and accrue experience in applying these techniques and further enhance their comprehension of what constitutes educational research that adheres to ethical standards and displays scientific rigour.

The detailed content in both modules as well as the two practical examinations that student teachers must take as summative assessments seek to ensure they demonstrate that they are well prepared for researching their own classrooms in diverse, rigorous, and ethical ways (Leow, 2019; McDonough & McDonough, 2014; Pawlak, 2016).

3.9 Conclusion

The various standards and can-do descriptors in teacher education presented in this chapter, along with many others, demonstrate that the number of competences and sub-competences, abilities, and skills needed by professional language teachers is vast. They cannot all be delineated in this chapter; therefore, the aim has been to describe and explain the most vital classroom-related competences with regard to learners' competences and abilities that teachers need to develop and train in the language classroom. There are, of course, other dimensions of professional competence that are essential for all language learning processes. For instance, teachers need to be able to create rich and productive learning and working environments for their learners. This is an extremely important ability described in detail in Chapter 6. Moreover, in the twenty-first century, teachers need to be able to account for the digitality of cultural, communicative, and pedagogical processes and develop competences that are key to this cultural and pedagogical dimension. Therefore, teachers' digital competence, including their ability to use and design digital teaching materials and to handle electronic equipment, is described and discussed in Chapter 7. Ultimately, with regard to evaluating a teacher's abilities and competences, what counts is learners' success in learning the English language.

REFLECTION FOR ACTION

Student Teachers

- Think about your own language classroom in school and the way you were taught. Would you say your teacher was competent to teach English?
- Do you think that the current teacher education programme is helping you to develop the competences you need to demonstrate in the classroom?
- Apart from the competences that you are developing in your teacher education programme, do you think there are also natural/innate talents that you need to bring to the teaching job?
- Reflecting on your professional abilities and competences so far, which do you think you need to develop further?

Novice Teachers

- Do you think professional standards and can-do descriptors adequately define a teacher's competences?
- Reflect on your recent classroom teaching experiences; do you feel your professional discourse competence in English is fully developed?
- Do you think your teacher education programme has given you the abilities and competences required for your current job?
- Apart from the competences you developed in your teacher education programme, are there also natural/innate talents required in your job that you deem essential?

Experienced Teachers

- In light of your teaching and classroom experiences, do you think professional standards and can-do descriptors adequately define a teacher's competences?
- Reflect on your evaluation and assessment practices. Would you say you have developed reliable routines for assessing your learners' performance? Or is every assessment still a challenge? If so, in what sense?
- Learning to teach is a lifelong process. Which abilities and competences do you find most demanding?
- When developing your professional competences further on the job, how important is collaboration with your colleagues?

4 Reflective Practice and Teacher-Led Research
The Path to Teacher Professionalism

As discussed previously in Chapter 2, English language teachers are now expected to partake in reflective practice and teacher-led research continuously in order to utilise and increase their disciplinary knowledge (Section 2.2), contribute to the development of disciplinary theory, and enhance their understanding of the teaching–learning process. In so doing, they become responsible for their behaviour and practice as teachers through a systematic and refined analysis of their actions, the way in which they perform these, and their reasons for doing so. This ensures that reflective practice has professional and personal meaning (Farrell, 2015) and, moreover, helps ensure that the language teaching they provide is of a high standard. On a more general level, it bolsters the professional and personal development of teachers as a whole (e.g., Cirocki & Farrell, 2017a; Crandall & Christison, 2016; Farrell, 2013, 2015; McGregor & Cartwright, 2011; Nurkamto & Sarosa, 2020).

The primary purposes of this chapter are to ensure English language teachers become conversant with the nature of reflective practice and make several recommendations as to ways in which they can engage in reflective practice, including classroom-based research, in an effective manner. The chapter comprises five sections. It first explains what is meant by reflective practice and what this entails. It then considers different forms of reflective practice and introduces the theoretical framework developed by Farrell to support this practice. Next, it presents and describes a collection of tools teachers can utilise to engage in reflective practice. The chapter ends with a brief discussion of teacher-led research.

4.1   Defining Reflective Practice

As a theoretical construct, reflective practice is difficult to unpack, mirrored in the range of definitions scholars offer. Lyons (1998), for instance, perceives it as relating to how teachers scrutinise their practices, the extent to which these are effective, and how such practices can be enhanced to meet the disparate requirements of students. Conversely, Finlay (2008) construes reflective practice as a process through which novel personal and professional insights are acquired through experience. By contrast, Zwozdiak-Myers (2012) characterises reflective practice as involving a tendency for teachers to engage in inquiry – reshaping what they do, know, and believe with respect to teaching to enhance both their professional and personal development. Farrell (2015, p. 123), however, defines reflective practice as 'a cognitive process accompanied by a set of attitudes in which teachers systematically collect data about their practice, and while engaging in dialogue with others use the data to make informed decisions about their practice both inside and outside the classroom' (see Chapter 9 for more details). More recently, however, Farrell (2018, p. 17) has argued that insufficient clarity regarding the way in which reflective practice is defined within the field of ELT means it can be more usefully construed as a multidimensional construct comprising six specific elements: *practical* (i.e., reflection that is deemed genuine), *cognitive* (i.e., the processes it entails), *meta-cognitive* (i.e., teachers' reflections on their personal beliefs), *critical* (i.e., broader reflections on the social and political facets of teaching), *moral* (i.e., reflections on moral facets), and *learner-related* (i.e., reflections on students and how they learn).

This review of definitions indicates two key points. First, it confirms that there are three distinct facets of reflective practice: (1) the *experiences* that affect teachers, (2) the *reflective processes* which form the foundation upon which teachers are able to practise, and (3) the *action* that arises from the new possibilities that emerge (Jasper, 2013). Second, rather than being seen as an individual and linear process, reflective practice is usually multifaceted and collaborative. For instance, it intertwines contextual components and pedagogical content knowledge (Section 2.2) with a professional environment of group culture in which teachers exchange, scrutinise, and discuss their classroom practice and experiences. For this to be effective, teachers must be willing to analyse significant events as well as listen to and comprehend other colleagues' perspectives (Fook & Gardner, 2007).

The variety of definitions presented suggests that, alone or with others, reflective practitioners need to consider how to develop their teaching by drawing on empirical, practical, and theoretical forms of knowledge. Moreover, they must scrutinise their teaching from alternative perspectives and embed new, innovative approaches into practice to enhance classroom-based learning while improving their teaching (Cirocki & Farrell, 2017a). What is problematic about these definitions is that they do not give explicit attention to disciplinary knowledge, the specialised understanding of ELT, and the theories, concepts, and practices that underpin it. As will be seen in the following sections, classroom practitioners who engage in critical reflection are always steeped in the knowledge of their field.

4.2 Reflection, Critical Reflection, and Reflexivity

It is essential for teachers to construe *reflection* and *critical reflection* as distinct concepts. For instance, reflection is an activity in which everyone can engage. It involves drawing on feelings and thoughts and has a distinct purpose (Boud et al., 1985). Conversely, critical reflection involves the utilisation of *critical reason*, *critical memory*, and *creative imagination* (Brookfield, 2017; Fook & Gardner, 2007; Groome, 1980; McNiff & Whitehead, 2011). Critical reason is required to assess the present, critical memory requires scrutiny of past events, and creative imagination requires envisioning the future.

As such, critical reflection allows teachers to construct knowledge that is of practical use by pinpointing the assumptions that guide what they do (Baldwin, 2004) and endowing them with the ability to identify avenues for change at both a personal and social level (Fook, 2002). Because it is deliberate and methodical in nature, critical reflection allows teachers to '[identify and check] the accuracy and validity of [their instructional] assumptions … that … guide them through new situations' (Brookfield, 2017, p. 3). Moreover, it is a process that permits teachers to make a comparison between theory and practice, undertake in-depth scrutiny of the teaching–learning process, identify the causal relationships embedded in this process, and formulate the best resolutions to difficulties they encounter in the classroom (Cirocki & Farrell, 2017b). The latter draw on disciplinary knowledge and theories teachers developed during their study of, for instance, psycholinguistics, pragmatics, and second language acquisition courses, offered as part of their teacher education programmes.

It is also important to distinguish between *critical reflection* and *reflexivity* as these concepts are often (incorrectly) seen as interchangeable. However, a detailed clarification of these two notions – key elements of reflective practice – is beyond the scope of this chapter. Nevertheless, it is vital that reflective practice experts consider this in their future publications to ensure consistency in the field. To summarise briefly, even though both ethical and political aspects of practice are addressed in critical reflection and reflexivity, reflexivity has a more limited focus and concentrates on self-awareness (Mann, 2016). In addition, reflection-in-action is emphasised, which refers to reflecting in the here and now as circumstances evolve (D'Cruz & Jones, 2014; D'Cruz et al., 2007). As such, reflexivity requires an instant and reactive critical awareness of one's positioning and practice (Fook, 2002; McGregor & Cartwright, 2011; Moore, 2004).

Reflexivity is also a means of employing critical reflection (Bassot, 2016; Fook & Gardner, 2007). It involves careful and methodical consideration of how teachers can enhance the teaching–learning process and the broader effect of sociocultural factors on classroom teaching (Fook & Askeland, 2006).

Effective reflective practitioners can therefore take a detached view of themselves and their practice and approach it from alternative and perhaps novel perspectives. McGregor and Cartwright (2011, p. 236) argue that reflexivity endows reflective practitioners with the ability to (1) recall and relate important events and situations or occurrences, (2) explain why certain critical events happened and why they acted as they did, (3) demonstrate an awareness that alternative actions could have been taken, (4) develop a means of establishing which approach would be optimal in dealing with such events, and (5) review evidence to determine which approach was optimal, how best to prevent a recurrence of an event, and why this is the case. It is therefore clear that reflective practitioners need to be able to interrogate their experiences, beliefs, and the choices and actions they take and assess their effect on those in the classroom and the processes that are taking place. As such, reflective practitioners need to think about the way in which they reflect on novel circumstances (Moore, 2004).

Another perspective that reflexivity brings to reflective practice is that teachers must be aware of how they co-construct meaning within the classroom setting and the disparate tools available to them to draw on in order to construct novel knowledge and forms of understanding. Moreover, classroom environments and the incidents that take place within them can be highly complex and should therefore make use of sociological, psychological, and pedagogical insights (Cartwright, 2011). The first encompasses the social behaviours of teachers within schools, the second is concerned with the behaviour and emotions displayed by teachers as part of a pedagogical community, and the third refers to the practice of teaching and the effect of this on learning.

From this discussion, it is clear that reflective practice involves teachers methodically scrutinising, evaluating, and altering their teaching as part of a spiral process (Cirocki & Farrell, 2017a). For such practice to be critical, it must be founded on disciplinary knowledge and theories – as indicated in Wallace's (1991) reflective cycle model, which was developed specifically for language teachers – as well as teachers' beliefs, which are shaped by evidence-based investigation and enhanced by engaging in effective working partnerships. Furthermore, such practice also requires that teachers look at their reflective teaching through the lens of the professional standards (Sections 2.2 and 3.4) and competences (Section 3.5) they are expected to demonstrate at specific stages of their teaching careers and judge the extent to which they meet these requirements and whether their current professional profiles tally with their career stages.

In conclusion, to provide high-quality language teaching and reflect critically upon this, teachers need to be systematic and analytical in their approach, bridge theory and practice, and exhibit a capacity to reflect. It is therefore important to emphasise that 'the path to developing as a critically reflective teacher cannot be prescribed with an intervention formula. The route cannot be preplanned – it must be lived' (Larrivee, 2000, p. 306).

4.3 Types of Reflective Practice

Thus far, it has been established that reflective practice is founded upon critical reflection and reflexivity. It is essential for teachers to remember that the classroom environment is a multidimensional space and that those who occupy it are 'products of complex social and personal circumstances' (Hillier, 2009, p. 6). All actions and behaviours are thus manifested by individuals at a specific point in time. This implies that teachers need to engage in a process of ongoing reflection so that they can react effectively to specific incidents in the classroom, propose effective resolutions to any problems that arise, and make any necessary changes to ensure that the delivery of lessons and their performance as teachers is productive and successful.

Teachers are advised to engage in five categories of reflective practice: *reflection-in-action*, *reflection-on-action*, *exploratory practice*, *reflection-for-action*, and *classroom-based research*. Given that the last category has attracted particular attention in the field of ELT over the past three decades, it deserves careful consideration and is therefore discussed separately under the heading of teacher-led research at the end of this chapter. Consequently, this section focuses only on four categories of reflective practice. The first of these, reflection-in-action, is similar to the concept of theories-in-use, which refers to the theories that shape teachers' actions (Argyris & Schön, 1978; Zwozdiak-Myers, 2012). It is a form of reflection that encompasses the way in which teachers consider their actions in the classroom and implement such actions by drawing on pedagogical knowledge. It therefore relates to the ability of teachers to handle any difficulties that arise in the classroom. Its primary purpose is to enable teachers to react effectively to student learning at any given point in time. It is important to note that reflection-in-action relates to both positive and negative situations that may arise as part of the teaching–learning process. Thus, when unexpected events occur (Section 4.5), teachers can implement several on-the-spot methods until an optimal solution is identified. As part of this process, three elements are focused upon: the action, the instinctive knowledge that underpins the action, and the subsequent outcomes (Farrell, 2008a; Farrell & Baecher, 2017; Pollard, 2014).

The second category, reflection-on-action, refers to 'the retrospective contemplation of practice' (Peterson, 2016; Schön, 1987). Its function is to elucidate the steps taken to resolve an incident in the classroom by understanding and explaining the information recalled. In this way, reflection-on-action helps teachers to build a stock of available experiences upon which they can draw when deciding how to handle any future difficulties that might arise.

Reflection-on-action thus connects theory to practice. It is therefore retrospective thinking that enables teachers to build novel sets of meaning, alternatively described as theories of practice (Cirocki & Farrell, 2017b), that are founded upon disciplinary knowledge and theory, reflective discussions with others, and specific teaching events.

The third category of reflective practice is exploratory practice, where both learners and teachers are stimulated to examine their own engagement in learning and teaching while concomitantly perfecting the target language (Hanks, 2017). Exploratory practice views learners as individuals who are committed to learning, are able to make decisions independently, and are capable of becoming successful learning practitioners (Allwright & Hanks, 2009). Moreover, it enables learners and teachers to collaborate in reflecting upon and making sense of areas of classroom practice they find challenging by employing standard teaching, learning, and monitoring activities as instruments of investigation (Hanks, 2017; Slimani-Rolls & Kiely, 2019). Exploratory practice is primarily concerned with the calibre of the classroom environment for language teachers and learners and with making sense of their experiences in this setting. To successfully achieve this, all those participating in the classroom need to reflect and collaborate meaningfully on an ongoing basis.

The final category of reflective practice to be discussed in this section is reflection-for-action. In contrast to the previous three categories, reflection-for-action concerns the knowledge and skills that teachers employ to determine the actions they will take in the future (Chien, 2013). To achieve this, teachers need to self-assess their achievements to date and develop guidelines grounded in disciplinary knowledge and theory which they can draw upon to guarantee future success. Furthermore, the critical analysis of and reflection upon the achievements need to be set against the aforementioned professional standards and competences to either provide support to teachers or plan the next steps for their professional growth.

Recently, the reflection-in-action, reflection-on-action, and reflection-for-action categories have been combined by Cirocki and Widodo (2019) into a practitioner-friendly reflective practice model. This conceptualises teaching as founded upon a set of logically connected lessons in which reflection is defined as an ongoing task of reassessing teaching and learning that allows teachers to make linkages between their various experiences. In making distinctions between the four discrete elements discussed, the model focuses teachers' minds on the essential value of reflection in facilitating the delivery of lessons from initial planning to implementation.

Thus, when engaging in pre-lesson reflection, teachers ponder critically on the planning involved. This will encompass the aims, learning outcomes, teaching strategies, materials, activities, and general management of the classroom. The next stage, reflection-before-lesson, is one in which teachers picture the lesson and devise a structure, predict any potential difficulties, and decide how to incorporate students' needs into the teaching–learning process. The following stage, reflection-during-lesson, concerns both the *theories-in-use* that drive teachers' actions (Li, 2017) and teachers' reaction to unexpected events, positive and negative, along with their 'ability to deal with [them] when they occur' (Cirocki & Farrell, 2017b, p. 9). Reflection-after-lesson, the next stage, refers to when teachers evaluate their lessons to acquire an in-depth understanding of incidents in the classroom, how these arise at specific points, and also the reasons for those incidents (Farrell, 2015; Griffith, 2000; Schön, 1983). In so doing, teachers are able to consider what alternative actions they could take if similar situations were to arise in the future. Finally, the reflection-beyond-lesson stage aligns with Farrell's (2015) notion of beyond practice and provides teachers with a wealth of valuable opportunities to examine 'the moral, political and social issues' (p. 30) that impact on their teaching (Section 4.4).

The following section presents Farrell's influential framework for reflecting on teaching experience. Teachers are advised to use it in their practice and integrate the various types of reflection discussed in this chapter thus far.

4.4 Farrell's Framework for Reflecting on Teaching Experience

A variety of reflective practice frameworks currently exist in the literature (e.g., Farrell, 2015; Gibbs, 1988; Jasper, 2013; Kolb, 1984; Schön, 1991), all of which have value; however, there is only space in this section to focus on Farrell's (2015) framework, which was selected for three reasons. Firstly, it recommends adopting a holistic attitude to reflection. What demarcates this framework from earlier ones is that it combines cognitive, meta-cognitive, and intellectual facets of professional practice with the moral, emotional, and spiritual components of reflection (Farrell, 2015). Secondly, practitioners, whatever stage they are at in their careers, are perceived to be active in pursuing their learning trajectories. This includes an in-depth evaluation of their values and how they relate to the pedagogical practices they employ. Thus, they not only take responsibility for their learning but can also make vital connections between practice and theory, enhancing their understanding of procedures, strategies, and difficulties within the classroom (Farrell, 2015). Finally, Farrell's framework is explicitly aimed at language teachers.

Embedded within the framework are five discrete stages of reflection: philosophy, principles, theory, practice, and beyond practice (Figure 4.1). The first, *philosophy*, requires a teacher-as-person perspective, the implication of which is that professional practice (Section 2.2) is shaped by the philosophies teachers hold, which continue to evolve throughout their lives. For instance,

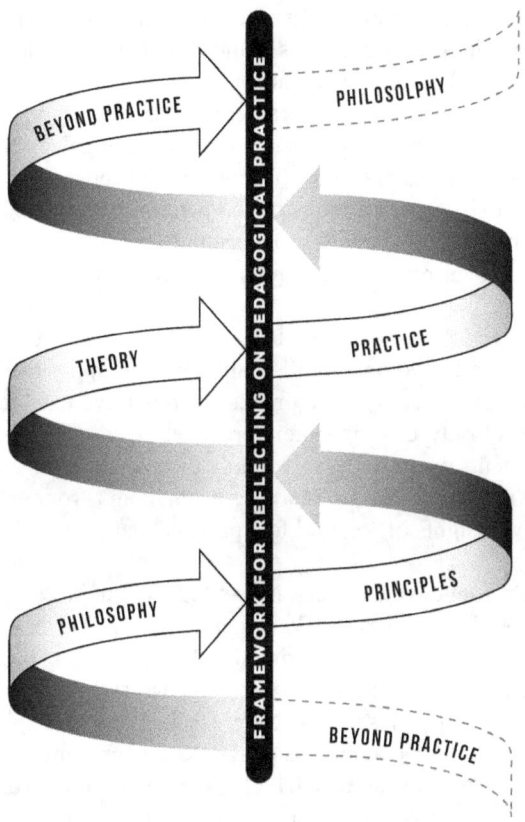

Figure 4.1 Five discrete stages of reflection: Farrell's framework

teachers can discuss how their experiences in the past have helped shape and develop their philosophies with respect to practice. The second level, *principles*, is one in which teachers reflect on their *beliefs*, *conceptions*, and *assumptions* with respect to teaching–learning. These are largely similar and are thus seen as constituting a unified system. Specifically, beliefs are perceived as personal views, evaluations, inferences, or conclusions. In contrast, conceptions are expositions and narratives pertaining to 'overall approaches and decision making in the classroom', and assumptions are principles of which the teacher is not consciously aware (Farrell & Kennedy, 2019, p. 3). The third level, *theory*, involves teachers reflecting on the decisions they make regarding the language systems or specific skills they teach. This enables teachers to convert their theoretical knowledge into practice. At the fourth level, *practice*, teachers partake in the process of reflection-in-action both during and after teaching (Section 4.3). The former requires stepping back while teaching and implementing changes in response to the situations that arise, while the latter involves reflecting upon classroom incidents once the lessons have been completed. Finally, the *beyond practice* level is where teachers reflect on the moral, political, and social factors that shape their professional practice. Moreover, such reflection can be extended to explore how political agendas and economic considerations shape existing perceptions of and patterns in English language education. In so doing, teachers become cognisant of the mutual relationships between their professional practice and the social world that exists outside schools.

Teachers are advised to adhere closely to these stages when embarking on their reflective trajectories. Doing so will enable them to apply theory-into-practice and practice-into-theory to the process of reflective teaching. In so doing, practitioners closely examine their practice, strive to make refinements and improvements where necessary, apply these in both the classroom and the wider school, and partake in 'learning through and from experience towards gaining new insights of self and for [professional] practice' (Finlay, 2008, p. 1).

Although Farrell's framework is very influential (Tajeddin & Watanabe, 2022), it is not without its weaknesses. For instance, the third level – theory – has a very narrow scope; it is about exploring the choices teachers make about the material they teach in the classroom (i.e., language skills, language systems) or 'how to put their theories into practice' (Farrell & Kennedy, 2019, p. 3). It needs to be clarified here that professional reflective practitioners require a wider perspective of theory than this. The broader definition needs to subsume ELT discipline-specific theories and theories pertaining to general education, as proposed in the model in Chapter 1. Professional teachers not only reflect on the teaching–learning process through this lens, they also rationalise their reflective practice and their reflective practice outcomes through these theories. It is therefore crucial that teacher educators and CPD providers consider emphasising the role of theory and disciplinary knowledge in reflective practice and instilling in pre- and in-service teachers three fundamental convictions: the purpose of educational theory is classroom action, effective classroom practices are grounded in diverse theories, and professional reflective practice always takes into account the interdependence between theory and practice.

A second critique concerns the *beyond practice* level in Farrell's framework. It assumes 'a sociocultural dimension to teaching and learning, and entails exploring and examining the moral, political, and social issues that impact a teacher's practice both inside and outside the classroom' (Farrell & Kennedy, 2019, p. 3). It is vital that this level also addresses the professional–ethical aspects of teaching (Section, 2.4) and does so explicitly. For instance, the impact of teacher education programmes, CPD events, or context-specific requirements for teaching (e.g., standards, competences) should all be considered.

4.5 Instruments for Reflective Practice

Having considered the theoretical basis of reflective practice, the next step is to examine some of the instruments available to help stimulate critical reflection and embed it into professional practice. The tools covered in this section are *teacher journals, collaborative blogging, critical incident focus groups, peer coaching, post-observation conferences*, and *lesson study projects*. These tools can also be used as data collection instruments in teacher-led research, discussed at the end of this chapter.

4.5.1 Teacher Journals

Journals are employed widely in the field of education (Stevens & Cooper, 2009). They are primarily employed as tools to collect qualitative data rather than being utilised for reflective practice. Through reflective journals, teachers keep a record of their daily practice (Bassot, 2013) and can thus examine and chronicle their teaching. This can include the use of objective data (e.g., attendance, lesson plans) alongside subjective accounts and individual reflections on classroom experiences. The process of keeping a journal fosters methodical analysis, rigorous evaluation, and planning in both the short and long term (Cirocki & Farrell, 2017b).

Critical reflection on all the data recorded enhances teachers' insights into the teaching–learning process, enabling them to evaluate its relative merits and demerits. Moreover, it enables them to form associations between existing ideas, connect theoretical concepts to what happens in the classroom, and devise novel ideas. Reflection encourages practitioners to ruminate deeply on what they have learnt regarding their behaviours and actions in the classroom. Consequently, they acquire enhanced insights into themselves as teachers and their professional practice. An additional benefit is that critical reflection enables teachers to revisit experiences in the classroom that either were highly rewarding or caused considerable distress. Through a re-analysis of their behavioural and emotional responses to such situations, teachers can further develop their identities as professionals (Section 2.3).

The use of teacher journals in research on reflective practice has become increasingly commonplace (e.g., Chien, 2013; Farrell, 2016; Gadsby, 2022; Genc, 2010; Khanjani et al., 2018; Kömür & Çepik, 2015; Yee et al., 2022). Lee (2008) explored the types of information pre-service teachers incorporated into their journals and whether these demonstrated the development of an ability to reflect. In addition, she elicited the reactions of these teachers to the experience of writing a journal. The participants comprised thirteen female English major undergraduates from Hong Kong who had enrolled on a Diploma in Education course to become English language teachers. The findings revealed that pre-service teachers felt journals were of value as they gave them a voice and helped them to build their identities as professionals through the acquisition of qualities such as an ability to question and evaluate their own practice and to identify and test alternatives.

Yee et al.'s (2022) project was based on the premise that reflective writing, in general, and reflective journals, in particular, are utilised by pre-service teachers to think carefully about their professional learning and teaching experiences. Their Malaysian case study examined the stages of pre-service teachers' reflective practice using a six-stage framework. Derived from Jay and Johnson (2002), these stages are *Describing*, *Feeling*, *Associating*, *Analysing*, *Assessing*, and *Developing*. The results indicated that the participants reflected at all six stages, but some were deemed more popular than others. In descending order, the stages were ranked as follows by the participants: *Describing* (36.04 per cent), *Analysing* (26.00 per cent), *Associating* (21.15 per cent), *Feeling* (12.12 per cent), *Assessing* (2.78 per cent), and *Developing* (1.92 per cent). This demonstrates that the pre-service teachers reflected most at the lowest stage of the framework, *Describing*, and least at the highest stage of the framework, *Developing*.

4.5.2 Collaborative Blogging

Unlike traditional journals, blogs provide more scope for teachers to partake in reflection. Importantly, they transform the journal's unidirectional discourse into interactive discussions among bloggers (Cirocki & Farrell, 2017b; Tang, 2009; Too, 2013). Collaborative blogs therefore provide teachers with a platform in which to critically reflect on issues relevant to teaching (e.g., formative assessment, classroom management); exchange experiences, knowledge, and teaching materials; devise and disseminate novel pedagogical frameworks; and increase their awareness of the role and position of reflective practice in their professional development as teachers (Section 9.4). A further advantage of blog posts is that it allows teachers to include video clips of lessons to stimulate collaborative reflection and professional exchanges on issues in which they have a similar interest.

Research has revealed that teamwork can facilitate professional growth (Bener & Yıldız, 2019; Blankstein et al., 2007; Ciampa & Gallagher, 2015; Garrison & Akyol, 2009; Garza & Smith, 2015; Hall, 2018; Nelson & Slavit, 2008; Petko et al., 2017; Tajeddin & Aghababazadeh, 2018). Professional development is thus enhanced when opportunities are provided to participate in collaborative settings as learners. To that end, King and Newmann (2001) emphasise the importance of fostering an advanced understanding of collaboration among schools and professionals working in other schools and educational institutions. Technology such as blogging can be utilised to support this process (Ciampa & Gallagher, 2015; Hou et al., 2009; Yadav, 2011; Yang, 2009). King and Newmann (2001, p. 86) also note that 'teacher learning is most likely to occur when teachers have opportunities to collaborate, [both synchronously and asynchronously], with professional peers, both within and outside of their school, along with access to the expertise of external researchers and programme developers. Peer collaboration offers a powerful vehicle for teacher learning, a necessary supplement to published materials and advice from other authorities'.

More recently, blogging was incorporated into a collaborative inquiry project involving practitioners from both elementary and secondary schools in Canada. In this project, Ciampa and Gallagher (2015) investigated the nature and frequency of blog usage and perceptions of blogging among the participants. Quantitative and qualitative data were gathered from three groups of participants: twelve teachers, one lead facilitator (K-12 literacy consultant), and two literacy coaches, using individual semi-structured teacher interviews, blog entries, and a blog statistics-tracking tool. The results revealed the benefits and challenges of using the blog to facilitate teacher collaborative inquiry. According to teachers, the blog was construed as a device that enabled them to share pedagogical techniques, methods of assessment, and knowledge and develop networks with their peers. Teachers who were reflective, shy, and introverted were considered most likely to find this beneficial. Regarding the more problematic aspects, teachers flagged non-existent or inadequate in-service training on using the blog, technical issues, low perceived usefulness and ease of use, time constraints, and a poor degree of simultaneous engagement and immediacy.

4.5.3 Critical Incident Focus Groups

Another helpful tool that can assist teachers in reflecting on or researching their teaching is critical incident focus groups. These consist of approximately six colleagues working together to scrutinise critical incidents that take place while teaching (Farrell, 2008a; Farrell & Baecher, 2017). Such incidents can be defined as unplanned and unexpected events that, by their very nature, are readily and vividly recalled.

Through reflection on such incidents, teachers develop novel understandings of the teaching–learning process they had hitherto taken for granted. The benefits accruing from this process are of three types: *epistemological, pedagogical*, and *empirical* (Richards & Farrell, 2005). Included in the epistemological category are an increased familiarity with existing suppositions pertaining to teaching and learning, critical interrogation of disparate elements of teaching, and further scrutiny of deeply held beliefs. In terms of pedagogical advantages, reflection allows teachers to hone their practices in response to feedback from learners, form a network of practitioners who are critically engaged, and share and appraise accumulated incidents with their colleagues. An additional benefit of joining such communities is that it enables teachers to conduct empirical studies, such as action research, to address ongoing issues relevant to teaching and learning.

Collective reflection involves teachers exploring their practice by narrating accounts of their experience to members of focus groups. In so doing, teachers are able to make sense of events that appear to be random as they possess innate personal knowledge and expertise acquired over years spent teaching the English language (Johnson & Golombek, 2002). Self-reflective narratives thus constitute an abundant source of information that enables teachers to reflect on how they have achieved the position they have attained, the way in which they implement their practice, the cognitive and problem-solving strategies they employ, and the fundamental presumptions, beliefs, and values that have formed and dictate their classroom practices (Farrell, 2013; Farrell & Baecher, 2017; Karimi & Nazari, 2019; Richards & Farrell, 2011).

Irrespective of whether narratives are spoken or written, analysis and discussion of critical incidents should follow the four steps outlined by Thiel (1999):

1. *Self-observation* – identification by teachers of significant incidents that have taken place in the classroom.
2. *Rich description of the event that has taken place* – what happened, what caused it, and what happened next.
3. *Self-awareness* – an analysis by the teacher of why the event happened.
4. *Self-evaluation* – an assessment by the teacher of how the event altered their understanding of teaching.

Such a four-step framework ensures that the stories teachers relate are consistent and adhere to the same basic structure. This enables the focus group to consider, reflect upon, scrutinise, and explore the narratives in a more systematic manner.

However, in the field of ELT, few research studies have focused on critical incidents. One such study was conducted by Farrell (2008a), who asked eighteen trainee English language teachers in Singapore to reflect on their teaching and describe a minimum of two critical incidents. From their reflections, the following categories emerged: language proficiency, class participation, behaviour, gender, classroom space, lesson objectives, classroom activities, attention spans, and additional class assistance. Farrell concluded that formal reflection on critical thinking would equip teachers with the skills needed to deal with changes throughout their careers.

In another study, Shapira-Lishchinsky (2012) focused on the ethical dilemmas that arise in relation to critical incidents and the way in which teachers responded to them. She created a taxonomy of critical incidents upon which a multidimensional model of ethical dilemmas, such as conflict with school rules or norms, was devised. She concluded that analysing critical incidents can help elucidate how teachers construe classroom incidents.

Atai and Nejadghanbar (2016) conducted a study to explore how six in-service English as a foreign language (EFL) teachers reflected, retrospectively and introspectively, on critical incidents. Throughout twelve sessions, these participants wrote about the incidents they had experienced in a blog they shared with their colleagues. A grounded theory analysis of the data provided valuable insights into the *what* and *why* of reflections on critical incidents.

In their study, Serna-Gutiérrez and Mora Pablo (2018) employed a narrative analysis to identify the most impactful changes and decisions that have taken place in the lives of BA TESOL transnational students teaching English in central Mexico. They aimed to determine what motivated the participants to study English language teaching (or languages). The findings revealed that through such critical incidents, participants could examine how their identity as teachers was constructed.

Mirzaee and Aliakbari (2017) examined similar processes of identity formation in a study of an Iranian EFL teacher. The researchers employed a life history approach focusing on critical incidents to gather data which were then analysed using the social ecology of identity. The findings revealed that the identities of the teacher were fundamentally socially constructed, and hence there was little scope for them to exercise personal autonomy (Chapter 5). Moreover, forged through years spent learning how to teach, the agency they were able to exhibit was principally exercised in a manner that had been carefully prescribed.

In the final study, Kılıç and Cinkara (2020) employed a mixed-methods approach to examine the ways in which forty-nine pre-service EFL teachers construed, made sense of, and viewed the vital events that had taken place during the process of learning English and how these impacted both their learning and the formation of their identity as teachers. A quantitative analysis indicated that these could be classified into three themes: contexts (e.g., educational, non-educational), people (e.g., teacher-related, peer-related), and outcomes (e.g., positive, negative). The primary conclusion drawn by the researchers was that such events had powerful and far-reaching impacts on language learning among the participants, as well as the means by which they constructed their identity as teachers.

4.5.4 Peer Coaching

Peer coaching is an approach in which two teachers work together (Gottesman, 2009; Lu, 2007; Robbins, 2015), one of whom adopts the role of a coach whose responsibility is to provide feedback and make recommendations to their partner, such as implementing a novel teaching method. As part of this co-teaching strategy, teachers partake in a productive professional discourse (Vidmar, 2006) that aligns with the five elements enshrined in Showers' (1984, pp. 74–78) model of peer coaching (Figure 4.2).

These are as follows:

1. *Companionship* – teachers use an alternative teaching model to discuss their successes and failures. This helps ameliorate feelings of isolation.
2. *Feedback* – teachers provide each other with objective, non-judgemental feedback on implementing the skills required by the new model.
3. *Analysis* – teachers offer mutual assistance in enhancing their control over the new method so that it becomes personalised, voluntary, and flexible.
4. *Adaptation* – teachers collaborate to align a teaching model to the specific needs of students.
5. *Support* – the coach furnishes appropriate support for the peer teacher when they implement a novel strategy.

For teachers engaged in reflective practice, there are valuable benefits to be accrued from peer coaching. For instance, engaging in such reflection helps both the coach and the peer teacher to enhance their knowledge and understanding of pedagogical practice (Richards & Farrell, 2005; Robbins, 2015). Their joint analysis of teaching and decision-making involves consciously modifying skills or methods to provide optimal learning experiences for students. Peer teachers, in particular, receive support and inspiration from coaches that enable them to appraise their experiences, discuss their frustrations, and fine-tune their teaching based on the helpful feedback and technical support

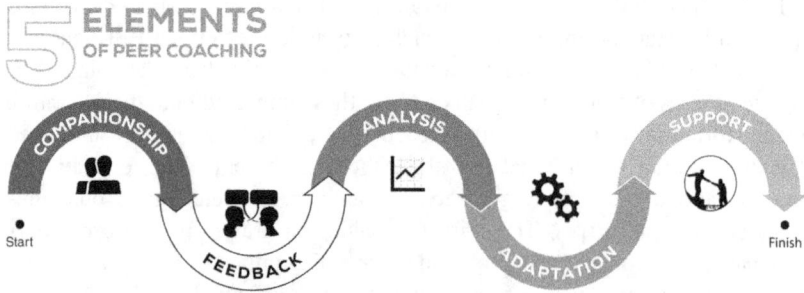

Figure 4.2 Five elements of peer coaching

they receive from practitioners with substantive experience (Koh & Neuman, 2006). This would particularly help novice teachers whose initial stages of their teaching journey may be somewhat turbulent. Peer coaching can also provide valuable data for teacher-researchers (Section 4.6) about practitioners' critical, analytical, reflective, and strategic types of thinking, in terms of not only how they are executed in classroom practice but also how they shape practitioners' capacity to be school leaders (Chapter 8).

Several research studies have been conducted on the utilisation of a peer-coaching strategy in language education. For instance, Kuru Gonen (2016) conducted a mixed-methods study that assessed how much peer coaching influenced reflexivity among twelve Turkish pre-service EFL teachers. The measures employed were a quantitative profile of the reflective thinking attributes scale and qualitative data obtained from reflective diaries, focus group discussions, and video recordings of post-conference sessions. The results showed that peer coaching practice increased reflexivity among pre-service teachers and that this was beneficial prior to beginning their pre-teaching careers proper.

Further notable studies on peer coaching have been conducted by Vacilotto and Cummings (2007), Soisangwarn and Wongwanich (2014), Alsaleh et al. (2017), and Porras et al. (2018). The aim of Vacilotto and Cummings' (2007) study was to examine whether the peer coaching model could be successfully employed as a tool for the professional development of pre-service TESOL teachers and whether it could be applied to binational centres in Brazil and teacher development programmes more broadly. Their results suggested that peer coaching helped nurture the development of teaching skills, provided opportunities for teachers to share instructional materials and methods, and encouraged those taking part to reconsider their teaching styles and methods.

Peer coaching was also used by Soisangwarn and Wongwanich (2014) to advocate reflective teaching and enhance the teaching skills of a group of professional teachers in Thailand. This mixed-methods study consisted of three separate stages: (1) conceptual transformation, (2) practising being a reflective teacher and facilitating mutual coaching (clear advantages are derived from allowing peers to work together and exchange ideas, opinions, and observations), and (3) evaluating and reflecting upon pedagogical expertise. The results revealed that as a consequence of peer coaching, teachers' individual reflections on their practices were considerably enhanced, and they benefitted from advice from their colleagues on how to improve their instruction. A community of teachers was also established (Section 9.4); its members were dedicated to enhancing and revitalising their pedagogical expertise.

A qualitative study conducted in Kuwait by Alsaleh et al. (2017) examined how peer coaching in the context of supervision impacted the professional development of pre-service teachers and how such coaching can be provided with institutional support by head department supervisors to enhance the professional development of teachers. The results indicated, among other things, that the professional development of teachers was nurtured through peer coaching with respect to team cooperation, teaching practices, and an increase in the enthusiasm, self-confidence, and autonomy of teachers (Chapter 5).

In another mixed-methods study, Porras et al. (2018) assessed the extent to which both peer coaching and reverse mentoring positively impacted the professional development of Colombian EFL teachers. The results indicated the effectiveness of both approaches in allowing participants to share instructional tools and pedagogical experiences in a cooperative and trusting environment. Moreover, there was an increase in teaching knowledge among the participants, who then trialled novel classroom strategies and methods to optimise learning.

4.5.5 Post-Observation Conferences

Another valuable tool that can be employed to support reflection and research on teaching practice is that of a post-observation conference. The aim, in this case, is to reflect on any lessons that have been observed and furnish teachers with helpful feedback to enhance their performance in the classroom (Bailey, 2006; Danielson & McGreal, 2000; Korthagen & Vasalos, 2010). This reflection usually encompasses what, when, why, and how an activity took place or why it did not take place. Post-observation conferences must also focus on future changes, such as potential improvements in elements of teaching practice (Cirocki & Farrell, 2017b).

A recent focus of discussions has been the use of video recordings of lessons to supplement post-observation conferences (e.g., Eröz-Tuğa, 2013; Kong, 2010; Marsh & Mitchell, 2014; Mercado & Baecher, 2014). Such recordings are considered more helpful in stimulating critical reflection and facilitating insightful analysis of lessons than written feedback from observers, which can be partial in nature and often biased (Wang & Hartley, 2003). Moreover, video recordings provide teachers with robust evidence of events taking place in the classroom and the dynamics therein (Hamilton, 2012; Marsh & Mitchell, 2014). This enables teachers to observe first-hand how they act in the classroom and use body language (e.g., facial expressions, gaze, posture) and speech to react to the actions of others. Because they can be watched repeatedly, teachers can focus closely on different elements of their practice, deepening their reflection and the extent to which they understand what is taking place in their practice (Borko et al., 2008; Wang & Hartley, 2003).

It is also essential for conferences to encourage open and frank discussions that utilise searching and focused questions to challenge the original thoughts and beliefs of the teacher. The ideas from such discussions produce the conditions necessary for transformative learning and facilitate teacher growth (Donovan et al., 2007). Teachers must then be motivated to consciously develop the elements of their practice that have been focused upon.

Irrespective of the feedback they receive, which can be perceived as extremely critical or disheartening, teachers must learn how to react accordingly. For example, such feedback should be perceived as the primary means of professional growth. To further improve teaching practice and enhance effectiveness, practitioners need 'to be open to listening, accepting, reflecting on, and acting on feedback' (Glendenning & Cartwright, 2011, p. 175). Common responses are to react defensively, disagree, or focus on other teachers; however, these are impediments to learning.

Finally, it is also essential to link post-observation conferences to research conducted in the classroom (see Section 4.6 for details). Among the interesting studies in this respect is a multiple-case project on the affordances of reflective dialogues in post-observation group feedback sessions by Kurtoğlu-Hooton (2016a). Specifically, she looked into confirmatory feedback – typically given as praise, summarising what a teacher did well – and how this type of feedback contributed to student teachers' professional learning during initial teacher training courses at a UK university. An important finding from her study was that group feedback sessions, offered by experienced teachers to student teachers after their teaching practice, operated as interactive learning fora (Kurtoğlu-Hooton, 2016b). Specifically, confirmatory feedback provided to one student teacher was also observed and acted upon by the other student teachers present in the feedback session, which had direct implications for teacher education. Additionally, Kurtoğlu-Hooton's (2016a) observation also aligns well with Farrell's (2015, p. 123) definition of reflective practice, where he states that 'reflective practice ... [is] [a] cognitive process accompanied by a set of attitudes in which teachers systematically collect data about their practice, and, while engaging in dialogue with others, use the data to make informed decisions about their practice both inside and outside the classroom'.

4.5.6 *Lesson Study Projects*

Another means of stimulating critical reflection is through lesson study projects. These teacher-driven fora employ collaborative inquiry to examine the curriculum, teaching practices, and student learning (Akiba et al., 2019; Collet, 2019; Dudley, 2015; Kager et al., 2023). They constitute a professional teacher-learning community model within which teachers engage in an organised and integrated cycle of planning, teaching, and reflecting, the overarching purpose of which is to identify ways to optimise opportunities and outcomes for students (Dudley, 2015; Vescio et al., 2008). Essentially, they comprise teams of teachers whose remit is to engage in research and assist student learning.

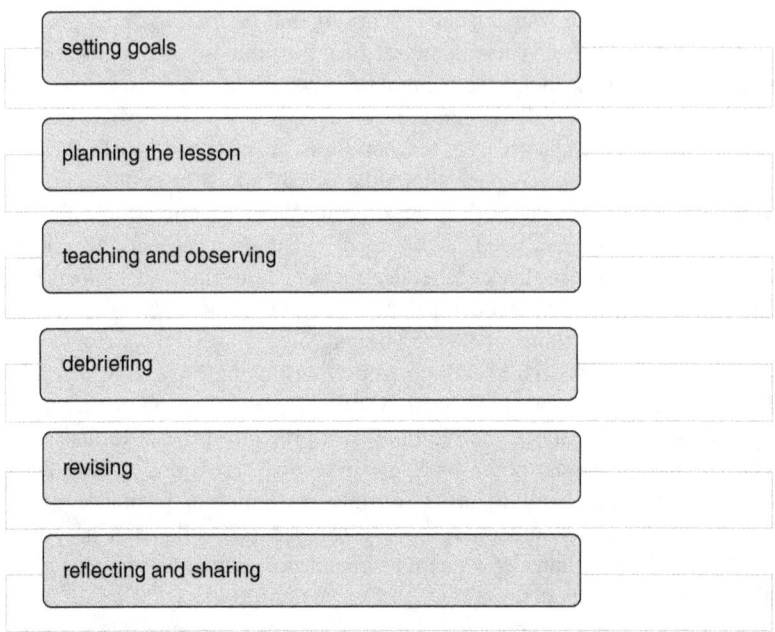

Figure 4.3 Six stages of a lesson study project

In line with the framework developed by Education Scotland (2015), an effectively designed project comprises the following six stages (Figure 4.3): *setting goals* (i.e., developing a theme relevant to the subject and establishing wide-ranging long-term aims for the lesson study cycle), *planning the lesson* (i.e., utilising current knowledge pertaining to existing conditions in the class), *teaching and observing* (i.e., one team member teaches the lesson while others observe students' responses and derive evidence as to their thoughts), *debriefing* (i.e., disseminating evidence on student learning), *revising* (i.e., a different team member then teaches the lesson to another group of students utilising the evidence gathered), and *reflecting and sharing* (i.e., proactively disseminating what has been learnt, ensuring that it is applied wherever it supports learning).

Like action research (Section 4.6), it is essential to reflect upon the lessons as this encourages teachers to change their presuppositions regarding teaching–learning and allows them to countenance new ways of implementing instruction in their own classrooms (Cirocki & Widodo, 2019). It also helps teachers to feel an elevated degree of ownership over their thoughts and ideas. However, they must be clear about the differences between lesson study and action research. For instance, whereas individuals can carry out action research, lesson study projects are always team-oriented; whereas action research often focuses on relatively open research questions, lesson study research focuses firmly on the needs of learners' and the attainment of learning outcomes. Furthermore, the remit of action research projects is broad and encompasses all issues pertaining to students, teachers, parents, learning, teaching, and school policies (Hanfstingl et al., 2018; Widodo, 2015).

Recent research in both general and English language education reveals myriad significant benefits of lesson study projects, including the development of new insights among pre- and in-service teachers into students' needs and how to enhance their teaching (Kıncal et al., 2019; Nashruddin & Nurrachman, 2016; van Halem et al., 2016), increased awareness of different teaching strategies (Nashruddin & Nurrachman, 2016; Vrikki et al., 2017), the development of agency (Lamb & Aldous, 2016), engagement in reflective practice (Soto Gómez et al., 2016), enhanced facilitation of discussion (Kohlmeier & Saye, 2017), grasping the importance of collaboration (Nashruddin & Nurrachman, 2016), and changes in beliefs and attitudes (e.g., Schipper et al., 2017). However, challenges relating to the implementation of lesson study have also been reported. For instance, in Nashruddin and Nurrachman's (2016) study, time and school administrative structures impeded teacher collaboration.

4.6 Teachers as Researchers

Previous sections have demonstrated that different types of reflective practice may occur in the language classroom. No matter what classroom aspects these reflective practices focus on, professional teachers will always approach them with curiosity, rigour, and commitment. They will engage in *critical* reflection, which, as explained earlier in this chapter, differs from teacher pedagogical tact, or teacher intuitive qualities, where 'the professional unconscious provides information about what is important and what should be done' in a particular classroom situation (Sipman et al., 2019, p. 1188). At times, critical reflection concerns solving classroom problems by bridging theory and practice. However, these theory–practice-oriented reflections sometimes lead to more profound, more systematic, and empirically focused studies of classroom practices and processes. Such reflections require that teachers act as researchers – the theme of this section.

Teacher-led classroom research is defined as an activity in which professional teachers engage to support standardised and methodical reflective practice, improve their teaching and that of their colleagues, scrutinise the assumptions that underpin the implementation of educational theory, examine the positive and negative impacts of educational practice, explore different components of the way in which students learn, and/or assess and enact the priorities of the school as a whole. The word *research*, as opposed to classroom inquiry, has been deliberately chosen as a heading for this section:

1. to emphasise that professional practitioners are not only capable of but are also expected to conduct rigorous, systematic, and theory-based investigations related to classroom life;
2. to indicate the importance of ethnographic research that professional teachers carry out to explore anglophone or world cultures to be able to introduce them to their students in the classroom;
3. to conceptualise classroom-based research as investigations that rely on concepts and theories derived from the disciplines of education and applied linguistics, thus connecting theories of learning and teaching languages with classroom practices;
4. to clarify that professional teacher-researchers, just like educational researchers or applied linguists, can produce high-quality research outputs;
5. to emphasise that teacher-led systematic investigations have a substantial impact on and far-reaching implications for language education, teacher education, and policy and should therefore not be overlooked; and
6. to encourage change in the current educational discourse and give professional teacher-researchers and their research outputs their rightful place, as their work is no less significant than that produced by educational researchers or applied linguists.

Similarly, recent literature emphasises the benefits and need for teachers to examine their own practice to serve as the driving force of change (Benitt, 2015; Burns, 2010; Burns et al., 2022; Cirocki & Burns, 2019). It promotes a perception of teaching as research conducted for teachers by teachers. Even though it is challenging for teachers to reflect on and examine their own practice and to make use of different kinds of reflection (Section 4.3), it is essential for them to participate in action research as this has an immediate effect on their teaching, as well as serving to prioritise and personalise what they learn.

Action research is an organised and reciprocal process that 'allows teachers to study their own classrooms…in order to better understand them and improve their quality or effectiveness' (Mertler, 2012, p. 4). Thus, it involves teachers scrutinising and questioning the actions they take in the classroom so that they can learn from these and improve upon them in the future (Biebighäuser et al., 2012; Burns, 2010; Kemmis & McTaggart, 1988; Mertler, 2009, p. 29). This process is spiralling or cyclical (Figure 4.4) as it involves practitioners methodically implementing the following eight steps:

1. *Clarify the problem* (e.g., EFL students lack the motivation to read in English).
2. *Acquire relevant information* (e.g., through holding informal conversations with students and conducting classroom observations).

Figure 4.4 Action research steps

3. *Review existing literature* (i.e., through analysing research on motivation to identify potential resolutions).
4. *Construct a research plan* (e.g., through holding a meeting with co-researchers).
5. *Execute the plan and collect data* (e.g., through distributing questionnaires and conducting interviews).
6. *Analyse the data* (e.g., through carrying out content and statistical analyses, etc.).
7. *Devise an action plan* (e.g., through enacting a creative and novel strategy to resolve the issue, like an online reading club).
8. *Disseminate results* (e.g., through attending conferences and workshops or publishing in journals and school reports).

This framework is especially valuable as it guides practitioners through every step in the action research process. However, practitioner researchers must bear in mind the following: (1) action research usually requires the application of mixed methodologies, which will be determined by the research questions (Creswell & Tashakkori, 2007; McNiff & Whitehead, 2011; Parsons & Brown, 2002), and (2) they are ethically obliged to share their results to help improve student well-being and instructional practices within classrooms and to devise strategies that will improve the quality of language education more generally.

Another type of research that is beneficial to the ELT classroom, yet is relatively rare, is that of ethnography. It is therefore included here as an innovative approach to researching English language classrooms. It is vital that it be promoted during teacher education programmes so that classroom practitioners feel more confident about it and utilise it while exploring their multidimensional classrooms. As a qualitative research method, ethnography focuses on the broad and long-term study of culture and is both a process and a product (Cohen et al., 2018; Pole & Morrison, 2003). As Dörnyei (2007, p. 130) further clarifies:

> Originating in cultural anthropology, ethnographic research aims at describing and analysing the practices and beliefs of cultures. 'Culture' is not limited to ethnic groups but can be related to any 'bounded units' such as organizations, programmes and even distinct communities ... The main goal of most ethnographic research is to provide a 'thick description' of the target culture, that is, a narrative that describes richly and in great detail the daily life of the community as well as cultural meanings and beliefs the participants attach to their activities, events and behaviours.

As this definition suggests, the classroom and the learners within it are 'distinct communities' that can be studied ethnographically (e.g., Bloome et al., 2005; Dörnyei, 2007; van Lier, 1988), and this is the first type of ethnography that teachers are encouraged to pursue in their classrooms to create reliable and valid knowledge and understanding of both learners and the teaching–learning process.

A second type of ethnography refers to developments and issues beyond the classroom. First and foremost, in times of highly dynamic social, cultural, and political developments and rapid change, this concerns the learners' lifeworlds and their cultural, communicative, and media practices, particularly digital environments. To appropriately connect learners' classroom work to their experiences and abilities, it is crucial that teachers be equipped with the ability to 'read' current cultural developments, the living conditions of their students, their ways of thinking, and their cultural practices. Such attempts at exploring the lives of people must rely on classical ethnography as a method for researching cultures in anthropology, as this offers 'a focused approach ... to study[ing] particular aspects of everyday life and cultural practices of social groups' (Green & Bloome, 2004, p. 183).

However, if ethnographic observation concerns the lives of learners directly, knowledge about cultural and social lives needs to be generated in direct collaboration with the students themselves. It can therefore be regarded as a contemporary reflexive epistemology of contact (Slembrouck, 2010). This implies that knowledge is embedded within and gradually formed during the long-term process of communicating and engaging with the arenas that constitute the research subject. Moreover, this kind of ethnographic teacher–learner collaboration is, in ethical terms, always committed to the perspective of those affected, that is, the learners as participants in the exploratory research so that observing is not transformed into spying (e.g., Slembrouck, 2010; van Lier, 1988). The high value placed on contact within ethnography is accompanied by a dedication to and clear foregrounding of the participant as a knowledge source and as offering a particular view of the world which cannot be easily made intelligible (Slembrouck, 2010). Such a participatory research approach can guide teachers and their learners to adopt a distanced, critical, and reflective attitude towards their own experiences and beliefs by actively and systematically researching their own worlds.

A third type of ethnography that merits consideration is exploratory in nature and relates to cultural learning in the ELT classroom. In an age of rapid cultural and media changes, ready-made knowledge about anglophone societies and cultures acquired in teacher education or presented in coursebooks or materials will quickly become obsolete. Therefore, teachers and learners need to have the capacity to create that kind of cultural knowledge autonomously. They need to be able to continuously study current issues and developments in the multitude of English-speaking societies, cultures, and sub-cultures about which they are teaching and learning (Bloome, 2012; Hallet, 2020a; König, 2020). Finally, teachers must be able to determine relevant cultural, transcultural, and global processes in order to define research foci that make it possible for them to explore the target language cultures and societies.

To account for ethnographic types of research outside ethnography and in other professional fields, Green and Bloome (2004, p. 183; Street, 2010) proposed a gradated system comprising three levels:

1. *Doing ethnography* is similar to the process of ethnography in cultural anthropology as it involves formulating, making sense of, writing about, and reporting the findings of a wide-ranging, comprehensive, and lengthy study of a particular social or cultural group, thereby aligning with the benchmarks for ethnography as conceived within a particular disciplinary field.
2. *Adopting an ethnographic perspective* denotes the study of the cultural practices and specific characteristics evident in the quotidian lives of a social group. Even though it is not specialist in nature, it must be guided by theories of culture and research employed in the fields of anthropology or sociology.

3. *Using ethnographic tools* alludes to the use of strategies and approaches typically employed in fieldwork to examine particular features of a given culture; as such, it does not need to be driven by theory.

In this vein, when choosing between the aforementioned second and third options, teachers need to decide what type of ethnographic research they would like to perform and how they would like to engage their students in this. Inevitably, in such research, teachers must familiarise themselves with ethnographic methods and tools that can be applied to studying and understanding English-speaking cultures (Hallet, 2020c). Such tools include, for example, questionnaires and interviews, observation and thick description, field notes and documents, and sources and data retrieved from archives and online sources. Because this research is conducted in the target language, the processes involved in designing questionnaires, preparing and conducting interviews, formulating interview questions for street or schoolyard surveys or questions for narrative interviews, and studying documents or online sources always and almost naturally result in a considerable amount of language learning. Moreover, these ethnographic tools are highly suited to enhancing and further developing linguistic and discourse competences in the English language of both teachers and students.

Overall, recent research reveals that teachers engaged with classroom-based research deliver better-quality teaching (Cirocki & Burns, 2019; Wyatt & Dikilitaş, 2016). Teacher engagement in research contributes not only to individual teacher development and enhanced pedagogical practices (Liu & Wang, 2018; Sato & Loewen, 2019) but also to broader improvements within schools and classrooms (Borg, 2010). By researching classrooms, teachers gain insights into their students' learning (Edwards & Burns, 2016a) and experience shifts in their professional identities, often towards identifying themselves as teacher-researchers or leaders (Edwards & Burns, 2016b; Yuan & Burns, 2017). Therefore, understanding teacher engagement in research is crucial as it generates deeper insights into the teacher-researcher identity (Edwards & Burns, 2016a) and into practitioners' motivation to partake in research (Yuan et al., 2016).

4.7 Conclusion

The focus of this chapter has been on analysing the notions of reflective practice and teacher-led research in the field of ELT. It has expounded on what they involve, reviewed an effective framework for reflective practice, and engaged in a brief discussion of tools that can be utilised to help teachers not only reflect on their instructional practice but also collect meaningful data on it. The aim has been to inspire English language teachers to utilise these tools at certain times and show how they can help them build reflective teacher identities. It is essential for teachers to engage in a process of ongoing professional development through the application of critical reflection and integrating research projects into their pedagogical practice. This will require teachers to:

- scrutinise their philosophies, principles, and concepts of practice;
- extend their reflections on these aspects to incorporate their students, primarily by conducting observations on, or researching, how they learn, interact, and behave in classroom scenarios;
- update and further their professional knowledge to include colleagues in their reflections on personal philosophies, principles, practice, and student learning and engagement in the teaching–learning process;
- build a solid bridge between their classroom practices and disciplinary knowledge and theory to be able to demonstrate their professional abilities and competences to employ evidence to enhance their grasp of key concepts, rationalise their decisions and choices, inform future practice, and contribute to the development of their discipline more broadly;
- invite administrative colleagues to enhance further their reflections through top-down development initiatives that will be beneficial to schools and teachers, students, or parents; and
- identify like-minded teachers in other professional organisations (e.g., TESOL International Association, International Association of Teachers of English as a Foreign Language, The Regional Language Centre, The Association of Teaching English as a Foreign Language in Indonesia) locally and globally, with whom reflections can be shared.

REFLECTION FOR ACTION

Future Teachers

- Reflect on the content of this chapter and discuss with your peers why it is crucial for teachers to engage in reflective practice.
- How does the teacher education programme you are currently undertaking help you to develop reflective competence?
- Reflect on Section 4.5 and the extent to which the assessments on your teacher education programme are reflective. Which of the instruments would you like to be integrated into your assessments?
- Think about the content of this chapter and explain how lesson study differs from action research.

Novice Teachers

- Reflect on the definitions of *reflection* and *critical reflection*. Explain how they differ and articulate the extent to which you perceive your reflective practice to be critical in nature.
- Think about the five stages in Farrell's framework and describe how these are reflected in your practice.
- What benefits do *individual* and *collective* forms of reflection provide? Which do you prefer engaging in, and why?
- Which of the six instruments presented in this chapter have you applied in your practice? How have these assisted you in reflecting on your teaching?

Experienced Teachers

- Reflect on the definitions of *critical reflection* and *reflexivity*. Explain how they differ and how much you feel you demonstrate the latter.
- Talk to a more experienced colleague and explain the extent to which and how the *philosophy* and *beyond practice* stages in Farrell's framework are integrated into your practice.
- Reflect on your professional learning and describe how much it has benefitted from collective reflection.
- Choose one of the six instruments presented in this chapter and discuss its usefulness.

5 Teacher Autonomy
The Professional Independence of Teachers

To a greater or lesser extent, the notion of teacher autonomy has been addressed by scholars since the early 1990s. However, it has recently been eclipsed by the concept of *learner autonomy*. A possible reason for this is that language educators have achieved no consensus on a definition of teacher autonomy that is sufficiently accurate to shape debates in the field of education (Pearson & Moomaw, 2006). This conceptual ambiguity has had a negative impact on the extent to which teacher autonomy can be theoretically understood, its appropriate utilisation in educational discourse, and the ramifications for education research, schooling, and relevant stakeholders (Cirocki & Anam, 2024; Lamb, 2008; Manzano Vázquez, 2018; Usma Wilches, 2007).

This lack of theoretical certainty can partly be explained by the fact that, in conceptual terms, the origins of autonomy lie in various fields, including philosophy and psychology. The former, for example, engages in discussions of *moral*, *personal*, and *political autonomy*. Philosophers define moral autonomy as the ability to reflect and apply a moral law to oneself instead of simply following other people's demands (Sprod, 2003). By contrast, philosophers define personal autonomy as the ability to make individual decisions and follow corresponding actions irrespective of the moral issues that may be involved (Berofsky, 1995; Lomelino, 2015; Raz, 1986). Finally, political autonomy is defined as the feeling that the decisions made in a political environment are valued, acknowledged, and listened to (Lomelino, 2015).

In the domain of psychology, autonomy has its roots in Roger's experiential learning theory and Vygotsky's sociocultural theory. The former advocates a holistic learning process in which teachers are continually involved in the dynamic creation of knowledge. This occurs at both intellectual and psychological levels (Rogers, 1969) and involves teachers completing a range of tasks while adopting various roles. By contrast, sociocultural theory construes learning as a social and collaborative activity that relies on support from wider society and culture and those with greater knowledge (Vygotsky, 1978). It is clear from this formulation that Vygotsky perceives language as a general tool for learning, a medium through which learners can engage in problem-solving, and a means for enabling different members of a culture to work together to develop a shared understanding and negotiate different forms of meaning (Cirocki, 2016; Lantolf, 2000; Lantolf & Poehner, 2014). Solving problems stimulates learners to engage in innovative, useful, reflective, and critical thinking. This enables learners to take responsibility for their behavioural choices and helps them to acquire leadership skills, which are typical attributes of individuals with autonomy. In essence, Vygotsky conceptualises learners as individuals who become autonomous due to their engagement in social interaction.

However, because the concept of teacher autonomy was previously considered largely theoretical, there have been few empirical studies on this concept in the field of ELT. This situation has now changed following teacher autonomy's integration into a teacher's professional identity (Section 2.3), with an increasing amount of research now conducted in a range of disparate contexts. The resultant findings are used to inform and improve English language teacher education programmes and initiatives for in-service professional development. Nevertheless, in numerous countries, the situation is by no means optimal. Teacher autonomy must therefore be established globally as a leading educational goal, while professional development training and teacher education programmes must generate teachers who exhibit professional autonomy and foster this in their students. To achieve this, teachers must be able to freely choose, design, enact, and evaluate their ideas to deliver instruction that is captivating, creative, effective, and sustainable and that aligns with students' objective (i.e., age, gender, level of language proficiency) and subjective (i.e., confidence, attitudes, expectations) needs.

Against this background, this chapter begins by defining the construct of teacher autonomy and presenting a profile of an autonomous teacher. This is followed by an overview of existing empirical projects on teacher autonomy. The focus then shifts to pedagogical strategies used to promote teacher autonomy in teacher education programmes and professional development events. An overview of the effective strategies draws this chapter to a close.

5.1 Defining Teacher Autonomy and Teacher Agency

It is clear from the literature that scholars understand teacher autonomy in different ways (Cárdenas Ramos, 2006; Cirocki & Anam, 2024; Dikilitaş & Griffiths, 2017; Lamb, 2008; Littlewood, 1997; Manzano Vázquez, 2018). The multitude of definitions that have been proposed means teacher autonomy is a wide-ranging and multidimensional concept. This is mainly because the evolution of the concept has been vigorous and non-linear, encompassing the attitudes, beliefs, abilities, decision-making processes, choices, independent behaviours, and critical reflection of teachers and the environments in which they work (Little, 1995; Usma Wilches, 2007; Wermke & Höstfält, 2014).

A teacher's capacity to control their work, which characterises teacher autonomy, consists of three components: *ability*, *willingness*, and *freedom* (Huang,

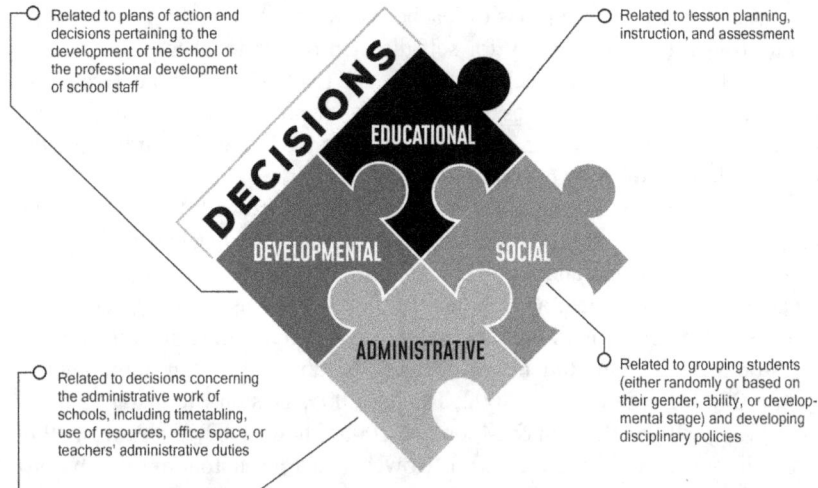

Figure 5.1 Types of teachers' decisions

2005; Huang & Benson, 2013). Ability alludes to the professional knowledge base of teachers (Section 2.2) and critical reflection (Section 4.2) on teaching practice. Willingness denotes the motivation teachers have to control their work. Finally, freedom refers to the space teachers are provided within which to think and act. Benson and Huang (2008, p. 431) also assert that 'professional freedom should not simply be "granted"'. This implies that teachers value and seek freedom only when they understand its worth. If freedom is granted, they may fail to use it effectively.

Teacher autonomy is also perceived in terms of decision-making. It is therefore essential to clarify that teachers' decisions (Figure 5.1) usually relate to different domains within the school and are made either individually or collectively with varying external constraints (Benson, 2000; Wermke & Höstfält, 2014; Wermke et al., 2018).

Such decisions can be categorised as follows:

- *educational* – related to lesson planning, instruction, and assessment;
- *social* – related to grouping students (either randomly or based on their gender, ability, or developmental stage) and developing disciplinary policies;
- *developmental* – related to plans of action and decisions pertaining to the development of the school or the professional development of school staff; and
- *administrative* – related to decisions concerning the administrative work of schools, including timetabling, use of resources, office space, or teachers' administrative duties (Wermke et al., 2018, p. 8).

Thus, the various definitions of teacher autonomy can be divided into three main groups: (1) the capacity for self-directed professional teaching, (2) the capacity for self-directed teacher learning, and (3) freedom from external control in relation to either professional teaching or professional learning (Smith & Erdoğan, 2008). However, definitions exist in the literature that include two or even all three of these perceptions.

The first group of definitions is principally concerned with the way in which autonomy is exercised when teaching. It encapsulates a teacher's willingness and ability to manage and take responsibility for daily schedules, to teach in whatever way they deem appropriate, to make decisions with respect to their roles in the teaching–learning process, to adapt to fluctuating situations within classrooms, and help students to develop the ability to learn autonomously (Aoki, 2002; Barfield et al., 2002; Huang, 2005; Hyslop-Margison & Sears, 2010; Little, 1995; Pearson & Moomaw, 2006; Shaw, 2002; Thavenius, 1999; Tort-Moloney, 1997; Vieira, 2006). However, learner autonomy can be promoted in classrooms only if teachers perceive themselves to be autonomous. Little (2000, p. 45) expands further on this idea, explaining that (1) 'it is unreasonable to expect teachers to foster the growth of autonomy in their learners if they themselves do not know what it is to be an autonomous learner' and (2) 'in determining the initiatives they take in the classrooms, teachers must be able to exploit their professional skills autonomously, applying to their teaching those same reflective and self-managing processes that they apply to their learning'.

Teacher autonomy is now increasingly being defined as the potential a teacher has in order to undertake self-directed teaching. Jumani and Malik (2017) state that this can be facilitated through *professional autonomy* (i.e., teachers' choices regarding professional tasks, including regulations/laws and CPD), *collegial professional autonomy* (i.e., collective decisions with respect to pedagogical practice), and *individual autonomy* (i.e., individual choices regarding classroom teaching).

The second set of definitions construe teacher autonomy as an ability to engage in self-directed professional learning (Dierking & Fox, 2013; Gu, 2014; Huang, 2005). McGrath (2000, p. 109) describes teacher autonomy as a form of 'self-directed professional development' that encompasses teachers' individual and collective engagement in classroom-based instruction and reflective practice. However, Nakata (2009, p. 210) contends: 'In the development of teacher autonomy...teachers set professional autonomy as their lifelong professional goal, and then start the endeavor to improve "self" toward that goal – of becoming truly autonomous professionals – in their own way and at their own pace'. This definition furnishes the notion of teacher autonomy with practitioner engagement as part of a more comprehensive lifelong learning process. Thus, learning among teachers involves expanding their professional knowledge, stimulating reflective thinking, and ensuring that their teaching is critically informed, appealing, and up to date. Furthermore, teachers engage in this form of learning to '[improve] knowledge, skills and competences within a personal, civic, social and/or employment-related perspective' (European Commission, 2001, p. 9).

To help develop teacher autonomy, Dikilitaş and Griffiths (2017) emphasise the advantages of engaging in action research. Doing so actively empowers teachers to create their level of freedom whereby they become self-directed and, as learner-teachers, produce practical knowledge through an examination of their contexts, reflection on their instructional practices, and interrogation of the way in which they teach in the classroom (Cirocki & Burns, 2019; Cirocki & Farrelly, 2016).

As discussed, several definitions of teacher autonomy cover more than one perspective. One such example is the recent definition of teacher autonomy presented by Cirocki and Anam (2024). This includes both perspectives discussed here – self-directed teaching and self-directed professional learning – and reads as follows:

Teacher autonomy is the teacher's capacity to willingly and freely engage in: (1) self-directed teaching, where they plan, deliver, and evaluate their pedagogical practice with a view to making it attractive, effective, and sustainable; and (2) self-directed lifelong professional learning, where they choose and participate in activities that enhance the pedagogical skills and content knowledge that directly affect student learning and achievements. This involves partaking in broadly-defined reflective practice and the curriculum design/evaluation process so that their voice is included in educational policies and reforms. (Cirocki & Anam, 2024, p. 444)

The third group of definitions – teachers' freedom from external control in relation to either professional action or professional development – is concerned with teachers' rights within the education system. For instance, teachers have the right to exercise their own choices in teaching and learning and therefore cannot become '[victims] of choices' made by others (Crabbe, 1993, p. 44). Because teachers' work is highly dependent on collective decisions that affect individual choices, a degree of individual freedom must be permitted within the overall constraints required by the education system and its various institutions (Benson, 2001, 2010; Freire, 1970).

Importantly, learning is essentially a social activity shaped by interaction, language, and environment (Cirocki & Anam, 2024; Lantolf, 2000; Lantolf & Poehner, 2014). As such, it is a lively and generative process in which contributions from those involved result in new information being acquired through the everyday experiences of teachers. It is predicated on the cognisance and understanding teachers have of their schools, the profession, and the range of sociopolitical factors that may impact both their pedagogical practice and professional learning (Cirocki et al., 2019a, 2019b). There must therefore be no limits on the extent to which teachers can exert control over their teaching and professional learning (Benson, 2001). They need to have confidence in their ability to make informed choices with respect to their classrooms and 'freely direct the course of [their professional lives]' (Young, 1986, p. 1). Therefore, administrative staff and school management teams are advised to motivate and support teachers in their decisions and in implementing change in their classrooms. Furthermore, teachers must devise and implement their theory according to their professional abilities, creativity, and confidence level (Bell, 2011; Kumaravadivelu, 2001).

The definitions of teacher autonomy presented in all three groups clearly demonstrate that it is a concept closely linked to teacher agency, which is broader in scope. It is essentially defined as teachers' potential to influence their professional contexts (i.e., classrooms, schools, the profession), as opposed to passively reacting to them, as part of a continuing relationship of mutual causality where the focus is on the intricate, vigorous interplay between both components (Mercer, 2011, p. 428). The level of agency teachers achieve is dependent on the scope of action they perceive themselves as possessing (Erss, 2018) and is attained through a consideration of the decisions and actions they take, given the cultural, material, and social circumstances of their working environment (Biesta et al., 2017).

Because agency is viewed as a temporal relational phenomenon, its achievement is best explained through *iterational*, *projective*, and *practical-evaluative* dimensions (Priestley et al., 2015). The iterational dimension denotes how patterns of past thoughts and actions are built up and then embedded into practical activities that stabilise and sustain the identities of teachers and educational institutions. The projective dimension encompasses both short-term and long-term aspirations that shape teachers' actions in accordance with possible future pathways. The practical-evaluative dimension refers to the ability of teachers in existing scenarios to make deliberate choices while working in specific structural, material, and cultural circumstances. The possible options derive from the preceding dimensions, which denote the past and the predicted future, enabling teachers to maintain but also alter practices used in the past (Biesta et al., 2015; Priestley et al., 2015).

Thus, at a conceptual level, agency is substantially more complex than autonomy, as it characterises people as social beings with distinct histories who are embodied, have the capacity to think and feel, and possess identities that drive them to attain particular goals and fulfil specific interests at certain places and times. It is influenced by society and culture and extends beyond volitional control over one's behaviour, including the capacity to ascribe meaning and significance to one's experiences and actions (van Compernolle, 2014). Moreover, teacher autonomy is fundamentally dependent on having agency in terms of being able to take actions in the world that have particular outcomes. Such agency is a vital prerequisite for behaviour aimed at achieving set goals, and hence the ability to regulate oneself.

Scrutiny of the various definitions and the way in which the notion of teacher autonomy has evolved through time indicates that the focus from independence through isolation and alienation has shifted to collective decision-making and collaborative agency. Proponents of *relational autonomy* argue that teacher autonomy is constantly developed with and shaped by others (e.g., Paradis et al., 2019). Thus, not independence but interdependence lies at the heart of the relational notion of autonomy. The context in which teachers work and the socially embedded network of others they engage with enable them to develop a robust capacity for self-determination and form a professional identity. Being part of the social network makes teachers interdependent; however, this interdependence does not infringe upon their autonomy. Instead, it should be considered an inherent part of their professional identity.

The preceding discussion additionally reveals that teacher autonomy is also a prerequisite for teacher empowerment, which is conceptualised as a process of enabling practitioners to believe and feel that they can make sense of their classrooms, schools, and teaching contexts more broadly and have the power to transform them. Consequently, at a micro level, teacher empowerment is equated with giving teachers the privilege to exercise professional reasoning and judgement while implementing the daily curriculum and planning and delivering English language instruction. At a macro level, it is viewed as an administrative investment in teachers that affords them the opportunity and freedom to actively manage and control their school objectives, policies, strategies, and plans (Bleumers et al., 2012).

Overall, the definitions presented here reveal that autonomous teachers have complex personality profiles, and thus complex professional identities (Section 2.3). In their teaching and professional learning, they are expected to demonstrate the qualities presented in Figure 5.2. These qualities derive from and

Figure 5.2 Attributes of autonomous teachers

summarise the foregoing theoretical overview and recent literature on teacher autonomy.

Furthermore, teachers who demonstrate autonomy consider themselves to be lifelong learners who oversee and critically evaluate not only their own learning but also that of other people.

5.2 Research Findings on Teacher Autonomy

Extensive research has been carried out on autonomy within educational contexts. Although several studies are relevant to ELT, most focus on learner autonomy; there are relatively few on teacher autonomy. Additional studies are therefore needed, and these must be in-depth, covering the way teachers participate in decision-making, the types of decisions made, the difficulties they face when exhibiting autonomy when teaching, and the ways in which schools encourage and support teacher autonomy.

The research that does exist on teacher autonomy forms two distinct strands. The first explores factors influencing the professional development of teacher autonomy. This concerns teacher affect (e.g., attitudes, emotions) and is thus strongly associated with teachers' beliefs, satisfaction levels, anxiety/stress, and burnout (Borg, 2006, 2009; Pearson & Moomaw, 2006; Warfield et al., 2005). The second strand evaluates the extent to which educational practices contribute to developing teacher autonomy. Even though such studies have been carried out in a variety of contexts, the results have primarily been indeterminate. The following summary focuses on research conducted with EFL teachers in Iran and Norway.

Javadi (2014) explored the relationship between teacher autonomy and feelings of burnout among 143 teachers working in a variety of private language institutions. A Burnout Inventory and a Teaching Autonomy Scale were employed to collect the data. The results demonstrated that teacher autonomy was significantly and inversely associated with feelings of burnout ($r = 53$, $p < 0.05$). A multiple regression analysis also indicated that teacher autonomy was significantly predicted by the following elements of burnout – emotional exhaustion, depersonalisation, and reduced personal accomplishment.

Esfandiari and Kamali (2016) recruited a convenience sample of 207 EFL teachers whose experience ranged from one to forty years. They divided them into five different age groups to explore the relationship between job satisfaction, teacher burnout, and teacher autonomy. The Minnesota Job Satisfaction Questionnaire, the Maslach Burnout Inventory, and the Teacher Autonomy Questionnaire were administered to collect the data. The results indicated that job satisfaction was negatively and weakly associated with teacher burnout and negatively associated with teacher autonomy. No significant relationship was found between teacher autonomy and teacher burnout.

Skaalvik and Skaalvik (2014) recruited a sample of 2,569 teachers from both elementary and middle schools to ascertain whether teacher autonomy and self-efficacy were independently related to engagement, job satisfaction, and emotional exhaustion. Data were collected by administering the Norwegian Teacher Self-Efficacy Scale, the Teacher Autonomy Scale, the Utrecht Work Engagement Scale, the Teacher Job Satisfaction Scale, and the Maslach Burnout Inventory. The results indicated that engagement, job satisfaction, and emotional exhaustion were independently predicted by both teacher autonomy and self-efficacy.

The second strand of research focuses on the interaction between the pedagogical practices teachers employ and teacher autonomy. For instance, Benson (2010) investigated factors limiting teacher autonomy when teaching the English language in four Hong Kong secondary schools. This was a case study employed to explore the decisions made by teachers daily regarding processes of teaching and learning within classrooms. The findings indicated that the different school work schemes primarily drove such decisions. The interviewees felt that these schemes, in conjunction with supervision and monitoring at work, limited their decision-making ability. Nevertheless, by altering, construing, or ignoring the duties inherent in such schemes, they were able to fashion a space in which to exercise autonomy.

It is also essential to discuss projects that utilise collaboration and partnership to enhance professional autonomy (Chapter 9). This relates to existing debates concerning whether collaboration between teachers within and across schools provides conditions that promote professional learning (Honigsfeld & Dove, 2010; La Ganza, 2008; Tajino et al., 2016). For instance, a comparative study conducted in Portugal by Vieira (2003) focused on collaboration with respect to reflective writing. She explored two instances where pedagogical knowledge was created through collaborative writing between experienced and inexperienced teachers. The first example involved the creation of practical knowledge, and the second the creation of practical–critical knowledge. With respect to inexperienced teachers, Vieira (2003, p. 76) found that 'autonomy starts with awareness on the workings of technical-practical action, on meaning given to action, fuelled by inquiry, dialogue, and confrontation of perspectives'. Conversely, with respect to experienced teachers, autonomy was reflected in 'an increased awareness of the purpose and implications of pedagogical action, also fuelled by the same processes, leading to an improved sense of direction' (p. 76).

Another case study project by Xu (2015) recruited four novice EFL teachers in China to determine (1) the effect of joint lesson preparation on the development of teacher autonomy and (2) the effect of collaboration and autonomy on the professional development of teachers. An analysis of classroom observations, one-to-one interviews, and journals indicated that collaborative lesson preparation had various levels of influence on the development of teacher autonomy. Such variation was attributed to the amount of anxiety teachers felt when engaging in such collaboration.

Vigorous discussions have also been conducted on the relative value of classroom-based research and teachers either working as researchers or participating in projects undertaken by researchers (Burns, 2010; Cirocki & Burns, 2019). Such debates have sometimes explored whether and how teacher autonomy can be developed through action research, giving rise to a series of projects on this theme. For example, Mello et al. (2008) conducted a project with Brazilian EFL teachers working in public schools who were engaged in The Continuing Education Program organised by the Universidade Federal de Minas Gerais (Federal University of Minas Gerais). The researchers motivated the teachers to participate in classroom inquiry, which increased the level of reflection and autonomy teachers were able to exercise in their professional practice. Consequently, these teachers came to appreciate the vast importance such practices have for their teaching. Moreover, they became cognisant of the possibilities classroom practices offer in terms of research and what it was like to undertake the role of a researcher.

Another collaborative action research project was conducted in China by Wang and Zhang (2013) with both university researchers and senior secondary school English language teachers. They examined the processes engaged in by teachers when learning to carry out research and the impact action research had on the development of teacher autonomy. Their results indicated that conducting the project gave pre-service teachers a more sophisticated comprehension of their roles and responsibilities in the classroom. Furthermore, actively engaging in the project gave teachers numerous opportunities to exercise different facets of autonomy.

Several studies have also found that reflective practice enhances the ability of teachers to take ownership of the teaching process and facilitates learner autonomy (Camilleri Grima, 1999; Osterman & Kottkamp, 2004). To support reflective practice, teachers can draw on various tools such as post-observation conferences, collaborative blogging, journals, and peer sharing (Cirocki & Farrell, 2017b). As part of a related project, Cakir and Balcikanli (2012) strived to enhance teacher autonomy at a Turkish university by employing the European Portfolio for Student Teachers of Languages (EPOSTL). Their research comprised four distinct stages: (1) ensuring student teachers became familiar with the EPOSTL, (2) eliciting their expectations regarding the EPOSTL, (3) applying the EPOSTL, and (4) conducting interviews with student teachers and their trainers on their experiences using the EPOSTL. The findings indicated that all participants felt the EPOSTL was a valuable tool. They especially highlighted its benefits with respect to reflection, self-assessment, and enhanced cognisance of both their teaching and professional learning. Other projects that have utilised portfolios to enhance teacher autonomy include those by Burkert and Schwienhorst (2008), Yildirim (2013), and Gámiz-Sánchez et al. (2016).

The remainder of this section focuses on four projects exploring practitioners' views of teacher autonomy. The first study by Khezerlou (2013) examined perceptions of teacher autonomy among Iranian and Turkish secondary school EFL practitioners ($N = 360$). The specific areas addressed were (1) the selection of pedagogical methods and techniques in conjunction with the implementation of the curriculum, (2) the extent to which teachers were involved in decision-making, and (3) the initiative exhibited by teachers to resolve problems at work. The results indicated that Iranian teachers' perceived teacher autonomy scores were lower than those of Turkish teachers. Moreover, the scores of male teachers and those holding a master's degree were higher than those of female teachers and those holding a bachelor's degree. Of the three dimensions explored, decision-making was the strongest predictor of teacher autonomy for both Iranian and Turkish teachers.

In the second study, Gabryś-Barker (2017) interviewed twenty-eight pre-service teachers of English from a Polish university to explore five inductive categories: (1) definitions of teacher autonomy, (2) the profile of an autonomous teacher, (3) the relationship between teacher and learner autonomy, (4) limitations on teacher autonomy, and (5) self-assessing the extent of autonomy. A qualitative data analysis suggested that teachers understood what was involved in teacher autonomy and perceived the concept positively. For instance, they viewed independent practitioners as 'fully competent, motivated by having a calling and a positive attitude to his or her students, which allows him or her to facilitate the learning process by creating a favorable classroom atmosphere' (Gabryś-Barker, 2017, p. 175). The findings also indicated that specific character traits, most notably self-esteem and self-confidence, were perceived as enhancing teacher autonomy. The participants saw the growth of teacher autonomy as a longitudinal process that developed with experience.

In the third study, Khalil and Lewis (2019) explored the understanding and development of teacher autonomy among EFL teachers in Turkish schools. Their principal purpose was to uncover the mechanisms that underlie these concepts. Through an analysis of various forms of data, they found that teachers generally experienced autonomy when teaching and assessing students, even though they were subjected to pressure from school managers and parents. However, although the participants believed they played a role in decision-making processes, they felt strongly that they needed to be given greater freedom with respect to their professional development.

Finally, in the fourth study, Cirocki and Anam (2024) strived to pinpoint areas of improvement in Indonesian secondary schools that would provide teachers with more autonomy when teaching or performing teaching-related tasks. It also strived to determine whether correlations between 185 teachers' perceptions of teacher autonomy and gender, teaching experience, school status, and school location were observed. Two methods of data collection were employed: a closed-ended questionnaire and a focus group. The results indicated that teachers' perceived autonomy was relatively strong with respect to teaching methodology, instructional materials, course content, assessment, and lesson planning. The results also indicated that teachers felt dismayed at their exclusion from involvement in decision-making with respect to the school curriculum. They would also like to have received more support regarding professional development and the provision of teaching facilities.

The discussion thus far reveals that various aspects of teacher autonomy require further exploration. Some of these need to be investigated on a larger scale to make the results more generalisable. Others should be analysed from alternative angles to shed more light on the notion of teacher autonomy, how it affects teachers' work and students' learning, and the extent to which it changes the environments in which teachers work. The findings reveal useful information that, when combined with research results from the fields of education or educational psychology, allow recommendations on how teacher autonomy can be effectively promoted. These are presented in the next section.

5.3 Strategies for Developing Teacher Autonomy

Teacher autonomy and learner autonomy are usually addressed together as they are strongly associated (Lamb & Reinders, 2008; Little, 1995) and need to be considered simultaneously when 'teachers and learners engage in the construction of more democratic pedagogies' (Manzano Vázquez, 2018, p. 387). Scholars extensively consider teachers' vital function in enabling learners to develop autonomy (Benson, 2001; Cirocki, 2016). By contrast, an issue that has received much less attention is how professional development initiatives and teacher education programmes enable teachers to exercise autonomy in both instructional practice and professional learning.

The concept of teacher autonomy therefore needs to form an integral part of teacher education programmes and professional development initiatives. Indeed, several studies have indicated that if teachers are not themselves autonomous learners, this will have a negative effect on the extent to which learners can develop autonomy in classrooms (Burkert & Schwienhorst, 2008; Sert, 2006). It is therefore important for schools to ensure that their teachers can make effective and independent decisions with respect to teaching, can critically reflect on these decisions, can respond carefully to any difficulties that arise, and, when changes need to be made, can adapt in a flexible and innovative way. Consequently, a great deal of effort has been invested over the past thirty years in ensuring that teachers in Europe are taught to be autonomous. This has primarily been driven by initiatives developed by the Council of Europe (European Commission, 2008; Newby et al., 2007). Outside the European Union, however, there remain a substantial number of countries where teacher autonomy is largely neglected.

A variety of methods can be employed in professional development initiatives targeted at English language teachers to enhance teacher autonomy. From a sociocultural point of view (Chapter 9), teacher learning is perceived as a vibrant social activity that takes place in physical and social contexts (Cirocki & Golombek, 2020; Johnson, 2009; Lantolf, 2000; Lave & Wenger, 1991; Leont'ev, 1981; Vygotsky, 1978). Within such environments, teachers engage in social interaction to 'trace the inherent complexities that make up the sum of…teachers' learning and teaching experiences, and make visible what those experiences ultimately lead to' (Johnson, 2009, p. x). Consequently, teachers develop into 'active users and producers of theory in their own right, for their own means, and as appropriate for their instructional contexts' (Johnson, 2006, p. 240). In so doing, both pre- and in-service teachers have the chance to take part in forms of professional development located within the contexts in which they teach (Johnson & Golombek, 2011).

Through the concept of *collective autonomy*, Little (1990, p. 519) identified a clear association between teacher collaboration and teacher autonomy (Chapter 9). He defines collective autonomy as 'teachers' decisions to pursue a single course of action in concert or, alternatively, to decide on a set of basic priorities that in turn guide the independent choice of individual teachers'. Clement and Vandenberghe (2000, p. 91) recently identified a similarly close relationship, explaining that 'collegial interactions are a source for the autonomous work and autonomous initiatives often lead to meaningful collegial contacts'.

Because teacher autonomy forms such an invaluable part of the professional identity of a teacher, professional development activities must involve both pre- and in-service teachers in realistic activities where they work together to develop both their teaching and professional learning. During such tasks, teachers must be allowed a substantial amount of freedom to take risks, implement initiatives, generate rational decisions, exhibit leadership, construct both short-term and long-term plans, and carry out reflective and objective evaluation of the programmes they teach, the wider school curriculum, and the processes of assessment implemented within their schools. Several productive strategies that can be employed to enhance teacher autonomy when undergoing professional development are presented in Table 5.1.

The success and importance of such practices, most of which are collaborative in nature, have been widely considered by many scholars (e.g., Burns, 2010; Hall, 2018; Li & Edwards, 2010; Searle & Swartz, 2015; Tajino et al., 2016). Workshops and group discussions, for instance, motivate teachers to reflect on what they do (Chapter 4), increasing their awareness of their individual

Table 5.1 *Strategies for developing teacher autonomy*

Strategies	Description
Collaborative workshops	*Focus on ELT theory and practice.* Teachers design and run two-hour workshops. Working in groups of three, they plan the workshop, negotiating its topic, aims, stages, content, and materials. They also decide which teacher is responsible for delivering which part of the workshop as work must be equally shared. They need to ensure that the workshop is well planned and runs smoothly. A detailed rationale for the workshop is required. A reflective group podcast detailing the planning and delivery processes should be recorded and submitted after the workshop.
Group discussions	*Focus on lesson planning.* Teachers design lesson plans without restrictions. They focus on the decisions they have to make before teaching these lessons. A justification for all decisions is required. Links to appropriate literature must be made. A written response to peer feedback must be submitted after the lesson has been taught.
Teacher portfolios (pen/paper or online)	*Focus on strengths and weaknesses of own teaching.* Teachers complete reflective portfolios in which they reflect on their teaching practice and identify strengths and weaknesses. A brief description of strengths and a detailed plan for improving weaknesses need to be provided.
Action research/ case study research	*Focus on specific aspects of teaching individually selected by teachers.* Teachers design and conduct mini action research/case study projects and share the results with peers. A rationale for the conducted study must be included. The methodology must be clearly explained with links to appropriate literature.
Co-teaching	*Focus on receptive/productive skills.* Teachers work in pairs, planning a lesson they can teach together. They negotiate the topic, aims, stages, content, and materials and decide which teacher is responsible for each lesson stage as work must be equally shared. The lesson must be well planned and run smoothly when taught. A detailed rationale is required. A reflective commentary detailing the planning process must be submitted before the lesson is delivered.
Peer teaching	*Focus on educational technology.* Teachers work in groups of four. They choose one aspect of educational technology (e.g., a blog, a podcast, a wiki) each and consider its implementation in the classroom. They read widely about the selected problem and teach it to the other three group members. The demonstration must combine theory, research, and practice. The teachers take turns and learn four new items of information in one session.
Reflective blogging	*Focus on lesson delivery.* Teachers reflect on the specific weaknesses of a lesson they recently taught with a view to improving it. They individually select the problematic aspects and post brief comments about them. Suggestions for improvement need to be provided with links to appropriate literature. Teachers engage in pedagogical discourse with peers who accept or reject their suggestions. Logical, critical, creative, and reflective thinking should underpin the blogging experience. Each teacher must comment on at least two posts submitted by other teachers. Posts with two feedback responses cannot be commented on again.

Table 5.1 (cont.)

Strategies	Description
Teamwork	*Focus on running school-wide competitions for English language learners.* Teachers working for the same school collaborate in the design of a school-wide competition for English language learners. School competitions can have different aims, formats, and foci. The latter may include English debating, an English language olympiad, an English poetry recitation, an English language spelling bee, or an English language translation bee. Teachers decide on the specific type of competition they would like to run in their school and plan the following: (1) purpose, format, and date of the event; (2) event venue; (3) types of awards; (4) the committee and its responsibilities; (5) registration procedure; (6) event advert/website; (7) competition schedule. Teachers plan the various stages in small groups and decide who works with whom and what each member is responsible for. They meet regularly to update colleagues on their progress, raise issues of concern, and then solve these creatively. When all the stages are ready, teachers meet with the management team to show them the final product.
Focus groups for pre- and in-service teachers	*Focus on critical incidents.* Pre- and in-service teachers work together to focus on critical incidents that occurred during lessons delivered by teacher trainees. Pre-service teachers briefly introduce the incidents. Pre- and in-service teachers reflect on the incidents in separate groups and devise a strategy that could be employed in the future should a similar situation happen again. All group members contribute to the discussion. Each group selects a representative to present their ideas. A different member presents each critical incident. The content and format of each presentation are negotiated within the individual groups. Both pre- and in-service teacher groups then meet to discuss the incidents. Pre-service teachers start first, followed by the in-service teachers. Finally, the best ideas/solutions are negotiated between pre- and in-service groups.
Interschool project work	*Focus on developing leadership skills in teachers.* To become influential leaders, teachers need to be proactive and step outside their comfort zone – the classroom – and become involved in wider school issues such as cyberbullying, anti-smoking/drug campaigns, or poor parent attendance at consultation evenings. To enable teachers to demonstrate autonomy and leadership skills, they work in pairs on wider school issues. If they come from different schools, they should focus on a problematic issue in both schools. They then explore the problem, study available literature and research on the topic, and prepare a report with recommendations for schools to consider resolving the problematic issue. After sharing the report with colleagues in their schools, teachers present it at a conference to share their findings/observations with the wider community of teachers.
Teacher-led workshops	*Focus on best practices.* English language teachers in the same school plan *Best Practices* workshops. Each workshop is devoted to a specific topic related to either ELT instruction or teacher professional development. Initially, teachers work individually and plan the delivery of their workshops. They make decisions regarding (1) the purpose, format, and outcome of the workshop, (2) the design of the presentation (e.g., theory, research, practice) and handouts for the participants, and (3) how to engage the audience in the workshop (e.g., in the warm-up stage, in the planned activities, or while sharing ideas in the discussion). Having planned their workshops, teachers reconvene and collaborate in designing a feedback form that participants will be asked to complete at the end of each workshop.

Note: Adapted with permission from Cirocki and Anam (2024, p. 465). Copyright 2021 by the authors.

teaching and learning practices (Camilleri Grima, 1997; Little et al., 2002). Conversely, portfolios enable teachers to oversee and reflect on their teaching expertise, styles, and abilities, evaluate their practice (Burkert & Schwienhorst, 2008; Cakir & Balcikanli, 2012), assist pre-service teachers in learning how to self-regulate and self-direct (Martins, 2009), and engage in autonomous learning first-hand (Miliander, 2008; Yildirim, 2013).

By contrast, action research and case studies enable teachers to reflect critically on their teaching, learn much more about their students and make use of empirical data 'to explain and evaluate their [pedagogical] actions' (Wang & Zhang, 2013, p. 232). The collaboration process also ensures recognition of the teacher as someone who can engender change when interacting with fellow professionals (Chapter 9). This promotes best practice, enhances student learning, and refines the overall performance of the school (Cirocki & Burns, 2019; Cochran-Smith & Lytle, 2009; Dikilitaş & Griffiths, 2017; Mockler & Groundwater-Smith, 2015).

Co-teaching encourages both collaboration and reflection, two vital components of professional learning. Teachers engage in a process of mutual learning when co-planning, co-teaching, co-reflecting, and co-evaluating their lessons (Hoekstra et al., 2009; van Velzen et al., 2012). Conversely, like teacher-led professional development, peer teaching increases the level of responsibility teachers have for learning, the strategies they employ to enhance students' learning, and the degree of collaboration among those involved in the teaching–learning process (Benson & Ying, 2013). An alternative to the standard top-down approach to professional development, which cannot offer teachers the requisite support and development, is to run teacher-led workshops (Patton et al., 2015). This form of professional development is valued and indeed preferred by teachers because it focuses directly on their needs, improves their content knowledge and teaching-related skills, recognises that learning is essentially a social activity, and construes teachers as active learners.

Finally, blogging provides teachers with opportunities to engage in social networking and participate in continuing discussions of their work as teachers (Fleming et al., 2011). For instance, it allows them to present their ideas about their teaching, ask questions, and elicit feedback from an extensive community, resulting in exposure to diverse views and experiences. Furthermore, proactively engaging in reflective writing will increase teachers' overall level of pedagogical knowledge as well as enhance their teaching.

5.4   Conclusion

The purpose of this chapter has been to explore the concept of teacher autonomy. The picture that emerges from the preceding discussion reveals two essential points. Firstly, teacher autonomy is multifaceted in nature and encompasses teachers' personal and professional lives. Secondly, additional research on teacher autonomy is required to contribute to a fuller understanding of the concept among practitioners. It will also raise their awareness of the benefits autonomy can bring to their professional practice. Most importantly, it is vital for future studies to focus on how teacher autonomy is promoted through professional development initiatives targeted at both pre- and in-service teachers, how teachers at different career stages develop autonomy, and the challenges teachers encounter in different contexts.

This chapter has proposed several effective strategies that can be easily integrated into any teacher education programme or professional development initiative. These seek to engage practitioners in the development of autonomous behaviours and help them to acquire 'a position from which to engage with the world, a way of being in it' (Breen & Mann, 1997, p. 134). This will make them feel more in control of their teaching and help them to learn a wide range of information pertaining to different areas of professional knowledge. It will also enable them to deport themselves with a more positive attitude, both in and out of school. Additionally, the chapter clarifies that teacher autonomy hardly ever exists without teacher collaboration, reinforced by social interaction. Paradoxical though it may sound, it is true. In fact, both social interaction and collaboration are prerequisites for achieving autonomy (Chapter 9).

In the classroom context, teacher autonomy is highly likely to encourage learner autonomy. The latter should therefore be regarded not only as 'a matter of control over learning activities and resources' but also as 'a matter of a particular orientation towards language learning' (Nunan, 2013, p. 211), whereby 'for the truly autonomous learner, each occasion of language use is an occasion of language learning, and vice versa' (Little, 1997, p. 99).

REFLECTION FOR ACTION

Future Teachers

- Reflect on your learning experiences and the teachers you had in the past. To what extent do you think they were independent in their pedagogical practices?
- How do you imagine yourself as an autonomous teacher? What would that entail?
- Can you identify any aspects of teacher autonomy integrated into your teacher education programme?
- How will the identified aspects of teacher autonomy help you to demonstrate independence in your teaching career?

Novice Teachers

- Reflect on the concept of teacher autonomy and your teaching journey. What features do you typically share with autonomous teachers? Briefly discuss these with your mentor.
- Considering the different definitions of teacher autonomy, can you relate these to the ways in which you take control of both your teaching and professional learning? Are there any ways in which this can be improved?
- Which strategies proposed for developing teacher autonomy should you use and why?
- Reflect on your teaching journey and the way in which your school supports you in becoming a more autonomous teacher. How happy are you with the level of support provided?

Experienced Teachers

- Which characteristic features of an autonomous teacher do you demonstrate? Briefly describe these to your colleague teacher and suggest how the current situation could be improved.
- Reflect on the definitions of teacher autonomy and relate these to the way in which you take control of your professional learning. Are there any ways in which this can be improved?
- Reflect on the strategies proposed for developing teacher autonomy and discuss with other colleagues how you could promote collaborative autonomy in your school.
- Select and implement one of the strategies you think will work particularly well in your current context. Having completed the task, discuss with colleagues how you, your students, and your school benefitted from the strategy.

6 Materials Development and Task Design
A Professional Challenge

Language learning occurs in an environment in which the learner needs to comprehend and produce texts and utterances in the target language and in various forms. To construct learning environments that allow learners to work autonomously and with agency (Chapter 5), such spaces must be carefully created to ensure that they align with course learning outcomes and learners' needs. While *exercises* focus on language (e.g., grammar, vocabulary, pronunciation), *activities* enable selected language items to be practised in communicative situations. *Tasks*, in turn, focus on meaningful communication modelled on real-life interactions where any specific language items do not restrict discourse. As such, tasks define the overall design of a whole learning environment, how learners are supposed to work, the goal(s) they are expected to pursue, and the outcomes they are instructed to produce. Given this crucial role of tasks in a pedagogical environment, this chapter focuses on tasks that determine the ways in which, and ends to which, the texts and materials are used. The exercises and activities defined earlier may be instrumental to working with such tasks. Still, their position in the learning process is subordinate, whereas the role of tasks is superordinate to the selection of materials and all other classroom practices.

There are two significant reasons why textual and medial environments must be pedagogically constructed. Firstly, language learning does not usually happen in a natural environment where learners can meet and interact with the target language users and their cultures. However, as an exception, natural language learning (Krashen, 1983) could happen while studying abroad. Because such experiences are relatively scarce, most learners have access to the other language only in the classroom, which is a pedagogical environment constructed for the purpose of language learning by imitating or suggesting some similarity to natural discursive and cultural environments. For this reason, natural discursive environments are comprehensively represented by presenting learners with all kinds of discourse, from listening materials that present dialogic conversations to newspaper articles or multimodal advertising flyers (Sections 3.1 and 6.3.1). Visual images, maps, and diagrams add to a consistent representation of the original cultural environment. The language classroom is thus a space that (re-)creates primary (natural) cultural and discursive elements of the focal societies by representing them in a recognisable way through textual and medial artefacts (Hallet, 2011).

Secondly, texts and materials must be geared to the needs and abilities of respective learners (Tomlinson, 2011). Apart from very advanced stages of language learning, the language classroom needs to account for the various levels of proficiency that correspond to the linguistic and cognitive complexities of input texts and materials. Whereas original texts may well be introduced and used in the advanced language classroom, at all earlier stages of language learning, materials and texts need to be adapted to the required comprehensibility levels (Krashen, 1985). Such comprehensibility encompasses linguistic structures and devices, the syntax and the length of texts, the cognitively demanding complexity of content, and the degree of abstraction.

This chapter examines ways in which teachers develop materials and design tasks for the language classroom. It strives to demonstrate why materials and tasks are always closely interconnected. Given that coursebook-based teaching is a common practice, this chapter first discusses the roles and functions of coursebooks and ready-made materials in the language classroom. It then explores the value of a teacher's independent development of materials and design of tasks and reflects upon and discusses criteria and principles for selecting texts and compiling materials for the ELT classroom. Following this, the philosophy, purposes, and functions of task approaches are examined, after which a model and a planning tool for a complex task that integrates materials into the task design are presented. Finally, potential strategies are proposed for assessing the outcomes of complex tasks.

6.1 Coursebooks and Ready-Made Materials

Most language courses and lessons are based on coursebooks and possibly other ready-made materials. These provide the teacher with selected materials and broadly defined classroom activities (i.e., exercises, activities, and tasks, as specified earlier). Still, for students and teachers alike, coursebooks are 'their main experience of using materials' (Tomlinson, 2011, p. 2). For this reason, a critical reflection on the role of coursebooks and the materials they offer is as important as the ability to develop one's own materials.

6.1.1 Common Practice

Critical reflection is a step towards furnishing teachers with a higher degree of autonomy in exercising professional judgement on the function and quality of pedagogical materials (Section 4.2, Chapter 5). Professional autonomy is fully exercised only when teachers can create and evaluate materials, exercises, activities, and tasks based on key principles. There are good reasons why high-quality coursebooks published by well-established publishers have attained such a central role in the language classroom. These are as follows:

1. *Coursebooks correspond directly to the institutional contexts in which language learning takes place.* They organise and structure a language course which Ur (2012, 2015) refers to as the function of a framework and provide linguistic and textual means geared to the needs of a course in the given institution. In such curricular (often defined by state administrations) and institutional (schools, adult education, university language courses) contexts, coursebooks serve as a syllabus (Ur, 2015) and prepare learners for tests or exams that certify their proficiency and structure the number of years or the time available so that they can steadily progress towards the defined goals of a course.
2. *Coursebook materials, including exercises, activities, and tasks, are part of larger, progressive learning units.* These units combine textual or medial input with language systems, as well as exercises, activities, and tasks. Such units often assess learners' progress in working with coursebook materials.
3. *Coursebooks define the purpose of input materials, exercises, activities, and tasks.* Whether they are selected from the cultural repertoire of texts and discourses or didactically created for the specific purposes of language learning, coursebook input materials are carefully geared to the respective learners' language proficiency levels and cognitive abilities. As such, coursebooks structure and grade learners in terms of progress and increasing proficiency and thus support the language learning process (Ur, 2015).
4. *Coursebook input materials encourage learners to engage in language production.* Production is broadly defined here and subsumes carrying out both speaking and writing activities for communicative purposes and completing language exercises in written form. Such materials provide learners with guidelines on how to work with texts and models of language use, such as conversational dialogues, stories, and descriptions of persons, objects, or places.
5. *Coursebook content is structured thematically.* Input materials are organised around thematic clusters so that learners acquire cultural and content knowledge about, for example, family life, school education, travelling, and leisure time. Such thematic orientations go hand in hand with the lexical work and learning words in the respective content areas.

All these purposes are challenging for teachers when they develop their own materials, including exercises, activities, or tasks, in a manner similar to coursebooks. A teacher or a teaching team cannot engage in the complex work of creating materials that aim to provide everything needed in an entire course's curricular context. Such work is not only very time-consuming (Ur, 2015) but also requires a well-developed familiarity with language learning and language acquisition theories (Tomlinson, 2011, 2016). It involves defining learners' needs at the respective level of language learning and against the cultural repertoire of texts and media from which selections or adaptations for the language classroom can be made.

As complete and perfect as texts, materials, and media in coursebooks may seem, they have certain limitations. Firstly, they are not tailor-made for learners and groups in terms of abilities, progress, and pace; instead, they rely on more general assumptions regarding each learner's age and stage of language proficiency and their corresponding needs and the support they require. However, to efficiently enhance language learning proficiency, ready-made materials, as a rule, require further adaptation, along with the teacher's pedagogical decisions and their implementation in the actual learning process. This may require selection procedures or the creation of additional materials.

Secondly, coursebook materials pre-define the content that is addressed. It is complicated to anticipate their relevance to learners, as students' interests and learning preferences may vary and depend on collective and individual factors (prior knowledge, cultural background, current cognitive development). This is also why learners' roles in shaping and designing topics and materials are minimal if a coursebook is the only language learning resource. In coursebook-based courses, learners are exposed to materials, texts, and content, the selection and criteria of which are external to the actual learning process. To some extent, this is driven by considerations and interests such as commercial or administrative factors that do not directly refer to language learning and acquisition processes.

Overall, in using a coursebook, the teacher is not completely in control of the learning process and how it is organised, structured, and thematically defined. Therefore, using a coursebook effectively may be more demanding than anticipated, as teachers need to account for the needs and wants of the learning group or individual learners. The 'increasing diversity of users and contexts' (Masuhara, 2011, p. 249) and the heterogeneity of classrooms compel the teacher to continually adapt coursebooks and other ready-made materials to the needs of learners and the respective purpose of use in a specific teaching–learning process.

6.1.2 *Evaluating Coursebooks and Published Materials*

The previous section explained that coursebooks are popular and teachers use them for various reasons. However, to select high-quality coursebooks, teachers need to be able to evaluate pedagogical materials in general, which is a demanding professional endeavour. Tomlinson (2013a, 2013b) has observed that the evaluation of materials is often intuitive and experiential at best but almost always somewhat subjective. This applies to pre-use evaluation in particular, as such materials have not yet been tested and used in classrooms, so any conducted evaluation can make assumptions and predictions about future use. Consequently, Tomlinson (2013a, 2013b) argues firmly in favour of more systematic, criterion-based evaluation processes, as this will mean that evaluation results can be shared intersubjectively, and various instances can be compared. The same criteria can be applied by several teachers and used for different materials.

In this way, evaluation may become a professional routine and, as such, be incorporated into teacher education. In his proposal, Tomlinson (2013a, p. 40) presents numerous evaluative questions and criteria which are too numerous to present in full in this chapter. However, he also proposes extremely useful 'possible categories for universal criteria' from which more specific criteria can be derived. These are learning principles, cultural perspective, topic content, teaching points, texts, activities, methodology, instructions, and design and layout. The results of such categorical evaluations may still be subjective, but they at least make it possible to depart from rather general impressions and judgements and agree on the aspects or features of the material or coursebook in question, which should be the focus of the evaluation.

Tomlinson (2013a) also proposes to cluster criteria along certain functions specific to a particular type of material or their use. According to this system, the criteria should be:

- *media-specific*: These criteria are explicitly developed for books, videos, and visual or multimodal materials regarding their functionality and effects on learning.
- *content-specific*: These criteria relate to the content and the topics of books and materials and the specific target group for whom they are produced. For instance, there should be 'a set of topic-related criteria which would be relevant to the evaluation of a business English textbook but not to a general English coursebook' (Tomlinson, 2013a, p. 41).
- *age-specific*: Learning processes, cognitive abilities, and learning strategies differ substantially, depending on the learner's age. For instance, the materials and input a Year 5 student needs vary considerably from those offered to adult learners.
- *local*: These criteria are not directly concerned with the features and quality of the materials 'but rather with measuring the value of the materials for particular learners in particular circumstances' and the specific context in which they are used. (Tomlinson, 2013a, p. 42)

There are, of course, other clusters of criteria one could imagine and bring to the materials, depending on the institutional context or specific language learning purposes. For example, Tomlinson (2013a, p. 43) mentions 'teacher-specific, administrator-specific, gender-specific, or culture-specific' criteria clusters, which must be specified further according to the backgrounds and purposes of use.

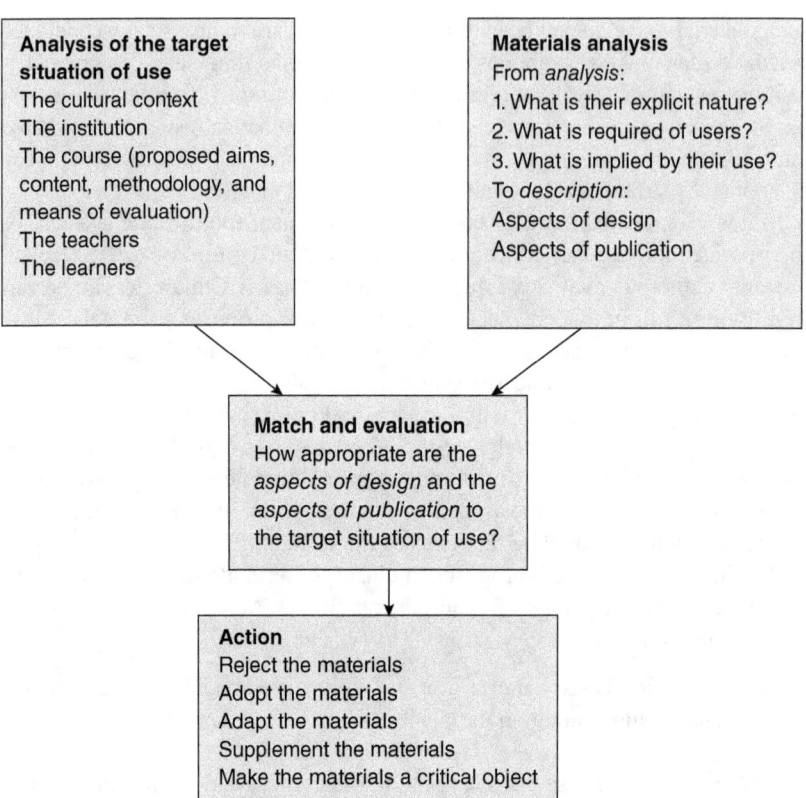

Figure 6.1 A framework of materials analysis, evaluation, and action
Note: Reprinted with permission from Littlejohn (2011, p. 202). Copyright 2011 by Cambridge University Press.

One of the problems of materials evaluation, which often results in rather intuitive, subjective, or hypothetical judgements, is that as a process it can be rather unsystematic and unstructured. This is why Littlejohn (2011) and Tomlinson (2013a) propose that teachers proceed in a sequence of steps, beginning with an analysis suitable for preparing evaluative judgements. In such a procedural approach, the actual evaluation is the final stage and is fully prepared by the preceding stages. Littlejohn (2011, p. 201) proposes the following four steps:

1. an analysis of the materials;
2. an analysis of the proposed situation of use;
3. the process of matching (the purpose of the materials and its actual use) and evaluation; and
4. subsequent action.

In his framework of materials analysis (Figure 6.1), Littlejohn (2011) provides the details and criteria he suggests for the various steps. While most of the criteria in the various stages are quite transparent and self-explanatory, subsequent actions range from rejecting proposed materials to creating supplements and transforming them into objects of critical analysis in the classroom.

This analytical and evaluative approach is an essential component of teacher professionalisation, as careful consideration of materials will assist teachers in making sense of their teaching style and why they prefer (or do not prefer) the particular mode of working required by such materials (Littlejohn, 2011). This critical evaluation of externally produced materials endows teachers with greater autonomy and supports their decision-making in the teaching–learning process (Section 5.1).

6.2 Materials Development and Task Design by Teachers

One of the general conclusions drawn from Chapter 5 is that a teacher's professional autonomy is fully exercised when they are able to not only evaluate but also create materials in general and in exercises, activities, and tasks based on set principles. The following discussion reflects on the advantages of teachers developing materials and designing tasks and highlights several challenges that can be overcome only with a professional approach. Consideration is also given to the collaborative design of materials and tasks. Finally, this section explains why materials development and task design are regarded as stepping stones to teacher autonomy and agency.

6.2.1 Advantages

As may be deduced from the demanding endeavour of materials analysis and evaluation, a teacher's ability to design materials and tasks independently must be regarded as a core professional competence and a sign of professional reflection on their practice (Tomlinson, 2001, 2013b). First and foremost, teacher-made materials and tasks have multiple advantages over published ones that are directly related to the processes and conditions of language teaching and learning. Specifically, materials and tasks developed by teachers:

- rely on the teacher's observation of their class and individual learners' needs and wants. In this sense, materials and tasks developed by teachers are learner-oriented and tailored to the needs of learners in their respective groups or classes;
- account for their students' specific interests, individual abilities, pre-knowledge, or cultural backgrounds. This kind of adaptivity can be achieved only through the teacher's own development of materials and tasks, not by

externally produced coursebooks, which are inevitably targeted at large and abstract learner populations; and
- respond to the broad scope of different learning styles, the pace of learning and work, and preferred working strategies.

Learners can be expected to appreciate such adaptivity of the materials, texts, and tasks in the learning process; for instance, they will be more motivated by texts and input materials tailored to their needs and interests. They may even actively select texts, topics, and tasks they would like to see and do in the language classroom. Materials creation can thus be a participative endeavour in which the teacher and learners commonly engage. However, the role of materials in the language learning process cannot be determined if they are not connected to tasks and there are no clear working instructions. The latter assign a function to the materials by defining the objectives for their use and ascribing them a place and function in the learning process (e.g., practising communicative skills, developing linguistic knowledge, acquiring cultural awareness, deepening content knowledge). Therefore, as represented in the stage of pedagogical realisation in the framework model in Figure 6.1, tasks and instructions are indispensable components of materials, and vice versa. Tasks can make sense only if directly connected with the materials to which the instructions refer.

6.2.2 Challenges

As demonstrated in Section 6.1.1, materials development, including task design, is a complex professional undertaking. Task and materials design must account not only 'for the needs and wants of learners' (Tomlinson, 2013a, p. 7) but also for those of language teachers (Masuhara, 2011) and administrators who seek to ensure alignment and standardisation with respect to a theory of language learning, a syllabus, examination requirements, and the specific policies a government adopts with respect to language (Tomlinson, 2013c, p. 3). For professional materials developers and publishers, the working conditions in terms of resources, time, and expertise are all geared towards the published and marketed products. For teachers, these conditions are inevitably less favourable and supportive. It is therefore essential to reduce the complexity of materials development for teachers by systematising and structuring the materials design and production processes. This also makes it possible to integrate task design and materials development into teacher education and to prepare teachers on the job for this professional activity. However, due to the absence of an institutional framework, as is often the case for published materials, it is advisable that, whenever possible, it should not be the individual teacher who develops materials but rather a group of teachers. Collaboratively developed materials (Tomlinson, 2011, 2013d) allow teachers to not only exchange and discuss various ideas but also reach an agreement concerning their teaching philosophy and course objectives on types and points of assessment and ensure consultation throughout the development process.

Jolly and Bolitho (2011) have developed a framework for materials writing which guides materials design on the part of a teacher or a group of teachers so that they can offer their students language materials and input that enhance the language learning process (Tomlinson, 2013d). The various stages and decisions in the design process cannot be described in detail in this chapter; instead, they are briefly defined as a tool that can be utilised when creating materials specifically for the language classroom (Jolly & Bolitho, 2011). This comprises the following stages:

- *Identification of the need for materials*: The teacher and/or the learner(s) identify a need in the language learning process or a problem (grammar, skills development, understanding authentic utterances, language production) that may be solved by creating materials.
- *Exploration of need*: This stage specifies and particularises the need, the problem, or the language learning area the materials are intended to meet and develop. In addition, the goals and purposes of creating and introducing certain materials for the language classroom are defined. These may concern, among others, language issues, content and meanings, skills, and communicative language production.
- *Contextual realisation*: This is the step in materials development in which the ideas, texts, and contexts (content areas) with which students are supposed to work are identified, selected, or produced.
- *Pedagogical realisation*: Materials must be integrated into the teaching–learning process through tasks and instructions that initiate and structure learners' work.
- *Physical production*: This stage addresses the actual material or digital production of the materials and the corresponding tasks; it encompasses layout, font types, and sizes, visual components if printed, and other components of the media in question (e.g., videos, audio materials).
- *Student use of materials*: This is the stage in which students must engage in the learning process by appropriating and integrating the materials into their own language repertoire or content knowledge. Here, the viability of the materials must be tested and demonstrated in terms of progress in language knowledge.

Evaluation of materials: The term *development* makes sense because creating materials is a continuous process and cycle that involves designing materials, applying them in the learning process, and evaluating their successful use. Apart from the criteria for a systematic analysis and evaluation introduced earlier (Section 6.1.2), there is an almost endless list of criteria and questions that may be brought to the materials and their wanted, but also unintended, effects in the classroom. Particular attention should be paid to learners' feedback on and evaluation of the materials (Jolly & Bolitho, 2011) based on questions such as: To what extent do classroom materials appeal to learners? To what extent do learners find classroom materials interesting and motivating? How do learners perceive pedagogical materials and evaluate them? (Tomlinson, 2013a).

It is the complexity and intricacy of the processes of creating materials and designing tasks that challenge a teacher's professional knowledge and competence. However, materials development and task design are pivotal in the language learning process and in how teaching and learning are organised in classrooms. They are therefore essential components of a teacher's professional competence (Section 3.7).

6.2.3 The Interdependence between Materials and Tasks

Materials must always have a pedagogical purpose (e.g., presenting students with a cultural topic or introducing them to a specific type of interaction). This is often defined through curricular and teaching contexts (Section 6.1.2) and by the teacher in particular, as materials structure the learning process and facilitate students' work. Students are thus rarely exposed to materials per se, but they are instructed on how to work with them and for which purposes. This is why, as a rule, materials are always connected with or form part of a task that defines a purpose for their active use by students. Reciprocally, whenever a task is designed (or used), the teacher needs to reflect and decide on the input materials the students should use while working on the task.

As a stage in creating materials and tasks, there may be immense value to be gained in reflecting systematically on the respective correspondences between materials and tasks. These can be seen as reciprocally functional; materials have a purpose for the task, and the task can be defined as functional to the materials addressed in the task. The functional correspondences are manifold, and those in Table 6.1 provide examples of frequent instances. These correspondences also pave the way for developing a more advanced concept of materials and task development in which materials are an integrated component of a complex task (Section 6.5). The closer the correspondences are, the

Table 6.1 *Correspondences between materials and tasks*

Text(s) and materials	Tasks
content, topic, thematic discourse	comprehension and content questions, extracting information, making meaning, interpretative tasks
textual features, rhetoric	analysis questions, description of textual discourse
non-verbal semiotic modes in the materials (photos, diagrams, maps, etc.)	understanding and making meaning of other modes, interrelating non-verbal with verbal components of the text
genre	genre analysis questions, identifying generic conventions, and applying genre conventions in language production tasks (e.g., essay writing, family conversation, online application video)
type of interaction	understanding discourse, engaging in similar types of social interaction
linguistic features, syntax, lexico-grammar	language aspects, vocabulary

more evident it becomes that in a more holistic approach both materials and tasks must be conceptualised as defining components of a rich learning environment in which learners' language abilities, knowledge, and personalities have the opportunity to unfold.

This is why, in the model of the complex task, materials are integrated into the concept and development process. They are just one of the components in the design of the task, and their development goes hand in hand with all the other components, all of which constitute a learning and working environment and framework in which students are enabled to work autonomously and in an agentic manner (Chapter 5).

6.2.4 *Collaborative Design of Materials and Tasks*

Although the individual teacher can accomplish the creation of tasks and materials, the effort and energy required for their construction are exceptionally high. However, beyond reducing the individual teacher's workload, the collaboration of several teachers in creating tasks and materials has several other advantages. First and foremost, several teachers' expertise and knowledge are superior to one's; therefore, collaborative work is not only an option but almost an imperative. As Tomlinson (2011, p. 25) notes: 'We all have constraints on our time and our actions, but it must be possible and potentially valuable for us to get together to pool our resources and share our expertise in a joint endeavour to develop materials which offer language learners maximum opportunities for successful learning'.

While teacher collaboration is an established practice, other types of collaboration are also worth considering. Adopting a broader approach, collaborating with external experts such as professional materials writers working for publishers or experts and researchers from academia, at least temporarily, may be highly productive and supportive, as it allows other experiences and backgrounds to find their way into the classroom. In addition, it would be innovative to collaborate with students in class and have them participate actively in the choice and compilation of materials for their own use and purposes. After all, if students can make their own choices, they are more likely to work with the materials in a motivated and engaged manner.

In addition to multiplied professional expertise, the joint creation of tasks and materials by teachers is an important way of aligning levels of learning and performance requirements that may generate a consensus among English language teachers concerning the appropriateness, degrees of difficulty, and complexity, as well as language standards of materials and tasks. The same applies to the standard definition of competence goals and their alignment with general educational standards, curricular frameworks, or the school curriculum. Indeed, this is a precondition for developing reliable assessment standards on which English language teachers should agree (Section 3.6). To summarise, collaborative task and materials development can be regarded as an essential avenue of professional learning and individual professional development, as well as one of the areas in which the English language unit of a school can develop into a professional development community (see Chapter 9 for details).

6.2.5 Materials and Task Design as Stepping Stones to Teacher Autonomy and Agency

Developing the competence to critically evaluate coursebooks and other published materials and to design tasks and materials has often been described as an essential component of a teacher's professional development and a pathway to teacher autonomy and agency (Chapter 5). Writing materials and using, evaluating, and designing materials and tasks give rise to various issues pertinent to becoming a teacher, including language awareness, selecting and grading a language, sociocultural appropriation, and knowledge of learning theories (Jolly & Bolitho, 2011).

Teacher autonomy is believed to be associated with the process of critical reflection (Section 4.2) and is generally construed as an eagerness and capacity to deal with limitations within a perspective on education that views it as empowering and liberating (Vieira et al., 2002). Because of this, all professional practices that are concerned with teaching and learning processes in the classroom and constant reflection upon these are suitable for contributing to a teacher's professional independence and agency. The teacher's insight into learning processes and the ability to design them equips instructors with a certain amount of freedom to make pedagogical decisions, determine the directions the learning processes take, and, more generally, gain power over what happens in the classroom. Broadly speaking, if task and materials design is an important component of teacher professionalisation, it also engenders a higher degree of autonomy in the institutional contexts of education (Chapter 5). Task and materials design therefore comes close to 'squaring the circle – reconciling materials as constraints with materials as empowerment' (Maley, 2011, p. 379).

What happens in the classroom is customarily regulated by cascades of political and administrative frameworks such as curricula at several levels (national, local), implementation procedures, and examination regulations. However, it is precisely within such institutional and professional frameworks (Yukselir & Ozer, 2022) that teacher autonomy is required to claim, gain, and sustain a certain level of freedom, independence, and individuality in decision-making and positioning (Chapter 5). This also applies to the freedom to use materials and tasks of one's own choice, as this avoids subjecting classes and learners to exclusively external curricular or pedagogical demands and requirements, while it is in the teacher's hands to reject, adapt, and modify published materials according to the individual and also the cultural needs of the learners.

Materials development and task design contribute to teacher autonomy and agency in the following ways:

- A highly developed and advanced professional knowledge and awareness of factors underpinning language learning empower the teacher to independently design and guide the teaching and learning processes. This can 'facilitate teachers' deep understanding of what is involved in the teaching-learning relationship' (Littlejohn, 2011, p. 204) and, in so doing, enhance independent decision-making on the part of teachers.
- In light of their development and use of materials, teachers need to constantly reflect not only on their effects but also on their pedagogical orientations and their particular approach to teaching and why they may prefer (or not prefer) the mode of working required for such materials (Littlejohn, 2011, p. 204). Therefore, materials development and task design are essential elements of teaching as reflective practice (Chapter 4) and of a teacher's autonomy and agency (Chapter 5).
- As demonstrated in Chapter 4, reflective classroom practices are also a pathway to teacher and classroom research. The analysis of and reflection on questions such as the expectations of the learner with respect to what they are required to do, with what, and with whom are central to the objectives of learning activities and thus may form the structural basis for collecting

data via, for instance, observations taking place in the classroom (Littlejohn, 2011). Such a reflective approach to the use of materials leads to greater independence of judgement and decision-making – essential components of the agency and autonomy of teachers.

The interconnectedness of materials and task development (Section 6.2.3), along with an increasing and constantly developing teacher autonomy, leads to the conclusion that the competences required to analyse, design, and utilise materials and tasks effectively are key to the language teaching profession. Therefore, materials development and task design should be established as 'a key component of initial training courses and a regular feature of in-service training programmes ... not only in order to reduce their dependence on published materials, but also as a means of professional development' (Jolly & Bolitho, 2011, p. 129).

6.3 The Selection of Texts and Compilation of Materials

Whether in the form of coursebooks, published materials, or self-created compilations, the variety and range of texts and materials offered to students are extremely broad, ranging, for instance, from family dialogues, newspaper articles, and stories to pop songs, photos, and flyers. Because all are effective in acts of communication and cultural discourses, it makes sense to classify all these artefacts as *texts* that can produce and share meaning in acts of communication and social interaction. In a meaning-focused, semiotic sense, photos, videos, and songs must be regarded as texts akin to any verbal text (texts in the narrow and traditional sense). It follows that photos and other visual images are not just decorations or illustrations but meaningful texts in their own right. Such a definition facilitates reflection upon the effect that all texts and materials introduced into the classroom may have and, from the teacher's point of view, enables them to anticipate the meaning they produce in the interplay with all kinds of other texts.

6.3.1 Criteria and Principles for Selecting and Combining Texts and Materials

There are several criteria and principles that need to be considered whenever materials are selected, adapted, or created for the language classroom (e.g., Grimm et al., 2015; McGrath, 2013; Tomlinson, 2011). All materials introduced as learning input must be comprehensible and processible for learners. Texts and materials need to be carefully graded and, for most stages of language learning, specifically created to align with each learner's level of language proficiency. Furthermore, it has become common to use the proficiency levels of the skills descriptions of the CEFR (Council of Europe, 2020) to classify the language level of texts and materials, from the basic level of A1 to the most advanced level of C2, which denotes completely authentic materials with no constraints (Cirocki, 2016). This section discusses the most important criteria to be considered when creating or selecting texts and materials.

Texts and materials can, of course, be classified globally, as suggested, for instance, in the 'overall reading comprehension chapter' of the CEFR (Council of Europe, 2020, p. 54). However, it is advisable to specify such classifications according to various features of the text and material. The features and criteria that need to be considered are as complex and multifarious as any communicative act to which the most important criteria would have to refer:

- *grammar*: the syntax structures and linguistic devices of the text in question;
- *the lexicon*: the number and level of new words in a text;
- *textual complexity and length*: the way a text is structured and unfolds (as an argument, a story, etc.) and the amount of time it takes to read and understand it;
- *content*: the age-appropriateness of a text and the way in which it relates to learners' pre-knowledge and experiences; moreover, it should meet their interests and be motivating; and
- *cognitive complexity*: the cognitive demands a text makes of learners, including degrees of experientiality, abstraction, and thinking skills.

Regarding language learning as a cognitively constructive process, it is important to note that the language level of the input materials and the language learner should not match exactly. This may sound surprising, but given that it is essential to provide textual input in the classroom that allows learners to incrementally increase their level of proficiency in a language (Cirocki, 2016), the materials should linguistically and cognitively reside at a level that makes it possible for learners to appropriate these and advance to a language level slightly higher than when they initially encounter a new text. This conviction originates in the general cognitive theory of learning developed by Vygotsky (1978), which describes a zone of proximal development (ZPD) as the space in which learning happens (Section 9.1). Applied to language learning, this zone can be defined as 'the distance between the actual development level of learners' learning as determined by independent performance in the target language and the level of potential development as determined through language generated with other class participants in a collaborative undertaking' (Cirocki, 2016, p. 35). Working with texts and materials is part of an interactive endeavour in which a text provides the linguistic and cognitive level the learner seeks to accomplish, or at least to approach. In that sense, texts and materials establish a rich learning environment that offers ample opportunities for language learners to advance their language abilities.

A few other criteria and principles need to be considered whenever materials are selected, adapted, or created for the language classroom (e.g., McGrath, 2013; Tomlinson, 2011). Cirocki (2016) proposes four such criteria for materials and text selection: *connectivity, suitability for personalisation, exploitability*, and *variety*.

Connectivity is defined as learners' potential to make connections between themselves and the textual worlds that texts always represent. There are three types of connections. First, *text-to-self* connections denote the extremely personal connections made by learners between the texts they seek to understand and their own life experiences. Second, *text-to-text* connections allude to the connections learners make between the text they are currently decoding and those already processed. Third, *text-to-world* connections are those formed by learners between texts and the concepts, topics, and events that lie substantially outside the scope of their individual experiences. Connectivity accounts for the fact that text comprehension and processing cannot be successful if learners cannot connect to textual representations of the world in some way. It thus ensures that texts are relevant and meaningful for learners and can thus enhance learning processes.

Personalisation responds to the heterogeneity and diversity of today's classrooms by accounting for the high degree of individuality by which all learning is characterised. It refers to instruction that aligns with individual ZPDs and individual learners' abilities, preferences, needs, interests, learning styles, and cultural backgrounds (Cirocki, 2016). Learners must be offered ways to engage with texts in their way and style; hence, the criterion of personalisation is well suited for the individualisation of learning in twenty-first-century heterogeneous classrooms (Armstrong, 2009; Ur, 2012). However, given that it is difficult to imagine that a single text can be appropriated in an individual manner by all members of a class or group, personalisation also refers to the need to create a rich textual environment in which learners have individual options and can make choices. Therefore, other constructs, such as *multiperspectivity* (introduced later), come into play which serve as guiding principles for creating such textual environments for language learning.

Exploitability refers to those features of texts and materials that offer a sound foundation for devising innovative, interactive, and stimulating tasks for learners whose levels of language proficiency may differ substantially (Cirocki, 2016). It thus accounts for the close interrelatedness of materials and tasks delineated in Section 6.2.3. However, there is never a one-to-one mapping of tasks on materials or vice versa, as every text can be made productive for language and content learning in manifold ways. For instance, the exact text may be utilised to teach a set of grammar structures, promote intercultural learning, or teach receptive skills. It follows that exploitability requires a high degree of professional reflection and the teacher's familiarity with factors and dimensions of and within language learning that may be an option when selecting materials and designing tasks.

Variety refers to the wide range of issues, text types, and contexts to which learners must be exposed regularly. This is vital as texts are categorised according to their intrinsic features, and thus the demands they place on learners vary enormously (Cirocki, 2016). Variety is indispensable when diverse and controversial topics are to be represented in the classroom in all cultural learning contexts. It also concerns types of texts, genres, and a range of semiotic modes beyond the verbal mode by which today's texts and layouts are typically characterised. Variety in textual environments therefore also has a representational function; it imitates the way texts occur in the lifeworld, how cultural agents make meaning of the world, and, more generally, how they negotiate meaning. The basis is always a multitude of topical or otherwise interrelated texts and never a single text.

When selecting and compiling materials for a specific classroom and group of learners, the criteria discussed earlier should be extended into, or mirrored in, principles which can be generalised and which apply more or less universally. Regarding the general philosophy of school education, as *Bildung*, discussed in Sections 1.3 and 3.1, the principles of selecting and compiling materials aim to prepare students to deal with the enormous quantity of texts to which they are constantly exposed in the real world, digital environments in particular. These texts also represent a broad scope of cultural, ethical, or political views and perspectives. Such principles also account for the fact that most texts in the lifeworld are based not only on words but also on several other semiotic modes, photographic and other visual modes in particular, which are often combined into a single text or act of communication (e.g., multimodality as in a flyer, a WhatsApp message, or a news magazine).

The three core principles are *multitextuality, multimodality,* and *multiperspectivity*. They are briefly described here.

Multitextuality: This principle specifies the cultural dimension of textual variety when working with texts in the classroom (Hallet, 2002). In the lifeworld, topical discourses are always constituted through a multitude of thematically interrelated texts and utterances. Speakers in the lifeworld are therefore constantly engaged in identifying commonalities or oppositions between large numbers of texts, utterances, and medial representations, determining an individual speaker's position among many other utterances, and positioning their utterances among a plethora of others. This is how cultural agents in the lifeworld make meaning of the world and, more generally, negotiate meanings and positions; the basis is always a multitude of topically or otherwise interrelated texts and utterances and never a single text.

As is often the case, working with a single text is a common practice in coursebooks and other published materials. This kind of reduction may be appropriate for the purposes of teaching text-based competences such as reading, comprehension, or all kinds of text production where a single text may serve as a model or reference. For instance, a letter to the editor would refer to a particular newspaper article and argue for or against aspects or elements of that article. Beyond such pedagogical purposes of language learning, students also need to learn how to deal with and handle a multitude of texts, as multitextuality is expected in the lifeworld, especially in digital environments. This is why the ability to process meanings based on several texts and the ability to recognise, establish, and exploit relations between texts is also a competence – intertextual competence – that teachers need to develop in the language classroom.

Multimodality: Whenever references are made to texts, it is spoken or written (and printed) texts that are denoted as a rule. However, in cultural discourses, especially digital environments, numerous other textual entities possess all the qualities of word texts and function like verbal texts in communicative acts but are not necessarily word texts themselves (Kress, 2010; Kress & van Leeuwen, 2001; van Leeuwen, 2005). An example of these textual features of non-verbal texts are photographs; they communicate content and represent a particular slice of the world, are complete message entities, and establish a relationship between the author of the image and the viewer. As coherent units that produce meaning, they function communicatively in the same way as texts in the word mode. Moreover, like all verbal utterances, they never appear without contextualising discourse; photos are defined by captions which often explain their content further or, as in the case of journalistic photos, serve to illustrate a word text and represent a specific cultural matter.

Multimodality is about selecting and combining texts for the language classroom because combining images and texts or other multiple semiotic modes in a single act of communication is culturally established (Hallet, 2006b). As explained in Section 3.2, a teacher needs to be aware of the cultural work of all kinds of images in cultural discourses and that photos and images should not be treated as decorations. Therefore, whenever materials are compiled for the classroom, the whole range of semiotic modes, from photos to maps and diagrams, and multimodal forms of representation such as newspaper articles, posters, or brochures must be integrated into the language classroom and be part of the communicative practices employed in language learning. The professional ability to select and combine texts and materials of different semiotic modes for the communicative classroom lies in determining the way in which they can be interrelated in effective ways and how learners can make meaning of them across modes and media when exploring issues and topics.

Multiperspectivity: Multiple materials and textual input in the language classroom seek to represent the polyphony of voices in every cultural discourse, that is, the pluralisation of discourses according to the cultural spheres and domains in which they emerge. Multiperspectivity accounts for the multiplication of

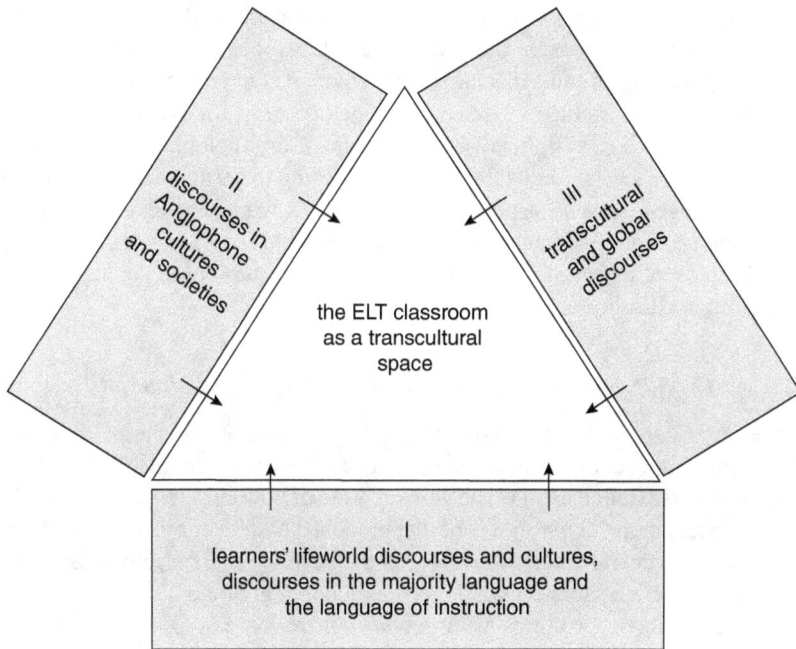

Figure 6.2 Three discourse spheres constituting the ELT classroom as a transcultural space
Note: Adapted and translated with permission from Hallet (2002, p. 48). Copyright 2002 by Wolfgang Hallet.

perspectives that different cultural backgrounds, including learners' lifeworlds and various cultural, ethical, or political orientations and positions, bring to the classroom.

The cultural spheres of discourse (Figure 6.2) from which texts and materials, in all semiotic modes, can be classified are as follows:

- students' and teacher's lifeworlds, including discourses in the language of schooling;
- discourses in anglophone cultures and societies around the world, including African, Asian, and other anglophone communities and societies with English as a national language; and
- transcultural, multicultural, and global discourses.

As depicted in Figure 6.2, these spheres all intersect and merge in the language classroom and constitute a transcultural (or hybrid) space that makes it possible to encounter and consider a broad scope of cultural perspectives across languages, societies, and cultures. Regarding pedagogical materials, texts and utterances may be selected to represent these different discourse spheres and thus account for the diversity and heterogeneity of discourses and different positions within a discourse. Moreover, distinguishing between these spheres makes it possible to focus on just one of them – for example, on a racism discourse or a civil rights discourse in one of the anglophone countries or societies, or the teacher and their students choosing to participate in the global climate change discourse as part of their classroom work. The texts and materials (including videos, diagrams, statistics) selected for such a teaching unit would represent the myriad of different, and sometimes controversial, voices in the climate discourse.

6.3.2 The Representation of Cultures through Texts and Materials

Representing anglophone cultures in the ELT classroom is one of the most challenging aspects of the professional work of teachers, coursebook writers, and publishers (Hallet, 2011). The general issue of how cultures are best taught and presented in the classroom is best approached by reflecting on how culture is defined. A general discussion exceeds the purpose and space of this book, but a few reflections are necessary. As the model in Figure 6.2 suggests, imagining and conceiving cultures as discursive spheres help avoid the misleading assumption that cultures are closed, homogenous, entities that can be represented as an overarching whole in the classroom. In their most advanced form, cultures are equated with nations so that general statements can be made about the United States or Australia and how their citizens think and live (Welsch, 1999). Often, such statements are stereotypical, ignoring the broad scope of cultural formations, communities, and orientations in any anglophone society.

This cultural diversity, plurality, and openness to all cultures (Andersen, 1983; Appiah, 2018; Hallet, 2020a, 2022; Posner, 2004) is the real challenge when it comes to decisions on how texts and materials in diverse semiotic modes, and visual images in particular, might best represent a culture. After all, one cannot contend that a text that has been selected or a visual image that is presented in the classroom can possibly represent a whole culture. Instead, cultural diversity and plurality, and the dynamics and the polyphony of cultural discourses, are best represented through a wide variety and plurality of texts and materials, which learners must then process and use to create meaning as to what these materials offer them. Therefore, teaching culture is always underpinned by the general criteria and principles delineated in Section 6.3.1.

First and foremost, it is not possible to teach cultures as a unitary whole. Instead, it is crucial to offer learners ways of understanding the cultural diversity, plurality, and openness of societies and to avoid homogenising assumptions or beliefs about other cultures and their internal heterogeneity. In the classroom, such cultural diversity, heterogeneity, and openness, and indeed any society's discursive polyphony, are best modelled and represented through many texts, different semiotic modes, and multiple perspectives. This is why the principles of multitextuality, multimodality, and multiperspectivity apply in culture-oriented classrooms in particular. They are best suited to giving learners a sense of the plurality of voices, different positions in a discourse, and controversies and ongoing cultural negotiations in a society (Hallet, 2011).

Modelling cultural discourses in this way constitutes a cultural space in the classroom where the students become cultural agents themselves, studying texts and listening to voices for orientation, making meaning of a range of different utterances, and positioning themselves within these. Conceiving the role of students in the language classroom can be regarded as learner orientation at its best; students are themselves the agents of meaning-making and cultural negotiations. Along with Kramsch (2009), this definition of students' position in the language learning process as cultural agency can be regarded as symbolic empowerment; the English language offers students access to and active participation in discourses in communities and cultures 'as connotations multiply across codes and additional meanings thrive in the interstices of different linguistic systems' (Kramsch, 2009, pp. 12–13).

It is important to emphasise that this pedagogical strategy of cultural representation places an ethical and cultural burden on the teacher's shoulders. Nobody can claim to present and represent whole cultures definitively; hence, it is evident that choices must be made, that only thin slices of complex cultural constellations can be presented, and that, due to various constraining factors, the language classroom can offer only small glimpses into anglophone cultures. The fact that this kind of insight is limited or is even, at its worst, biased must be openly addressed and discussed with students. After all, in the digital age, they have access to ongoing anglophone discourses and utterances in specific cultural contexts or worldwide, independent of the kind of insight the language classroom offers them.

6.3.3   Texts and Materials in the Digital Age

All the features of cultural discourses described in Section 6.3.2 can be observed not just in analogue environments. Rather, there are immense and endless quantities of information and utterances, texts, and materials available in the digital world (the effect of multiplication through digitisation) that intensify and reinforce all of the phenomena surrounding the emergence of cultural discourses (the effect of amplification through digitisation). Vast numbers of materials are 'newly produced that did not even exist before digitization and networking or did not leave the private sphere' (Stalder, 2016, p. 112). The real pedagogical challenge lies in how our students can be optimally taught to handle such textual and medial amounts of information and the diversity of orientations in digital environments. In an EU document on digital education, the respective competence area is defined as searching and filtering data and information and as information and data literacy, scaled with proficiency levels (Carretero Gomez et al., 2017).

However, the sheer number of texts and information produced and circulated in digital environments worldwide is not simply a quantitative phenomenon. It also has a qualitative dimension, as digital data can be stored, organised, and accessed in ways substantially different from those of handling analogue data. This technological feature results in entirely new forms of knowledge and archiving; cultural knowledge is now accessible in databases, digital archives, or online reference works. Furthermore, multimodal genres of representation and communication now prevail: YouTubing, Instagramming, and chatting on platforms such as WhatsApp and Telegram are now well-established standard social and communicative practices. It is therefore part and parcel of teachers' professional competences to familiarise themselves with working and communicating in digital environments and to possess the competence to teach their students the digital dimension of communication and social life in the language classroom (Carrier et al., 2017; Darvin & Hafner, 2022; Lütge, 2022).

Evidently, in the digital age, the learner's position vis-à-vis sources, data, and information has been transformed; the students are notably autonomous when accessing and processing information. Autonomy in digital environments even implies that institutional frameworks in schools and universities for providing information, accessing and acquiring knowledge, and processing or sharing it are losing authority and weight. They may even become obsolete, as the teacher and the educational institution are no longer gatekeepers. Instead, online environments and whole communities are now emerging through shared interests, communicative and social practices (e.g., gaming, Instagramming), or standard creative digital practices (e.g., programming, commenting on online games). All these developments may well lead to relatively informal types of language learning.

In conclusion, teachers, curricula, and coursebook writers need to develop strategies for integrating such types of learning into the language classroom. Jones' (2018) proposal is to define a (digital) video game literacy to be introduced and developed in the language classroom. This is just one example of how reflections on working and communicating in digital environments may well result in the definition of new competences and literacies and the redefinition of established skills and competences in the language classroom. Consequently, there is a whole new area of competences that teachers need to acquire and develop in order to guide and train their students when working and communicating digitally (Chapter 7).

6.4 Approaches to Tasks

The interconnectedness of materials and tasks that was addressed in the preceding sections, particularly in Section 6.2.3, made it apparent that exercises, activities, and tasks initiate all learning in the language classroom in connection with textual input. As explained in Section 6.3.1, the exploitability of materials and the various options they offer for learning are defined by corresponding exercises, activities, and tasks, ranging from acquiring new words to cultural learning. It follows that if language learning processes must be designed in terms of systematic teaching and learning, the purposes and functions of these at certain points and in specific contexts of language learning must be clearly defined in order to prepare the ground for the teacher's pedagogical decisions and their planning of an entire unit or teaching sequence. Section 6.4.1 discusses some of the approaches to conceptualising and systematising the description of purposes and functions of tasks, which, historically, has resulted in task typologies (Section 6.4.2) and the comprehensive approach of task-based language teaching and learning (Section 6.4.3).

6.4.1 Purposes and Functions of Tasks in the English Language Teaching Classroom

As familiar and natural as the presence of exercises, activities, and tasks in educational institutions in general, and the ELT classroom in particular, may appear, the more specific functions of tasks came to the fore in connection with two paradigmatic changes in the language classroom (Hallet & Legutke, 2013). From a historical perspective, the communicative turn in the early 1980s shifted the focus from the transmission of formal linguistic knowledge (e.g., grammar rules) and training language skills to designing the language classroom as a space for communication and social interaction (Breen & Candlin, 1980; Canale & Swain, 1980; Candlin, 1981; Howatt, 1984). The challenges and questions raised by this paradigm shift towards communicative competence were precisely those addressed in the earlier sections on materials development: What are the issues and topics that make it possible for learners to engage in communicative acts that are relevant and meaningful? What types of tasks are suited to initiating meaningful communication in the English language? How can the classroom allow for authentic and meaningful communication, simultaneously leading to language learning through language use?

This turn to the communicative classroom also led to a re-definition of the position and role of the learner. Learners were now seen as situated at the centre of all classroom processes. They were supposed to speak for themselves in an authentic manner akin to acts of communication in the real world outside the classroom. These two shifts defined communicative processes and social interaction as the overarching goal of the language classroom. However, given that the classroom remains a pedagogical and largely fictional communicative space, based on the pretence that learners were real speakers of English and had to use English for actual purposes in terms of authentic communication, it was clear from the outset that a rich textual or medial environment had to be created and that communicative and social interaction had to be initiated through tasks. Furthermore, in the early stages of language learning in particular, it was apparent that, besides authentic communication, there would also be phases of language learning in which the focus would rather be on linguistic forms and on training or exercising rather than on true communication. Therefore, the communicative turn was a period when communicative tasks were introduced but also when, simultaneously, other types of tasks, now categorised as activities or exercises with a different and more limited purpose, were distinguished more systematically.

6.4.2 Types of Tasks

The literature has so far proposed several typologies of communicative tasks (e.g., Hallet, 2011; Hallet & Legutke, 2013; Long, 2015; Müller-Hartmann & Schocker, 2011; van den Branden et al., 2007), indicating in general that the main objective of a task is to enable learners to use language in a meaningful way. However, because various task concepts have evolved over the years, early typologies are very different from today's understanding of tasks, as is the terminology. For instance, early classifications of tasks (e.g., Legutke & Thomas, 1991) in the vein of the communicative turn also designate as tasks all exercises and activities classified as such in this book.

6.4.2.1 Tasks in the Communicative Classroom In the following typology from the early 1990s, Legutke and Thomas (1991, pp. 33–34) categorise classroom tasks in the following ways:

- *Language learning tasks* aim to train and develop discrete language skills and are often denoted as (grammar, pronunciation, or vocabulary) exercises.
- *Pre-communicative tasks* aim to help and enable students to learn how to deal with different kinds of language input autonomously and produce meaningful utterances in communicative situations.
- *Communicative tasks* (*proper*) initiate learners' autonomous and meaningful use of the target language in negotiating and problem-solving processes. Meaningful content, communicative needs, and purposeful objectives are the core of these tasks.
- *Instrumental and management tasks* are used and needed to organise and manage learners' (individual or collaborative) problem-solving and working processes, activating a range of skills (self-access, social, media, or organisational).

This and other similar typologies account for the fact that in the communicative classroom, authentic, meaningful communication in the target language is the clear and significant objective. However, such typologies also acknowledge that to prepare students for autonomous communication in the real world, explicit stages of language learning and training need to be implemented in the learning process. In the history of task-based approaches (Section 6.4.3), the relation between real-world communicative tasks and pedagogical tasks was further systematised and specified. Long (2015) presents a typology of ten different pedagogical tasks, all of which serve to reduce the complexity of target tasks (i.e., those performed in the real world, outside the classroom) such as closed tasks that 'require students to find the correct solution' or convergent tasks that 'require learners to reach agreement on the solution to a problem' (Long, 2015, p. 242). Systematisations such as Long's account for the fact that tasks modelled on real-world discursive interaction need to account for learners' respective cognitive abilities and their linguistic proficiency at the respective state of language learning.

6.4.2.2 Tasks in the Literary Classroom More specific typologies that account for different domains of the language classroom, such as reading literary texts or cultural learning, have also been developed. For instance, Freitag-Hild's (2010, pp. 120–121) typology of tasks for an intercultural and transcultural approach to teaching literature classifies tasks along with their functions and purposes in terms of different ways of working with literary texts (Table 6.2). These different task types do not necessarily build upon each other but all are interrelated and can be combined to explore literary texts in different directions and for different reasons.

Numerous tasks in this typology also lend themselves to other domains of the language classroom as analysis, negotiations or reflection, or standard components of all language classrooms can serve different purposes beyond working with literary texts. It is no surprise that another typology useful for task design adopts Freitag-Hild's classification and applies it to cultural learning and diversity education. This very recent typology developed by Merse (2021) concerns cultural learning in the ELT classroom, the notion of discourse competence in general, and students' ability to participate in lesbian, gay, bisexual, transgender, and queer (LGBTQ) discourses. In such an approach, students are defined as cultural agents who engage in and learn to participate in LGBTQ discourses in ways that are specific to the language classroom. The task types of this 'queer- and diversity-oriented typology' (Merse, 2021, p. 98) are described in more detail here.

Merse's (2021) proposal is another example of a task typology that applies the classification concept of more general typologies to cultural learning, where typologies are scarce or non-existent. However, as specific as this typology

Table 6.2 *Task types for the intercultural and transcultural literature classroom*

Task types	Functions	Task formats
Tuning-in tasks	Developing and preparing the willingness to engage in intercultural encounters	Pre-reading tasks, activating or developing pre-knowledge or the reader's expectations
Self-perception tasks	A conscious perception of and reflection on one's own perspectives	Articulating, discussing, or reflecting on experiences in the reception of the literary text
Interpretation and empathy tasks	Identifying, appropriating, or co-ordinating perspectives in the literary text	While-reading tasks for character analysis and the reconstruction of characters' perspectives and character relationships
Analysis and reflection tasks	Analysis of ways of creating the fictional world	An analysis of literary devices, their meaning-making, and functional potential
Negotiation and participation tasks	Negotiating meanings and differences	Interpretative classroom discourse; exchanging and comparing cultural views, experiences, and interpretative schemata; comments
Contextualisation and transfer tasks	The contextualisation of the literary text and the constitution of relations between these and the reader	Research tasks, intertextual tasks, identifying or constituting relations to other texts, anglophone discourses, or learners' lifeworlds
Reflection tasks	Co-ordinating different perspectives, self-reflection, and reflections at a meta-level	Tasks for co-ordinating perspectives, reflections on the intercultural learning process, and the conditions and problems of intercultural learning

Note: Adapted and translated with permission from Freitag-Hild (2010, pp. 120–121). Copyright 2010 by the author.

seems, it is worth considering with respect to systematising tasks in the whole area of cultural learning and not just in queer discourses; hence, the typology may be applied not only to other diversity discourses but also to other cultural discourses such as civil rights discourses, climate change discourses, or racism discourses. As demonstrated in the task typology for literary learning, the advantage of such a domain-specific typology is that it is ideal for systematising a specific learning area in the language classroom that may otherwise be (and often is) approached in a relatively intuitive and less systematic way or is ignored.

In the context of such task typologies, it is worth reflecting on the position of the complex task discussed and presented in Section 6.5. One of its notable features is its integrative design. On the one hand, it is clearly a communicative task as it defines a communicative purpose and a specific type of meaningful discursive and social interaction as a task outcome learners accomplish through largely autonomous work. On the other hand, it accounts for the fact that some learners may need support, that grammar rules or linguistic devices need to be acquired, and that learners need to complete exercises before they can produce the pre-defined discursive and communicative outcome autonomously. Therefore, the complex task may be regarded as a task design built on various typologies, accounting for the disparate needs and purposes in the learning process and in the communicative classroom to which different types of tasks respond.

6.4.2.3 Accounting for Diversity through Tasks and Materials The discussion of task typologies would not be complete without mentioning task types that account for heterogeneity and diversity. The concepts of personalisation (Section 6.3.2) and adaptivity (Section 6.3.1) in connection with materials development aim to respond to the cultural and individual heterogeneity and diversity of contemporary classrooms. More recently, the concept of diversity has been taken up in ELT pedagogy (Banegas et al., 2021; Cirocki & Motschenbacher, 2022; Ludwig & Eisenmann, 2018; Lütge et al., 2020) as learning in general and the development of discourse competence in the language classroom must account for diversity, both as individual dispositions in the learning process and as a cultural discourse in which speakers of the English language engage. Therefore, diversity and heterogeneity are highly important aspects in the design of tasks that initiate the learning and working processes in the language classroom, which must address different individual predispositions, diverse learning preferences, and an array of abilities and talents that must be taken up and developed further.

For instance, Merse's (2021) typology of tasks strives to introduce diversity and queerness as topics in the culture classroom, using the umbrella concept of LGBTQ*, which includes intersex and any other sex or gender identity. It is worth noting that this typology was devised and enacted to support teacher education in Germany (Merse, 2021) and can therefore be regarded as a tool aimed at professionalisation and a strategy of accounting for diversity in task design as a principle. Like other typologies, it is a tool for task design, part of which is always a reflection on the functions and purposes of a specific task in the learning process and the accomplishment of objectives. Merse's (2021, pp. 98–105) proposal lists seven types of tasks for diversity learning:

- tasks for drawing learners into an LGBTIQ* topic;
- tasks for contextualising an LGBTIQ*-related topic in terms of its historical and cultural dimensions;
- tasks for LGBTIQ*-focused language enrichment;
- tasks for identifying and laying open the power of heteronormativity;

- tasks for changing one's perspective into that of an LGBTIQ* identity;
- tasks for reflection and de-centring; and
- tasks for communicative and creative follow-ups.

Applied to cultural learning and as explained and illustrated by Merse (2021), almost all these tasks are directly connected to input materials that are selected, presented, or accessed, serving the specific purpose of the respective task. For instance, when working on the task of changing one's perspective, the students access an online archive that chronicles life stories across the 'full range of the acronym LGBTIQ*; for example, by including transgender perspectives that are often rare to find' (Merse, 2021, p. 102). In that sense, and as explained in Section 6.4.2, task types serve the purpose of materials development and the selection of texts and materials; they are professional tools that support the creation and design of tasks.

6.4.3 Task-Based Language Learning

In the 1990s and 2000s, the concept of tasks in terms of initiating meaningful communication and authentic social interaction in the classroom was developed into a comprehensive and holistic approach to language teaching and learning, one designed to create learning environments that were wholly based and oriented on tasks (Nunan, 1989, 2004; van den Branden, 2006; Willis, 1996; Willis & Willis, 2007). The task concept has now become an established approach designated as task-based language learning and/or teaching (TBLT, Ahmadian & García Mayo, 2018), and in its most advanced (but also controversial) form, the entire language curriculum may be task-based.

Moreover, so many varieties of task-based teaching and learning have emerged that '"task-based" has come to be rather loosely applied as an umbrella term to refer to any context in which tasks are used' (Samuda & Bygate, 2008, p. 57). This may lead to terminological problems and the need to define in what sense the term *task* is used. In the context of this book, TBLT is defined as a comprehensive approach that focuses on using authentic language to complete meaningful tasks in the target language and defines all classroom processes (Bygate et al., 2022).

One of the varieties of TBLT, task-supported language learning (TSLL), responds to the problem addressed in Sections 6.1.1 and 6.1.2. If a coursebook is used, there is almost no space for a teacher's own decisions and alternative teaching approaches and vice versa. Adopting a comprehensive task approach leaves no room for other language teaching and learning forms, such as using a coursebook. The TSLL approach accounts for attempts to open up opportunities to use tasks in a way that recognises they are an essential component employed to structure learning, albeit not the only one (Müller-Hartmann & Schocker, 2011). In this approach, tasks may be used in addition to a coursebook or to replace a unit in a pre-defined syllabus, or they may be an extension of an activity that the coursebook offers. TSLL accounts for many (mainly institutional) language learning contexts. However, the tasks themselves manifest all features of complex tasks designed in TBLT contexts or the concept of the complex competence task, as presented in Section 6.5.

Willis' (1996) task approach may serve as an example of the task philosophy and the comprehensive character of other approaches to TBLT. This framework divides learners' work into an introductory stage called the pre-task, the task cycle at the centre of the actual working processes (individual work, pair work, group work), preparing the presentation of task outcomes in class (planning), and the presentation itself (report). In addition to focusing on the content by which the actual task is defined, Willis' model also includes an optional focus on form for language analysis and teacher-led exercises (practice). What is most intriguing about this task concept is the fundamental idea that in order for it to be completed successfully, a complex task must be translated into a process structure on the part of the teacher as well as learners.

In more recent TBLT approaches, it is widely agreed that while task outcomes are modelled on real-world interactions and the needs that can be identified for them, there is also a requirement for pedagogical tasks that can guide and support the learners in the production of target tasks (Long, 2015). In such approaches, the entire task process is organised as a task syllabus that proceeds from a needs analysis of the real-world situation and demands (e.g., a flight attendant's duties and routines before take-off) to target tasks that are directly derived from this analysis and the definition of more abstract task types that categorise and model the real-world task (e.g., service, security checks, prepare for take-off) for the classroom. Target tasks are embedded in a system of pedagogical tasks directly derived from target task types to determine what students need to learn to complete the assigned tasks. Such pedagogical tasks 'are simpler, sometimes much simpler, versions of the target task-type or of one or more of its components' and 'gradually increase in complexity ... until they reach the full complexity of the target task' (Long, 2015, p. 225; see also Section 6.4.2).

What TBLT approaches have in common is that they are oriented towards the actual cognitive and sociocultural classroom learning conditions. However, most do not conceive of learners as cultural subjects participating in cultural and social developments and processes. Therefore, in a genuine task approach, the learners' values, interests, and attitudes are crucial when planning and performing tasks. In particular, this concerns the way a task addresses thematic questions and their connectedness to lifeworld discourses, as tasks can be relevant and meaningful only if they refer to lifeworlds, to learners' real-world experiences, and to their ideas, ways of thinking, and cultural practices (Figure 6.3). These cannot be ignored because they are activated in all processes of understanding and meaning-making, as Legutke

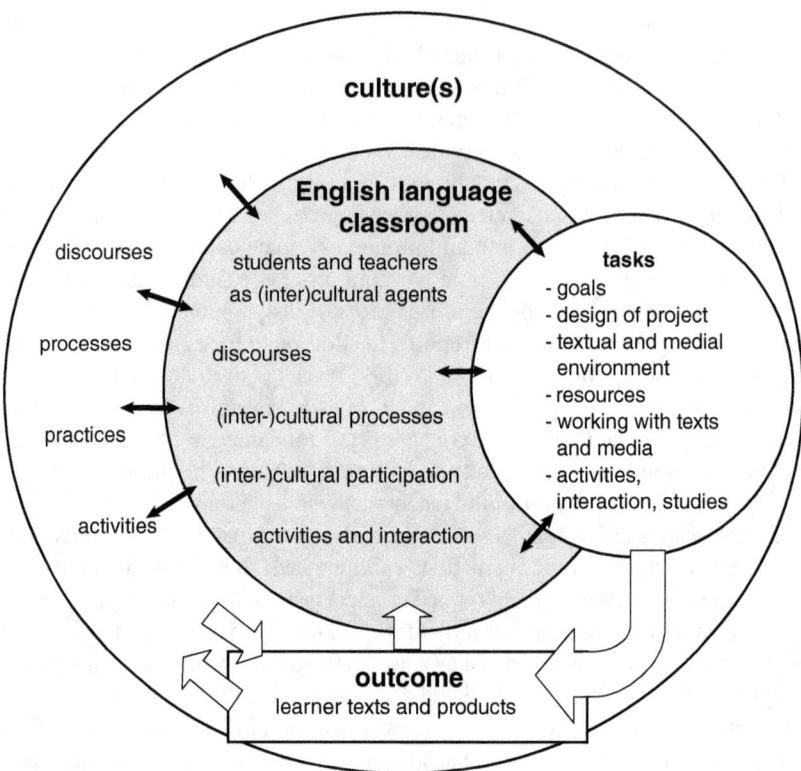

Figure 6.3 Classroom discourse and cultural discourses intertwined through tasks
Note: Reprinted with permission from Hallet (2006b, p. 77). Copyright 2006 by Narr.

and Thomas (1991, p. 61) note: 'Learners will also mobilize their views of the world, their personal values and own experience content'.

Finally, considering real-life conditions is relevant because robust, complex, and competence-developing tasks can be designed only if they are modelled on the requirements of real-life situations and problem-solving. The task model in Section 6.5 considers all these aspects and aims to integrate them into the complex competence task concept.

6.4.4 A Model for the Procedure of Task Design

Because task design is a complex professional process, the ability to engage in such a professional endeavour is anything but natural or based on intuition. Rather,

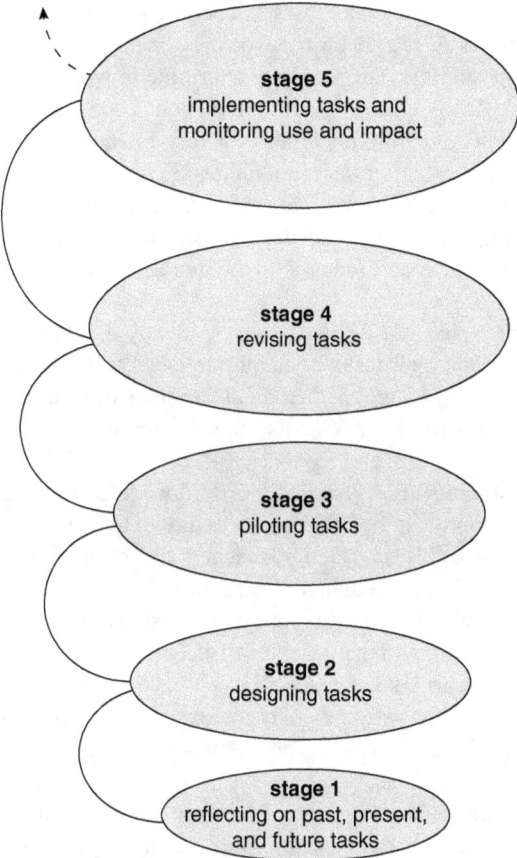

Figure 6.4 Stages of task development
Note: Reprinted with permission from Cirocki (2016, p. 208). Copyright 2016 by the author.

complex processes such as designing tasks must be operationalised and structured to make the process lucid and teachable. It is advisable to break down the entire process into steps and stages so that the complexity of the procedure is reduced and designing a task is a sequence of decisions and reflections. Especially important is the fact that a stage model runs counter to the idea that a task is drafted and then ready for classroom use. Cirocki (2016) presents a task development model as a helix (Figure 6.4) deliberately created to represent a seamless flow of transitions across all model stages. The model also stimulates a teacher's constant reflection on their teaching practices and designs (Chapter 4) and helps to build up professional expertise and develop it further, as represented in its upward form.

For instance, *Stage 1* of the model aims to encourage teachers and professional ELT communities to reflect on the weaknesses and strengths of tasks that have been used or that they are using to determine in what direction they should be developed. Along with Taggart and Wilson (2005), Cirocki (2016) proposes activating reflective thinking on three levels. First, the technical level focuses on choosing and enacting instructional tasks. At the contextual level, teachers analyse and reflect upon the theory and conceptual approaches that underpin their teaching practices. The third level, dialectical, concerns the broader sociocultural context and focuses on the moral, ethical, or sociopolitical issues implied in using a task.

Stage 2 is the actual phase of designing tasks, ideally a collaborative process where teachers create their tasks or adapt published tasks to the needs of their learners. At this level, several pedagogical variables of task design come into play, namely learner needs, task goals, input materials, task procedures, teacher roles, classroom setting, and feedback.

Stages 3 and *4* distinguish the systematic procedure of task design from a more or less intuitive approach; before actually deciding to use a task in classroom routines, it is thoroughly analysed by teachers reflecting on and answering questions that concern the challenges that a task poses, what scaffolding should be provided, or whether and in what way a task responds to learners' needs. Stage 3 is experimental in that teachers distribute a newly designed task among small groups of learners and teachers to observe and evaluate whether and to what extent they work and to display the expected effects. This evaluation must be criterion-based and systematic, employing research instruments such as questionnaires, checklists, or interviews. Stage 4 then serves to analyse the feedback and insight gained in Stage 3. Aspects and parts of a task that appear problematic in terms of content or form are modified, developed, or even replaced before a task is finalised for classroom use.

Stage 5 represents the use of a task in the classroom. As expected in such a reflective approach to task design, the processes and procedures of working with a task are constantly monitored, focusing on usability, effectiveness, and impact.

Using this model of the reflective and systematic design of tasks, it becomes evident that in the creation of tasks a teacher's professional theoretical expertise and competences culminate and materialise in practice and that task design is a constant process of reflecting upon the theory and practices of an instructor's methods of teaching.

6.5 The Complex Task: A Model and Planning Tool

While Section 6.2.4 proposed a systematic procedure for the collaborative design of tasks, this section elaborates on the actual content of a task and the various components that must be considered or anticipated when planning it.

The most general reflection and question that needs to be asked is whether and how a task develops learners' discourse competence in the English language. As explained in Section 3.1, discourse competence is a core concept of language learning. It is by no means delimited to language learning as it serves to encompass and develop all the skills (e.g., handling a phone), abilities (e.g., writing an email), and competences (e.g., contributing to an ongoing discourse) needed in social interaction to master situations and solve problems in real-world contexts. Learners are therefore expected to activate all their knowledge and abilities whenever they interact in the target language to participate in ongoing discourses and negotiate meanings in real-world contexts (Figure 6.3). This is why the task type presented here is a competence task (Section 6.5.2), not only in terms of language abilities but also in the broad sense of problem-solving, engaging in social interaction, and mastering social and interactional situations.

6.5.1 The Purpose of Task Complexity

Because the competences acquired in the language classroom serve the purpose of mastering social and interactional situations, solving problems in the real world, and participating in real ongoing discourses, the concept of competence underlying language learning needs to be broad and complex. Based on such a maxim, competence can be understood as a collection of 'cognitive skills and abilities that are available to or learnable for the individual to solve specific problems' and as 'a disposition that enables individuals to successfully solve specific types of problems' or concrete situations (Weinert, 2001, pp. 27–28, our translation).

Competences are thus always complex and multidimensional, and language learning cannot be reduced to acquiring simple abilities or skills. From this, it follows that competence tasks in the language classroom must be complex, developing all the skills, types of knowledge, and cognitive dispositions necessary for an individual's participation in lifeworld social and cultural discourses (Hallet & Legutke, 2013). Therefore, the complexity of such real-world challenges must be modelled in tasks that imitate or simulate the challenges of real-world interactive and discursive situations. The issue of complexity (Long, 2015) is therefore always directly 'connected with task demands and task support' (Cirocki, 2016, p. 114) and the features that may impact the complexity of a task which includes the number of components involved, the degree to which they differ, and whether there is a shared perspective and/or context (Long, 2015).

It becomes evident that a task that meets the demand of modelling real-life challenges will be necessarily complex. Consequently, students will not be empowered to master them if they are constantly faced with highly didactic, reductive, or simplifying demands, as is the case for numerous exercises and activities in the language classroom. Therefore, the main purpose of complex tasks is to model the complexity of real-world communication and interaction.

6.5.2 The Model of the Complex Task

The model of the complex competence task presented in Figure 6.5 represents an attempt to integrate all the elements discussed earlier in a task concept that is suited to representing the holistic and complex character of lifeworld problem-solving and situations involving social and discursive interaction. Simultaneously, it accounts for the need to structure the task process and to support learners in developing and enhancing their language skills and discourse competences.

The various components are designed to account for the double focus of complex tasks addressed earlier. Firstly, a task imitates real-world problem-solving. Secondly, it responds to the need to structure (or pre-structure) learning and working processes in the language classroom. In brief, the functions

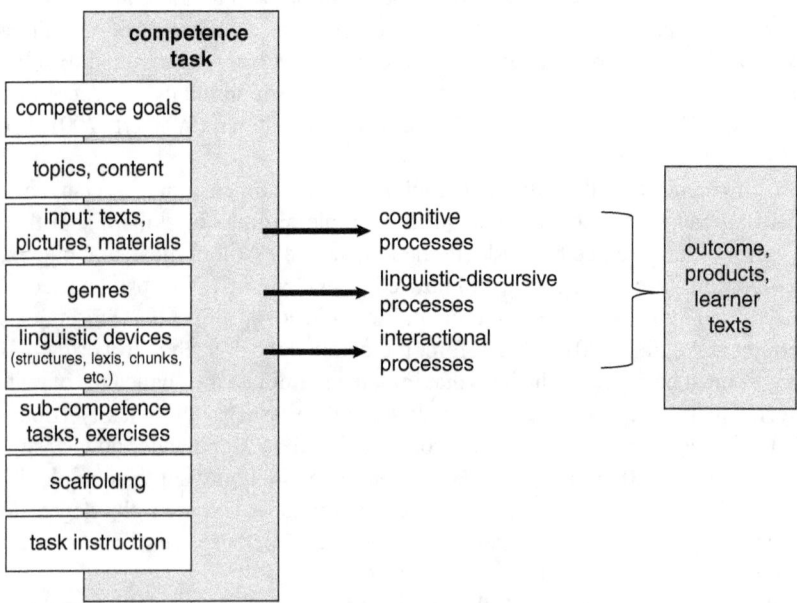

Figure 6.5 The model of the complex competence task
Note: Reprinted with permission from Hallet (2011 p. 153). Copyright 2011 by Klett Kallmeyer.

and purposes of the various components of the model (see also Hallet & Legutke, 2013) can be defined as follows:

The competence goals: These define the outcome of the students' task work in terms of the abilities and skills that are needed and acquired to engage in problem-solving and successfully master discursive interaction in the other language. They define the outcome abilities and the type of discourse that should result from the initiated cognitive, social-interactional, and language-discursive processes. Thus, the definition of the task's overarching competence goal depends on the kind of lifeworld problem or interactional situation on which the task focuses. This is why, in the complex task, competence goals reach far beyond traditional language skills. In addition, competence tasks clearly address the key aspects of cognition in terms of the targeted levels of knowledge or understanding and of language learning in terms of proficiency.

Topic and content: The complex task is characterised by an overarching topic that connects to the learners' experiential world and lifeworld discourses. The choices that are made require careful reflection and cultural knowledge on the part of a teacher or a community of practice to decide whether a topic is meaningful and relevant in society and for learners.

Input texts, images, and materials: The compilation of materials and texts represents the slice of the cultural discourse that defines the topic and the multitude of voices and medial forms of real-world discourses. This multiplicity of texts, materials, and media mirrors the complexity of the problem and the polyphony of cultural discourses and negotiations. Pedagogically, the input material forms the basis for the entire work process and the classroom discourse.

Genres: In the language classroom, the outcome product of a task is pre-defined as a type of interaction or utterance that can always be described as a genre (Hallet, 2016). Therefore, learners should be given generic models of the utterances and the texts they are expected to produce. The genres of social and communicative interaction represent language in use and give the learner a clear idea of the utterances they should produce.

Linguistic forms and devices: The concept of the competence task follows a functional approach. The linguistic forms and devices learners are expected to acquire or learn are therefore pre-determined by the goal and purposes of communication.

Sub-competence tasks, activities, and exercises: When new or difficult linguistic forms (i.e., sub-competences below the level of discourse competence) are needed to perform successfully when working with tasks, learners must be offered specific exercises and activities to help them to train, practise, and internalise the new forms. Language exercises, communicative activities, and sub-competence tasks (e.g., asking questions correctly) also help meet learners' individual needs.

Scaffolding: Regarding its *natural* complexity, scaffolding and task support must be an integral part of the complex task. Therefore, a whole support framework must be created around the learning and working process to support learners according to their needs. Scaffolding devices may range from specifically targeted input materials (e.g., images that help comprehend the verbal text) to specific tips for understanding and working with resources.

Cognitive, interactional, and discursive processes: It is essential that the concept of the task can distinguish between the different types of initiated processes and the way in which competence acquisition is attributed to them. The pertinent questions are: What should be understood and learnt (content and cognition)? In which social and interactional forms are learners supposed to work? In which linguistic-discursive or generic forms are students supposed to negotiate and communicate?

Outcome: The discursive and interactional outcome is the goal of all learning and working processes that the task initiates and also pre-defines. Everything that happens and is done while working through the task is determined by this pre-defined outcome (backward planning).

Task instruction: The task's complexity and entire work process are anticipated, described, and explained to the learners in the task instruction. This must provide the students with clear directions and tips for all elements and stages of the working process.

The components of the model are, of course, all parts of established professional routines of materials development and task design (also applied to materials and tasks in, for example, coursebooks), conducted in a systematic manner so that the components of the model can also be used as factors that can be used as checks when designing a task. However, after working with the model for some time, teachers will internalise its components and develop planning routines, automatising the various components of the model as stages in the process of designing a task.

6.5.3   The Model as a Tool for Task Design

As specified in Section 6.5.2, the complex competence task is a model in various respects (Figure 6.5). First and foremost, it provides teachers with a practical tool that helps them to define the purpose and objectives of a task in terms of the competence goals and all the components needed to enable students to accomplish the requisite objectives. As such, it is a competence model that operationalises the acquisition of the target competences, knowledge, abilities, and skills during and through the production of the expected outcome.

The model is also a process model; it represents the various stages of the task process from planning and initiating the task process (left-hand part of the model) to the actual stages of work and classroom interaction (the three components in the middle) and, finally, the presentation and publication of the pre-defined discursive and interactional outcome in generic form (the outcome component on the right).

Finally, the model is a planning tool as it serves as an instrument for task-based classroom planning by choosing themes, materials, and targeted student products in a systematic manner. It systematises and structures the process of planning the various components of a task, including selecting or creating materials, sub-competence tasks (i.e., a fill-in exercise), and the task instruction that serve to prepare, monitor, and follow up on the process of task-initiated learning and the working processes (e.g., joint construction of texts) during which learners collaborate and negotiate. To facilitate the professional design and creation of tasks and materials, systematic and functional reflection on a task by the teacher, as presented in the various components of the model, is advisable.

6.6 Assessing the Outcomes of Complex Tasks

Complex tasks revolve around lifeworld interactions and situations and also problem-solving. As explained in Section 6.5, one of the implications of this is that there is a wide, holistic concept of underlying competence so that a complete bundle of competences (e.g., linguistic proficiency, interaction, problem-solving, motivation) and skills (e.g., using communication technology) is activated and trained, as is the case in real-world situations. In institutional contexts of language learning, which are obliged to assess, test, or certify proficiency levels or the progress of language learning, this raises the problem of how learners' achievements and task outcomes – meaningful, discursive communication and interaction – can be assessed. The core problem is that established forms of testing and assessment do not account for the complexities of real-world communication and interaction and 'over-attribute value to the well-formedness of messages and to the completion of the functional acts' (Purpura, 2016, p. 4). Therefore, for complex competence tasks and task approaches in general, assessment strategies that correspond with the features of complex tasks need to be developed, but they also account for the need to develop reliable forms of assessment in institutional and curricular contexts. For more detailed information on task-based language assessment, see the overview in Norris and East (2022).

The first strategy accounts for the holistic character of tasks by creating forms of task-based language assessment 'where assessment revolves around the examinee's ability to use language meaningfully to accomplish tasks, designed as contextualised, real-world activities' (Purpura, 2016, p. 22). In such an approach, competences are drawn from 'the specific knowledge, skills, and abilities needed to accomplish the task at different performance levels' (Purpura, 2016, p. 23). The advantage of task-based assessment is that the criteria students adhere to when producing the task outcome are also those underlying the assessment, including sociocultural and interactional knowledge, communicative abilities, and technological skills.

The second strategy reduces the complexity of tasks by defining just one or two of the competences that are activated for the purpose of testing or assessment (the focus skills). For instance, if the target task is a panel discussion involving several students, individual contributions are always dialogic by nature as they depend on interlocutors' interaction, content knowledge, rhetorical abilities, and personalities. Consequently, it is extremely difficult, if not impossible, to assess an individual's abilities and contributions reliably. However, it is perfectly possible to develop an assessment task that defines a specific language skill and levels of proficiency and can therefore be employed to assess an individual's communicative competence in the context of the specific task. In the example of the panel discussion, a learner's speaking skills can be assessed by presenting them with a speaking task in which they are expected to produce an opinion statement on one of the central issues. These monologic utterances can be assessed according to pre-defined criteria such as content and knowledge and the appropriateness of the generic form of the argument (the opinion statement) and also in terms of coherence and cohesion. Accuracy and fluency are also assessment criteria – alongside others that are task-specific (e.g., familiarity with the controversial topic that is debated).

Because complex tasks always involve a bundle of competences and skills, the focus skill may be one of the planning factors from the outset. For instance, if the teacher wants or needs to account for a mandatory form of classroom-based assessment or an external exam, a pre-defined focus skill (the speaking skill in the example) may also be used to define the target task. Arguments can be produced in various written or spoken forms; if speaking skills must be tested or assessed, the language outcome defined in the task would therefore be a task developing speaking. All other skills and competences involved in the complex task would then be functional to the focus skill, for example, making notes and reading content materials. From the assessment perspective, complex tasks would therefore comprise a collection of functional skills (reading, writing, etc.) that are needed and serve to produce the linguistic and interactional outcome of the task and its focus skill, in this case, speaking.

6.7 Conclusion

To summarise, materials development and task design are professional and, preferably, collaborative practices which activate and integrate the entirety of a teacher's knowledge, competences, and reflections, as described in detail in the preceding chapters and the various sections of this chapter. Because materials and tasks define everything that happens in a classroom, particularly learners' language learning styles, materials development and task design constitute the essence of the professionalism of a teacher and a teacher community. This communal aspect needs to be considered because, as a rule, tasks must be embedded into curricular contexts and account for institutional frameworks such as classroom assessment (i.e., formatives and summatives) and externally prepared language and proficiency exams.

REFLECTION FOR ACTION

Future Teachers

- Reflect on your English language learning experiences. How would you describe the role of a coursebook from the perspective of a learner?
- Are *materials development* and *task design* integrated into your current teacher education programme? As a future teacher, are you prepared to develop materials and design tasks?
- Thinking about selecting texts and materials for your future ELT classrooms, what significant challenges do you envisage?
- Do you believe you are well prepared to work with digital materials in your future job? What immediate needs come to mind? What training would you sign up for?

Novice Teachers

- To what degree do you believe the coursebooks you currently use are effective language teaching and learning tools?
- Do you develop materials and tasks for your classrooms? What benefits have you identified so far? What challenges have you faced?
- Do you think you are well prepared to develop materials and tasks? Which competences discussed in this chapter do you need to develop further?
- Have you been engaged in collaborative materials and task development? What were the benefits? What were the challenges?

Experienced Teachers

- How would you describe the role of coursebooks and published materials in your teaching practice? Do you rely on them? Why/why not?
- Do coursebooks and published materials facilitate your students' learning processes? Are they helpful and supportive? Can you think of any disadvantages?
- To what extent do you agree that the coursebooks and other published materials you are currently using are effective tools for language teaching and learning?
- Do you find task approaches convincing? Have you ever tried to implement a task approach in your teaching? Why/why not?

7   Teaching English in the Digital Age
Professional and Cultural Intricacies

The professional challenges teachers face in the digital age are by no means new. The widespread use of personal computers and the emergence of popular worldwide electronic communication on the internet date back to the early 1990s. Since that time, schools have gradually been equipped with digital technologies and hardware, such as computer labs and laptops, as well as early educational software designed to support learning in various school subjects. However, for an extended period, digital teaching and learning were regarded as a pedagogical specialisation for which information technology experts were responsible. As a result, the digitisation of teaching and learning was not firmly established as a regular part of teacher education or ELT pedagogy until recently. It may even be assumed that the entire field of digitisation in ELT has, to date, been somewhat unstructured and that digital education is not fully implemented in the classroom as a regular dimension of teaching and learning.

However, since the 1990s, digitisation has developed at an incredible speed. It has permeated all spheres of cultural life; new, hitherto unseen, formats and technologies of communication and representation have emerged, and the mobile technology that is now used in smartphones has made it possible to access digital sources, contact other users, and disseminate digital data, messages, and artefacts at any time from and to anywhere in the world. Moreover, everybody has the capacity to produce any digital product – a blog, a video, a tweet that includes photos and video snippets – and instantly circulate it worldwide. As promising as this democratised access to and use of digital (and mobile) technologies seems, this popularisation of cultural production and dissemination has led to the worrying observation that it is becoming increasingly difficult to distinguish between reliable information and fake news and between authentic authorship and aliases (Hallet, 2020d). The most recent turn is now being discussed worldwide. Artificial Intelligence has reached a stage at which it has become complex and sometimes impossible to distinguish between human artefacts and non-human, machine-generated, texts and products. This includes photos and films that do not display reliable correspondences with empirical reality but instead may be presenting a completely realistic, albeit fictional, reality. In other words, digitisation is now such a complex cultural phenomenon that all attempts to integrate it into school education, particularly in the language classroom, are struggling with a large number of intricacies for which convincing answers must be found to develop systematic, structured, and effective pedagogical strategies and professional responses.

It appears that in light of some of the pertinent approaches in English language education, teachers are inadequately prepared for these intricacies. The substantial cultural transformations delineated earlier are rarely reflected in English language pedagogy and are not usually modelled for the language classroom. Instead, the pedagogical concepts or frameworks currently available and predominant such as computer assisted language learning or technology enhanced language learning, are relatively narrow and of the technological kind. Generally speaking, these approaches regard digital technologies as instrumental to language learning and share the following features:

- They focus on the technology or the hardware (technological infrastructure, computers, Wi-Fi).
- These concepts emerged as a general pedagogical, cross-curricular framework, irrespective of disciplinary or subject-specific purposes.
- In these approaches, language teaching and learning, content, meaning, and communication are separated or regarded as being separable from the instruments (or media) used for the transmission of information; hardware is regarded as instrumental, whereas new and culturally established digital formats of communication are often ignored.
- All these approaches regard the value of technology or media as complementary or supportive to using a language or as external to the learning process; computers and digital technologies *assist in* or *enhance* language learning, while the cultural transformations of language and communication detailed later are widely ignored.

However, because the communication of content between interlocutors in given situations and interactions is the core of language use in language education, language teachers have to be prepared to account for digital forms of communication which represent new social and discursive practices. The latter practices stress the need to define the discursive competences that teachers have to teach and learners need to learn. These cultural transformations, new discursive and social practices in the lifeworlds of whole societies, and even new ways of thinking are explored in Section 7.1. What happens in the classroom and teacher education to respond to these cultural transformations must be derived from these cultural observations.

To approach teaching digital communication in a structured manner, it is essential to reflect upon the various levels and dimensions of ELT teacher education that are affected by or need to be developed by considering the digitisation of everyday life and all domains of the lifeworld, the transformations of communication in particular. Such a systematisation is offered in Section 7.2. All these transformations raise many questions concerning the knowledge and competences associated with digitality in society and in the classroom that teachers need to acquire (Lütge, 2022; Lütge & Merse, 2021). These are addressed in Section 7.3. The pedagogical concepts that must be developed to account for the cultural digitisation in the language classroom and provide ELT students with the competences that they need to be proficient language users and agents in digital environments are described in Section 7.4.

7.1 Cultural Transformations: The Digitality of Culture and Digital Deep Structures

To avoid pedagogical discourses that continue to revolve primarily around technologies and hardware, it is crucial to at least try to understand the cultural transformations that go hand in hand with digitisation in more depth. Felix Stalder's (2016) theorisation of the sociocultural implications is one of the first and most convincing approaches employed to hypothesise that digitisation is penetrating all areas of cultural life and spheres of society and that digitality has captured and transformed our cultures in their entirety. For this reason, Stalder (2016, p. 10) speaks of the *digitality of culture*. One of the central characteristics of this digitality is the multiplication of cultural choices, which Stalder (2016, p. 11) explains as follows:

More and more people are participating in cultural processes, more and more dimensions of existence are becoming fields of cultural confrontation and social action is being embedded in increasingly complex technologies without which these processes could hardly be thought of, let alone accomplished. The number of competing cultural projects, works, points of reference and systems is growing rapidly, which in turn has triggered a worsening crisis of established forms and institutions of culture that are not geared to deal with this flood of claims to meaning.

Therefore, the educational mission of developing a digital discourse competence does not primarily relate to digital technologies. Instead, it is the ability to orientate oneself within the enormously diverse cultural choices, multiple social contexts, and enormous numbers of texts and artefacts that are circulated, to position oneself within all these masses of information, and to communicate appropriately and in a goal-oriented manner. Language teaching, the active production of texts and communication in the English language, must prepare teachers and students alike for how to orient themselves in discourses, cope with enormously vast quantities of texts, including images, recognise positions in discourses, and determine their position within them (Section 3.1). However, advancing digital technologies, apparatuses, and applications (apps) are somehow transforming the deep structures of societal, social, and individual thought and action. Stalder (2016) identifies three central forms of digitality that guide cultural ways of thinking and action.

7.1.1 Referentiality

Referentiality refers to the complex process of retrieving information, meanings, and artefacts from one cultural context to apply them in another. This adoption and reproduction of cultural artefacts is an essential feature of the numerous strategies by which individuals imprint themselves into cultural activities (Stalder, 2016, p. 13). In so doing, cultural agents 'constitute [themselves] as producers' of meaning who 'inscribe [themselves] into cultural processes' (Stalder, 2016, p. 95). The production of (new) references is a fundamental method by which people engage, separately or with others, in collectively establishing meaning (Stalder, 2016, p. 96). Translated into language education, this digital cultural practice, which materialises in the practices of sharing, forwarding, or creating memes, results in the pedagogical imperative that language teachers and learners alike have to be able to navigate vast numbers of texts and artefacts such as photos and videos and to identify discourses as thematic processes of negotiating meaning. As Stalder (2016, p. 13) puts it, 'In the context of an unmanageable mass of unstable and meaningless reference points, selecting and merging become basic acts of producing meaning and of constituting the self'. As cultural agents, teachers and their students need to determine how they wish to negotiate meanings and actively participate in a discourse with their own contributions.

7.1.2 Communality

The digitisation of all areas of life has produced new 'forms of communality that develop in the ramifications of networked life' (Stalder, 2016, p. 134). Exchange and communication within defined fields of practice (sports, religious groups, political movements, online video games) establish the frames of reference central to such communities' constitution and preservation. In these collective frameworks, meanings become fixed, choices arise with respect to action, and resources are made available (Stalder, 2016, p. 13) through a large number of communicative acts and in digital discursive interaction. Only with the assistance of digital technologies can it generate and process the required volume of tweets, emails, updates, shared images, blogs, and entries on collaborative platforms, texts, and databases (Stalder, 2016, p. 137). Therefore, to enable language learners to participate digitally, the discourse competence that is taught and learnt in the language classroom must integrate the digital channels that are circulating and producing meaning and the growing number of digital formats of communication and interaction.

7.1.3 Algorithmicity

Algorithms are machine-based methods for creating orders and valences in otherwise inaccessible vast amounts of data (such as those used by search engines to find websites – sometimes known as Big Data). They make it possible to find and use what is hidden in immeasurable large data networks and translate this into forms of information that are readily comprehensible (Small Data) (Stalder, 2016, p. 96). Algorithms are thus the prerequisite for participation in a 'culture based on digital technologies' (p. 6). However, they are highly problematic because they are power-based (Google, Amazon), create hierarchies, and are evaluative in that they 'pre-sort ... the (informational) world' (p. 96). In other words, algorithms are culturally formative.

As far as the educational mission of schools and language teaching is concerned, this is the broadest and most challenging area to work on. It can be conceived in terms of how individuals can maintain a degree of self-determination in the face of these omnipresent and extremely effective machine-based procedures and controllers of political, commercial, and social action while sustaining a self-determined life that is indispensable for authentic cultural participation. Continually reflecting on this challenging question must become an integral part of school education and *Bildung* (Section 1.3) and reflective discourses on digitisation in the language classroom.

Stalder (2016) does not contend that his description of the substantial cultural transformations is comprehensive and all-encompassing. However, new procedural ways of using available resources by referencing and re-contextualising artefacts, a new understanding and novel ways of constituting social bonds and communities, for instance, by re-defining friendship, and the machine-based operations on which cultural agents need to rely, as is the case with search engines, clearly concern almost all daily social and cultural practices. Stalder (2016) even concludes and gives evidence to suggest that these transformations that occur in the digital world and digital processes affect all that happens in the offline lifeworld. Moreover, he contends that digitality also concerns ways of treating artefacts, defining friends and friendship, and establishing algorithmic principles in everyday thinking – for example, by creating lists or samples or expressing likes and dislikes as a communicative routine.

The issue of communicative routines raises the question of why, in Stalder's theory of the digitality of culture, communication is neither thematised nor elaborated upon as one of the cultural dimensions undergoing substantial transformations. For language teacher education and the language classroom, such reflections are of paramount relevance, and therefore, the impact of digitisation on communication cannot be ignored. This is discussed in the following section.

7.1.4 Communication

As is the case with reference or communality, it seems evident that, from a cultural perspective, digitisation is not just yet another technological twist. Instead, digital communication opens up a large number of new cultural options, redefines an individual's position amid an enormous mass of meaning-making processes, and offers individuals and whole communities new channels that make it possible to share meanings and artefacts, participate in ever more meaning-making processes, and constitute social bonds and communities based on the digital exchange by communicating with others. Therefore, it is not surprising that digitisation has transformed, and is constantly transforming, ways of communicating. The formats introduced into cultural discourses, such as tweets, online comments, and online video channels, are just some new formats that have emerged from or even constitute digital environments.

One of the most fundamental cultural and social changes caused by digitisation and mobile digital devices concerns our communication concept, traditionally defined as exchanging signals between a sender and a receiver in a bounded context or situation. However, because communication and interaction have traditionally occurred in the physical world and face-to-face, the advent of digital communication, particularly its mobile version, has led to a constant bipolarity of communication, the permanent presence of interlocutors in at least two worlds, one in the physical empirical environment and the other in a distant context. As Bauman in Bauman and Lyon (2013, p. 37) puts it:

> Our life (and to a growing degree as we move from older to younger generations) is split between two universes, 'online' and 'offline', and is irreparably bi-centred. With our lives spanning two universes, each with substantive content and procedural rules of its own, we tend to deploy the same linguistic material when we move to and fro, without noticing the change of its semantic field at each crossing of the boundary. [...] Virtually every notion related to present-day life processes inevitably bears a mark of their bipolarity.

The impact of this shift to a dual communicative life, with a digital second life permanently entangled in our empirical world and our first life entangled in the second, is so fundamental that current standard communication models may have to be re-conceptualised. Instead of a simple sender–receiver relationship in a single situation or context, communication is now almost bi- or multidirectional, with a constant co-presence of at least two or even more contexts in which interlocutors communicate simultaneously. This bipolarity and the permanent challenge to contextualise what is communicated in distant situations, in particular, must be regarded as one of the most apparent communicative, interactional, and cultural problems in the digital age for which strategies must be taught and learnt in language classrooms.

Another substantial communication transformation concerns the modes of communication and the position of the alphabetic language in the broad scope of other sign languages. The multimodality of communication and discourse is not a phenomenon that is necessarily tied to digitisation. On the contrary, semiotic modes such as photographs, diagrams, and maps and their combinations in artefacts have a long tradition, not least in the layout of newspapers, magazines, brochures, and posters in print (Kress & van Leeuwen, 2001). However, the rise and popularisation of computer and electronic communication have established multimodality as a cultural and communicative normality practised by virtually all cultural agents. The design of websites, the creation of blog posts, and messaging in social media cannot possibly be imagined as relying solely on the spoken or written word. Instead, messenger and chat platforms are designed to integrate other modes, including videos and music (Lim & Tan-Chia, 2022).

These modes can be regarded as languages in their own right, as they are suited and designed to express and communicate meaning so that, for instance, the black and white wedding photograph, the interactive digital map, or the online self-video can be understood as texts. They serve very specific communicative or signifying purposes in clearly defined and bounded social and cultural contexts and employ different sign systems through which they engage in meaning-making. Furthermore, all these modes are tied to medial carriers or channels employed in each communicative situation or context according to the purpose and the addressee(s) of an utterance (Kress, 2010). If such modes are regarded as (and taught and learnt like) languages, they must also be characterised by a specific communicative efficiency and a capacity to produce meaning in a way that is specific to a particular mode and distinct from other 'languages'. This unique communicative capacity of a semiotic mode is called affordance and is why maps or diagrams are employed in everyday communication, online and offline, sometimes replacing the verbal mode, sometimes in addition to it, and sometimes in combination.

Multimodality therefore designates two ways of making meaning. The first refers to cultural discourses constituted through the combination and interplay of various semiotic modes (Kress, 2010). For instance, photographs, films, informal conversations, newspaper articles (digital and print alike), maps, and statistics may all contribute to the migration discourse. The second refers to the fact that single utterances or communicative acts (individual contributions to a discourse) may themselves be multimodal as various semiotic modes can be combined in that single communicative act. Examples of such multimodality may be a photo with a caption, a brochure with verbal text and visual images, or, as a most advanced form, the film which fully integrates moving images, spoken language, music, sound, and sometimes also written text into the single text of the film.

Thus, in the digital age, multimodality has become a general feature and principle of everyday communication and specific domains such as school education. All coursebooks in the language classroom are now highly multimodal, combining all previously mentioned modes. Unfortunately, this does not imply that the multimodality of communication is also taught. This remains a high-priority goal; hence, it is necessary to integrate the multimodality of everyday communication into language learning.

The first response to the increasing multimodality of cultural discourses and digitisation in school education – not specified for English as a foreign or second language – was developed in the 1990s and resulted in a proposal titled *Multiliteracies: Literacy Learning and the Design of Social Futures* (Cope & Kalantzis, 2000). This approach rightly argued that to enable learners to actively participate in cultural processes and shape the futures of societies, a whole range of linguistic, discursive, and medial competences (literacies) is required, as well as proficiency in the use of a variety of symbolic forms, codes, and languages. Reading and writing (traditional literacy) now also refer to electronic environments (electronic literacy) and must encompass the use of other semiotic modes such as photos and films or maps and diagrams (hence, photographic literacy, visual literacy, cartographic literacy, diagrammatic literacy, and multiliteracies). Education must therefore follow the cultural shift from the written word to other media and modes of cognition and communication. The overarching goal is to enable learners to participate in multimedial, multimodal, and multilingual exchange processes of society (Cope & Kalantzis, 2000). This shift from reading and writing to multiple literacies encompassing, for instance, photographic or diagrammatic communication and representation is further elaborated in Section 7.2, which focuses on the language classroom.

A cultural theory of digitality, including the transformations of communication elucidated previously, is one of several approaches that are needed to understand the true nature of digitisation. Based on theories of culture and explanatory models (Posner, 2004), language teaching and teacher education depend on such findings to ensure that school and language education do not fall short of these recent developments. Thus, digitisation cannot be negotiated and processed (only) at the level of technologies, suitable end devices, and the latest digital educational applications. Instead, it is essential to understand how digitisation permeates the social and personal lives of all those whose discourse abilities teachers intend to develop and enhance. If digital practices are not simultaneously understood as cultural, social, and communicative practices and as cognitive imprints, it will be difficult for the teacher to engage in learner-oriented ways of language teaching and to integrate lifeworld experiences into the classroom.

7.2 Levels of Digitisation

In view of the extreme complexity of all processes of digitisation analysed in the previous section, it is vital to define as clearly as possible the aspects or phenomena that are addressed whenever *digitisation* is thematised to clearly explore the cultural and professional challenges and the competences that language teachers need to integrate the digital dimension into the language classroom. For pedagogical discourses in teacher education, it is helpful to distinguish between six levels of digitisation as specified in the following sections.

7.2.1 The Digitisation of Information, Representation, and Communication in the Lifeworld

Digitisation causes but also results from complex global, economic, cultural, and personal exchange transformations. All these processes have undergone (and are still undergoing) fundamental changes which can briefly be summarised as globalisation, the multiplication and individualisation of cultural, ethical, or religious orientations, the multiplication of textual information and presentation (hypertextualisation), the pluralisation and acceleration of the distribution of information, and the use of a large variety of modes in acts of representation and communication, including visual, diagrammatic, and cartographic languages. As has been elucidated in Section 7.1, because digitisation principally concerns fundamental cultural and communicative practices, these must be integrated into language learning, and the English language in particular, as *the* language of worldwide communication, via the internet, as this is a forum in which learners and teachers already participate actively in their everyday lives – for example, YouTubing or gaming. Digital education must therefore be conceived as part of a larger pedagogical framework that draws upon social, cultural, and societal changes, processes, and conditions in which future generations live and which they must be able to actively design and create, as discussed in detail in the first seminal volume on multiliteracies (Cope & Kalantzis, 2000).

Because digitisation in the lifeworld concerns all domains of cultural and social interaction and communication, complemented by mobile communication devices (such as the smartphone or the spread of internet communication facilities), language teachers need to be proficient in all the digital practices of cultural communication and social interaction if they are to teach them to their students. These include:

- communicative practices in (and their extension into) digital environments such as online chats, emailing, tweeting, blogging, Instagramming, and YouTubing;
- resenting and positioning the self online in ongoing discourses;
- producing and constituting social constellations and communities (e.g., online friendship, video game communities);
- the use of digital designs of presentation and representation in private and professional contexts, characterised by the co-presence of various media and semiotic modes (images, verbal language, sound), as in electronic slides, websites, or digital photography;
- the collaborative online production of texts and artefacts on electronic platforms, fora, wikis, or shared online documents;
- the use of digital genres in communication and information such as blog entries, vlogs (or video blogs), explainer videos, formal or informal email letters, online chats, and instant messaging;
- online search for information, online research, and the retrieval of digital knowledge; and
- the use of digital genres (artefacts) of communication and representation as building blocks of discourses.

It is clear that most teachers are familiar with new and emerging digital practices and formats of exchange. In that sense, they should be well prepared to teach their students how to communicate and interact in the digital world. However, as has been demonstrated in Section 7.1, because digital practices have broader implications and cultural and cognitive effects, pedagogical decisions must be made regarding how the digitality of culture and communication can be integrated into the language classroom. In particular, strategies have to be developed to account for new and specific formats of digital communication and interaction and how competences in digital communication can be taught and acquired. Relevant suggestions are provided in Sections 7.3 and 7.4.

7.2.2 *From the Traditional Four Language Skills to Multiple Literacies*

As opposed to technology-oriented concepts, at a very early stage the multiliteracies approach (The New London Group, 2000) developed a pedagogical framework that was derived from the social and cultural changes caused by the spread of digital communication, production, and design in the domains of private lives, the world of work, and public life. The literacies concept points to the fact that an individual's capacity to pursue their happiness and participate in societal negotiations depends mainly on their ability to make meaning of signs, acquire and share knowledge, articulate thoughts, emotions, and experiences, and engage in all sorts of communicative interaction – in other words, the ability to be literate, not least when communicating in the English language.

This is why the English classroom and, more generally, digital education in terms of a personality-oriented and holistic concept of *Bildung* (Section 1.3) must account for the digital dimension of discourses in the English language and the individual's cultural, political, and social participation in lifeworld discourses. School education therefore needs to equip the students with digital competences and literacy (Walker & White, 2013; see also Section 7.4 in this volume). For the English classroom, this must be specified as digital discourse competence, which encompasses proficiency in a wide range of digital communicative genres across sign systems and languages with the main focus on verbal language (Hallet, 2014, 2016), their combination in a single act of communication (multimodality, as in electronic slides or videos), and the ability to reflect critically upon their own and others' digital practices and ways of self-constitution, social interaction, and sociality. More traditional concepts and approaches to teaching communication must be expanded beyond traditional notions of speaking and writing towards using manifold digital communicative and representational formats and genres, including new digital genres of oral communication such as the explainer video or the podcast. Section 7.4 proposes ways of conceptualising abilities beyond traditional language skills.

7.2.3 The Digitisation of Classroom Technologies

Teaching digitised communication is, of course, possible only if the classroom is also digitised. This digitisation needs to materialise in the technological equipment and the communicative or informational practices that these technologies entail. The technologies and devices, also referred to as tools, which are or should be or will be available in school classrooms and communicative classrooms in particular, encompass:

- internet access;
- electronic interactive whiteboards;
- personal computers or tablets and hand-held devices (e.g., smartphones);
- electronic teaching and learning platforms (e.g., learning management system or LMS, Moodle, Coursera); and
- clouds and other online solutions that make it possible to store and share data and materials in a safe environment.

These technologies are not directly tied to, or intrinsic to, language learning and use, not least because they also occur in content subjects and other classrooms. This is why they can be conceptualised as assisting or enhancing learning across the curriculum. However, language teachers need to be able to handle digital classroom technologies efficiently and effectively and use a digital classroom infrastructure to maximise language learning in schools.

7.2.4 The Digitisation of Language Learning

The aforementioned digital technologies are an essential precondition for any software and digital application that has been developed and designed for the purpose of digital language learning. Language teachers need to be aware of and be proficient users of diverse software and applications that are designed to support and enhance language teaching and learning (Kasemsap, 2019; Kim et al., 2019; Stockwell, 2021). These fall into three major types:

1. Digital coursebooks, digital language learning materials, and software designed for classroom use, generally at the teacher's disposal, for example, interactive whiteboard software, personal computer classroom software (e.g., computer-assisted grammar training), pedagogical tablet applications, or WebQuest software.
2. Language learning software, often commercial, designed for individual and independent learning, primarily online and with feedback or tracking options in terms of individualised levels and progress reports (increasingly also based on Artificial Intelligence), and language learning games.
3. Digital environments designed for non-pedagogical purposes and use in the medial lifeworld such as video platforms, social network platforms, blogs, or fora, all of which can be connected to the language classroom, adding to it an extremely authentic, real-world dimension, while offering the option of connecting the classroom to the lifeworld; teachers also need to be aware that nowadays their students increasingly engage in online communication and communities, partaking in activities that go hand in hand with using English as a global language. As a result, students acquire a substantial amount of language in non-institutional contexts and may be more proficient in using the English language than they appear to be. Part of a professional approach to language teaching is to account for such non-institutional and informal ways of language learning and integrate them into the classroom.

The dimension of the digitisation of the language classroom refers directly to the digitisation of cultural and social life and communication addressed earlier. In terms of education and experiential learning, this may be regarded as one of the most promising paths of digitised language learning as students will be familiar with English in such environments and may be eager to learn more quickly and systematically. Teachers need to be aware that this kind of autonomous language learning affects the way English is taught and learnt in the classroom, as students' digital ways of doing things and their communicative and social practices are almost natural to them. As a result, they may find conventional and highly didacticised ways of language learning to be unproductive, if not useless.

7.2.5 The Digitisation of Classroom Communication and Discourse

In pedagogical approaches such as the multiliteracies concept, the three domains of personal, public, and work life are defined as the relevant spheres in which cultural and communicative changes occur. However, it is evident that because digitisation changes communication in all spheres of life, it also affects the domain of education in schools and universities. In that sense, the education system represents a fourth domain of change. The digitisation of the classroom becomes manifest mainly in the growing use of electronic learning and working tools and digital classroom infrastructure. As many ways in which knowledge and experiences are accessed, retrieved, represented, circulated, shared, and acquired in the classroom are also digitised, classroom discourse as a whole is regularly taking on a digital dimension and is no longer necessarily tied to the physical presence of learners in a physical room; moreover, classroom communication and discourse no longer need to be synchronous.

As a result, language teachers must be trained to apply new forms of distance or blended learning and have to be able to design new types of classrooms, such as a virtual classroom, in which teaching and learning happen in an exclusively digital space or a flipped or inverted classroom which combines working at a distance in a non-institutional context such as home and family with teaching and learning inside a physical classroom. In such an approach, students are supposed to work autonomously, while the physical classroom and the teacher monitor, support, evaluate, and reflect upon their work and develop it further (Hallet, 2020e; Hallet et al., 2020). Therefore, teachers should be able to make productive use of and integrate digital and non-digital types of classroom discourse.

The digitisation of classroom communication and discourse leads to a wide range of other forms of access to knowledge and classroom communication that teachers have at their disposal:

- individual, mobile, and almost universal access to information and knowledge, for example, instant online verification or falsification of facts inside the physical classroom; online research by accessing online archives, online resources and sources, electronic libraries, or databases;
- collaborative online and offline creation and production of digital communicative artefacts (e.g., designing a comic, creating a video);

- the multimodality of presenting and communicating knowledge and results of classroom work (e.g., electronic slides, digital explainer videos, using electronic notice boards); and
- asynchronous and distance communication, including teacher instructions and tasks or feedback.

These new types of classroom discourse develop rapidly as electronic formats (genres) of communication and classroom discourse due to the extreme dynamics of the creation and commercial promotion of new technologies and devices, which constantly change and are transformed along with new hardware and communication technologies.

7.2.6 Reflections and Discourses on Digitisation

In a pedagogical approach to digitisation, it is crucial to enable teachers to reflect upon and research the permanent cultural and pedagogical challenges of digitisation, both in students' and teachers' lifeworlds and in anglophone cultures and societies (Chapter 4). The language classroom is an essential space for negotiations and discussions and a training ground that meets individuals' needs and supports their ability to position themselves in often controversial discourses on cultural and pedagogical digitisation (Gee & Hayes, 2011; Mansfield, 2017). Given that students are also cultural agents of digital practices and digital communication, a teacher's reflections on digitisation should always be shared and negotiated with students, not least because such reflections and cultural discourses are conducted in English. There is a whole language of digitisation as well as a technical and critical vocabulary in which those who want to participate in these discourses must be proficient. The language classroom is the pedagogical space in which teachers and students learn to reflect critically and discuss digitisation.

All the levels of digitisation addressed here require specific pedagogical concepts and responses, as well as teachers' and teacher educators' professional expertise, so digitality becomes a transversal dimension of the language classroom. The levels may serve as guidelines for integrating digitisation into teacher education systematically and define the objectives of that part of teacher education.

7.3   Teacher Digital Literacy

In most teacher education contexts, teachers' digital competences (described in detail in this section) and skills (e.g., sending an email) are not defined in a systematic manner. Therefore, to a substantial extent, teacher education cannot rely on teachers' systematically acquired digital proficiency and knowledge but only on what they have learnt informally for personal reasons and purposes. As there is now a digital dimension to all areas of school education, and the language classroom in particular (Section 7.4), strategies are required to integrate digital competence into the education of language teachers in a comprehensive manner (Nascimbeni, 2018). To systematise the knowledge and expertise teachers need to account for the digitality of culture and communication, it is necessary to reflect on and describe the competences and knowledge they need to acquire. Two primary objectives can be defined for this purpose: firstly, language teachers have to be able to move, communicate, and interact in digital environments professionally, and secondly, they have to be prepared to educate their students to communicate and interact digitally.

The most advanced concepts of the description of digital competences in a professional context were published in the context of the European Union's citizenship policy and education policy. The official documents are titled *The Digital Competence Framework for Citizens* (Carretero Gomez et al., 2017) and the *European Framework for the Digital Competence of Educators* (Punie & Redecker, 2017). These systematise the competences required to be proficient users of digital technologies in everyday life (the citizens framework) and in education (the educators framework). These frameworks are a productive and inspiring approach that can be specified for language education, where a similar approach can be applied to equip teachers and teacher educators with guidelines and foci for integrating the digital dimension of communication and representation into language education. In this section, the various competences defined in these two documents are adapted and integrated to provide a systematic framework of language teachers' digital competences.

The *Framework for Citizens* (Carretero Gomez et al., 2017, p. 11) proposes five different areas of digital competence and defines them with eight different proficiency levels and examples of use. These areas are as follows:

- *Information and data literacy* refers to practices of searching, filtering, and evaluating data, information, and digital content and the respective competences.
- *Communication and collaboration* concern the competences needed to interact, share, and collaborate digitally.
- *Digital content creation* addresses the competences in developing and re-elaborating digital content.
- *Safety* concerns protecting personal data, privacy, health, and competences.
- *Problem-solving* concerns the ability to identify and solve technical problems or to ask for support when needed.

The *European Framework for the Digital Competence of Educators* (Punie & Redecker, 2017) is a pedagogical proposal (across subjects) that profiles education and educators in the pedagogical field in terms of teachers' professional digital competences (Figure 7.1).

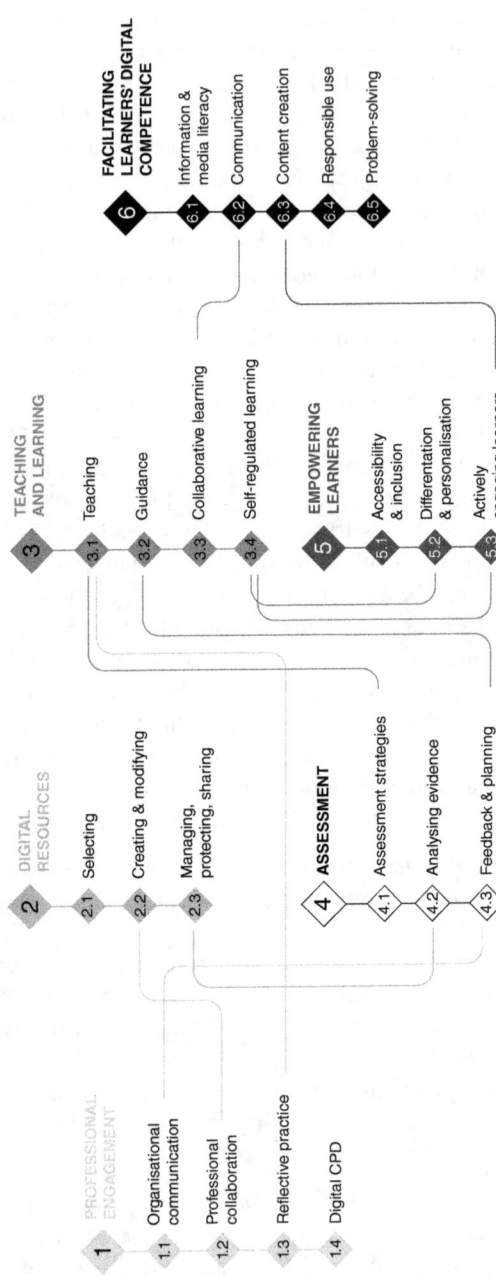

Figure 7.1 DigCompEdu – digital competences and their connections
Note: Reprinted with permission from Punie and Redecker (2017, p. 16). Copyright 2017 by Publications Office of the European Union.

This pedagogical approach presents a total of twenty-two competences and distinguishes the following six competence areas:

- *Professional engagement*: using digital technologies for communication, collaboration and professional development;
- *Digital resources*: sourcing, creating, and sharing digital resources;
- *Teaching and learning*: managing and orchestrating the use of digital technologies in teaching and learning;
- *Assessment*: using digital technologies and strategies to enhance assessment;
- *Empowering learners*: using digital technologies to enhance inclusion, personalisation, and learners' active engagement; and
- *Facilitating learners' digital competence*: enabling learners to creatively and responsibly use digital technologies for information, communication, content creation, well-being, and problem-solving (Punie & Redecker, 2017, p. 16).

Due to space constraints, the competence descriptions cannot be presented in detail. Both European Commission documents provide plausible competence descriptions and, to some extent, are self-explanatory (Lütge et al., 2021). Nevertheless, systematic categorical approaches always raise questions. For instance, why are 'communication and collaboration' defined as one competence area in the *Framework for Citizens* (Carretero Gomez et al., 2017) when the competences needed to communicate digitally or in digital environments differ considerably from those required for professional collaboration? Similarly, one could ask why *empowering learners* and *facilitating learners' digital competence* are different competence areas. After all, learners' empowerment may be defined as one of the primary goals of school and language education.

The following descriptions of language teachers' professional digital competences are a synthesis, sometimes an adaptation, and sometimes an addition to the competences proposed in the European documents. This is necessary because none of these documents is geared towards the specific requirements of language educators and language teaching. In any case, the competences based on the European documents must be adapted to the specific needs of English language education and professional language teaching, as they are designed for non-pedagogical or cross-curricular purposes. Moreover, all the competences have a dual focus: professional and pedagogical. The former concerns the teacher's professional work and contexts so that they develop the abilities that are somehow related to digital professional competences. The latter aims at the competences that a teacher needs to teach, initiate, evaluate, and assess all students' learning processes related to digitality or in which digital devices or digital artefacts are involved (pedagogical competences).

7.3.1 Competence 1: Digital Information, Resources, and Data Literacy

Professional: Language teachers need to be able to browse, search, and filter data concerning all areas of their professional expertise in language teaching and to retrieve all kinds of information and content from digital sources for their professional use and their classrooms. Retrieving information applies to more general social and cultural developments in their own and their learners' society, in anglophone societies, and other societies that are addressed in global discourses conducted in English. Evaluating these data or content and accessing the respective sources are as important as managing the retrieved data and information. Nowadays, a whole range of online resources is available for language work, including bilingual online dictionaries, monolingual collocation dictionaries or thesauruses, translation platforms (Artificial Intelligence-driven), and online encyclopaedias. Using digital resources also requires the ability to fact-check and verify digital information and knowledge (Hallet, 2020d) and manage data, for instance, to download, save, and store or process data to provide them to students.

Pedagogical: Principally speaking, teachers must be able to apply all their knowledge and digital proficiency to their classrooms by instructing their students to use digital resources and environments effectively. Students must also be enabled to use online resources for their ethnographic research (Section 4.6). One of the pedagogical precautions taken when retrieving information from digital sources is to employ critical inspection and the principle of selection and critical evaluation, making decisions as to what information and which online resources should be made accessible to the students, not only in terms of pertinent content but also in terms of cognitive, linguistic, and age-related and ethical appropriateness. Furthermore, students need to be taught how to navigate in digital environments and masses of information and texts (Section 7.1).

7.3.2 Competence 2: Digital Communication

Professional: Above all else, language teachers need to be able to use digital technologies to communicate in the language they are teaching for two purposes. In their professional contexts and networks, they need to communicate proficiently with colleagues and other members of their professional community (Chapter 9). Digital communicative competence is essential, as a lack thereof results in exclusion from these contexts and communities (Sections 3.1 and 7.4). It is also part of a language teacher's professional competence to be able to teach their students all the methods, formats, and techniques that are needed to communicate efficiently and purposefully in digital environments.

Pedagogical: Given that the overall purpose of the language classroom is to equip learners with all the competences and abilities that they need to communicate in the target language successfully, the teacher's mission is to integrate all digital options and formats of communication into the language classroom (Hallet, 2018). The methods for equipping the students with digital communicative competences and integrating them into the classroom are described in Section 7.4.

7.3.3 Competence 3: Digital Content Creation

Professional: Developing digital content is one of the core competences that language teachers need when creating their materials or tasks. When using or even publishing digital artefacts and materials online, whether for pedagogical, professional, or more personal purposes, teachers need to be aware of and evaluate copyright and licence issues. If language teachers are proficient users, they may be able to use more complex digital technologies, as is the case when they prepare lessons for the smartboard, integrating all kinds of modes of presentation such as exercises, activities, and tasks from the textbook, photos, and videos or audio files for listening comprehension. Most coursebook publishers offer such packages for digital classroom technologies. Also, part of the digital dimension of language teaching involves teachers being able to use learning and working platforms (including, e.g., online solutions such as WebQuests) where they can offer materials and tasks to their students or share them with colleagues.

In addition, teachers must be able to create digital spaces that their students can use to publish and share their work or their task products. Furthermore, teachers may also wish to demonstrate to their students how digital devices and software can be used for their creative work beyond word processing software and what the digital end product of such a work – a comic, a multimodal page in a youth magazine, or an interactive map – will look like. In particular, the multimodality of communication (Section 7.1) makes it necessary for the teacher to use multiple modes in acts of communication, from the written text and the photo to the map and the video, so that they can teach these to the students and support them in their creation of digital content (Menna, 2016). Finally, there are areas of content creation in the classroom that may require the ability to program. For instance, digital interactive storytelling, which is challenging and motivating for students (e.g., as a pre-stage to online gaming), is possible only if accessible forms of programming are applied to create an interactive, algorithmic kind of story (Nami, 2020; Raffone, 2020).

Pedagogical: All that was said about digital artefacts and the everyday use of digital technologies in Section 7.1 needs to result in creating products in the target language. In other words, learners have to be introduced to and become proficient producers of digital messages, texts, and all kinds of multimodal artefacts to participate digitally in all kinds of discourses. There is a whole world of digital artefacts that are not available in analogue communication and representation, such as animated cartoons, video clips, podcasts, and many others. Also, students must be taught how to create more complex products such as a digital youth magazine, an online application video, a blog post, or online comments.

7.3.4 Competence 4: Digital Collaboration

Professional: Language teachers need to be able to interact through digital technologies inside and outside the classroom and share data and information with their students or colleagues. They are also expected to use digital environments to engage in citizenship and position themselves online in cultural and political discourses. Online fora and platforms, including Twitter staff rooms (Eutsler et al., 2022), YouTube, and blogs, have become valuable spaces of professional collaboration where language teachers share experiences and ideas, discuss approaches and proposals, or chat informally at a more personal level. Online collaboration makes it possible to join and establish professional communities beyond one's staffroom and school (Chapter 9), encounter new ideas, exchange materials and teaching proposals, and contribute to pedagogical discourses that might otherwise not even be initiated in one's school or, more specifically, in the English language unit. The community effect in digitised societies described in Section 7.1 directly affects the constitution of ELT professional communities, as such communities do not necessarily rely on personal relations or shared physical social spaces (Section 9.4).

Pedagogical: In the digital age, collaboration as a pedagogical concept is facilitated substantially through digital technologies and through software. The pandemic era produced not only online solutions and routines of collaboration at a distance but also the knowledge of how these technologies can be implemented sustainably in the analogue classroom. As a result, students can now quickly contact other students, share, display, and publish their products (e.g., using online notice boards such as Padlet), and collaborate at a distance if needed. All these digital options have substantially expanded students' ways of collaborating and enhanced their autonomous work.

7.3.5 Competence 5: Safety and Protection in Digital Environments

Professional: All activities in digital environments require a high degree of safety awareness, as well as safety precautions and practices. This applies not only to the way hardware is handled but also to personal data and all issues of privacy, both for teachers and for their students. All online activities are particularly vulnerable as they are inevitably connected with sharing data, potentially leading to data mining, and creating more or less permanent online profiles that users cannot easily remove or manipulate.

Pedagogical: Teaching safety must be part of students' digital education and the way the teacher instructs them to use their hardware and software, access online sources, and save data for their personal use. Therefore, it may be a good idea to develop a whole set of dos and don'ts in conjunction with the students, not least to create the kind of safety awareness and the need to permanently monitor themselves that will ensure they are using safe digital spaces. Using digital technologies also concerns environmental issues, for instance, using electricity and producing as little waste as possible to reduce environmental damage.

7.3.6 Competence 6: Digital Technological Troubleshooting and Problem-Solving

Professional: Language teachers cannot be, and usually are not, information technology experts; nevertheless, to a certain degree, they should be able to solve technical problems or help their students to do so. At a minimum level of expertise, teachers need the ability to identify technical problems such as online access or installing software, communicate problems to more experienced users or experts, and respond to their solutions or proposals. It is also helpful if teachers can identify competence gaps so that more experienced users (sometimes their students!) or experts can be consulted.

Pedagogical: What has been said about teachers regarding troubleshooting and problem-solving also applies to learners. They cannot be expected to be information technology experts or to do any repair work themselves. On the contrary, it may transpire that some students do not even have the basic knowledge needed to access digital environments. Among the basics that at least some learners need to be taught are the safe creation and use of a password, using URLs properly, and how to save documents and create backups of their digital products. Inevitably, most of the routines concerning the problems of using digital technologies and solving them are not subject-specific and should therefore be a cross-curricular endeavour. One of the aspects of the modern-day heterogeneity of classrooms is the observation that there may always be some students who have developed advanced forms of digital expertise concerning hardware and software alike. Of course, it is highly desirable to integrate their expertise into the language classroom so that other students (and the teacher!) may benefit from their skills and knowledge.

7.3.7 Competence 7: Cultural Empowerment – Participation, Critical Reflection, and Content Evaluation

Professional: The notion of empowerment connects digital education to the humanistic personality-oriented principle of *Bildung* as an overarching goal of school education and the language classroom (Sections 1.3 and 3.1). Viewed negatively, the lack of digital proficiency and knowledge is bound to produce exclusion as discourse, negotiations, knowledge, and an individual's cultural or political positions are now, to a substantial extent, negotiated in digital environments. Proficient users of digital technologies can access environments, contact institutions and other individuals, and position themselves in online discourses. Therefore, it is not overly far-fetched to conclude that digitally proficient teachers are culturally empowered as they are able to access contexts and contribute actively to ongoing discourses, evaluate digital content critically, and be active cultural agents in digital environments. This kind of empowerment entails critical reflections on the cultural effects of digitisation, the attendant risks and challenges, and the value of using digital technologies.

Pedagogical: The preceding discussion about teachers' empowerment also applies to the students, not least because their empowerment is one of the prime goals of school education and language learning and should take place in a comprehensive, inclusive manner that empowers learners of all abilities and backgrounds (Conley et al., 2018). However, critical reflection and evaluation need to be taught. Proficient users of digital technologies may not often reflect, and so the school classroom is a space in which they can encounter other views, benefit from other people's experiences, and consider positions different from their own. For professional teachers, it is evident that all digital competence areas must be developed in an advanced manner and implemented in teacher education programmes (Beck, 2016; Kosnik et al., 2016). However, levels of proficiency as proposed in the European Union's citizenship framework (Carretero Gomez et al., 2017) may serve as a pedagogical guideline when decisions must be made as to how and to what extent (at what proficiency level) they educate their learners with respect to digital competences. These are described in more detail in Section 7.4, taking up the concept of literacy established to denote the competences needed to become proficient users of digital technologies.

7.4   Teaching Digital Literacy: The Languages of Digital Communication

With regard to teacher education, categorising and systematising language learners' digital skills, abilities, and competences all integrated into the pedagogical concept of literacy (OECD, 2021) are indispensable. This is important as what has been stated about language learners' discourse competence in general also applies to their digital proficiency. Proficient users have access to many discourses and a large amount of knowledge; those who are neither proficient nor trained have limited or no access.

As discussed previously, when attempts are made to systematise and define the competences and skills that must be taught in the language classroom, official documents and curricula concerning language learning may not always be helpful. For instance, it is striking that language curricula have, thus far, paid little attention to the digital dimension of everyday communication. Even in the latest version of the CEFR (Council of Europe, 2020), the concept of digitality plays no role. In particular, the descriptions of the skills ignore digital communication almost completely. All that exists is a small separate section in the chapter 'Interaction' which presents descriptors and scales for 'online interaction' in the skills areas of 'online conversation and discussion' and 'online goal-oriented transaction and collaboration' (Council of Europe, 2020, pp. 84–87). This is a remarkable finding for a language policy document that intends to model and describe language skills for the twenty-first century in a seemingly comprehensive and detailed way.

In view of what has been said about the digitisation of communication in Section 7.3, it should have become apparent to the reader that the ability to express oneself in the English language in digital forms and environments is only one of the dimensions of discourse competence. Yet there are specific abilities (e.g., retrieving information online) and competences (e.g., communicating digitally) that are needed when communicating in digital environments and which should be taught and learnt in the language classroom. Therefore, Walker and White (2013) propose to define a digital competence that accounts for the use of digital technologies efficiently in addition to the communicative competence that is acquired in the language classroom. They divide digital competence into four separate competences:

1. *Procedural competence* refers to the ability 'to manipulate the technology in terms of the hardware and applications' (Walker & White, 2013, p. 8).
2. *Socio-digital competence* is defined as the ability to understand what is suitable to employ in disparate social settings or fields of knowledge (Walker & White, 2013), for instance, when and how to communicate in social media or to write a formal email.
3. *Digital discourse competence* denotes the ability 'to manage an extended task' (Walker & White, 2013, p. 9), such as creating a digital video or other digital artefacts.
4. *Strategic competence* accounts for the need to resolve issues and further extend technological understanding and abilities (Walker & White, 2013).

It is evident that what Walker and White (2013) define as digital discourse competence lies at the core of digitising the language classroom. Also, it is necessary, as Walker and White (2013) do, to connect forms of digital discourse with traditional modes of communication such as speaking and writing. However, to entirely and more systematically integrate digital communication into language learning, it is helpful to consider the generic forms of communication in a methodical manner so that the English classroom accounts for the large number of different sign languages and semiotic modes that are now involved in discourses (Hallet, 2020f).

Following the Australian (Sydney School) genre approach (Bawarshi & Reiff, 2010; Johns, 2002), basic generic patterns of communication can be distinguished, including narratives, argumentations, and expository texts (e.g., descriptions) with inherent characteristics that can be found in all modes of communication; for instance, features of oral, written, or multimodal storytelling (as in comics or films) can be found in both analogue and digital modes of communication. In this sense, the digitality of communication is an extension that draws upon the correspondences and analogies of non-digital communication formats. Teachers can therefore facilitate and promote the learning of digital forms by connecting them to learners' awareness and knowledge of analogue genres. Digital discourse competence can then be taught by instructing learners to produce texts in the digital mode as target tasks (Table 7.1).

Such a generic approach is also useful as new and previously non-existent communication formats are constantly being created on the internet or emerge because of constant online practices. These new forms follow their conventions and have structural, textual, and social-communicative characteristics that teachers need to be aware of and teach. Genres that are already frequently used include online comments, podcasts, informative or opinion pieces in digital magazines (such as fanzines and teen magazines), digital photos, or application videos. Such digital target formats not only are ideal as target products of complex tasks which the learners develop autonomously (Section 6.5) but are also associated with the use of digital environments, tools, and applications (e.g., Book Creator for the design of digital magazines). Furthermore, a teacher and their students may decide to whom such digital creations are made accessible beyond the members of a learning group or class; for instance, digital texts of all kinds may be addressed to other members of the school community or a broader public when published online. Consequently, these products lose the character of a pedagogically defined task outcome and instead assume a high degree of personal and cultural authenticity. Using digital genres, teachers can integrate frequently used digital forms and practices of everyday communication into the language classroom.

Digital literacy, in this sense, does not refer to developing an area of competence in the language classroom that can be separated from developing learners' discourse competence. Rather, it refers to the development and acquisition of discourse skills that integrate digital forms of communication in addition to analogue ones. For this dimension of discourse competence to be developed, the specifics of digital genres, the environments in which they are produced and used, and the technical tools (hardware and software, platforms, applications) needed to produce them must be part of teaching and learning the language. Moreover, because of the overlap with and connection to the analogue

Table 7.1 Conventional and digital modes and genres of communication

Macro genre	Genre	Oral mode	Written mode	Multimodal mode	Digital mode
Expository (factual) texts	Description	**Conversation**: A new apartment	Estate agents **exposé**: A new apartment	Estate agents **brochure**: A new apartment	**Website presentation**: a new apartment
	Report	**Presentation**: Aborigines in contemporary Australia	**Written report**: Aborigines in contemporary Australia	A **wall poster**: Aborigines in contemporary Australia	A **multimedia presentation**: Aborigines in contemporary Australia
	Explanation	**Oral explanation**: How an electric bike works	**Written explanation**: How an electric bike works	**Illustrated magazine page**: How an electric bike works	An **encyclopaedic wiki text**: How an electric bike works
	Procedure	**Instruction**: How to build a paper plane	**Instruction**: How to build a paper plane	**Illustrated manual**: How to build a paper plane	**Step by step video**: How to build a paper plane
	Protocol	**Introducing rules** for new members: 10 dos and don'ts in the theatre club	**Written rules** for new members: 10 dos and don'ts in the theatre club	A **booklet** for new members: 10 dos and don'ts in the theatre club	**Social network group post**: 10 dos and don'ts in the theatre club

Note: Reprinted with permission from Hallet (2016, p. 82). Copyright 2016 by Klett Kallmeyer.

components of discourse, digital literacy is not considered a competence of its own but a regular and essential dimension of discourse competence. Therefore, language teachers must develop ways, means, and strategies to integrate the digital dimension into language learning and train learners' digital competence as part of their general literacy in the English language.

7.5 Conclusion

As has been demonstrated in this chapter, the digitality of culture and communication has led, and is constantly leading, not only to multiple transformations in terms of social, cultural, and communicative practices but also to the emergence of new cultural deep structures (e.g., communality) and substantial re-definitions of what constitutes discursive and social interaction. One of the recent and most exciting developments in the field of digital technologies could not be discussed in this chapter, namely, the rise and popularisation of Artificial Intelligence (Bashir, 2022), which directly concerns the use of languages and the production of texts (including visual images, videos, and a whole range of meaning-producing artefacts) in the language classroom in the future. The implications for the language classroom and teacher education are far-reaching (Strasser, 2021) but extremely difficult to gauge at the current stage. This means it is impossible to make reliable proposals in this emerging field. Nevertheless, Artificial Intelligence needs to be integrated gradually and efficiently into what has been described in this chapter as teachers' and learners' digital literacy.

REFLECTION FOR ACTION

Future Teachers

- Reflect on your own experiences as a language learner. To what extent was digitisation a dimension of learning in your school classroom? Were the ways of using digital technologies that you encountered efficient?
- As a future teacher, how can you prepare yourself to educate and train your students to become proficient users of digital technologies and communicate digitally competently?
- What significant challenges do you envisage when working in digital environments in the classroom? What are your priorities?
- Do you believe whether you and your students work with digital or print materials makes a substantial difference?

Novice Teachers

- How do you integrate the digital dimension of language learning into your language classroom? Do you think you are doing this in a systematic manner?
- Do you regularly develop and use digital materials and tasks for your classrooms? Have you been engaged in developing them in a collaborative manner?
- Are you teaching your students to use digital formats and genres when communicating in the target language?
- Do you think that the ways in which digitality is integrated into your classroom connect to your students' lifeworld digital practices?

Experienced Teachers

- How would you describe the role of digital materials, a digital coursebook, or digital technologies such as a smartboard in your teaching practice? Do you believe that you have developed effective routines?
- To what extent do you account for students' digital lifeworld practices in your classroom? Would you say that you do so systematically? Why/why not?
- Do you agree that digitisation has substantially changed the ways in which people communicate? In what way does the language classroom have to account for these cultural and communicative transformations?
- Do you use software or online resources to assess your students' language competences? What is your experience of these? Do you or your students benefit from such digital assessment tools?

8 Teacher Leadership
Reinforcing Professional Practice in Schools

Over the past thirty years, there has been a growing emphasis on the need for both school and teacher leadership in formulating educational policies (Harris & Muijs, 2005). Likewise, in academic literature and in schools, the association between teacher professionalism and teacher leadership has been highlighted, with teacher leaders being increasingly responsible for enhancing achievement levels, raising teaching standards, and improving the overall quality of schools (Chapter 2).

Recent debates also reveal that teacher leadership is not necessarily about formal roles or demonstrating power (Cirocki & Coombe, 2023; Maggin & Tejero Hughes, 2021). For instance, it involves teachers identifying new challenges and opportunities for growth beyond the classroom. This may involve disseminating examples of best practices, working with the community, or mentoring novice teachers, all of which contribute to fostering teacher leadership development (Danielson, 2006; Levin & Schrum, 2017; Petrie, 1995).

Like other concepts included in this volume – for instance, teacher autonomy (Chapter 5) – teacher leadership is difficult to define. There is no common conceptualisation of this notion in the field of ELT, yet teacher leadership is universally regarded as a critical aspect of school success and teacher professionalism (Danielson, 2006; Grimsæth et al., 2008; Levin & Schrum, 2017; Rizvi & Elliot, 2005). Therefore, it is essential to allow teachers to step outside their classrooms and work with others to develop leadership capacity (Dozier, 2007). Several scholars contend that teacher leadership involves undertaking formal administrative roles, whereas others assert that the tasks performed by teacher leaders are mainly informal and classroom-based (Zepeda et al., 2003). Despite this divergence of views, all generally agree the capacity for teacher leadership has not been widely explored in schools (Brubaker, 2004; Greenlee, 2007; Strike et al., 2019). This is especially the case with respect to ELT.

It is important to emphasise that this chapter defines teacher leaders by the exact nature of their school work and therefore alludes to formal and informal leadership types. All teachers have the capacity to become leaders; however, the development process must be appropriately promoted and generously supported by workplaces. Specifically, this chapter begins by defining teacher leadership and presenting a profile of a teacher leader. A discussion of the development of teacher leadership in schools follows this. This section revolves around types of leadership, types of power in leadership, and strategies for helping teachers to develop as leaders. Next, the principles of successful teacher leadership are presented. A brief discussion of leadership through mentoring teachers concludes the chapter.

8.1 Teacher Leadership and Teacher Leaders

Although it is by no means new, the notion of teacher leadership has recently acquired greater importance. Current definitions suggest that teacher leadership is context-bound and thus means different things to different teachers in different settings (Cooper et al., 2016; Cosenza, 2015; Harris & Muijs, 2003; Wenner & Campbell, 2017). Areas of divergence are apparent in the following definitions. For instance, Miller et al. (2000, p. 4) define teacher leadership as 'actions by teachers outside their classrooms that involve an explicit or implicit responsibility to provide professional development to their colleagues, to influence … policies, or … to support changes in classroom practices among teachers'. Childs-Bowen et al. (2000, p. 28) describe it as the way in which teachers 'function … in professional learning communities to affect student learning; contribute to school improvement; inspire excellence in practice; and empower stakeholders to participate in educational improvement'. According to Andrews and Crowther (2002) teacher leadership is a form of principled behaviour through which teacher leaders strive to ensure the success of the entire school. This is based on the underlying strength teaching has in widely disseminating sets of meanings among children, young people, and adults. In so doing, it has an enduring and positive impact on the standard of life in the community. York-Barr and Duke (2004, pp. 287–288) construe teacher leadership as a 'process by which teachers, individually or collectively, influence their colleagues, principals, and other members of school communities to improve teaching and learning practices with the aim of increased student learning and achievement'.

Alternatively, Katzenmeyer and Moller (2009, p. 6) define teacher leadership as a form of behaviour in which teachers lead both inside and outside the classroom, become part of and make contributions to a wider community of teacher learners and leaders, help others to enhance their pedagogical practice, and are responsible for ensuring the expected outcomes are achieved. More succinctly, Wenner and Campbell (2017, p. 140) define teacher leadership as a capacity to 'maintain … classroom-based teaching responsibilities, while also taking on leadership responsibilities outside of the classroom'.

These definitions indicate that teacher leaders need to demonstrate several competences (Figure 8.1).

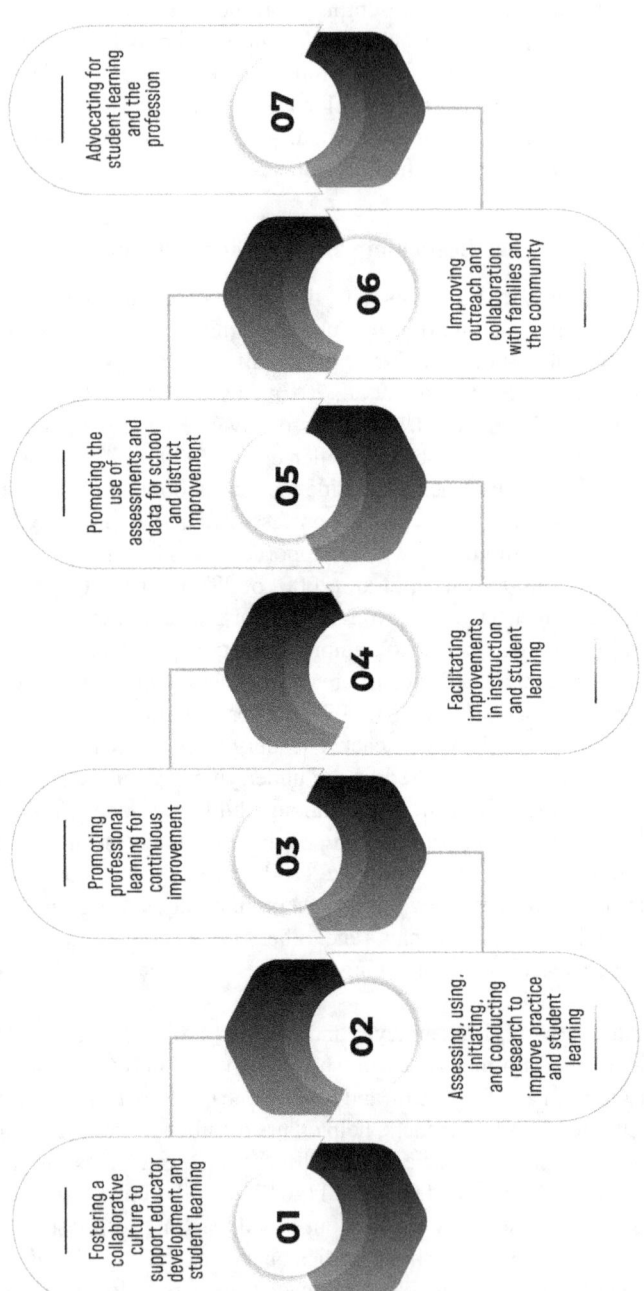

Figure 8.1 Teacher leadership competences

In line with recent literature (e.g., Benegas & Stolpestad, 2020; Cirocki & Coombe, 2023; Levin & Schrum, 2017) and the *Teacher Leader Model Standards* developed by the Teacher Leadership Exploratory Consortium (2011, p. 9; 2011, as cited in Doraiswamy et al., 2022, pp. 50–52), the competences of teacher leaders can be summarised as belonging to seven domains:

1. *Fostering a collaborative culture to support educator development and student learning*
   Teacher leaders should:
   - assist teachers in working together in problem-solving and decision-making and advocate for effective changes in teaching and learning;
   - demonstrate impactful strategies for achieving common objectives and professional learning;
   - utilise their ability to develop trust among fellow workers and promote both student and teacher learning through active practice and the promotion of ownership of their work; and
   - build a culture of inclusion that embraces diverse views and promotes meaningful engagement among colleagues.

2. *Accessing, using as well as initiating, and conducting research to improve practice and student learning*
   Teacher leaders should:
   - assist colleagues in accessing and making use of research to pinpoint techniques effective for improving student learning;
   - initiate and conduct classroom-based research projects on various aspects of the teaching–learning process;
   - create a structure for analysing data on student learning, collectively interpreting the results and applying these to enhance the teaching–learning process; and
   - assist colleagues in disseminating classroom-based data to spread knowledge and to inform and change classroom practice.

3. *Promoting professional learning for continuous improvement*
   Teacher leaders should:
   - work with fellow teachers and school administrators to design a framework of professional learning that is sustainable and collaborative and targets the needs of students;
   - utilise data on adult learning to address the diverse learning requirements of teachers by promoting distinctive modes of professional learning enhanced by the use of technology; and
   - improve instructional practice and enhance student learning by providing teachers with effective feedback.

4. *Facilitating improvements in instruction and student learning*
   Teacher leaders should:
   - create a structure for collecting, analysing, and utilising data obtained from classrooms and schools to determine how curricula, teaching, assessment, school organisation, and the school culture can be improved;
   - participate in and promote reflective dialogue with colleagues based on student work, teaching observations, and data on assessments and help to make links to productive practice based on research;
   - utilise information on established and new technologies to direct colleagues in assisting students to effectively and correctly traverse the wealth of information accessible via the internet, as well as employ social media to support collaborative learning and be able to engage with people and resources across the world; and
   - facilitate the use of pedagogical techniques that tackle diversity and equity issues within classrooms while ensuring that the central focus of teaching is to meet the individual learning requirements of students.

5. *Promoting the use of assessments and data for school and district improvement*
   Teacher leaders should:
   - enhance the ability of colleagues to locate and utilise numerous tools for assessment that comply with local, national, and international standards;
   - work with teachers in designing, implementing, scoring, and interpreting student data to enhance pedagogical practice and student learning;
   - foster an environment of trust and critical reflection (Chapter 4) on which to embark on searching discussions regarding data on student learning to resolve any problems that may emerge; and
   - collaborate with teachers in utilising assessment and data results to effect pedagogical practices or institutional framework changes to enhance student learning.

6. *Improving outreach and collaboration with families and community*
   Teacher leaders should:
   - utilise what they know and understand about diversity within the school community to facilitate meaningful engagement among co-workers, families, and the community at large;
   - enable colleagues to scrutinise their comprehension of culture and diversity in the community and the ways in which they can employ culturally sensitive techniques to enhance educational experiences and ensure high standards of learning for all students;
   - create a shared understanding among co-workers of the diverse educational requirements of families and the wider community; and

- work alongside families, communities, and colleagues to create all-encompassing methods that meet the diverse educational requirements of families and the community at large.

7. *Advocating for student learning and the profession*
   Teacher leaders should:
   - disseminate data to teachers within and/or beyond the school concerning how patterns and policies may affect pedagogical practices, as well as expectations with respect to student learning;
   - collaborate with colleagues to pinpoint and utilise research to promote teaching and learning activities that address the needs of every student;
   - facilitate access to financial support, along with human and material resources, so that teachers can engage in extensive learning regarding useful practices; and
   - establish professional development communities (Chapter 9) to improve teaching and learning processes within schools.

These competences correspond closely with Danielson's (2006) dispositions of teacher leaders. These include:

- deep commitment to student learning;
- optimism and enthusiasm;
- open-mindedness and humility;
- courage and a willingness to take risks;
- confidence and decisiveness;
- tolerance of ambiguity;
- creativity and flexibility;
- perseverance; and
- willingness to work hard.

Three principal conclusions can be drawn from this discussion. Firstly, teacher leadership addresses disparate 'forms of empowerment and agency' (Harris, 2003, p. 316) and is thus believed to comprise three principal tasks. According to Katzenmeyer and Moller (2009) these are (1) *leadership of students or other teachers* (e.g., facilitator, coach, mentor, trainer, curriculum specialist), (2) *leadership of operational tasks* (e.g., maintaining good organisation of the school and striving to achieve targets through their roles as an action researcher or task force member), and (3) *leadership through decision-making or partnership* (e.g., membership of school improvement teams, committees, or parent–teacher associations). Secondly, teacher leadership is a complex task driven by the beliefs, personality, and experiences of teachers and the occupational environment (Ackerman & Mackenzie, 2007; Katzenmeyer & Moller, 2009; Savage & Savage, 2010). Finally, workplaces are venues where leaders, followers, and circumstances are intrinsically bound up with individual, social, and organisational processes. They are places where leaders and followers have the capacity to change how they behave, and each situation will have its idiosyncratic requirements. Therefore, it is difficult and demanding to be a leader. Leaders must be able to assess the circumstances correctly and their followers to identify and implement the leadership style that will yield optimal outcomes.

8.2 Fostering Teacher Leadership in Schools

Teacher leaders are needed in schools as the functions of the schools are continually altering. A school is no longer a step towards a job; it now plays a vital role in enabling young people to become informed and active members of wider society. This means that schools must rapidly adapt to a continually changing world. Moreover, teacher leaders are urgently required due to the myriad roles principals are expected to fulfil (e.g., delivering pedagogical leadership, maintaining the school site, engaging with the wider community and the political, social, economic, and cultural milieu) (Danielson, 2007). In a role that requires them to be innovative thinkers, effective managers, and pedagogical leaders, they must work alongside teachers to ensure that schools operate effectively and autonomously. Finally, it is important to remember that school leaders are human, and there are limits to their abilities and skills. Thus, the requirement is for teacher leaders or 'teacherpreneurs' (Bell et al., 2011; Berry et al., 2013, p. xvii), who are skilled, charming, inspirational, effectual, and empowering, to build a platform on which students can achieve academic success and to nurture leadership in their colleagues.

There are several indicators of readiness for teacher leadership. Such teachers are expected to:

- have developed a clear philosophy of teaching and a broad outlook on the school they work for;
- have begun to offer peers (e.g., teachers, administrators) valuable opinions, advice, and guidance;
- have begun to actively participate in school meetings and CPD events within and beyond the school;
- have begun volunteering for leadership roles (e.g., establishing student discipline procedures);
- take creative risks while teaching (e.g., experimenting with new technology);
- exhibit confidence and not hesitate to act on their beliefs, values, dispositions, and principles;
- handle crises well;
- seek more responsibility and authority to empower others;
- motivate colleagues to become more skilled and thoughtful regarding their work;

- inspire and encourage peers to overcome challenges; and
- mobilise teacher colleagues to improve the performance of schools through their crucial teaching and learning responsibilities.

Having identified these practitioners, it is vital for schools to invest in their development. The process through which classroom practitioners transform into teacher leaders is unique and depends on various factors (e.g., school culture, teacher personality, teacher personal life, school support, school philosophy), making the process organic for some and encouraged or strategically led for others. It is therefore recommended that teachers are wholeheartedly supported on their leadership journeys and are provided with frequent opportunities to engage in different types of leadership.

8.2.1 Types of Leadership

There are different methods of achieving teacher leadership; however, discussing them all is beyond the scope of this chapter. The following discussion therefore focuses on six types of leadership – formal, informal, hybrid, instructional, policy, and association – teachers are encouraged to engage with on their journey to becoming successful leaders.

Teachers generally take on two fundamental leadership roles: formal and informal (Ackerman & Mackenzie, 2007; Hunzicker, 2018; Zepeda et al., 2003). *Formal leadership* refers to roles such as lead teachers or co-ordinators allocated and overseen by school principals. It can also include roles without any specific title, such as serving on a school committee or acting as a mentor to a less experienced teacher. By contrast, *informal leadership* refers to teachers spontaneously deciding to tackle a particular issue not part of a designated role, such as disseminating knowledge and experience with colleagues, engaging in professional development, or participating in community events.

It is also possible for teachers to engage in both types of leadership, commonly referred to as *hybrid leadership*. In addition to everyday teaching responsibilities, this can involve mentoring colleagues by sharing useful resources, offering feedback on lesson plans, and observing the classes they teach (Barnwell, 2015). This is a valuable role as it enables them to '[bring] together school and university-based teacher educators and practitioner and academic knowledge in new ways to enhance the learning of prospective teachers' (Zeichner, 2010, p. 486).

Instructional leadership refers to engagement with the processes that shape teaching and learning. This could involve setting up a reading club or reviewing and assessing textbooks and associated materials when deciding which books to adopt for a particular course (Zepeda et al., 2003). It is therefore important to emphasise that this type of leadership goes beyond the need to be an outstanding teacher. To be effective, such leaders need to share best practices with their colleagues to benefit all students rather than just those they teach directly. Timperley's (2011) view of instructional leadership is that it has a moral underpinning in that it seeks to advance professional inquiry, build trusting relationships, promote deep student learning, and identify instances of evidence in action.

Policy leadership is exhibited by teachers who are prepared to form and enact policies to enhance the teaching–learning process. Their value lies in implementing pedagogical policies directly and providing the crucial insider's perspective from classrooms. This helps generate robust and effective norms and regulations to support student learning. Such policy decisions can have instant ramifications for the way in which classroom practice is improved (Center for Teaching Quality, National Board for Professional Teaching Standards, & the National Education Association, 2014).

The final form of leadership is *association leadership*, which refers to developing and shaping meaningful and robust collaborative action within and across schools. Such leaders guide the activities of collective groups of students, teachers, or a combination of the two along the path towards the required change. This involves forging close links with administrators and other important stakeholders to develop effective policies to ensure high-quality pedagogical practice (Center for Teaching Quality, National Board for Professional Teaching Standards, & the National Education Association, 2014). Among other tasks, this could entail sharing best practices within and across schools or taking the lead in promoting lesson study sessions (Section 4.5).

8.2.2 Types of Power

As discussed previously, successful teacher leadership requires power to be redistributed from principals to teachers (Levin & Schrum, 2017; Muijs & Harris, 2006). Through such power, teacher leaders are able to 'influence their colleagues and often assist in making changes in practices at the classroom and school levels' (Katzenmeyer & Moller, 2009, p. 102). As the literature reveals (Hersey et al., 1979; Raven & Kruglanski, 1970; Savage & Savage, 2010; Zepeda et al., 2003), the most common forms of power (Figure 8.2) leaders have at their disposal include the following:

- *expert power* – a teacher leader is perceived to have a high level of knowledge or a specific skill set that others do not possess;
- *referent power* – a teacher leader is able to shape what their followers do as a result of their appreciation, regard, or identification with the leader;
- *connection power* – a teacher leader is perceived to have influential connections within and outside the school;
- *informational power* – a teacher leader is perceived to have control of the information other teachers need or want;

Figure 8.2 The power of teacher leaders

- *legitimate power* – a teacher leader is perceived as having a formal right to make specific demands and to expect those following to comply and obey; and
- *reward power* – a teacher leader employs rewards to ensure their instructions or orders are adhered to; their power thus resides in their ability to withhold such rewards.

Power therefore plays an extremely important role in teacher leadership and is essential in ensuring goals at every level – individual, team, and institution – are achieved. Such leaders must be able to inspire others to produce their optimal performance, their superiors and colleagues to make crucial decisions, and stakeholders to maintain the strength and vigour of the school. However, an overzealous use of power may harm working relationships and damage their status as professionals.

8.2.3   Helping Teachers to Develop as Leaders

The literature reveals that teachers increasingly take on formal and informal leadership roles (Danielson, 2006; Katzenmeyer & Moller, 2009; Krovetz & Arriaza, 2006; Levin & Schrum, 2017). However, schools must provide teachers with generous and continued support to succeed as leaders. This could include creating a leadership-dense school culture, promoting collaborative leadership, and offering effective professional development regarding teacher leadership. Each of these is now addressed in turn.

The first form of support is creating a leadership-dense school culture. Within such schools, administration teams need to be established that are enthusiastic and prepared to share power with instructors and possess the requisite abilities and characteristics to nurture teacher leaders. Furthermore, a detailed conceptualisation and effective method for promoting teacher leadership is required, which teachers themselves play an active part in creating. Moreover, it is essential for schools to ensure teachers are given the opportunity to learn and lead so that they can disseminate their expertise and enhance student performance.

Schools that promote teacher leadership must therefore forge an environment where all teachers are invited to take on formal and informal leadership positions. In addition to its principal focus on the teaching–learning process, teacher leadership in schools should also promote job-embedded professional learning, which encompasses several different aspects of leadership (Krovetz & Arriaza, 2006). The leadership initiatives schools support should also nurture the building of trust, risk-taking, accountability, and an ability to adapt to, as well as initiate and foster, change and development, all of which are essential traits of a skilled leader.

Creating an effective environment that fosters and promotes successful collaborative leadership is an extremely difficult (but not impossible) undertaking for school management teams. In the educational climate of the twenty-first century, teacher leaders must exhibit an extensive suite of skills and competences (Section 8.1), be responsible for leading disparate teams, nurture the development of various stakeholders within the school community, and strive to ensure productive, inclusive, and real-world collaboration among teachers, students, administrators, and parents. It is thus imperative for schools to ensure teachers are given as many opportunities as possible to lead projects and activities that are collaborative in nature, such as dealing with problems within the school or external promotion of the school. This form of leadership can have multiple benefits as it involves the utilisation of collective intelligence. This is predicated on the notion that members of the school community are cleverer, more innovative, and more capable together than they are alone. Regarding their nature and focus, some projects will be only for teachers, while others will be for teachers and students. Some will be highly formal (e.g., designing a set of electronic English language tests for a specific grade) and have a substantial effect on the teaching–learning process. In contrast, others will be informal and enjoyable (e.g., designing a newsletter for prospective students).

Table 8.1 presents an example of a collaborative project prepared with a teacher leader in mind. It demonstrates how a teacher leader can build and lead a team around their project, converting their ideas into reality. This consists of three major processes: recruiting the right team, coaching team members, and managing their performance. It is important to emphasise that motivation and critical reflection form an inevitable part of coaching and managing

Table 8.1 *Designing a welcome newsletter for prospective students: a collaborative project*

	Stages	Activities
1.	Attracting the right team	Consider: – involving teachers, students, administrators, and parents
2.	Introducing the project and motivating the team	Consider: – presenting the project to the team in detail, including its aims, scope, stages, and deadlines – discussing intrinsic/extrinsic rewards, the value and recognition of the project – creating a sense of community and belonging
3.	Delegating effectively	Consider: – checking the experience, knowledge, and skills of individual team members – discussing their preferred work style – checking the current workload of team members – delegating tasks and providing adequate support – being available to answer questions
4.	Preparing the team for performance	Consider: – clarifying what you want to achieve – allowing individual team members to lay out their tasks as they see them – encouraging individual team members to explore a range of options and choose the most sensible way forward – helping individual team members to identify/prepare for obstacles and deal with them in advance – checking individual team members' understanding of their tasks
5.	Monitoring performance	Consider: – monitoring the work of the individual team members – checking individual members' progress – motivating individual team members – providing adequate support – being available to answer questions
6.	Submitting and reflecting on first drafts	Consider: – reflecting on tasks with individual team members – inviting the entire team to reflect on the individual tasks – providing detailed feedback on the tasks – clarifying the revision process with the individual team members – checking individual team members' understanding of their tasks
7.	Revising first drafts	Consider: – monitoring the work of individual team members – checking individual members' progress – motivating individual team members – providing adequate support – being available to answer questions

Table 8.1 (*cont.*)

Stages	Activities
8. Resubmitting and reflecting on first drafts	Consider: – reflecting on resubmitted tasks with individual team members – inviting the entire team to reflect on the resubmitted tasks – providing detailed feedback on the revised tasks If needed: – clarify the revision process with individual team members – check individual team members' understanding of their tasks
9. Finalising the project	Consider: – discussing the layout of the newsletter with the entire team – negotiating the final version of the layout – discussing the graphic design with the entire team – negotiating the final version of the graphic design with the entire team – printing the newsletter for review
10. Participating in post-project reflection	Consider: – reflecting on the process of designing the newsletter with the entire group – discussing the advantages and disadvantages of teamwork – analysing the lessons learnt – reflecting for future action – completing a feedback form assessing the leader's performance – planning a new project

performance. The Activities column provides valuable guidelines for a teacher leader with regard to planning and executing the individual stages of the project.

While working in collaborative environments, teacher leaders must ensure that:

- the available information, skills, and talents are widely shared;
- broadly defined diversity is greatly appreciated;
- decisions are made by the entire team, either through consensus or co-creation;
- all members actively participate in teamwork and take responsibility for the effective functioning of the group; and
- all members work with a view to contributing to the school's success and are aware that this success depends on creating an environment of trust, mutual respect, and shared aspiration.

Thus, to develop collaborative leadership in schools, teacher leaders need to concentrate on the relationships among participants, the outcomes, and the importance of social interaction in facilitating collaborative leadership (Sections 9.1 and 9.2).

The final form of support is professional development. As discussed previously, all teachers have the ability to take on numerous roles to improve schools. However, this needs to be facilitated through ongoing professional development (Cirocki et al., 2023). Events that schools can provide to support this include taking part in collaborative tasks that involve serving as an appropriate role model, offering helpful feedback, providing mutual encouragement, and engaging in critical reflection. It is therefore paramount to motivate teachers to partake in quality training that delivers a broad suite of leadership experiences and provides recommendations regarding particular sectors of professional practice in which they can lead or mentor others to do so. Therefore, to ensure teachers are fully prepared for such roles and to develop an effective and clear plan for leadership, such training should focus on the following:

- **Teacher learning**
  Learning is a social phenomenon within social relationships (Lantolf, 2000; Johnson, 2009). Teachers learn how to teach by watching knowledgeable others engage in instructional practice. Through a process of mutual engagement, teachers are supported in their learning while also supporting others.
- **Effective instruction**
  Multiple components of instructional practice mutually augment one another. This is an intricate process based on the belief that students are motivated to learn when they are in an environment in which they feel safe, understand the purpose and importance of learning, are given chances to practise, are given lucid feedback, and undertake complex, purposeful thinking (Harmer, 2007; Scrivener, 2011; Ur, 2012). Teachers need to understand the nature of this process and ensure their knowledge of teaching is continually kept up to date by utilising educational technology that can optimise the learning experience for students.
- **Accurate assessment**
  One of the most essential elements of the teaching–learning process is assessment. Well-designed and containing formative and summative elements, assessment can stimulate learning, provide students with appropriate guidance, and assess their progress (Al-Mahrooqi et al., 2017; Brown & Abeywickrama, 2018; Cheng & Fox, 2017). Carried out often enough, it also enables practitioners to evaluate the effectiveness of their teaching. Schools must therefore establish rigorous assessment procedures that generate valid and reliable data. This involves taking part in ongoing discussions on assessment in which significant decisions are made with respect to the purposes

of different assessment tools and how the data produced are used, how such data shapes decisions regarding the teaching–learning process, and issues pertaining to workload and marking consistency.

- **Reward systems for teacher accomplishments**
Teachers should be rewarded for excellent work and the particular roles they take on both inside and outside schools. Allocating such rewards is usually based on clearly specified criteria, such as outstanding performance, length of service, or achievements in a team. Establishing an effective reward system will motivate teachers to develop and accomplish new goals; it also helps establish a school environment centred on growth (Andrews, 2006; OECD, 2009). To enhance their efficacy, an effective monitoring system needs to be put in place.

- **Teacher autonomy**
Teachers need to be motivated to exhibit autonomy (Chapter 5) in both their teaching and their professional learning. To ensure they are able to determine their instructional practice and make knowledgeable decisions regarding their participation in professional development events, teachers need to be taught a diverse range of strategies they can draw on. The development of teacher autonomy requires a high level of skill and commitment. Therefore, teacher leaders must understand what it means to be autonomous learners; they must be able to utilise their professional knowledge in an autonomous manner and be trained to generate and exhibit an array of autonomous practices in schools (Little, 2007).

- **Teacher reflection**
To develop novel insights into themselves, their instructional practices, and their teaching careers, teachers need to be motivated to reflect and learn from their experiences. Such reflection can take multiple forms and be documented using various tools (Section 4.5); it involves critiquing, generating alternatives, and reshaping instructional practices. To enhance teaching and increase confidence among practitioners, schools are advised to adopt a critical friendship approach (Gonzalez Smith, 2019; Farrell, 2008b). This will facilitate more profound self-evaluation and practical thinking, support the development of collaborative pedagogical practices, increase knowledge, and create spaces in which difficult questions can be asked with respect to teaching practices within and across schools (Costa & Kallick, 1993; Schuck & Russell, 2005; Farrell, 2001) and the potential for reframing such practices where necessary.

- **Collegiality**
Collegiality alludes to the nature of the relationships between professional colleagues and the extent to which they are encouraged to feel they are part of a wider community in which everyone's contribution has value, suggestions can be exchanged and discussed, and there is a collective responsibility

for ensuring that shared objectives are met (Gappa et al., 2007; Hoerr, 2005). Collaborative activities among teachers concentrate on enhancing the learning/development of students, developing and implementing creative school initiatives, participating in collaborative action research, and establishing inclusive classrooms. Collegiality can be expressed through the exchange of instructional materials, peer observations, or reflective discussions on lessons (planned and taught). This is essential in providing teachers with moral support, enhancing their effectiveness, raising levels of pedagogical reflection, and establishing a programme of ongoing professional learning. It is therefore essential to encourage strong collegiality.

- **Honest communication**
Irrespective of whether communication occurs between teachers, students, teachers and students, or teachers and parents, effective communication skills are essential (Dempster & Robbins, 2017; Kowalski, 2015). For relationships in schools to remain productive, open, and stress-free, teachers and administrators must be transparent in how they convey and receive information and be fully informed about what is taking place within schools. Based on an established communication etiquette, opinions and feelings can be readily and comfortably shared. This will promote inclusion and loyalty and increase levels of engagement among all members of the school community. Schools should therefore consider honest communication a key priority.

- **Diversity, equity, and inclusion**
Three values – diversity, equity, and inclusion – are crucial to define workplace environments in the twenty-first century. Such environments are desirable because they support individuals from all walks of life, enabling them to bring their whole selves to the workplace and feel valued and respected. Diversity is about who is represented in the workforce (e.g., gender, age, ethnicity, physical ability). Equity denotes just practices, equal opportunities, and fair treatment for all, considering individuals' unique circumstances. Inclusion is about embracing all individuals and creating non-discriminatory conditions for all to thrive. As these three values are closely linked, education leaders are expected to implement them in schools to build sustainable cultures (Marques & Dhiman, 2022; Netolicky, 2022). These cultures should not only offer their members a sense of belonging and a voice but also benefit from permanent and transient individual differences (i.e., skills, values, emotions) within them.

- **Friendly environment**
To facilitate personal and professional growth, dedication, trust, respect, high levels of achievement, and happiness, the working environment needs to be both friendly and positive (Massey, 2012; Norton Scott, 2008). This increases the morale of teams and fosters active and productive collaboration. Effective and supportive working environments are those in which

management teams are cognisant of the school culture as a whole, promoting the growth of all members and ensuring they feel respected and cared for. Thus, methods for establishing a friendly environment need to be developed and reviewed on a regular basis.

Teacher leaders must perceive the development of leadership as ongoing. They should view themselves as lifelong learners with a strong desire to acquire additional information and new skills while acknowledging that it will never be possible to know everything. As such, teachers permit themselves to become experts in specific fields. Thus, by encouraging colleagues to engage in novel modes of thinking and explicitly asking for advice, strategic leaders enable colleagues to share their thoughts and suggestions. In addition, teacher leaders must also be principled, as discussed in the following section.

8.2.4 Five Principles of Successful Teacher Leadership

In the contemporary educational environment, schools look for principled leaders who clearly articulate their values, make decisions guided by these values, engage in critical reflection (Chapter 4), and take account of ethical considerations (Dantley, 2003, 2008), all while adhering to existing professional standards in their schools. This section discusses five principles successful teacher leaders are expected to follow. At an individual level, these principles guide teacher leaders in influencing, engaging, and encouraging their school community to act towards common goals. At a team level, they drive the entire community towards success.

8.2.4.1 Leadership Is about Behaviour and Dispositions Leadership does not refer to positions or titles; it is a group of behaviours and dispositions teacher leaders are expected to exhibit. For instance, before they can lead others, they must be able to manage themselves. Before taking on leadership roles, teacher leaders will have been assessed based on their attitudes, behaviours, and the actions they take (or have taken). The traits perceived as most desirable among teacher leaders include altruism, perceptiveness, the ability to support others, integrity, empathy, approachability, fairness, resourcefulness, and decisiveness (Gabriel, 2005).

8.2.4.2 Leadership Is about Pursuing a Vision The primary focus of teacher leaders should be on a long-term and measurable vision. This should be one they are able to clearly define, which forms the basis for a strategic plan for the school and is communicated to followers in a manner that motivates them to achieve shared objectives (Bell et al., 2011). A workable vision should thus be derived from teacher leaders' past experiences, look towards the future, and handle the everyday reality of school life. Vision is thus vital because it motivates followers to act and progress. Thus, from the outset, followers should be involved in helping leaders to develop their vision. This enables it to be reshaped and reformulated while team members make productive contributions towards achieving the set targets. If they have a sound understanding of what to do to attain this vision, along with a sense of when, how, and why, they will feel motivated to embark on their learning journeys with a clear sense of purpose.

8.2.4.3 Leadership Is about People Leadership involves enabling peer teachers and students to attain their maximum potential. To realise this goal, they must be supplied with the tools and methods needed to optimise the success of the school and enhance both their personal and professional lives (Danielson, 2006; Katzenmeyer & Moller, 2009; Zepeda et al., 2003). Through leadership that is people-oriented, teacher leaders can establish a learning culture that motivates and engages both teachers and students and ensures they feel both valued and respected. Given that motivation is what drives individuals to success, it is important that teacher leaders:

- show they care for all members of the learning culture;
- have a clear vision for each member's development;
- delegate work appropriately to increase the trust and commitment of their followers;
- recognise the efforts and achievements of their followers;
- inspire mutual trust between themselves and their followers; and
- set clear expectations that inspire excellence in their followers.

8.2.4.4 Leadership Is about Influence One of the most critical skills teacher leaders must possess is to be able to influence others, for example, teachers, students, administrators, or parents (Bond, 2015). To exert such influence requires them to have a direct or indirect effect on the behaviours, attitudes, and choices made by others. Unlike power and control, influencing involves identifying the factors that stimulate teacher commitment and applying this to enhance performance and generate positive outcomes (Katzenmeyer & Moller, 2009).

There are several ways in which teacher leaders can exert influence within the school community, three of which are now discussed here (Bond, 2015). Firstly, *strategic influence* refers to the long-term holistic exertion of influence over a diverse array of people, the majority of whom possess little authority. This could include convincing these people of the utility of a specific proposal to engender authentic commitment rather than mere compliance or even resistance. The initial fuel for this process occurs when teacher leaders establish moral goals that transform ideals into action plans. By drawing on a collection of values and a shared language, they can formulate and contextualise their vision in a manner others can readily subscribe to (Davies & Davies, 2010).

To obtain the support of particular people for specific purposes, teacher leaders can also employ *tactical influence* (Cohen & Bradford, 2005; Stanford, 2019), which can include proactive behaviour (i.e., taking the lead on an important issue and rallying others to the cause) and reciprocity (i.e., doing favours for others in anticipation that they will be returned).

Finally, *reverse psychology* can be exerted by teacher leaders. This involves expressing beliefs opposite to what is desired to provoke followers to adopt the desired behaviour (Woods, 2020).

8.2.4.5 Leadership Is about Transformation Teacher leadership directly impacts on the success of schools. As crucial agents of change, teacher leaders can be characterised as teacherpreneurs who can inspire and encourage members of the school community to make changes that will ensure schools become fairer, more sustainable, and more successful. Through collaboration with followers, teacher leaders can engender a shift in school culture from one predicated on self-interest to one where collective efforts towards a common good are afforded priority and buttressed by collaboration, transparent communication, and legitimacy. To enact pedagogical change (e.g., blended learning courses) and thus impact students and teachers throughout schools necessitates critical reflection on existing theory, research, and practice in the field of education. It also requires teacher leaders to be willing to employ their skills and networks to devise out-of-the-box solutions.

For teacherpreneurs, the teaching–learning process is transformative in nature, the purpose being to promote positive changes in students' lives. This ensures that teacher leaders do not simply limit themselves to imparting information to students but instead change how their students learn and live. Accordingly, transformative learning refers to a form of in-depth learning that involves much more than the straightforward acquisition of knowledge; it involves interpreting and reflecting on experiences and then situating them in a wider context, thereby assisting learners in changing the assumptions they hold about both themselves and the world in which they live (Yacek, 2021). More specifically, as Taylor (2009a, pp. 5–13; 2009b) notes, transformative learning consists of the following core elements:

1. *individual experiences* – prior experiences that learners bring to the teaching–learning process;
2. *critical reflection* – questioning the integrity of deeply held assumptions and beliefs based on prior experiences;

3. *dialogue* (with the self and others) – the medium through which transformation is promoted and critical reflection is enacted, experiences are reflected upon, assumptions and beliefs are questioned, and habits of mind are ultimately transformed;
4. *holistic orientation* – the approach that encourages engagement with other ways of knowing, both the affective (i.e., feelings and emotions in the learning process) and expressive (i.e., engagement with music in the classroom or art more broadly);
5. *awareness of context* – appreciation and understanding of the personal and sociocultural factors that influence the learning process; and
6. *authentic relationships* – meaningful, genuine, positive, and trusting relationships with classroom community members.

It is essential to acknowledge that these core elements are systematically integrated by teacherpreneurs into their instructional activities. They are cognisant that these elements are entrenched in robust assumptions regarding the use of teaching to promote change, a process in which both instructors and students – alone or with their peers – challenge, scrutinise, and fundamentally alter the world inside and outside the classroom.

Furthermore, Lieberman (2011, p. 16) argues that teacher leaders are in a unique position to make change happen because:

[t]hey have learned a great deal about how to teach well and know how to build ... school and classroom conditions that can help transform schools. They have not only 'been there,' [they have also] successfully worked with all kinds of students and have learned how to facilitate adult learning as well. They have learned to teach well in the context of a classroom and have developed ... knowledge that teachers trust and believe.

Nevertheless, teacher leaders must be mindful of the complexity of educational change. It takes time and skilled leadership, and is only feasible when 'it is embedded in a clear vision, strong leadership, resource investment, internal and external accountability, high-quality practice, collaboration, and continuous engagement by all [school] stakeholders' (Malone, 2013, p. 2).

Thus, teacher leaders need to instigate, manage, and reflect on change from three perspectives: *rational*, *political*, and *emotional*. Regarding the former, teacher leaders need to exert control and justify the reasons for change through rational argumentation and explanation. They must also explain the logic that underpins a particular initiative and its potential benefits. Adopting a political perspective on change requires taking into account their position, work-related duties, the extent of power, and their degree of influence on other school members. Finally, an emotional perspective involves considering psychological aspects such as shared values and norms pertaining to emotions and the principles that dictate which emotions are expressed by individuals and which are suppressed. Emotions thus play an essential role in shaping communication within schools and their subsequent engagement with the outside world.

8.3 Leadership through Mentoring

The discussion on teacher leadership would not be complete without briefly mentioning leadership that takes the form of mentoring teachers. Mentoring is a structured, sustained, and dyadic relationship for supporting professional learners in transforming their practices as well as being one of the formal roles of teacher leadership in terms of supporting colleagues at the early stage of their career, through a career transition, or when facing a particular challenge (Cirocki & Johnson, 2022; Dozier, 2007; Hester & Setzer, 2013; Mann & Hing Tang, 2012; Nguyen, 2017; Othman & Senom, 2020). More specifically, experts from the State of Victoria Department of Education and Training (2014, p. 8) list the following roles of teacher mentors:

- offering an ear to listen – being interested rather than interesting;
- identifying, acknowledging, and appreciating what a new teacher brings to the school;
- being passionate, positive, and professional while working with new teachers – offering strong role modelling while becoming a trusted colleague;
- being approachable, accessible, and available when needed (new teachers identify these qualities in their mentors as being extremely important);
- assisting teachers to navigate and find their way through the school culture – and to understand how things are done in this context;
- encouraging new colleagues to make decisions and exercise an appropriate degree of autonomy so that they can develop their approach to teaching;
- encouraging new teachers to experiment with their practice; and
- fostering positive, productive relationships with all members of staff, students, their families and the wider community, thus demonstrating respect for culture and diversity.

For instance, Johnson (2022) contends that the development of new teachers is usually mediated through social interactions with those who possess greater knowledge, such as teacher educators and/or mentors, and by familiarisation with relevant theory. Therefore, the processes involved in learning-to-teach can be understood and supported only through the mediational function of theoretical concepts and the calibre of mentoring in relation to these. Thus, mentoring as mediation can be defined as novice teachers engaging in directed learning opportunities based on discussions with mentors that serve to enhance their development as professional teachers gradually. This is established as a type of leadership through the process of mediation, the successful implementation of the roles highlighted previously, the substantial way in which mentors nurture and refine the instructional practices of both novice and experienced teachers, and the ongoing enhancement of the school community (Ensher & Murphy, 2005; Katzenmeyer & Moller, 2009; Moyle, 2016).

It is also vital that mentor–mentee pairings are not established randomly (Jonson, 2008). They should be a consequence of a careful preparation process that considers, among other things, the goals of the mentoring programme, the pool of available mentors, the career stage of mentees, mentees' needs and preferences, and expected outcomes at the end of the process. Therefore, to set up successful pairings and effective collaboration, it is recommended that both teacher mentors and teachers address the following questions:

- What makes us a good match?
- Are we clear about what we hope to gain from the mentorship scheme?
- Have we checked that the mentee has a clear understanding of what mentoring is and what it entails?
- Do we know what our responsibilities in the mentoring scheme are?
- Have we agreed on short- and long-term objectives for the mentee's development? Does the mentee know what the objectives mean for them?
- Have we discussed possible ways of assessing the mentee's development? Are they aware of this, and what needs to be done, how, and when?
- Have we agreed on how the mentorship scheme will be documented?
- Have we clarified how often and for how long we are expected to meet?
- Have we clarified how the mentorship scheme can be terminated and how the termination can be formally requested?

Incontrovertible evidence exists for the advantages of teacher mentoring. Research indicates that a mentoring relationship can be valuable in supporting pre-service and novice teachers (e.g., Banegas, 2022; Mann & Hing Tang, 2012; Wu & Ware, 2022). It is also of value to the mentors (Hudson, 2013, 2016) as spending the time and energy to assist mentees can help expand their knowledge and inspire them (Ghosh et al., 2020). When mentoring takes place early on in a teacher's career, it can enable them to grow, visualise, and construct their teacher identity and become more resilient as professionals who are not yet fully prepared to teach (Henry & Mollstedt, 2021; Morettini et al., 2020; Varghese & Snyder, 2018). Such advantages will increase the extent to which they feel accepted into the teaching community (Morettini et al., 2020) while increasing their self-efficacy beliefs (Feng et al., 2019; Hobbs & Putnam, 2016). Past research has reported that mentoring has a positive impact on the outcomes for mentees (Chen et al., 2020; Zheng et al., 2020). Furthermore, mentoring is particularly successful when it involves dialogic engagement in an atmosphere of mutual trust, providing novice teachers with social and emotional support (Robnett et al., 2018).

Additionally, the literature suggests that successful teacher mentors are education leaders, implying that they not only demonstrate leadership competences

(Section 8.1) but also systematically follow principled leadership (Section 8.2.4) in the workplace. Notably, interpersonal skills for teacher mentors are of particular importance. These include forming strong working relationships, constructing collegiality with novice teachers, striving to enhance the school within the parameters of a reasonable workload, using conferencing and communication to build partnerships with parents, and understanding and implementing the school's philosophy (Jonson, 2008).

8.4 Conclusion

This chapter has aimed to unpack the concept of teacher leadership and emphasise its significance in the current school system. Contemporary schools heavily rely on teachers assuming various leadership roles, both formal and informal, to drive substantive school improvement, educational excellence, and the well-being of the entire school community. With this in mind, the chapter has clearly explained the notion of teacher leadership and what it entails. It has provided ideas on how to cultivate, empower, and support teacher leaders so that they can lead or mentor others in changing schools to become more robust learning and professional communities (Section 9.4). Such communities are underpinned by supportive and shared leadership, a collective vision and strategic intent, collaborative and reflective learning, and shared professional practice. Overall, the chapter has made teacher leadership a concrete and attainable goal for any teacher; however, this is only on the condition that schools are ready and willing to include and support teacher leadership as part of their strategic plan.

REFLECTION FOR ACTION

Future Teachers

- Reflect on your learning experiences at the secondary school level and identify one teacher leader. What, in your opinion, made him/her a leader?
- Think about the content of this chapter and decide which three competences are the most important for a teacher leader to have. Present them to your classmates and justify your choices.
- Do you plan to be a teacher leader in your future teaching career? How do you think you could demonstrate leadership in the workplace?
- Using this chapter's content, explain how leadership is linked to transformative learning.

Novice Teachers

- Reflect on your teaching and yourself as a teacher. Review the teacher leadership competences listed in this chapter and decide which you already demonstrate and which still need to be developed. How ready do you think you are to assume leadership roles?
- Think about your school community in terms of teacher leadership and prepare a list of suggestions (to share with your mentor/supervisor) on how your school management team could promote this on a larger scale. Divide your list into two categories, one for novice teachers and one for experienced teachers.
- Is it possible for teacher leaders to lead without power? If so, how can this be done? Invite another teacher colleague to discuss these questions.
- Which of the six types of power presented in this chapter have you exerted in the workplace thus far? Provide concrete examples and a context for each in your reflective journal. How did you feel while exercising power?

Experienced Teachers

- To what extent is teacher leadership embedded in your school community? What types of leadership discussed in this chapter are promoted? How could the present situation be improved?
- Evaluate your work with pre-service or less experienced teachers. How do you inspire and empower them? Compare your reflections with a colleague who also supervises pre-service teachers.
- List suggestions on how your school could support you in a formal leadership role. Discuss these ideas with your performance reviewer.
- Reflect on the role of teacher leadership in your school. Volunteer to become an advocate for teacher leaders. Prepare a description of the recruitment process, specifying how teacher leaders will be selected, how long their period of service will be, what will be contained in their role descriptions, and how they will be evaluated. Discuss your draft with two experienced teachers and follow their advice. When you are ready, share the document with your management team.

9 Building Professional English Language Teaching Development Communities

In order to develop a conceptual and reflective guide to English language teacher education, the preceding chapters have discussed specific aspects of teacher professionalism, as well as the specific competences that professional English language teachers are expected to demonstrate in the workplace in the twenty-first century. This discussion has revealed that being a professional teacher is a demanding undertaking and a deep responsibility, and the journey to acquiring the status of a professional teacher is complex and lengthy. This concluding chapter is different in nature. Although it is a product of critical reflection on current theory, research, and practice, it strives to innovate teacher professional learning and, hopefully, make it transformative and sustainable. Its specific purpose is fourfold: (1) to bring all the preceding chapters together to holistically conceptualise the notion of teachers as professionals and discuss the sociocultural underpinnings of this, (2) to reconsider the wider sociopolitical context within which teachers work and develop by looking outside the language classroom and into professional communities of practice, (3) to elucidate the process of building professional development communities within the field of ELT and exemplify what it entails, and (4) to suggest directions for future action with respect to professionalising English language teaching. All these aspects are elaborated upon in the following sections.

9.1 English Language Teacher Professional Learning: A Sociocultural Perspective

The preceding discussion reveals that becoming a professional teacher is not only the product of an enormous effort and an occupational achievement but also a sociocultural process. Such a process entails the formation of an individual's cognitive capacities as a result of interacting with those who possess more significant levels of knowledge and skills. Put another way, teacher learning and professional development are partly assisted by individuals serving as mentors, be they teacher educators or teachers with greater experience. Supplementing this, the values and beliefs of teacher learners are fostered through interpersonal engagement within specific social groups or by taking part in professional events such as conferences (Cirocki & Golombek, 2020; Cirocki et al., 2023; Johnson, 2009; Johnson & Golombek, 2016).

Three fundamental concepts define sociocultural theory: social interaction, language, and ZPD, all of which have appeared on several occasions with varying frequency and intensity in the preceding chapters. According to Vygotsky (1978), social interaction plays a crucial role in the learning process, as thinking originates from the social world; thus, it is impossible to understand cognitive development without considering the social milieu in which it is rooted. Put simply, the development of teaching expertise is mediated through engagement with pedagogical concepts and through social interactions (oral, written, face-to-face, virtual) with expert others (i.e., teacher educators, mentor teachers). It is therefore vital to view teaching as dialogic mediation. This developmental process initially takes place by collaborating with other people (other-regulation) and after that is controlled by the individual (self-regulation).

Vygotsky's (1978) concept of ZPD is closely related to the notion of *scaffolding* (Díaz Maggioli, 2012; Wood et al., 1976). It is viewed as a process that enables teacher learners to solve problems or achieve goals they could not otherwise accomplish without the help of others. The process is always learner-focused in that assistance from more experienced teachers is contingent on teacher learners' needs, the aim being to develop their specific competences, skills, or knowledge base. The role of expert others in this process is extremely important, as these more knowledgeable individuals increase learning among teacher learners by supporting them in accomplishing tasks that exceed their existing level of ability, even to a slight degree. It is this guidance that is referred to as scaffolding, which can take different formats and sometimes depends on the career stage teachers have reached. Some of these formats include (1) *linguistic scaffolding* to advance teacher learners' language skills; (2) *sensory scaffolding* to enable teacher learners to make connections between ideas and acquire new knowledge; (3) *interactive scaffolding* to enable teacher learners to develop communication and collaboration skills, acquire new knowledge through interacting with others, and nurture empathy and open-mindedness; (4) *graphic scaffolding* to facilitate learning among teacher learners through broadly defined graphic organisers (e.g., graphs, charts, mind maps); and (5) *procedural scaffolding* which promotes modelling and coaching.

In conclusion, sociocultural theory considers teacher learning and development to be a socially situated and collaboratively co-constructed process, one in which every action that occurs while working with others to construct knowledge is considered (Cirocki & Golombek, 2020; Lantolf & Thorne, 2006). As the previous chapters attest, it places a very precise emphasis on the way in which knowledge is co-constructed as a result of mutual support and cooperation among all participants, including teacher learners, experienced teachers, teacher educators, and teacher mentors, thereby enabling teacher learners to achieve what they cannot bring into fruition independently.

9.2 The Value of Teacher Collaboration for Professional Development

As clarified in the previous section, learning the craft of teaching is a social process. It occurs through social interactions between individuals bound to specific contexts, where social interactions result in high-value products, including changes in understanding and agency in the individuals involved that have become situated within the context in which such individuals reside. The outcomes of human interactions are referred to as *social capital*, defined in Coleman's tradition (1990) as a reservoir of shared values, norms, resources, and behaviour, as well as multifaceted social interrelationships which allow teachers to work together effectively to achieve desired outcomes. The latter may range from jointly designed syllabi and classroom materials through well-designed action research projects to reading clubs established in local libraries.

According to Coleman (1990), the construct of social capital is conceptualised as follows:

- Capital is a feature of the community; it is scrutinised with respect to the way individual teachers employ it.
- It places an emphasis on relationships and trust and therefore establishes a structure that empowers teachers to act effectively while fostering a positive and innovative school culture.
- The more potent the social bonds and sense of belonging among individual teachers within schools, the more closed their communities are and the more consolidated their networks to enact transformation in civic life for the common good.
- Capital is derived from the unintended outcomes of conscious and deliberate action; teachers do not act to create social capital but commit themselves to achieving particular professional goals. When teachers engage in collaborative work, they build social structures which aid them in satisfying their professional needs.

Given this evidence, it can be concluded that social capital is an essential part of teacher professional capital, comprising a multidimensional construct made up of *human*, *social*, and *decisional* types of capital (Hargreaves & Fullan, 2012; Osmond-Johnson, 2017). While human capital refers to classroom practitioners' education, qualifications, and experiences, decisional capital pertains to teachers' capacity to make independent, objective, and accurate decisions and judgements and improvise in the workplace. Social capital, by contrast, is constructed through meaningful interactions and collaborations with peers, which revolve around teaching and are contingent on positive emotions and feelings of closeness and trust (Hargreaves & Fullan, 2012; Nolan & Molla, 2017).

Having stressed collaborative work among teachers on a number of occasions in this book, it seems fitting to elaborate on the concept of social capital a little further. There are three types of social capital: *bonding social capital*, *bridging social capital*, and *linking social capital* (Lancee, 2010; Woolcock & Sweetser, 2002). The first type, bonding social capital, is about heightening the relationships and networks teachers already enjoy and which are valuable in developing a sense of shared identity and security. The second type, bridging social capital, refers to developing new links and networks beyond teachers' immediate social circles, for example, liaising with teachers from other schools, CPD providers, or community workers, all stimulating teachers' career advancement. The third type, linking social capital, pertains to creating social relationships between teachers and educational leaders or government officials to benefit from their power and influence.

It is therefore evident that the construct of social capital is extremely valuable in teachers' everyday jobs. Its distinctive types form the basis of professional collaboration among teachers, conceived as entailing participation in task-focused activities founded on volitional relationships in which the emphasis is placed on equality and joint accountability for the decisions made and the outcomes achieved (Bush & Grotjohann, 2020; Datnow & Park, 2019; Lassonde & Israel, 2010). All three types of social capital also serve to develop teacher learning, nurturing solidarity among teachers, including more senior teachers, to engender a more substantive understanding of the teaching–learning process. The most all-encompassing and potentially the most crucial recurrent feature is the objective of enhancing student learning.

Notably, collaborative culture in the workplace does not mean working together on a random task or compulsory school meetings. Instead, it is invariably interwoven into the everyday tasks, school events, and ceremonies in which teachers participate, formal and informal exchanges of ideas and experiences, and regular analyses of teachers' pedagogical practice. Needless to say, all these components of professional collaborative culture are inherently underpinned by trust, openness, collegiality, and support among teachers.

According to Little (1990), the following four steps need to be taken towards complete and productive collaboration: (1) storytelling and scanning for ideas, (2) aid and assistance, (3) sharing, and (4) joint work. The first step, characterised by weak levels of interdependence, relates to random exchanges of experiences among teachers in staffrooms, which are intended to offer informational and social support. The second step of teacher collaboration, with moderate levels of interdependence, pertains to teacher interactions, whereby classroom practitioners share ideas and advice, mainly on singular classroom situations.

In the third step, teachers share materials and methods in which they display a wide range of patterns and choices with regard to the curriculum and instruction, as well as the personal philosophies underpinning their pedagogical practice. In the final step, referred to as joint work, teachers engage in interactions with high levels of interdependence, as a result of which they feel collective responsibility and accountability for the teaching work.

The collective commitment to professional practice and joint work is the driving force behind successful teacher professional communities, which are discussed in the following section.

9.3 Professional Communities of English Language Teaching Practitioners

As outlined in the preceding sections of this chapter, professional collaboration is one of the catalysts of learning and innovation. This sounds more natural than it actually is in the context of teacher education and teachers' careers. Teacher education is, as a rule, focused on the individual teacher; professional collaboration methods and strategies do not generally form part of the teacher education curriculum. Consequently, a teacher's reflections, classroom and teaching practices, pedagogical decisions, and responses to students' behaviour, or pedagogical challenges, are all based on individual perceptions and judgements. By contrast, in their professional work, teachers experience collaboration as a daily practical requirement of managing classes, organising the school day, designing school curricula, and myriad other duties, activities, and routines. Thus, collaboration is experienced as a standard dimension of professional work. However, teachers are also aware of the limitations of this kind of collaboration. It mainly occurs at the level of daily duties or pragmatic responses to situations that concern more than one teacher – everyday pragmatic collaboration does not usually include a teacher's ideas for change and development, long-term perspectives, or innovations. However, it is clearly the case that structural changes, entire teaching philosophies, teachers' individual professional development, or a school's pedagogical transformation can happen only if new ideas and strategic thinking are systematised, structured, and shaped in a goal-oriented manner.

Because this chapter proposes creating and establishing professional communities in schools or other educational institutions and beyond, it is necessary to scrutinise a range of approaches which all revolve around the notion of professional communities whose intention is to both structure the professionalisation of developmental processes and enhance collaboration. The assumptions underlying the creation of professional communities are manifold. First and foremost is the belief that, as a rule, institutions as a whole must identify the need for innovation and transformation and that, normally, this is a task that is beyond the potential and capacity of an individual. Secondly, an institution cannot fully develop if its members do not consider themselves responsible as a social group for how the institution develops and its directions. Thirdly, there is certainly a considerable advantage if the members of a community collaborate and are thus able to take advantage of the professional knowledge, ideas, and skills – not just of individuals but also of the entire community. Finally, these approaches rely on the observation that individual professionals develop best if a community develops as a whole and, in so doing, actively contribute to a common goal and accomplishment. Therefore, as has been argued in almost all the chapters of this book, collaboration is one of the core concepts of professionalisation and of working in a professional manner.

Three approaches in particular have emerged since the 1990s, some in pedagogy and some in other domains of professional training and learning; these are the concepts of *professional learning communities* (PLCs), *professional communities of practice* (CoPs), and *professional communities of inquiry*. These three concepts are examined and discussed in the following sections in order to identify the essentials and commonalities that need to form part of the endeavour of creating and establishing a professional community in the realm of ELT. In fact, there are numerous commonalities between these three approaches, professional collaboration in particular but also change and innovation in institutions and the need to design and structure processes suited to further developing an institution. Sometimes, the differences may appear to be of minor importance, but, as the names of the communities indicate (learning, practice, inquiry), each places emphasis on a different aspect of developmental processes, as closer consideration of the following three sections reveals.

9.3.1   *Professional Learning Communities*

The notion of a professional community is associated with the idea that teachers at various institutional levels, such as at the level of a whole school or educational institution, or of a specific grade, or freely formed teams of teachers of a given subject form a team or a community to discuss, initiate, and agree upon future developments in the respective field. The goals of such collaborative initiatives may focus on the quality and improvement of teaching practices, agreements on the institution's philosophy and mission statement, or efforts to develop a school community. The PLC concept was the focus of a large empirical study on teacher collaboration in Great Britain by Bolam et al. (2005). One of the research findings was that in most cases studied teachers' collaboration triggered individual and collective learning processes, and enhanced communication and reflections led to forming a professional community for which key characteristics could be empirically identified. The following eight characteristics were regarded as crucial not only to create such a community but also to sustain, establish, and develop it further in an institution over time (Stoll et al., 2006):

> *Shared values and vision*: These were 'directed to the learning of all pupils and shared across the whole staff' and specifically comprised 'shared educational values' (Stoll et al., 2006, p. 4). In large schools and many secondary schools, values and visions were not always shared by all staff but by smaller groups or teams of teachers. Also, there could 'sometimes be disagreement about how best to achieve the learning goals' (Stoll et al., 2006, p. 4).
>
> *Collective responsibility for pupils' learning*: This feature referred to staff 'sharing a sense of responsibility for the learning of all pupils in the school' (Stoll et al., 2006, p. 5). Collective responsibility was found to occur at various levels, for instance, staff teaching particular subjects or age groups. Sharing data and information about pupils was also part of this collective practice, as was monitoring pupils' individual learning targets and staff discussions regarding better promotion of learning and raising achievement among students.
>
> *Reflective professional inquiry*: Schools needed to collect data and monitor pupils' progress to engage in such a research-oriented practice. However, in terms of pedagogical or action research and empirical classroom observation, professional inquiry required strategies to use the data systematically and apply them in a manner that was suited to transforming the learning conditions and improving pupils' learning outcomes.
>
> *Collaboration focused on learning*: This characteristic concerned collaborative activities 'focused on pupil learning and mutual professional learning' (Stoll et al., 2006, p. 5). Examples of such activities included planning teaching sessions, sharing learning resources, and discussing students' progress.
>
> *Group and individual professional learning*: Professional learning, both individual and collective, was a core characteristic of PLCs. In the study, teachers reported that they learnt through collaboration with colleagues but simultaneously were in charge of their learning.
>
> *Openness, networks, and partnerships*: Openness to new ideas and exchanging them with the community and staff in other schools was another key characteristic. Significantly, this feature prevented teachers from being 'inward looking or defensive' (Stoll et al., 2006, p. 6). Links and networks with other schools were regarded as productive and favourable for innovation.

Inclusive membership: This characteristic explained why the notion of community lay at the core of this kind of professional development. The idea was that such a community involved not only teachers but also support staff, school governors, and school council members. One of the essential conditions was that all members of a more comprehensive and extensive community needed to understand and share the school's values and mission.

Mutual trust, respect, and support: PLCs were 'characterised by trust and respect between colleagues and mutual support' (Stoll et al., 2006, p. 6). Members of a professional community had to be confident that colleagues would act in a professional manner.

Overall, the professionalisation of teaching and learning is a collective enterprise which requires shared visions and goals, research-led decisions, and teachers' willingness to learn and be open to innovation. However, for such a professional community, although collective learning should be one of the key factors or goals, it should not be the defining characteristic, as learning is only a means to an end. Moreover, learning and inquiry should focus not only on students' learning but potentially on everything that forms part of the school's pedagogical philosophy, its organisation, its resources and architecture, and numerous other factors pertaining to school life and learning. A second observation concerns the composition of a community's membership. In the PLCs approach, it appears to be somewhat contingent on the type of school and its actual community. For this reason, external professional expertise is absent and not part of the concept. Nevertheless, there can be no doubt that such expertise needs to be one of the pillars of a development community that needs to integrate and include academic and professional experts such as teacher educators or teacher trainers.

9.3.2 Professional Communities of Practice

The concept of CoPs focuses on practitioners in a specific domain, such as companies or schools, and thus lays emphasis on shared experiences, along with the visions that emerge from a daily common practice. This concept therefore primarily revolves around shared practice. The approach also evolved mainly during the 1990s (Wenger, 1998) and is closely related to the PLCs concept outlined in Section 9.3.1. Three key elements can be identified that have remained constant during different stages of the development of the approach and across a variety of concepts: the notion of building a community of professional practitioners, 'the location of the community in a domain of knowledge', and 'the sharing of practice' (McDonald & Mercieca, 2021a, p. 7). However, CoPs are also learning communities as 'a *shared practice* develops as members learn with and from each other to become effective in the domain' (McDonald & Mercieca, 2021a, p. 7, emphasis in the original). Notably, constant learning is here regarded as one of the factors that develops a shared practice and is part of reiterative classroom practice and learning loops. There is evidence that teachers benefit from joining such a community in the domain of teaching and learning in schools. In an empirical study of early career teachers, the authors found that 'belonging to these collaborative communities allowed them to thrive in their teaching practice as they participated in learning loops, taking ideas, and strategies gained from the Communities of Practice to the classroom and then back again to the community for further feedback and support' (McDonald & Mercieca, 2021b, p. 21).

It is important to note that one of the different types of CoPs that can be distinguished is an intentional community of practice 'created to satisfy a particular organisational need or strategy' (McDonald & Mercieca, 2021a, p. 9). Unlike more organic types of communities, such intentional community building can lead to a more systematic and structured composition of the membership so that, for example, the school principal, other experts in the community, or external academic experts may be invited to join, share their expertise, and learn and collaborate with others to develop the respective domain. Also, in such a community model, leadership and management can be established at various levels to ensure that the community as a working unit is sustainable (Mercieca & McDonald, 2021).

For a comprehensive approach to building professional communities, three conclusions can be drawn from experiences with CoPs, at least of the intentional type:

1. A professional community's membership needs to be carefully composed so that various levels and profiles of expertise are represented. In particular, the potential of external expertise (scholars, teacher educators, educational researchers) needs to be considered and incorporated.
2. The community needs a social structure so that leadership at various levels can be established and the community can be managed. This is a requisite for sustainability.
3. The learning process itself has to be managed and structured so that, for instance, learning loops are established that implement what has been learnt in classroom practice; such implementation needs to be evaluated and reflected upon in order to discuss the innovation with the community then. Following this, a refined or revised version of the new approach is applied to the classroom.

To sum up, the three crucial elements that must be integrated into the comprehensive concept of a professional community, as proposed in Section 9.4, are a carefully composed membership that focuses on professional expertise, the social structure and leadership of the community, and a strategy suited to structuring and systematising the community's learning processes. As the third approach in the next section reveals, other key elements that co-constitute professional development are inquiry and research.

9.3.3 Professional Communities of Inquiry

As the name of this type of professional community suggests, there is a specific need in professional communities to invite, consult, and integrate academic expertise and research into their professional work (Jaworski, 2008) and innovation processes. There are various ways to integrate research and inquiry into professional learning in the field. For instance, collaboration between researchers or scholars may be dialogic so that teachers can draw on researchers' expertise to formulate their conclusions. However, collaboration between researchers and teachers may also be more participative and continuous. Moreover, academic researchers may support teachers in designing classrooms or pedagogical research tailored to the needs of their schools or their learners and classrooms.

What is important in this approach is that inquiry and research are communal, social endeavours, which accounts for the fact that experience or subjective perceptions are helpful as starting points. However, impressions, perceptions, or more or less subjective hypotheses usually do not provide a reliable knowledge base for decisions or sustainable initiatives. Inquiry refers to processes involving a more systematic, more profound investigation of all sorts of phenomena observed in an institution, classrooms in particular, which typically involves collecting data or relying on the broader, more intersubjective scope of observations. Research goes further as it defines research objectives or foci and research questions based on theoretical and disciplinary concepts. The obvious advantage is that such pedagogical research serves a common purpose and that everyone in the school benefits from research that members of the community conduct. The notion of teacher research ties in directly with the approaches of teacher-led research and research-based reflective practice in Chapter 4 of this book. This is also why research is one of the crucial elements in the concept of professional development communities (PDCs) proposed in Section 9.4.

The focus on inquiry in this approach accounts for the fact that every shared practice is based on a joint knowledge base that, more often than not, remains implicit. Communal inquiry is a concept that renders professional knowledge, assumptions, and beliefs explicit and leads to the generation of new, more profound, and more systematic knowledge. The joint production of knowledge is therefore a specification of professional learning, but it is also an important dimension of shared practice whereby a meta-level is established from which learning and practice can be better assessed.

In sum, comparing the three approaches discussed here, it can be stated that, on the one hand, they emphasise different aspects of a professional community's work, as indicated in the labels they use: professional learning, practice, and inquiry. On the other hand, it is also apparent that they have a number of features in common, such as the core definition of what a professional community is and many of the key elements. In this sense, the names of the communities appear to be slightly contingent. For instance, in a recent German publication that explores the CoPs approach in the humanities in more detail, Kaufmann (2019) focuses almost exclusively on learning through research in cultural studies and ethnology, thereby integrating the core notions of communities of practice and learning and inquiry. However, given that, historically, the three concepts of professional communities have developed almost simultaneously for more than thirty years since the 1990s, it is not overly surprising that they have inspired each other and that each has integrated elements from the other concepts.

Although intriguing, these three initiatives are not without their limitations. Given recent perspectives, trends, and innovations in the field of ELT, as evidenced in the preceding chapters, it is necessary to make a fresh attempt to conceptualise professional communities. Without question, twenty-first-century communities must integrate all the shared key features of professional communities of the three approaches previously introduced. In conjunction with this, there is a compelling need for these new communities to account for interdisciplinary developments such as digitisation (Chapter 7), leadership and management (Chapter 8), effective communication (Section 1.3, Chapter 7), and the professionalisation of teacher education. This is developed further in the next section.

9.4 Creating Professional English Language Teaching Development Communities: A Principled Approach

The preceding section reveals that current approaches to professional communities hinge on sets of guidelines and characteristic features that vary across schools according to the literature (Brodie & Borko, 2016; Lomos et al., 2011; Stoll et al., 2006). To formalise and standardise such communities in the field of ELT, a principled approach needs to be devised. The approach proposed in this section is much broader in scope than the professional communities discussed earlier. It is aligned closely with the demands of twenty-first-century education and the concept of teacher professionalism discussed in the preceding chapters. To acknowledge this, it is vital that the present-day concept of professional communities be replaced by a new label, namely, professional development communities.

The process of building PDCs requires a principled approach which ensures that communities fulfil their roles, operate smoothly, and contribute to the

Table 9.1 *Key principles underpinning twenty-first-century PDCs*

Professional development communities should
1. have a clear purpose, vision, and mission of innovation and transformation;
2. create and establish the community with a clear intention, composing it carefully by recruiting relevant members and clarifying their roles;
3. identify and address the needs of their members and their school or educational institution;
4. define ethical values, compliance rules, and professional conduct to guide their work;
5. decide on and establish their structures and working formats;
6. specify their strategies, and plan and define procedures and activities to enact these;
7. engage in systematic inquiry and teacher-led research;
8. clarify, disseminate, and act on their outcomes;
9. create and implement detailed evaluation procedures;
10. reflect on the evaluation results and decide how they will inform the next cycle of their activities.

transformative and sustainable development of English language teachers and other educational stakeholders, as well as of schools and other educational institutions, and also their missions. There are ten key principles to which PDCs should adhere; these are listed in Table 9.1 and discussed in greater detail below.

As can be seen, some of the principles align with the three approaches described in Section 9.3. However, in the context of the developmental approach proposed here, new aspects must be rationalised and included. Consequently, present-day PDCs must have the following features:

> *Have a clear purpose, vision, and mission of innovation and transformation*: In the developmental approach, the defining factor is a clear idea of the direction in which an educational institution should develop. This implies that community members share several observations regarding the status quo and will reach a consensus on the kind of change and innovation they deem necessary in their particular contexts. The community is therefore defined by transformative goals for the future of the institutions and of individual members, that is, the teachers or other members of staff who need to engage in learning themselves, thus developing their teacher identities and professional competences. First and foremost, educational institutions are concerned with the learning processes of their students, which will therefore often be one of the foci of the community's work. It is also part of this first key principle that the community define its vision (i.e., what the community wants to achieve or become ultimately) and mission (i.e., the community's reason(s) for existence) clearly and more or less formally so that the goals of the respective community are explicitly defined and can be effectively evaluated.

Create a community that is carefully composed: Any community approach requires a definition of what actually constitutes a community. It may be regarded as a more or less naturally grown community, formed by teachers or other staff members of a given school or institution. In the developmental approach, these 'natural' members of an institution form the core of the community. However, given that such a professional community is also a working group, a (consensual) strategy is needed as to who will actually and intentionally be a member, who agrees to the vision, mission, and goals, and who is prepared to take an active part in the work of the community as a whole. In addition, depending on the goals, vision, and mission, it is almost always advisable to invite external experts to join the professional community so that the vision, mission, and goals can be supported by theoretical input as well as diverse perspectives and outlooks (academic, political, philosophical, moral, and social). Such expertise is also extremely helpful when it comes to defining a systematic inquiry or conducting research in the institution on any issues that are deemed relevant for the innovative work of the professional community. Other members of the school's professional network, such as school administration representatives, teacher educators, and others, should also be invited (Figure 9.1).

Moreover, it may be inspiring and productive to invite members of the larger institutional community, such as the school principal, students, parents, and other staff members, into the PDC. In so doing, it is necessary to clarify and define the expectations and their roles in the community so that they share its goals, values, vision, and mission. In the digital age, it is also necessary to consider whether and to what extent the community may be joined by more remote members who might contribute to its work digitally (Section 7.1). There is a large number of digital formats and platforms available that have been established for teachers' use, including digital staff rooms, teacher fora, digital pinboards, and clouds.

Identify and address the needs of their members and their school or educational institution: After defining the community's vision, mission, and goals and before the actual working process starts, it is essential for members to exchange and identify the personal views, interests, and needs that they define as forming the basis of their work in the group as individuals. This is important as it serves to avoid discrepancies, controversial expectations, and a lack of understanding of how every individual defines their role, perceptions of the school's needs, and the kind of contribution they have in mind. This is crucial because it represents the only way

Building Professional Development Communities 221

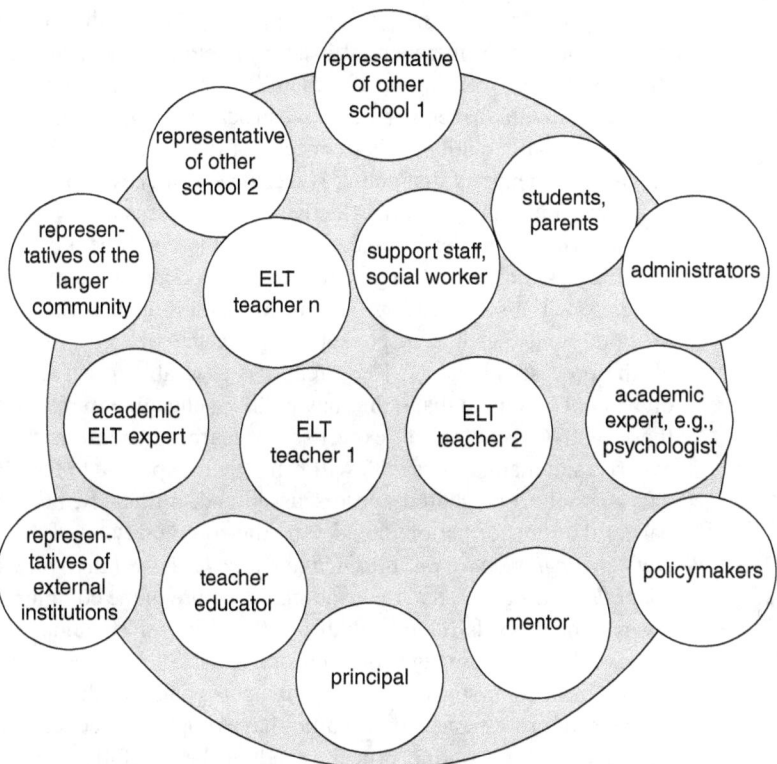

Figure 9.1 Potential members of a professional ELT development community consisting of selected members of the actual institutional community and the community's network

to develop a more or less formally constituted community into a socially and professionally coherent working group.

Define ethical values, compliance rules, and professional conduct that guide their work: A professional community's work requires an ethical foundation that is regarded as consensual and as guiding their work and professional conduct. Such values concern the actual work of the community in terms of openness, trust, and shared information. Still, it may also concern the institution as a whole so that solidarity, justice, and fairness for everyone and a promising future for the younger generation are established as values that guide the community's work. Rules of professional conduct and compliance make ethical orientations explicit and concretise them for the practical work of the professional community.

Decide on and establish structures and formats: Depending on the size and number of members, it is advisable to provide a clear-cut structure for the working processes and define the roles and place of each individual member in these structures. There can be no one-size-fits-all solution; it is the needs of the educational institution and its members that count. Nevertheless, it is evident that to make the community's work effective over time, it is highly advisable to structure it. For instance, as a rule, there will be a plenary meeting in which everything is discussed in a democratic manner, but there will also be leaders who fill more prominent positions in the community, such as a speaker or a manager who co-ordinates all the processes (Chapter 8). Often, it is advisable to agree on a division of labour so that there may be those engaging in research, those with psychological expertise in learning, administrative experts, and many others who will bring their expertise to the plenary session to be shared and discussed and, ultimately, become part of the transformation intended by the community.

Specify strategies and plan, and define procedures and activities to enact the strategies: The organisational structure of the community always corresponds directly with the definition of strategies, for instance, for various stages or cycles of work. Such a plan should also define a community's steps to pursue its goals. As all the other concepts of professional communities have proposed (Section 9.3), such a complex working process needs to be carefully planned, establishing a clear timeline and a precise definition of the stages in which the community intends to proceed, including monitoring, feedback loops, and potential revisions or adaptations of the plan. Figure 9.2 visualises the standard stages in such a working cycle, which can also inform the next work cycle.

Engage in systematic inquiry and teacher-led research: Systematic inquiry and teacher-led research can be valuable tools for acquiring more credible information about and an understanding of those issues in which a professional community is particularly interested as a knowledge base for their work. As argued in Chapter 4, teachers are professionals who may engage in such research, using ethnographic tools (e.g., questionnaires, interviews, field notes, journals) or creating statistics revealing more about learners, teaching practices, institutional structures, and so on. Because quantitative research and experimental studies require a higher degree of methodological expertise than classroom practitioners typically demonstrate, external academic experts could be invited, with whom the goals of a research project, the research

Building Professional Development Communities

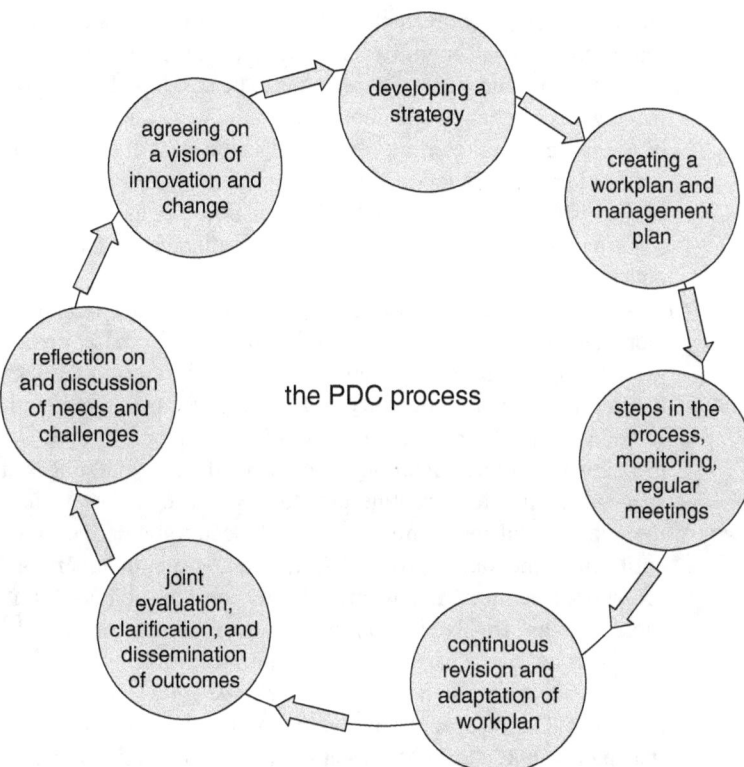

Figure 9.2 The PDC cycle: standard stages of the working process

design, and the data analysis stage are planned and executed. Whenever systematic inquiry and teacher-led research are conducted, there must be an agreement on ways of disseminating and evaluating the results and how these results inform the community's further work; otherwise, issues of professional misconduct may come into play.

Clarify, disseminate, and act on the outcomes: The last step of the whole process in Figure 9.2 naturally represents the most important stage, as the professional community needs to define and clarify, disseminate and communicate, and also seek agreement on how to act on the results of their work. This is the stage where the initial vision of innovation and change becomes real. Therefore, it cannot be completed without critical reflection (Chapter 4), effective communication, and negotiating everything with all institution members, including the principal and, potentially, the school administration or other external members or institutions. Given that it concerns all members and all levels of the institution, dissemination implies that a strategy has to be developed as to how all those who did not actively contribute to the work and the decisions of the professional community can be involved in the change process and how their work can be implemented in the daily practices of the institution. It may also be the case that, alongside this, a new working cycle is initiated to secure the continuous and sustainable development of the institution.

Create and implement evaluation procedures: Innovative ways of work and new practices are challenging for all those involved, particularly teachers and their students. As it is almost impossible to predict the functionality and success of innovative practices in educational settings, it is essential to continuously monitor and evaluate the implementation process to identify challenges and successes. Therefore, routine procedures and tools for evaluating the outcomes of the community's work need to be defined for the entire implementation process. At the same time, members of the professional community need to be in constant contact with all those who are involved in putting the community's new products into practice to receive and then act upon feedback.

Reflect on the evaluation results and decide on the next cycle of activities: The results of any evaluation require critical reflection (Chapter 4) and careful discussion as they constitute the basis for further decisions and, in terms of the PDC cycle, inform a second or third working cycle of the professional community. Such results need to be widely disseminated within the institution and discussed in detail with all those concerned or involved. Moreover, this stage may also be the beginning of a new working cycle designed to secure the institution's continuous and sustainable development, or the results may inspire a new cycle of inquiry or research to validate the evaluation. Reflection and discussion may also focus on the evaluation tools or procedures themselves so that they can be further developed or optimised.

The picture that emerges from the foregoing discussion reveals that a thriving professional ELT development community rests on ten principles. Valuable work within such a community is guaranteed by two explicit factors, fruitful collaboration and effective communication. These are integral to the ten principles discussed and all stages of work within PDCs (as depicted in Figure 9.2). They are crucial to PDC processes because a PDC's work always affects an entire institution, and sometimes also its professional network and external partners (companies, public institutions, services), hence it is a type of collaboration that becomes increasingly important and defines a school's or educational institution's position in the broader social community. Because a PDC devotes its work to the whole institution and all its members, all aspects of such work must be shared and well communicated among the members. Effective communication ensures that members are well connected, boosts their engagement and satisfaction, and drives better results for the individual member, the whole team, and the entire institution.

Additionally, a PDC's work can be regarded as an ongoing professional collaboration model that is always carefully planned, well structured, and underpinned by the PDC's vision, mission, and goals. Therefore, the work of such professional communities can inspire other teachers' or colleagues' attitudes and willingness to collaborate daily, demonstrating that collaboration is suited to producing outcomes that an individual alone cannot achieve.

It is also important to clarify that high-quality communication and collaboration in the workplace, or more specifically in a professional ELT development community, is contingent on other factors, including language proficiency (Section 1.5.1), critical reflection (Chapter 4), collective autonomy and agency (Chapter 5), and leadership (Chapter 8), all of which have been mentioned in this book on a number of occasions. Therefore, these factors implicitly underpin the ten principles of the proposed model of a PDC presented earlier. At a conceptual level, this demonstrates how the various theoretical, empirical, and practical deliberations in the individual chapters of this book feed into the innovative model of a professional ELT development community. At a structural level, it shows how the individual chapters build the argument that culminates in Chapter 9, thus ensuring the internal coherence of the entire book.

9.5 Professional Development as Lived Experience: Professional Development Communities in Action

Having discussed what creating PDCs entails, it seems fitting to exemplify the authors' engagement in teacher professional development. Therefore, this section, unlike the others, is more reflective and practical in nature. In this chapter, we have proposed to share with other colleagues in the field a principled approach to PDCs that sets out how we educate English language teachers and organise CPD activities to enable both pre- and in-service teachers to develop professionally. To make this approach more credible, three specific projects we have (co-)led in diverse ELT contexts, in which the creation of PDCs has been prioritised, are discussed.

PROJECT 1

Title

The National Centre for ELT Materials Development (NCELTMAD), Indonesia https://nceltmad.unesa.ac.id

Aims

The overarching purpose of establishing this English-based centre in 2022 was to build a sustainable PDC of Indonesian EFL teacher educators and teachers interested in designing pedagogical materials to support English language education in secondary schools across Indonesia. Since its establishment, the community has pursued the following aims:

- supporting teachers in teaching English in a creative way by providing them with a bank of effective activities and tasks that provide opportunities for students to negotiate meaning and partake in meaningful interpersonal exchanges in the target language;
- helping teachers to engage learners in social interaction and meaningful communication in the classroom through high-quality materials;
- offering teachers CPD programmes focusing on materials design so that they are able to supplement local coursebooks in the teaching–learning process; and
- reporting developments in ELT theory, research, practice, and policy to teachers and giving them an opportunity to contribute an independent voice to the profession.

Description

The centre is located at Universitas Negeri Surabaya, Indonesia, and brings together local EFL teacher educators and pre- and in-service teachers. Individuals who want to become members of the centre must submit an online form available on the NCELTMAD's website, and to maintain their membership, they must be actively involved in designing pedagogical materials. Initially, the materials in the centre were earmarked for promoting speaking skills only, but more recently, efforts have been made to develop materials which focus on extensive reading to contribute to English language learning and literacy development among Indonesian teenagers.

The members of the centre meet regularly, both face-to-face and online, to design new materials and collectively reflect on existing materials with a view to improving them so that they promote effective and innovative teaching while also allowing for the inclusion of contextual factors and local needs in the design process. During the meetings, teachers design worksheets, submit them for external review, and, if needed, revise them. The accepted classroom worksheets are then uploaded to the NCELTMAD's website and used by EFL teachers nationwide.

Strengths and Challenges

One of the strengths is that teacher educators and teachers assume the role of materials developers and belong to a professional community where they work together to improve English language education in Indonesia. The teachers bring their own teaching experiences to the table, collectively reflect on them, and ensure that these critical reflections inform the design of new materials, with clear instructions for classroom use to guide teachers. The centre also serves as a platform for some teachers to demonstrate their technological competence while using diverse apps and software to design attractive and engaging materials. Others then have multiple opportunities to learn from these classroom practitioners how to use new apps and software to design materials in a professional manner.

Regarding the challenges, some teachers struggle to design materials focusing on skills development as they mainly have experience in developing grammar and vocabulary exercises. Therefore, extra support is provided to remedy this situation. Another challenge lies in the low language proficiency of a large number of the teachers, which means centre leaders must carefully edit all their outputs before their worksheets are sent for external review. From time to time, teachers skip some of the centre sessions and therefore delay submitting their materials.

Outcomes

Indonesian teacher educators and teachers develop worksheets for classroom use, which are uploaded to the NCELTMAD's topic-based bank after a successful review process. The worksheets are downloadable and can be used instantly in classroom teaching. Additionally, workshops and conferences on developing pedagogical materials are organised by the leaders of the centre, not only to offer the community of Indonesian secondary school EFL teachers opportunities to learn to design high-quality materials but also to create a professional development forum whereby they can showcase their work and receive constructive feedback on their final products.

PROJECT 2

Title

TESOL Cafe Colombia

Aims

The general purpose of establishing this English-based virtual platform in 2022 was to create a viable PDC of Colombian EFL teacher educators and teachers to facilitate their professional growth with regard to TESOL methodology. More specifically, the community has pursued the following aims:

- offering teachers a platform to discuss teaching-related matters and share best practices;
- engaging teachers in a professional dialogue whereby they analyse and reflect on their teaching and link it to recent theory and research;
- improving the pedagogical competences of teachers to ensure that classroom instruction is current and innovative; and
- creating a community of practice which guides teachers in their pedagogical practice.

Description

This platform gathers EFL teacher educators and teachers at pre- and in-service levels. The community meets once a month. Each two-hour session begins with an invited talk relating to a topic of interest among community members, such as Enhancing Students' Reading Skills through XReading. The talk usually lasts one hour and combines theory and practice. The practice element showcases stimulating activities and tasks to give the audience specific examples of good practice, encouraging them to try them out in their pedagogical practice. After the talk, community members discuss the session topic in breakout rooms, usually for about forty-five minutes, and reflect on how they have already integrated it into their teaching and how they could improve the current state of affairs. Following this, all the members meet in one Zoom room for about fifteen minutes to reflect on their discussions, draw conclusions, and share action points with respect to their professional practice.

Strengths and Challenges

The main strength of this community is that there are a number of committed teacher educators and teachers who are determined to learn new things and improve their current classroom practices. In addition, they regularly attend the sessions as they consider this platform a perfect opportunity to practise English. The invited speakers are experienced teacher educators or teachers from international contexts, which enables the community members to find out how English is taught outside Colombia – an indisputable strength.

Regarding the challenges that have arisen, the major one lies in organising each virtual session timewise. The two leaders of this community live in Colombia and England, while the invited speakers live all over the globe. This means that morning sessions in Colombia may be scheduled for evenings and nights in Asian contexts, which is not always the most optimal solution.

Outcomes

This community directly enriches its members' teaching experiences by deepening their pedagogical content knowledge, providing valuable suggestions for improving their current teaching styles and engaging them in collective critical reflection on the teaching–learning process in the Colombian EFL classroom. Teachers leave each session feeling empowered and ready to enact positive classroom changes. Additionally, the participants practise English in authentic and meaningful situations, which they perceive as an excellent opportunity and a vital element of their professional learning.

PROJECT 3

Title

Talent Development in School Education, Germany

Aims

The nationwide collaborative research project Talent Development in School Education was initiated in 2018 by the German National Ministry of Education and all the ministries of the federal states. The first phase ended in 2023, and in July 2023, the transfer phase started, aiming to establish talent development in a much broader range of schools. The project's main goal is to enhance the identification and support of talented and high-achieving students and establish the development of all kinds of talent in daily school practice as a standard. The research undertaken for the English language project in eighteen schools revolved around the complex task (Section 6.5) as an instrument of talent identification and development in the English language classroom. In this project, teachers:

- were introduced to concepts and theories of talent development;
- introduced to the concept of the complex task as an instrument to identify individual talents, develop tasks that initiate talent development processes, and evaluate task outcomes in terms of visible talents and achievements;
- developed complex tasks specifically for their classes and groups, accounting for potential talents they had identified and then developing these further; and
- were expected to establish talent development through complex tasks in their own and their colleagues' daily classroom routines.

The project also sought to initiate and enhance change at institutional, organisational, and individual levels by professionalising the teachers and enhancing their willingness to innovate, communicate, and collaborate.

Description

In the research project, teachers were introduced to the complex task and its educational philosophy in terms of creating a space for the holistic development of students' personalities and an opportunity to unfold and display their capabilities and talents freely. Teachers were encouraged to engage in collaborative work when designing tasks and materials (Chapter 6) and to collaboratively evaluate the outcome of their designs, using tools such as lesson study and meetings to exchange and discuss their experiences and the outcomes of their teaching units based on their tasks and materials. The colleagues of the individual schools also became members of the national network of English language project schools. This enabled them to engage in further professionalisation by learning about complex task assessment and collaboration strategies and communicating the project in their school community and to other subjects. At a very practical level, they presented their work and tasks at national network conferences, exchanged experiences with colleagues from other schools, and made their tasks available to others by uploading them to the digital cloud of the national project. Teachers were also introduced to and actively participated in the ethnographic empirical classroom research, which included lesson videography, learners' task products, and teacher and student interviews. In the broader network of the national research cluster, they could attend interdisciplinary congresses and conferences, where they listened to recent developments and renowned speakers in, for instance, educational psychology, talent development models, and talent development in other subjects.

Strengths and Challenges

By joining the talent development project, teachers engaged in a process of professionalisation by expanding their knowledge about talent development as a daily routine and by employing the alternative, strictly student-oriented, methodology of working with complex tasks. First and foremost, however, they were able to develop their autonomy by creating tasks and materials that were geared towards the needs, interests, and talents of the respective group. This resulted in the experience of a new and more adaptive kind of teaching that differentiates and individualises students' learning and respects their personalities and agency.

Regarding the challenges that arose, the first was to convince the teachers that they are professionals who can design their own classroom practices and tasks autonomously and that, despite the initial investment of creating their tasks, they will ultimately benefit from this in the long run, not least because they have re-defined their role in the classroom as a facilitator rather than an instructor. Moreover, precisely because of their new roles and increased autonomy (Chapter 5), they also exhibited higher professional satisfaction and self-identification with their professional work. The second challenge that several teachers reported was the need to position themselves in their departments and schools, convincing their colleagues that it was worthwhile engaging in a complex endeavour such as this. The third challenge concerned how to engage in teaching and collaboration in the research network during the pandemic. In the end, it was satisfying for everyone to see how they managed to switch over to digital classroom work and digital collaboration in the research network within a short period of time and how, after the pandemic, working online and in digital environments enriched the other work and became the new normal.

Outcomes

The research project produced a wealth of evidence that this complex task is suited to addressing and evoking individual talents. It also

> convincingly demonstrated that the strategy to create PDCs composed of teachers, teacher educators, school administrators, representatives of the ministries, and, of course, scholars and researchers led to the desired professionalisation of teachers' daily work – provided spaces were created that encourage and enable this kind of collaborative professional work. In this project, teachers engaged (and had to engage) in much more than just professional learning. They were actively involved in research, collaborated with external academic experts and scholars, and developed their autonomy so that task and materials development and collaboration could be established as a sustainable practice and a professional capability that continues to be effective upon completion of the research project.

The three projects described here are just some recent examples of how teachers, scholars, and other members of the respective professional communities engaged in transformative collaboration, which the concept of the professional ELT development community presented in this chapter seeks to conceptualise and propose. They are also paradigmatic examples of innovation and development in language teaching that can only be accomplished in a collaborative endeavour borne by a community in terms of a socially coherent group of professionals that share common visions, define their goals, and engage in sustainable action and work. We are convinced that there are myriad such development communities in schools and countries around the world which promote professional collaboration to enhance students' learning, create better learning conditions for them, and improve their learning outcomes. We hope that future literature will shed more light on these professional communities in general and their effective practices more specifically.

9.6 Conclusion and Future Directions

The chapters in this conceptual and reflective guide to English language teacher education have proposed the professionalisation of ELT in the twenty-first century. They have presented fundamental concepts that ought to be included under the umbrella term of professionalisation and encouraged teachers to reflect on these concepts to understand them better and link them explicitly to their practice and the context in which they teach. It is hoped that this reflection has made them grasp where they are placed on the 'professional journey' continuum and encouraged them to make long-term workable plans for further professionalisation of their careers.

Regarding future directions, these need to be considered in terms of three meta-dimensions: (1) lifelong learning, (2) classroom ethnography, and (3) educational leadership.

9.6.1 Professional Teachers as Lifelong Learners

It is imperative that professional teachers are lifelong learners who stimulate themselves and others to acquire the knowledge, skills, and understandings they require throughout their lifetimes and apply them with confidence, creativity, and enthusiasm in diverse contexts. In addition, teachers need to be able to quickly adapt to changes, systematically innovate, and successfully sustain school-/university-wide transformations of curricula, materials, and assessments so that the latter not only meet students' needs but also accurately reflect and effectively respond to social developments. The other attributes of lifelong teachers include an ongoing examination of their understanding of themselves as professional teachers and an analysis of their flexibility and openness to critical reflection and self-renewal. Finally, a systematic mastery of teamwork skills (i.e., collaborating with others and serving as a good team player/role model), technological competence, and display of emotions such as empathy and compassion are indispensable. The ability to express these two emotions in a healthy way in the classroom will be of particular use to teachers who work with students who are marginalised or disabled, have learning difficulties, or suffer from mental health disorders.

9.6.2 Professional Teachers as Classroom Ethnographers

It is essential that professional teachers function as classroom ethnographers. This role requires them to systematically promote research in the classroom at two different levels. At the first level, they must utilise ethnographic, sociolinguistic, or discourse analytic methodologies to investigate classroom lives and meanings such that activities within the classroom are implemented and understood by the individuals tasked with performing them. Such research allows for a re-conceptualisation of a language classroom and describes what processes occur within this arena. The result of this type of research is a thick description (Geertz, 1973) or a detailed account of field experiences which integrates the views of classroom members and the researcher's interpretation of the social lives of these members within the classroom context. Notably, the ethnographer and the classroom members under study act as partners in co-constructing meanings within the context to which they belong.

At the second level, teachers are expected to promote ethnography as a learning approach to enhance, for instance, students' intercultural learning in the classroom (e.g., Byram & Cain, 1998; Byram & Fleming, 1998;

Kearney, 2016; McConachy et al., 2022). The purpose of such learning is to create opportunities for students not only to deepen their knowledge of the target language culture by scrutinising relevant resources and presenting their outcomes to the classroom community but also to participate in global classrooms (i.e., virtual classrooms located in two or more countries) such that students learn how to communicate appropriately with target language speakers and develop analytical understandings of their systems of meanings (Corbett, 2003). In so doing, learners-as-ethnographers, individually or in collaboration with their teachers, are stimulated to explore the target language and culture, which involves using ethnographic tools of data collection (e.g., field notes, participant observations, semi-structured interviews), gathering evidence to support their interpretations and disseminating their findings in the classroom or beyond.

As befits the twenty-first century, classroom ethnography necessitates the integration of technology and social media into its design. Therefore, both teachers-as-ethnographers and learners-as-ethnographers must demonstrate the capacity to utilise and interact with computer technologies to collect and analyse data, thereby integrating online information and operating multimedia resources. This includes 'information and data literacy, communication and collaboration, media literacy, digital content creation (including programming), security (including digital well-being and cybersecurity-related skills), intellectual property issues, problem-solving, and critical thinking' (Council of the European Union, 2018, p. 9).

9.6.3 Professional Teachers as Educational Leaders

It is paramount that professional teachers serve as educational leaders who systematically engage in the process of transforming classrooms and schools by effectively implementing their ambitious plans and visions. They should be able to solve problems creatively, initiate actions swiftly, adapt to change quickly, and go beyond their classroom responsibilities by collaborating professionally with education stakeholders, including teachers, teacher educators, parents, students, policymakers, designers of materials, and the public. Teacher leaders are expected to understand the importance of building communities and empowering classroom practitioners to confront the dilemmas their schools face. It is essential that they are able to conduct ethical research and utilise their findings to develop new teaching approaches to further students' academic success and have an awareness of how the process of English language learning is integrated into their students' lives and understanding of themselves (*Bildung*). In the same vein, teacher leaders should critically reflect on how their professional learning is embedded in their own lives and understanding of themselves. Last but not least, teacher leaders are obliged to act as advocates for social justice by willingly promoting both interactive and inclusive learning spaces and assuming the role of campaigners engaged in championing the needs of their students, the local communities, and the PLCs to which they belong.

This book also carries important and urgent messages for policymakers, teacher educators, and educational researchers. It is vital that the concepts discussed in the previous chapters are included in educational policies and teacher education curricula and syllabi so that teacher education programmes and CPD events raise teachers' awareness of the notion of professionalisation in relation to teaching careers and what it entails. Educational researchers, in turn, are encouraged to read this book with future research in mind, identify gaps in the chapters, and plan high-quality research accordingly so the concept of professionalisation is given more attention in empirical literature in the field of ELT.

REFLECTION FOR ACTION

Future Teachers

- In your future work as a teacher, would you benefit from belonging to a PDC? How?
- Do you find the PDC concept convincing compared to the other professional community concepts outlined in this chapter? Why (not)?
- As a future teacher, what kind of expertise/contribution do you think you could bring/make to the PDC in your school?
- From your experience of school education and, maybe, your current observation of schools and the language classroom, what challenges can creating a PDC pose?

Novice Teachers

- How could you and other English language teachers benefit from belonging to a PDC within your school?
- In light of your experiences as a language teacher, what immediate issue(s) should become a priority for PDCs at your school or institution?
- Reflect with two or three other English language teachers on a specific issue you want to address in your school. How would you integrate it into your school-based PDC?
- What external expertise do you consider crucial in PDCs? Why?

Experienced Teachers

- In the past, were you involved in one of the professional community concepts described in this chapter or any other professional collaboration to develop your school/institution or its members? What did you do? How successful was it? To what extent did you value the experience?
- According to your experience as a teacher, to what extent do you agree that teachers' engagement with PDCs should aim at transforming schools? What fundamental changes are required in your school/institution?
- What potential challenges would you envisage if your school or institution intended to establish a PDC? How would you respond to these challenges?
- Reflecting on your professional competences, how do you think you could contribute to a PDC in your institution to be considered an agent of change?

References

Abatayo, J. (2018). Developing communities of practice through language teacher associations in Oman. In A. Elsheikh, C. Coombe, & O. Effiong (Eds.), *The role of language teacher associations in professional development* (pp. 105–116). Springer.

Ackerman, R., & Mackenzie, S. (Eds.). (2007). *Uncovering teacher leadership: Essays and voices from the field.* Corwin Press.

Ahmadian, M. J., & García Mayo, M. P. (Eds.). (2018). *Recent perspectives on task-based language learning and teaching.* De Gruyter.

AITSL (Australian Institute for Teaching and School Leadership). (2022). *Australian professional standards for teachers.* AITSL.

Akiba, M., Murata, A., Howard, C. C., & Wilkinson, B. (2019). Lesson study design features for supporting collaborative teacher learning. *Teaching and Teacher Education, 77,* 352–365. https://doi.org/10.1016/j.tate.2018.10.012

Akkerman, S. F., & Meijer, P. C. (2011). A dialogical approach to conceptualizing teacher identity. *Teaching and Teacher Education, 27,* 308–319. https://doi.org/10.1016/j.tate.2010.08.013

Al-Issa, A. S. M. (2017). Qualities of the professional English language teacher educator: Implications for achieving quality and accountability. *Cogent Education, 4*(1), 1326652. https://doi.org/10.1080/2331186X.2017.1326652

Al-Mahrooqi, R., Coombe, C., Al-Maamari, F., & Thakur, V. (Eds.). (2017). *Revisiting EFL assessment: Critical perspectives.* Springer.

Allwright, D., & Hanks, J. (2009). *The developing language learner: An introduction to exploratory practice.* Palgrave Macmillan.

Alsaleh, A., Alabdulhadi, M., & Alrwaished, N. (2017). Impact of peer coaching strategy on pre-service teachers' professional development growth in Kuwait. *International Journal of Educational Research, 86,* 36–49. https://doi.org/10.1016/j.ijer.2017.07.011

Amzat, I. H., & Valdez, N. P. (2017). *Teacher empowerment toward professional development and practices: Perspectives across borders.* Springer.

Andersen, B. (1983). *Imagined communities: Reflections on the origin and spread of nationalism.* Verso.

Andrews, D., & Crowther, F. (2002). Parallel leadership: A clue to the contents of the 'black box' of school reform. *International Journal of Educational Management, 16*(1), 152–159. https://doi.org/10.1108/09513540210432128

Andrews, H. A. (2006). Supporting quality teachers with recognition. *Australian Journal of Teacher Education, 36,* 59–70. https://doi.org/10.14221/ajte.2011v36n12.5

Andrews, S. J. (2007). *Teacher language awareness.* Cambridge University Press.

Aoki, N. (2002). Aspects of teacher autonomy: Capacity, freedom, and responsibility. In P. Benson, & S. Toogood (Eds.), *Learner autonomy 7: Challenges to research and practice* (pp. 111–124). Authentik.

Appiah, K. A. (2018). *The lies that bind: Rethinking identity: Creed, country, colour, class, culture*. Profile Books.

Argyris, C., & Schön, D. (1978). *Organizational learning: A theory of action perspective*. Addison-Wesley.

Armstrong, T. (2009). *Multiple intelligences in the classroom* (3rd ed.). ASCD Publications.

Atai, M. R., & Nejadghanbar, H. (2016). Unpacking in-service EFL teachers' critical incidents: The case of Iran. *RELC Journal, 47*, 97–110. https://doi.org/10.1177/0033688216631177

Atjonen, P. (2012). Student teachers' outlooks upon the ethics of their mentors during teaching practice. *Scandinavian Journal of Educational Research, 56*, 39–53. https://doi.org/10.1080/00313831.2011.567395

Bailey, K. M. (2006). *Language teacher supervision: A case-based approach*. Cambridge University Press.

Baldwin, M. (2004). Critical reflection: Opportunities and threats to professional learning and service development in social work organisations. In N. Gould, & M. Baldwin (Eds.), *Social work, critical reflection and the learning organisation* (pp. 41–56). Ashgate.

Banegas, D. L. (Ed.). (2020). *Content knowledge in English language teacher education: International experiences*. Bloomsbury Academic.

Banegas, D. L. (2022). 'It's like starting all over again': Mentoring novice TESOL teachers in emergency online teaching. *The European Journal of Applied Linguistics and TEFL, 11*(1), 117–134.

Banegas, D. L., Beacon, G., & Pérez Berbain, M. (Eds.). (2021). *International perspectives on diversity in ELT*. Palgrave Macmillan.

Barfield, A., Ashwell, T., Carroll, M., Collins, K., Cowie, N., Critchley, M., Head, E., Nix, M., Obermeier, A., & Robertson, M. C. (2002). Exploring and defining teacher autonomy: A collaborative discussion. In A. S. Mackenzie, & E. McCafferty (Eds.), *Developing autonomy: Proceedings of the JALT CUE conference 2001* (pp. 217–222). The Japan Association for Language Teaching College and University Educators Special Interest Group.

Barkhuizen, G. (Ed.). (2017). *Reflections on language teacher identity research*. Routledge.

Barnwell, D. (2015). *Strategies to overcome barriers to a more effective leadership style* [Doctoral dissertation, Walden University]. https://scholarworks.waldenu.edu/cgi/viewcontent.cgi?referer=&httpsredir=1&article=2938&context=dissertations

Bashir, D. (2022). *AI literacy: Understanding shifts in our digital ecosystem*. New Degree Press.

Bassot, B. (2013). *The reflective journal*. Palgrave Macmillan.

Bassot, B. (2016). *The reflective practice guide: An interdisciplinary approach to critical reflection*. Routledge.

Bauer, K.-O. (2002). Vom Allroundtalent zum Professional. Was bedeutet Lehrerprofessionalisierung heute? [From allrounder to professional. What does teacher professionalisation mean today?]. *Pädagogik, 54*(11), 18–22.

Bauman, Z., & Lyon, D. (2013). *Liquid surveillance: A conversation*. Polity Press.

References

Bausch, K.-R., Burwitz-Melzer, E., Königs, F. G., & Krumm, H.-J. (Eds.). (2005). *Bildungsstandards für den Fremdsprachenunterricht auf dem Prüfstand. Arbeitspapiere der 25: Frühjahrskonferenz zur Erforschung des Fremdsprachenunterrichts* [Examining educational standards for foreign language learning: Working papers of the 25th spring conference for foreign language learning research]. Narr.

Bawarshi, A. S., & Reiff, M. J. (2010): *Genre: An introduction to history, theory, research, and pedagogy*. Parlor Press.

Beach, R., Thein, A. H., & Webb, A. (2016). *Teaching to exceed the English language arts common core state standards: A literacy practices approach for 6–12 classrooms*. Routledge.

Beck, C. (2016). Rethinking teacher education programs. In C. Kosnik, S. White, & C. Beck (Eds.), *Building bridges: Rethinking literacy teacher education in a digital era* (pp. 193–205). Sense Publishers.

Behrendt, M., & Franklin, T. (2014). A review of research on school field trips and their value in education. *International Journal of Environmental and Science Education, 9*, 235–245.

Bell, B. (2011). *Theorising teaching in secondary classrooms: Understanding our practice from a sociocultural perspective*. Routledge.

Bell, J. S., Thacker, T., & Schargel, F. P. (2011). *Schools where teachers lead: What successful leaders do?* Eye On Education.

Benegas, M., & Stolpestad, A. (2020). *Teacher leadership for school-wide English learning*. TESOL International Association.

Bener, E., & Yıldız, S. (2019). The use of blog activities to promote reflection in an ELT practicum. *Australian Journal of Teacher Education, 44*(8), 3. https://doi.org/10.14221/ajte.2019v44n8.3

Benitt, N. (2015). *Becoming a (better) language teacher: Classroom action research and teacher learning*. Narr.

Benson, P. (2000). Autonomy as a learners' and teachers' right. In B. Sinclair, I. McGrath, & T. Lamb (Eds.), *Learner autonomy, teacher autonomy: Future directions* (pp. 111–117). Longman.

Benson, P. (2001). *Teaching and researching autonomy in language learning*. Longman.

Benson, P. (2010). Teacher education and teacher autonomy: Creating spaces for experimentation in secondary school English language teaching. *Language Teaching Research, 14*(3), 259–275. https://doi.org/10.1177/1362168810365236

Benson, P., & Huang, J. (2008). Autonomy in the transition from foreign language learning to foreign language teaching. *D.E.L.T.A., 24*. www.scielo.br/j/delta/a/FHFnkGJY5jbgRCZdDGrF7vq/?lang=en#

Benson, P., & Ying, D. (2013). Peer teaching as a pedagogical strategy for autonomy in teacher education. *Chinese Journal of Applied Linguistics, 36*(1), 50–68. https://doi.org/10.1515/cjal-2013-0004

Berofsky, B. (1995). *Liberation from self*. Cambridge University Press.

Berry, B., Byrd, A., & Wieder, A. (2013). *Teacherpreneurs: Teachers who lead without leaving*. Jossey-Bass.

Bibri, S. E. (2018). *Smart sustainable cities of the future: The untapped potential of big data analytics and context aware computing for advancing sustainability*. Springer.

Biebighäuser, K., Zibelius, M., & Schmidt, T. (Eds.). (2012). *Aufgaben 2.0: Konzepte, Materialien und Methoden für das Fremdsprachenlehren und -lernen mit digitalen*

Medien [Tasks 2.0: Concepts, materials and methods for language learning and teaching with digital media]. Narr.

Biesta, G., Priestley, M., & Robinson, S. (2015). The role of beliefs in teacher agency. *Teachers and Teaching: Theory and Practice, 21*(6), 624–640. https://doi.org/10.1080/13540602.2015.1044325

Biesta, G., Priestley, M., & Robinson, S. (2017). Talking about education: Exploring the significance of teachers' talk for teacher agency. *Journal of Curriculum Studies, 49*(1), 38–54. https://doi.org/10.1080/00220272.2016.1205143

Blankstein, A. M., Houston, P. D., & Cole, R. W. (2007). *Soul of educational leadership: Sustaining professional learning communities*. Corwin Press.

Bleumers, L., All, A., Mariën, I., Schurmans, D., van Looy, J., Jacobs, A., Willaert, K., & de Grove, F. (2012). *State of play of digital games for empowerment and inclusion: A review of the literature and empirical cases*. Publications Office of the European Union.

Bloome, D. (2012). Classroom ethnography. In M. Grenfell, D. Bloom, C. Hardy, K. Pahl, J. Rowsell, & B. Street (Eds.), *Language, ethnography, and education: Bridging new literacy studies and Bourdieu* (pp. 7–26). Routledge.

Bloome, D., Power Carter, S., Beth, M. C., Otto, S., & Shuart-Farris, N. (2005). *Discourse analysis and the study of classroom language and literacy: A microethnographic perspective*. Lawrence Erlbaum.

Bolam, R., McMahon, A., Stoll, L., Thomas, S., & Wallace, M. (2005). *Creating and sustaining effective professional learning communities (DfES Research Report RR637)*. University of Bristol. http://dera.ioe.ac.uk/5622/1/RR637.pdf

Bond, N. (2015). *The power of teacher leaders: Their roles, influence and impact*. Routledge.

Bonnet, A., & Hericks, U. (2022). Professionalisierung in Schule und Fachunterricht aus der Perspektive der Praxeologischen Wissenssoziologie [Professionalisation in schools and specialist teaching from the perspective of the praxeological sociology of knowledge]. In R. Bohnsack, A. Bonnet, & U. Hericks (Eds.), *Praxeologisch-wissenssoziologische Professionsforschung: Perspektiven aus Früh- und Schulpädagogik, Fachdidaktik und Sozialer Arbeit* [*Praxeological-sociological professional research. Perspectives from early and school education, subject didactics and social work*] (pp. 59–85). Klinkhardt.

Borg, S. (2006). *Teacher cognition and language education: Research and practice*. Continuum.

Borg, S. (2009). Language teacher cognition. In A. Burns, & J. C. Richards (Eds.), *The Cambridge guide to second language teacher education* (pp. 163–171). Cambridge University Press.

Borg, S. (2010). Language teacher research engagement. *Language Teaching Journal, 43*(4), 391–429. https://doi.org/10.1017/S0261444810000170

Borg, S. (2013). *Teacher research in language teaching: A critical analysis*. Cambridge University Press.

Borko, H., Jacobs, J., Eiteljorg, E., & Pittman, M. E. (2008). Video as a tool for fostering productive discussions in mathematics professional development. *Teaching and Teacher Education, 24*, 417–436. https://doi.org/10.1016/j.tate.2006.11.012

Boud, D., Keogh, R., & Walker, D. (1985). *Reflection: Turning experience into learning*. Kogan Page.

Brater, M. (1997). Schule und Ausbildung im Zeichen der Individualisierung [School and education under the sign of individualisation]. In M. Beck (Ed.), *Kinder der Freiheit [Children of freedom]* (pp. 149–174). Suhrkamp.

Breen, M., & Candlin, C. (1980). The essentials of a communicative curriculum in language teaching. *Applied Linguistics, 1*, 89–112. http://dx.doi.org/10.1093/applin/1.2.89

Breen, M., & Mann, S. (1997). Shooting arrows at the sun: Perspectives on a pedagogy for autonomy. In P. Benson, & P. Voller (Eds.), *Autonomy and independence in language learning* (pp. 132–149). Addison Wesley-Longman.

Breidbach, S. (2007). *Bildung, Kultur, Wissenschaft: Reflexive Didaktik für den bilingualen Sachfachunterricht [Bildung, culture and the sciences. Reflexive didactics for content and language integrated learning]*. Waxmann.

Breidbach, S., Elsner, D., & Young, A. (2011). Language awareness in teacher education: Cultural-political and social-educational dimensions. In S. Breidbach, D. Elsner, & A. Young (Eds.), *Language awareness in teacher education: Cultural-political and social-educational perspectives* (pp. 11–19). Peter Lang.

British Educational Research Association-RSA. (2014). *The role of research in teacher education: Reviewing the evidence. Interim report of the BERA-RSA inquiry.* www.bera.ac.uk/wp-content/uploads/2014/02/BERA-RSA-Interim-Report.pdf

Brodie, K., & Borko, H. (Eds.). (2016). *Professional learning communities in South African schools and teacher education programmes.* HSRC Press.

Brookfield, S. D. (2017). *Becoming a critically reflective teacher* (2nd ed.). Jossey-Bass.

Brookhart, S. M. (2013). *How to create and use rubrics for formative assessment and grading.* Association for Supervision & Curriculum Development.

Brown, H. D., & Abeywickrama, P. (2018). *Language assessment: Principles and classroom practices* (3rd ed.). Pearson Education.

Brubaker, D. L. (2004). *Revitalizing curriculum leadership: Inspiring and empowering your school community.* Corwin Press.

Bukhatir, S. (2018). *Professionalism in education: An overview.* The London Centre for Leadership in Learning. https://discovery.ucl.ac.uk/id/eprint/10065143/1/Bukhatir_2018%20Professionalism%20in%20education%20-%20An%20overview%20-%20Safa%20Bukhatir.pdf

Burkert, A., & Schwienhorst, K. (2008). Focus on the student teacher: The European Portfolio for Student Teachers of Languages (EPOSTL) as a tool to develop teacher autonomy. *Innovation in Language Learning and Teaching, 2*(3), 238–252. https://doi.org/10.1080/17501220802158941

Burns, A. (2005). Action research: An evolving paradigm? *Language Teaching, 38*(2), 57–74. https://doi.org/10.1017/S0261444805002661

Burns, A. (2010). *Doing action research in English language teaching: A guide for practitioners.* Routledge.

Burns, A., Edwards, E., & Ellis, N. J. (2022). *Sustaining action research: A practical guide for institutional engagement.* Routledge.

Burns, A., & Richards, J. C. (Eds.). (2009). *The Cambridge guide to second language teacher education.* Cambridge University Press.

Bush, A., & Grotjohann, N. (2020). Collaboration in teacher education. A cross-sectional study on future teachers' attitudes towards collaboration, their intentions to collaborate and their performance of collaboration. *Teaching and Teacher Education, 88*, 102968. https://doi.org/10.1016/j.tate.2019.102968

Bygate, M., Samuda, V., & van den Branden, K. (2022). A pedagogical rationale for task-based language teaching for the acquisition of real-world language use. In M. J. Ahmadian, & M. H. Long (Eds.), *The Cambridge handbook of task-based language teaching* (pp. 27–52). Cambridge University Press.

Byram, M. (2021). *Teaching and assessing intercultural communicative competence: Revisited*. Multilingual Matters.

Byram, M., & Cain, A. (1998). Civilisation/cultural studies: An experiment in French and English schools. In M. Byram, & M. Fleming (Eds.), *Language learning in intercultural perspective* (pp. 32–44). Cambridge University Press.

Byram, M., & Fleming, M. (1998). *Language learning in intercultural perspective: Approaches through drama and ethnography*. Cambridge University Press.

Byram, M., & Wagner, M. (2018). Making a difference: Language teaching for intercultural and international dialogue. *Foreign Language Annals, 51*(1), 140–151. https://doi.org/10.1111/flan.12319

Cakir, A., & Balcikanli, C. (2012). The use of the EPOSTL to foster teacher autonomy: ELT student teachers' and teacher trainers' views. *Australian Journal of Teacher Education, 37*(3), 2. https://files.eric.ed.gov/fulltext/EJ969522.pdf

Cambridge Assessment English. (2018). *Cambridge English teaching framework competency statements*. UCLES.

Camilleri Grima, A. (1997). Introducing learner autonomy in initial teacher training. In H. Holec, & I. Huttumem (Eds.), *Learner autonomy in modern languages: Research and development* (pp. 87–101). Council of Europe.

Camilleri Grima, A. (1999). *Learner autonomy: The teachers' views*. http://archive.ecml.at/documents/pubCamilleriG_E.pdf

Canale, M., & Swain, M. (1980). Theoretical bases of communicative approaches to second language teaching and testing. *Applied Linguistics, 1*, 1–47. http://dx.doi.org/10.1093/applin/I.1.1

Candlin, C. (Ed.). (1981). *The communicative teaching of English: Principles and an exercise typology*. Longman.

Cárdenas Ramos, R. (2006). Considerations on the role of teacher autonomy. *Colombian Applied Linguistics Journal, 8*, 183–202. https://core.ac.uk/download/pdf/229141607.pdf

Carl, A. E. (2009). *Teacher empowerment through curriculum development: Theory into practice* (3rd ed.). Juta Legal and Academic Publishers.

Carr, D. (2000). *Professionalism and ethics in teaching*. Routledge.

Carretero Gomez, S., Vuorikari, R., & Punie, Y. (2017). *DigComp 2.1: The digital competence framework for citizens with eight proficiency levels and examples of use*. Publications Office of the European Union.

Carrier, M., Damerow, R. M., & Bailey, K. M. (Eds.). (2017). *Digital language learning and teaching: Research, theory and practice*. Routledge.

Cartwright, L. (2011). How consciously reflective are you? In D. McGregor, & L. Cartwright (Eds.), *Developing reflective practice: A guide for beginning teachers* (pp. 55–68). The McGraw-Hill Companies.

Caspari, D., & Grünewald, A. (2022). Fachdidaktisches Wissen in der Fremdsprachenlehrkraftebildung [Subject-specific knowledge in foreign language teacher education] [Special issue]. *ZFF, 33*(1), 160.

Center for Teaching Quality, National Board for Professional Teaching Standards, & the National Education Association. (2014). *The teacher leadership competences.* www.nbpts.org/wp-content/uploads/teacher_leadership_competencies_final.pdf

Chen, C., Wen, P., Chen, Z., Liao, S., & Shu, X. (2020). Formal mentoring support and protégé creativity: A self-regulatory perspective. *Asian Journal of Social Psychology, 11*, 12440. https://doi.org/10.1111/ajsp.12440

Cheng, L., & Fox, J., (2017). *Assessment in the language classroom: Teachers supporting student learning.* Palgrave Macmillan.

Cheung, Y. L., Said, S. B., & Park, K. (Eds.). (2015). *Advances and current trends in language teacher identity research.* Routledge.

Chien, C. (2013). Analysis of a language teacher's journal of classroom practice as reflective practice. *Reflective Practice, 14*(1), 131–143. https://doi.org/10.1080/14623943.2012.732951

Childs-Bowen, D., Moller, G., & Scrivner, J. (2000). Principals: Leaders of leaders. *National Association of Secondary School Principals (NASSP) Bulletin, 84*(616), 27–34. https://doi.org/10.1177/019263650008461606

Choo, S. S. (2013). *Reading the world, the globe, and the cosmos: Approaches to teaching literature for the twenty-first century.* Peter Lang.

Chowdhury, R. (Ed.). (2018). *Transformation and empowerment through education: Reconstructing our relationship with education.* Routledge.

Christison, M., & Murray, D. E. (Eds.). (2009). *Leadership in English language education: Theoretical foundations and practical skills for changing times.* Routledge.

Christodoulou, N. (2016). *Reflective development through the care model: Empowering teachers of English as a foreign language.* Cambridge Scholars Publishing.

Ciampa, K., & Gallagher, T. L. (2015). Blogging to enhance in-service teachers' professional learning and development during collaborative inquiry. *Educational Technology Research and Development, 63*(6), 883–913. https://doi.org/10.1007/s11423-015-9404-7

Cirocki, A. (2016). *Developing learner autonomy through tasks: Theory, research, practice.* LinguaBooks.

Cirocki, A., & Anam, S. (2024). How much freedom do we have? The perceived autonomy of secondary school EFL teachers in Indonesia. *Language Teaching Research, 28*(2), 440–465. https://doi.org/10.1177/13621688211007472

Cirocki, A., & Brown, J. D. (2021). Assessment in the ELT classroom [special issue]. *The European Journal of Applied Linguistics and TEFL, 10*(1).

Cirocki, A., & Burns, A. (2019). Language teachers as researchers [special issue]. *The European Journal of Applied Linguistics and TEFL, 8*(2).

Cirocki, A., & Coombe, C. (2023). Leadership and management in TESOL [special issue]. *The European Journal of Applied Linguistics and TEFL, 12*(2).

Cirocki, A., & Farrell, T. S. C. (2017a). Reflective practice in the ELT classroom [special issue]. *The European Journal of Applied Linguistics and TEFL, 6*(2).

Cirocki, A., & Farrell, T. S. C. (2017b). Reflective practice for professional development of TESOL practitioners. *The European Journal of Applied Linguistics and TEFL, 6*(2), 5–23.

Cirocki, A., & Farrell, T. S. C. (2019). Professional development of secondary school EFL teachers: Voices from Indonesia. *System, 85*, 1–14. www.sciencedirect.com/science/article/abs/pii/S0346251X18303932

Cirocki, A., & Farrelly, R. (2016). Research and reflective practice in the EFL classroom: Voices from Armenia. *Eurasian Journal of Applied Linguistics, 2*(1), 31–56. https://doi.org/10.32601/ejal.460995

Cirocki, A., & Farrelly, R. (2019). Current perspectives on teaching English to refugee-background students [special issue]. *The European Journal of Applied Linguistics and TEFL, 8*(1), 236.

Cirocki, A., & Golombek, P. (2020). Sociocultural theory in teacher education and development [special issue]. *The European Journal of Applied Linguistics and TEFL, 9*(2), 232.

Cirocki, A., & Johnson, K. E. (2022). Mentoring beginning TESOL teachers [special issue]. *The European Journal of Applied Linguistics and TEFL, 11*(1), 200.

Cirocki, A., & Levy, M. (2018). Educational technology in English language learning and teaching [special issue]. *The European Journal of Applied Linguistics and TEFL, 7*(2), 228.

Cirocki, A., & Motschenbacher, H. (2022). Diversity and representation in the ELT classroom [special issue]. *The European Journal of Applied Linguistics and TEFL, 11*(2), 202.

Cirocki, A., & Widodo, H. P. (2019). Reflective practice in English language teaching in Indonesia: Shared practices from two teacher educators. *Iranian Journal of Language Teaching Research, 7*(3), 15–35. https://doi.org/10.30466/IJLTR.2019.120734

Cirocki, A., Farrelly, R., & Buchanan, H. (Eds.). (2023). *Continuing professional development of TESOL practitioners: A global landscape*. Springer.

Cirocki, A., Maydarov, I., & Baecher, L. (Eds.). (2019a). *Current perspectives on the TESOL practicum: Cases from around the globe*. Springer.

Cirocki, A., Maydarov, I., & Baecher, L. (2019b). Contemporary perspectives on student teacher learning and the TESOL practicum. In A. Cirocki, I. Maydarov, & L. Baecher (Eds.), *Current perspectives on the TESOL practicum: Cases from around the globe* (pp. 1–20). Springer.

Cirocki, A., Parba, J., Caparoso, J., & Caday, C. A. (2019). Metacognitive reading strategies in the Filipino ESL classroom: Use and instruction. *Asian Journal of English Language Teaching, 28*, 29–60.

Clark, R., Livingstone, D. W., & Smaller, H. (2012). *Teacher learning and power in the knowledge society*. Sense Publishers.

Clement, M., & Vandenberghe, R. (2000). Teachers' professional development: A solitary or collegial (ad)venture? *Teaching and Teacher Education, 16*(1), 81–101. https://doi.org/10.1016/S0742-051X(99)00051-7

Cochran-Smith, M., & Lytle, S. L. (2009). *Inquiry as stance: Practitioner research for the next generation*. Teachers College Press.

Cohen, A. R., & Bradford, D. L. (2005). *Influence without authority* (2nd ed.). John Wiley & Sons.

Cohen, L., Manion, L., & Morrison, K. (2018). *Research methods in education* (8th ed.). Routledge.

Coleman, J. S. (1990). *The foundations of social theory*. Harvard University Press.

Coleman, M. R., Gallagher, J. J., & Job, J. (2012). Developing and sustaining professionalism within gifted education. *Gifted Child Today, 35*(1), 27–36. https://doi.org/10.1177/1076217511427511

Collet, V. S. (2019). *Collaborative lesson study: ReVisioning teacher professional development*. Teachers College Press.

References

Conley, Q., Scheufler, J., Persichini, G., Lowenthal, P. R., & Humphrey, M. (2018). Digital citizenship for all: Empowering young learners with disabilities to become digitally literate. *International Journal of Digital Literacy and Digital Competence, 9* (1), 1–20. https://doi.org/10.4018/IJDLDC.2018010101

Coombe, C., Anderson, N. J., & Stephenson, L. (Eds.). (2020). *Professionalizing your English language teaching.* Springer.

Cooper, K. S., Stanulis, R. N., Brondyk, S. K., Hamilton, E. R., Macaluso, M., & Meier, J. A. (2016). The teacher leadership process: Attempting change within embedded systems. *Journal of Educational Change, 17*(1), 85–113. https://doi.org/10.1007/s10833-015-9262-4

Cope, B., & Kalantzis, M. (Eds.). (2000). *Multiliteracies: Literacy learning and the design of social futures.* Routledge.

Corbett, J. (2003). *An intercultural approach to English language teaching.* Multilingual Matters.

Cosenza, M. N. (2015). Defining teacher leadership affirming the teacher leader model standards. *Issues in Teacher Education, 24*(2), 79–99. https://files.eric.ed.gov/fulltext/EJ1090327.pdf

Costa, A. L., & Kallick, B. (1993). Through the lens of a critical friend. *Educational Leadership, 3*, 49–51.

Council of Europe. (2001). *Common European framework of reference for languages: Learning, teaching, assessment.* Council of Europe.

Council of Europe. (2018). *Reference framework of competences for democratic culture (vol. 1): Context, concepts and model (vol. 2): Descriptors of competences for democratic culture (vol. 3): Guidance for implementation.* Council of Europe.

Council of Europe. (2020). *Common European framework of reference for languages: Companion volume.* Council of Europe.

Council of the European Union. (2018). Council recommendation of 22 May 2018 on key competences for lifelong learning. *Official Journal of the European Union, C 189*(1). https://eur-lex.europa.eu/legal-content/EN/TXT/PDF/?uri=CELEX:32018H0604(01)&rid=7

Crabbe, D. (1993). Fostering autonomy from within the classroom: The teacher's responsibility. *System, 21*(4), 443–452.

Crandall, J., & Christison, M. (Eds.). (2016). *Teacher education and professional development in TESOL: Global perspectives.* Routledge.

Creswell, J. W., & Tashakkori, A. (2007). Developing publishable mixed methods manuscripts. *Journal of Mixed Methods Research, 1*, 107–111. https://doi.org/10.1177/1558689806298644

Crookes, G. (2003). *A practicum in TESOL: Professional development through teaching practice.* Cambridge University Press.

Crookes, G. (2009). *Values, philosophies, and beliefs in TESOL: Making a statement.* Cambridge University Press.

Dahler-Larsen, P. (2009). Learning-oriented educational evaluation in contemporary society. In K. E. Ryan, & J. B. Cousins (Eds.), *The SAGE international handbook of educational evaluation* (1st ed., pp. 307–322). SAGE Publications.

Danielson, C. (2006). *Teacher leadership that strengthens professional practice.* Association for Supervision and Curriculum Development.

Danielson, C. (2007). The many faces of leadership. *Educational Leadership, 65*(1), 14–19. www.solonline.org/wp-content/uploads/2018/08/sol_reflections_2.1.pdf

Danielson, C., & McGreal, T. L. (2000). *Teacher evaluation to enhance professional learning*. Educational Testing Service.

Dantley, M. E. (2003). Principled, pragmatic, and purposive leadership: Reimagining educational leadership through prophetic spirituality. *Journal of School Leadership, 13*(3), 181–198. https://doi.org/10.1177/105268460301300203

Dantley, M. E. (2008). The 2007 Willower family lecture reconstructing leadership: Embracing a spiritual dimension. *Leadership and Policy in Schools, 7*, 451–460. https://doi.org/10.1080/15700760802247411

Darvin, R., & Hafner, C. A. (2022). Digital literacies in TESOL: Mapping out the terrain. *TESOL Quarterly, 56*(3), 865–882. https://doi.org/10.1002/tesq.3161

Datnow, A., & Park, V. (2019). *Professional collaboration with purpose: Teacher learning for equitable and excellent schools*. Routledge.

Davies, B., & Davies, B. J. (2010). Developing a strategic leadership perspective. In B. Davies, & M. Brundrett (Eds.), *Developing successful leadership* (pp. 11–26). Springer.

Davis, J. M., Norris, J. M., Malone, M. E., McKay, T. H., & Son, Y. (Eds.). (2018). *Useful assessment and evaluation in language education*. Georgetown University Press.

Day, C. (2002). School reform and transitions in teacher professionalism and identity. *International Journal of Educational Research, 37*, 677–692. https://doi.org/10.1016/S0883-0355(03)00065-X

Day, C. A., Gordon, K., & Sammons, P. (2006). The personal and professional selves of teachers: Stable and unstable identities. *British Educational Research Journal, 32*(4), 601–616. https://doi.org/10.1080/01411920600775316

D'Cruz, H., & Jones, M. (2014). *Social work research in practice: Ethical and political contexts* (2nd ed.). SAGE Publications.

D'Cruz, H., Gillingham, P., & Melendez, S. (2007). Reflexivity, its meanings and relevance for social work: A critical review of the literature. *British Journal of Social Work, 37*(1), 73–90. https://doi.org/10.1093/bjsw/bcl001

de Boer, I., de Vegt, F., Pluk, H., & Latijnhouwers, M. (2021). *Rubrics – A tool for feedback and assessment viewed from different perspectives: Enhancing learning and assessment quality*. Springer.

de Dios Martínez Agudo, J. (Ed.). (2018). *Emotions in second language teaching: Theory, research and teacher education*. Springer.

Dempster, K., & Robbins, J. (2017). *How to build communication success in your school: A guide for school leaders*. Routledge.

Dewey, J. (1929). *The quest for certainty: A study of the relation between knowledge and action*. Minton, Balch & Company.

Díaz Maggioli, G. (2012). *Teaching language teachers: Scaffolding professional learning*. R&L Education.

Dierking, R., & Fox, R. (2013). 'Changing the way I teach': Building teacher knowledge, confidence, and autonomy. *Journal of Teacher Education, 64*(2), 129–144. https://doi.org/10.1177/0022487112462893

Dikilitaş, K., & Griffiths, C. (2017). *Developing language teacher autonomy through action research*. Palgrave Macmillan.

Donovan, L., Meyer, S., & Fitzgerald, S. (2007). Transformative learning and appreciative inquiry: A more perfect union for deep organizational change. *Academy of Management Proceeding*. http://proceedings.aom.org/content/2007/1/1.28 2.full.pdf

Dörnyei, Z. (2007). *Research methods in applied linguistics: Quantitative, qualitative, and mixed methodologies.* Oxford University Press.

Dozier, T. (2007). Turning good teachers into great teachers. *Educational Leadership, 65*(1), 54–55. www.ascd.org/el/articles/turning-good-teachers-into-great-leaders

Dudeney, G., & Hockly, N. (2007). *How to teach English through technology.* Pearson Longman.

Dudley, P. (Ed.). (2015). *Lesson study: Professional learning for our time.* Routledge.

Doraiswamy, N., Wilson, G., Czerniak, C. M., Tuttle, N., Porter, K., & Czajkowski, K. (2022). Teacher leader model standards in context: Analyzing a program of teacher leadership development to contextual behaviours of teacher leaders. *European Journal of Educational Management, 5*(1), 49–62. https://doi.org/10.12973/eujem.5.1.49

Eckerth, J., & Leung, C. (2009). Talking to the other, and writing for oneself: Pursuing teacher professionalism through narrative inquiry. In M. A. Vyas, & Y. L. Patel (Eds.), *Teaching English as a second language: A new pedagogy for a new century* (pp. 194–211). PHI Learning Private Limited.

Education and Training Foundation. (2014). *Professional standards for teachers and trainers in education and training.* www.et-foundation.co.uk/wp-content/uploads/2014/05/ETF_Professional_Standards_Digital_FINAL.pdf

Education International, & UNESCO. (2019). *Global framework of professional teaching standards.* Education International. www.ei-ie.org/en/item/25734:global-framework-of-professional-teaching-standards

Education Scotland. (2015). *Lesson study.* Education Scotland.

Edwards, E., & Burns, A. (2016a). Action research to support teachers' classroom materials development. *Innovation in Language Learning and Teaching, 10*(2), 106–120. https://doi.org/10.1080/17501229.2015.1090995

Edwards, E., & Burns, A. (2016b). Language teacher researcher identity negotiation: An ecological perspective. *TESOL Quarterly, 50*(3), 735–745. https://doi.org/10.1002/tesq.313

Ellis, E. (2016). *The plurilingual TESOL teacher: The hidden languaged lives of TESOL teachers and why they matter.* De Gruyter Mouton.

Elsheikh, A., Coombe, C., & Effiong, O. (Eds.) (2018). *The role of language teacher associations in professional development.* Springer.

England, L. (2020). *TESOL career path development: Creating professional success.* Routledge.

Ensher, E. A., & Murphy, S. E. (2005). *Power mentoring: How successful mentors and proteges get the most out of their relationships.* Jossey-Bass.

Eröz-Tuğa, B. (2013). Reflective feedback sessions using video recordings. *ELT Journal Volume, 67*(2), 175–183. https://doi.org/10.1093/elt/ccs081

Erss, M. (2018). 'Complete freedom to choose within limits' – Teachers' views of curricular autonomy, agency and control in Estonia, Finland and Germany. *The Curriculum Journal, 29*(2), 238–256, https://doi.org/10.1080/09585176.2018.1445514

Esfandiari, R., & Kamali, M. (2016). On the relationship between job satisfaction, teacher burnout, and teacher autonomy. *Iranian Journal of Applied Language Studies, 8*(2), 73–98. https://doi.org/10.22111/IJALS.2016.3081

Eunson, B. (2015). *Communicating in the 21st century* (4th ed.). John Wiley & Sons.

European Commission. (2001). *Making a European area of lifelong learning a reality.* European Commission.

European Commission. (2008). *Levels of autonomy and responsibilities of teachers in Europe*. Eurydice.
Eutsler, L., Hancock, L., & Pettet, T. H. (2022). Twitter as a professional learning network in teacher preparation. *International Journal of Digital Literacy and Digital Competence, 13*(1), 1–16. https://doi.org/10.4018/IJDLDC.309101
Evans, L. (2011). The 'shape' of teacher professionalism in England: Professional standards, performance management, professional development and the changes proposed in the 2010 White Paper. *British Educational Research Journal, 37*(5), 851–870. https://doi.org//10.1080/01411926.2011.607231
Evans, M., & Esch, E. (2013). The elusive boundaries of second language teacher professional development. *The Language Learning Journal, 41*(2), 137–141. https://doi.org/10.1080/09571736.2013.790129
Evetts, J. (2008). The management of professionalism. In S. Gewirtz, P. Mahony, I. Hextall, & A. Cribb (Eds.), *Changing teacher professionalism: International trends, challenges and ways forward* (pp. 19–30). Routledge.
Evetts, J. (2011). A new professionalism? Challenges and opportunities. *Current Sociology, 59*(4), 406–422. https://doi.org/10.1177/0011392111402585
Faez, F., Karas, M., & Uchihara, T. (2021). Connecting language proficiency to teaching ability: A meta-analysis. *Language Teaching Research, 25*(5), 754–777. https://doi.org/10.1177/1362168819868667
Farr, F. (2015). *Practice in TESOL*. Edinburgh University Press.
Farrell, T. S. C. (2001). Critical friendships: Colleagues helping each other develop. *ELT Journal, 55*(4), 368–374. https://doi.org/10.1093/elt/55.4.368
Farrell, T. S. C. (2008a). Critical incidents in ELT initial teacher training. *ELT Journal, 62*(1), 3–10. https://doi.org/10.1093/elt/ccm072
Farrell, T. S. C. (2008b). *Reflective language teaching: From research to practice*. Continuum.
Farrell, T. S. C. (2013). *Reflective practice in ESL teacher development groups: From practices to principles*. Palgrave Macmillan.
Farrell, T. S. C. (2015). *Promoting teacher reflection in second language education: A framework for TESOL professionals*. Routledge.
Farrell, T. S. C. (2016). The practices of encouraging TESOL teachers to engage in reflective practice: An appraisal of recent research contributions. *Language Teaching Research, 20*(2), 223–247. https://doi.org/10.1177/1362168815617335
Farrell, T. S. C. (2018). *Research on reflective practice in TESOL*. Routledge.
Farrell, T. S. C., & Baecher, L. (2017). *Reflecting on critical incidents in language education*. Bloomsbury Academic.
Farrell, T. S. C., & Kennedy, B. (2019). Reflective practice framework for TESOL teachers: One teacher's reflective journey. *Reflective Practice, 20*(1), 1–12. https://doi.org/10.1080/14623943.2018.1539657
Feng, L., Hodges, T. S., Waxman, H. C. (2019). Discovering the impact of reading coursework and discipline-specific mentorship on first-year teachers' self-efficacy: A latent class analysis. *Annals of Dyslexia, 69*, 80–98. https://doi.org/10.1007/s11881-018-00167-1
Finlay, L. (2008). Reflecting on 'reflective practice'. *PBPL*, paper 52 (January), 1–27. https://oro.open.ac.uk/68945/1/Finlay-%282008%29-Reflecting-on-reflective-practice-PBPL-paper-52.pdf
Fleming, D., Bangou, F., & Fellus, O. (2011). ESL Teacher-candidates' beliefs about language. *TESL Canada Journal/Revue TESL du Canada, 29*(1), 39–56. https://doi.org/10.18806/tesl.v29i1.1088

References

Fook, J. (2002). *Critical social work*. SAGE Publications.
Fook, J., & Askeland, G. (2006). The 'critical' in critical reflection. In S. White, J. Fook, & F. Gardner (Eds.), *Critical reflection in health and social care* (pp. 40–53). Open University Press.
Fook, J., & Gardner, F. (2007). *Practising critical reflection: A resource handbook*. Open University Press.
Foucault, M. (1972). *The archaeology of knowledge*. Routledge.
Fox, E. M. (2019). Mobile technology: A tool to increase global competency among higher education students. *The International Review of Research in Open and Distributed Learning, 20*(2). https://doi.org/10.19173/irrodl.v20i2.3961
Freeman, D. (2016). *Educating second language teachers*. Oxford University Press.
Freeman, D. (2017). The case for teachers' classroom English proficiency. *RELC, 48*(1), 31–52. https://doi.org/10.1177/0033688217691073
Freeman, D., Katz, A., Garcia Gomez, P., & Burns, A. (2015). English-for-teaching: Rethinking teacher proficiency in the classroom. *ELT Journal, 69*(2), 129–139. https://doi.org/10.1093/elt/ccu074
Freire, P. (1970). *Pedagogy of the oppressed*. Continuum.
Freitag-Hild, B. (2010). *Theorie, Aufgabentypologie und Unterrichtspraxis inter- und transkultureller Literaturdidaktik: British Fictions of Migration im Fremdsprachenunterricht* [Theory, a task typology and classroom practices of an inter- and transcultural pedagogy of literature. British fictions of migration in the foreign language classroom]. WVT.
Gabriel, J. G. (2005). *How to thrive as a teacher leader*. ASCD Publications.
Gabryś-Barker, D. (2017). Preservice teachers' perceptions of teacher autonomy. In M. Pawlak, A. Mystkowska-Wiertelak, & J. Bielak (Eds.), *Autonomy in second language learning: Managing the resources, second language learning and teaching* (pp. 161–177). Springer.
Gadsby, H. (2022). Fostering reflective practice in post graduate certificate in education students through the use of reflective journals: Developing a typology for reflection. *Reflective Practice, 23*(3), 357–368. https://doi.org/10.1080/14623943.2022.2028612
Galante, A. (2015). Intercultural communicative competence in English language teaching: Towards validation of student identity. *BELT-Brazilian English Language Teaching Journal, 6*(1), 29–39. http://dx.doi.org/10.15448/2178-3640.2015.1.20188
Galloway, N., & Rose, H. (2015). *Introducing global Englishes*. Routledge.
Gámiz-Sánchez, V. M., Gallego-Arrufat, M. J., & Crisol-Moya, E. (2016). Impact of electronic portfolios on prospective teachers' participation, motivation, and autonomous learning. *Journal of Information Technology Education: Research, 15*, 517–533.www.jite.org/documents/Vol15/JITEv15ResearchP517-533Gamiz2896.pdf
Gappa, J. M., Austin, A. E., & Trice, A. G. (2007). *Rethinking faculty work: Higher Education's strategic imperative*. John Wiley & Sons.
Garrison, D. R., & Akyol, Z. (2009). Role of instructional technology in the transformation of higher education. *Journal of Computing in Higher Education, 21*(1), 19–30. https://doi.org/10.1007/s12528-009-9014-7
Garza, R., & Smith, S. F. (2015). Pre-service teachers' blog reflections: Illuminating their growth and development. *Cogent Education, 2*, 1066550. https://doi.org/10.1080/2331186X.2015.1066550
Gebhard, J. G. (2017). *Teaching English as a foreign or second language: A self-development and methodology guide* (3rd ed.). University of Michigan Press.

Gebril, A. (2021). *Learning-oriented language assessment: Putting theory into practice*. Routledge.
Gee, J. P., & Hayes, E. R. (2011). *Language and learning in the digital age*. Routledge.
Geertz, C. (1973). *The interpretation of cultures: Selected essays*. Basic Books.
Genc, Z. S. (2010). Teacher autonomy through reflective journals among teachers of English as a foreign language in Turkey. *Teacher Development, 14*(3), 397–409. https://doi.org/10.1080/13664530.2010.504028
Gerlach, D. (2020). *Zur Professionalität der Professionalisierenden: Was machen Lehrerbildner*innen im fremdsprachendidaktischen Vorbereitungsdienst?* [*On the professionalism of the professionalizers: What do teacher educators do in secondary FLT teacher education?*]. Narr.
Ghosh, R., Hutchins, H. M., Rose, K. J., & Manongsong, A. M. (2020). Exploring the lived experiences of mutuality in diverse formal faculty mentoring partnerships through the lens of mentoring schemas. *Human Resource Development Quarterly, 31*(3), 319–340. https://doi.org/10.1002/hrdq.21386
Gibbs, G. (1988). *Learning by doing: A guide to teaching and learning methods*. Oxford Further Education Unit.
Gill, B. (2005). *Schule in der Wissensgesellschaft: Ein soziologisches Studienbuch für Lehrerinnen und Lehrer* [*Schools in the knowledge society: A sociological reader for teachers*]. Verlag für Sozialwissenschaften.
Gitsaki, C., & Coombe, C. (Eds.). (2016). *Current issues in language evaluation, assessment and testing: Research and practice*. Cambridge Scholars Publishing.
Glendenning, F., & Cartwright, L. (2011). How can you make the best use of feedback on your teaching? In D. McGregor, & L. Cartwright (Eds.), *Developing reflective practice: A guide for beginning teachers* (pp. 165–185). The McGraw-Hill Companies.
Goldhaber, D., & Hannaway, J. (2009). *Creating a new teaching profession*. The Urban Institute.
Golombek, P., & Doran, M. (2014). Unifying cognition, emotion, and activity in language teacher professional development. *Teaching and Teacher Education: An International Journal of Research and Studies, 39*(1), 102–111. https://doi.org/10.1016/j.tate.2014.01.002
Gonzalez Smith, M. (2019). A video-mediated critical friendship reflection framework for ESL teacher education. *The Electronic Journal for English as a Second Language, 23*(1). www.tesl-ej.org/wordpress/issues/volume23/ej89/ej89a7/
Gottesman, B. L. (2009). *Peer coaching in higher education*. Rowman & Littlefield.
Gray, J., & Morton, T. (2018). *Social interaction and English language teacher identity: Studies in social interaction*. Edinburgh University Press.
Green, J., & Bloome, D. (2004). Ethnography and ethnographers of and in education: A situated perspective. In J. Flood, S. B. Heath, & D. Lapp (Eds.), *Handbook of research on teaching literacy through the communicative and visual arts* (pp. 181–202). Routledge.
Greenlee, B. J. (2007). Building teacher leadership capacity through educational leadership programs. *Journal of Research for Educational Leaders, 4*(1), 44–74. www2.education.uiowa.edu/archives/jrel/spring07/documents/greenlee_0705.pdf
Griffith, V. (2000). The reflective dimension in teacher education. *International Journal of Educational Research, 33*, 539–555. https://doi.org/10.1016/S0883-0355(00)00033-1
Grimm, N., Meyer, M., & Volkmann, L. (2015). *Teaching English*. Narr.

Grimsæth, G., Nordvik, G., & Bergsvik, E. (2008). The newly qualified teacher: A leader and a professional? A Norwegian study. *Professional Development in Education, 34*(2), 219–236. https://doi.org/10.1080/13674580801950873

Groome, T. H. (1980). *Christian religious education: Sharing our story and vision.* Harper and Row.

Gu, P. (2014). EFL teacher learning in the Chinese sociocultural context. In D. Coniam (Ed.), *English language education and assessment: Recent developments in Hong Kong and the Chinese mainland* (pp. 69–85). Springer.

Gutierrez, A., Alexander, C., & Fox, J. (2019). *Professionalism and teacher education: Voices from policy and practice.* Springer.

Hadar, L., & Brody, D. (2010). From isolation to symphonic harmony: Building a professional development community among teacher educators. *Teaching and Teacher Education, 26*(8), 1641–1651. https://doi.org/10.1016/j.tate.2010.06.015

Hall, L. A. (2018). Using blogs to support reflection in teacher education. *Literacy Research and Instruction, 57*(1), 26–43. https://doi.org/10.1080/19388071.2017.1367055

Hallet, W. (2002). *Fremdsprachenunterricht als Spiel der Texte und Kulturen: Intertextualität als Paradigma einer kulturwissenschaftlichen Didaktik* [*The foreign language classroom as an interplay of texts and cultures: Intertextuality as a paradigm of cultural studies-based pedagogy*]. WVT.

Hallet, W. (2006a). *Didaktische Kompetenzen: Lehr- und Lernprozesse erfolgreich gestalten* [*Didactic competences: Designing teaching and learning processes successfully*]. Klett.

Hallet, W. (2006b). *Tasks* in kulturwissenschaftlicher Perspektive: Kulturelle Partizipation und die Modellierung kultureller Diskurse durch *tasks* [*Tasks* in a cultural studies perspective: Cultural participation and modelling cultural discourses through *tasks*]. In K-R. Bausch, E. Burwitz-Melzer, F. Königs, & H.-J. Krumm (Eds.), *Aufgabenorientierung als Aufgabe: Arbeitspapiere der 26. Frühjahrskonferenz zur Erforschung des Fremdsprachenunterrichts* [*Task orientation as task: Working papers of the 26th spring conference for foreign language classroom research*] (pp. 72–83). Narr.

Hallet, W. (2011). *Lernen fördern: Englisch: Kompetenzorientierter Unterricht in der Sekundarstufe I* [*Enhancing learning: English in the competence-oriented secondary foreign language classroom*]. Klett Kallmeyer.

Hallet, W. (2014). Beyond speaking. Neue Mündlichkeiten [New forms of oral communication]. In E. Burwitz-Melzer, F. G. Königs, & C. Riemer (Eds.), *Perspektiven der Mündlichkeit* [*Perspectives of oral communication*] (pp. 69–78). Narr.

Hallet, W. (2016). *Genres im fremdsprachlichen und bilingualen Unterricht: Formen und Muster der sprachlichen Interaktion* [*Genres in the foreign language classroom and in CLIL: Forms and patterns of discursive interaction*]. Klett Kallmeyer.

Hallet, W. (2018). The multiple languages of digital communication. In J. Buendgens-Kosten, & D. Elsner (Eds.), *Multilingual computer assisted language learning* (pp. 3–17). Multilingual Matters.

Hallet, W. (2020a). Surveillance cultures: Theory, ethnographic research and discourse competence in the foreign language. In J. Kramer, & B. Lenz (Eds.), *How to do cultural studies: Ideas, approaches, scenarios* (pp. 107–134). Königshausen & Neumann.

Hallet, W. (2020b). Close reading and wide reading: Analyzing the cultural dimension of literary texts. In V. Nünning, & A. Nünning (Eds.), *Methods of textual analysis in literary studies: Approaches, basics, model interpretations* (pp. 197–227). Wvt Wissenschaftlicher Verlag Trier.

Hallet, W. (2020c). Instrumente forschenden Lernens [Tools for research-based learning]. In W. Hallet, F. G. Königs, & H. Martinez (Eds.), *Handbuch Methoden im Fremdsprachenunterricht [A handbook of methods in language classrooms]* (pp. 510–513). Friedrich-Klett Kallmeyer.

Hallet, W. (2020d). Be your own fact checker: Informationen überprüfen [Checking information]. *Der fremdsprachliche Unterricht Englisch, 54*(163), 8–9.

Hallet, W. (2020e). Komplexe Aufgaben für den digitalen Distanz- und Präsenzunterricht konzipieren [Complex tasks for digital and the analogue classroom]. *Der fremdsprachliche Unterricht Englisch, 54*(167), 10–13.

Hallet, W. (2020f). Die Digitalisierung der fremdsprachigen Diskursfähigkeit [The digitization of foreign language discourse competence]. In M. Eisenmann, & J. Steinbock (Eds.), *Sprachen, Kulturen, Identitäten: Umbrüche durch Digitalisierung? [Languages, cultures, identities: Transformation through digitization?]* (pp. 191–202). Schneider.

Hallet, W. (2022). Kulturelles Lernen im Fremdsprachenunterricht [Cultural learning in the foreign language classroom]. In L. König, B. Schädlich, & C. Surkamp (Eds.), *Unterricht_kultur_theorie: Kulturelles Lernen im Fremdsprachenunterricht gemeinsam anders denken [Classroom_culture_theory: Rethinking cultural learning in the foreign language classroom collaboratively]* (pp. 41–56). Metzler.

Hallet, W., & Legutke, M. K. (2013). Task-approaches revisited: New orientations, new perspectives. *The European Journal of Applied Linguistics and TEFL, 2*(2), 139–158.

Hallet, W., Surkamp, C., & Vogt, K. (2020). Digitales Englischlernen im Distanz- und Präsenzunterricht [Learning English digitally at a distance and in the analogue classroom]. *Der fremdsprachliche Unterricht Englisch, 54*(167), 2–7.

Halliday, M. A. K. (1981). Introduction. In M. A. K. Halliday, & J. R. Martin (Eds.), *Readings in systemic linguistics* (pp. 13–16). Batsford.

Hamilton, E. (2012). Video as a metaphorical eye: Images of positionality, pedagogy, and practice. *College Teaching, 60*(1), 10–16. https://doi.org/10.1080/87567555.20 11.604803

Hanfstingl, B., Abuja, G., Isak, G., Lechner, C., & Steigberger, E. (2018). Continuing professional development designed as second-order action research: Work-in-progress. *Educational Action Research*, 1–12. https://doi.org/10.1080/09650792.20 20.1850496

Hanks, J. (2017). *Exploratory practice in language teaching: Puzzling about principles and practices*. Palgrave Macmillan.

Hannula, M. S., Leder, G. C., Morselli, F., Vollstedt, M., & Zhang, Q. (Eds.). (2019). *Affect and mathematics education: Fresh perspectives on motivation engagement and identity*. Springer.

Hargreaves, A. (2000). Four ages of professionalism and professional learning. *Teachers and Teaching History and Practice, 6*, 151–182. https://doi.org/10.1080/713698714

Hargreaves, A., & Fullan, M. (2012). *Professional capital: Transforming teaching in every school*. Teachers College Press.

Harlen, W. (2007). *Assessment of learning*. SAGE Publications.

Harmer, J. (2007). *The practice of English language teaching* (5th ed). Pearson Longman.

Harrington, C., & Thomas, M. (2018). *Designing a motivational syllabus: Creating a learning path for student engagement*. Stylus Publishing, LLC.

Harris, A. (2003). Teacher leadership as distributed leadership: Heresy, fantasy or possibility? *School Leadership and Management, 23*(3), 313–324. https://doi.org/10.1080/1363243032000112801

Harris, A., & Muijs, D. (2003). Teacher leadership and school improvement. *Education Review, 16*, 39–42. www.researchgate.net/publication/238508986_Teacher_Leadership_A_Review_of_Research

Harris, A., & Muijs, D. (2005). *Improving schools through teacher leadership.* Open University Press.

Healey, J. F. (2020). *Diversity and society: Race, ethnicity, and gender* (6th ed.). SAGE Publications.

Hegarty, S. (2000). Teaching as a knowledge-based activity. *Oxford Review of Education, 26*(3/4), 451–465. www.jstor.org/stable/1050770

Heidt, I. (2015). Exploring the historical dimensions of Bildung and metamorphosis in the context of globalization. *L2 Journal, 7*(4), 2–16. https://doi.org/10.5070/L27425457

Helsby, G. (2000). *Changing teachers' work and culture.* Open University Press.

Henry, A., & Mollstedt, M. (2021). The other in the self: Mentoring relationships and adaptive dynamics in preservice teacher identity construction. *Learning, Culture and Social Interaction, 31*, 100568. https://doi.org/10.1016/j.lcsi.2021.100568

Herrera, S. (2016). *Biography-driven culturally responsive teaching* (2nd ed.). Teachers College Press.

Hersey, P., Blanchard, K. H., & Natemeyer, W. E. (1979). Situational leadership, perception, and the impact of power. *Group & Organization Management, 4*(4), 418–428. https://doi.org/10.1177/105960117900400404

Hester, J. P., & Setzer, R. (2013). Mentoring: Adding value to organizational culture. *The Journal of Values-Based Leadership, 6*(1), 4. https://scholar.valpo.edu/jvbl/vol6/iss1/4

Hidri, S. (Ed.). (2018). *Revisiting the assessment of second language abilities: From theory to practice.* Springer.

Hidri, S. (Ed.). (2020). *Perspectives on language assessment literacy: Challenges for improved student learning.* Routledge.

Hillier, Y. (2009). *Reflective teaching in further and adult education.* Continuum.

Hobbs, K. S., & Putnam, J. (2016). Beginning teachers' experiences working with a district-employed mentor in a North Carolina school district. *Journal of Organizational and Educational Leadership, 2*(1), 1–29. https://digitalcommons.gardner-webb.edu/joel/vol2/iss1/2/

Hoekstra, A., Korthagen, F., Brekelmans, M., Beijaard, D., & Imants, J. (2009). Experienced teachers' informal workplace learning and perceptions of workplace conditions. *Journal of Workplace Learning, 21*(4), 276–298. https://doi.org/10.1108/13665620910954193

Hoerr, T. R. (2005). *The art of school leadership.* Association for Supervision and Curriculum Development.

Hoinkes, U., & Weigand, P. (2016). Der Aufbau des fachspezifischen Professionswissens angehender Fremdsprachenlehrerinnen und -lehrer in der ersten Ausbildungsphase: Wege zur Entwicklung einer quantitativen Messung [The development of subject-specific professional knowledge of future language teachers during the first stage of teacher education for the purpose of quantitative assessment]. In M. Legutke, & M. Schart (Eds.), *Fremdsprachendidaktische Professionsforschung: Brennpunkt*

Lehrerbildung [*Researching the language teaching profession: Focus on teacher education*] (pp. 47–75). Narr Francke Attempto Verlag GmbH.

Honigsfeld, A., & Dove, M. G. (2010). *Collaboration and co-teaching: Strategies for English learners*. Corwin Press.

Hou, H-T., Chang, K-E., & Sung, Y-T. (2009). Using blogs as a professional development tool for teachers: Analysis of interaction behavioural patterns. *Interactive Learning Environments, 17*(4), 325–340. https://doi.org/10.1080/10494820903195215

Howatt, A. P. (1984). *A history of English language teaching*. Oxford University Press.

Hu, A. (2015). The idea of Bildung in the current educational discourse: A response to Irene Heidt. *L2 Journal, 7*(4), 17–19. https://doi.org/10.5070/L27428980

Huang, J. (2005). Teacher autonomy in language learning: A review of the research. *Research Studies in Education, 3*, 203–218.

Huang, J., & Benson, P. (2013). Autonomy, agency and identity in foreign and second language education. *Chinese Journal of Applied Linguistics, 36*(1), 7–28. https://doi.org/10.1515/cjal-2013-0002

Hudson, P. (2013). Mentoring as professional development: 'Growth for both' mentor and mentee. *Professional Development in Education, 39*(5), 771–783. https://doi.org/10.1080/19415257.2012.749415

Hudson, P. (2016). Forming the mentor-mentee relationship. *Mentoring & Tutoring: Partnership in Learning, 24*(1), 30–43. https://doi.org/10.1080/13611267.2016.1163637

Hudson, R. (2008). Linguistics theory. In B. Spolsky, & F. M. Hult, (Eds.). *The handbook of educational linguistics* (pp. 53–65). Blackwell Publishing.

Hughes, G. (2011). Aiming for personal best: A case for introducing ipsative assessment in higher education. *Studies in Higher Education, 36*(3), 353–367. https://doi.org/10.1080/03075079.2010.486859

Hughes, G. (2014). *Ipsative assessment: Motivation through marking progress*. Palgrave Macmillan.

Hughes, G. (2017). *Ipsative assessment and personal learning gain: Exploring international case studies*. Springer.

Hunzicker, J. (Ed.). (2018). *Teacher leadership in professional development schools*. Emerald Publishing Limited.

Hyslop-Margison, E. J., & Sears, A. M. (2010). Enhancing teacher performance: The role of professional autonomy. *Interchange, 41*(1), 1–15. https://doi.org/10.1007/s10780-010-9106-3

Illes, E. (2020). *Understanding context in language use and teaching: An ELF perspective*. Routledge.

Ingersoll, R. M., & Collins, G. J. (2018). The status of teaching as a profession. In J. Ballantine, J. Spade, & J. Stuber (Eds.), *Schools and society: A sociological approach to education* (6th ed., pp. 199–213). Pine Forge Press/SAGE Publications.

Ingersoll, R. M., & Perda, D. (2008). The status of teaching as a profession. In J. Ballantine, & J. Spade (Eds.), *Schools and society: A sociological approach to education* (pp. 106–118). Pine Forge Press.

Jackson, J. (Ed.). (2020). *The Routledge handbook of language and intercultural communication*. Routledge.

Jarvis, M. (2005). *The psychology of effective teaching and learning*. Nelson Thornes Ltd.

Jarvis, P. (2007). *Globalization, lifelong learning and the learning society: Sociological perspectives*. Routledge.

Jasper, M. (2013). *Beginning reflective practice* (2nd ed.). Nelson Thornes Ltd.
Javadi, F. (2014). On the relationship between teacher autonomy and feeling of burnout among Iranian EFL teachers. *Procedia Social and Behavioral Sciences, 98*, 770–774. https://doi.org/10.1016/j.sbspro.2014.03.480
Jaworski, B. (2008). Building and sustaining inquiry communities in mathematics teaching development: Teachers and didacticians in collaboration. In K. Krainer, & T. Wood (Eds.), *International handbook of mathematics teacher education: Volume 3: Participants in mathematics teacher education: Individuals, teams, communities and networks* (pp. 309–330). Sense Publishers.
Jay, J. K., & Johnson, K. L. (2002). Capturing complexity: A typology of reflective practice for teacher education. *Teaching and Teacher Education, 18*, 73–85. https://doi.org/10.1016/S0742-051X(01)00051-8
Jenks, C. J. (2020). *Researching classroom discourse: A student guide*. Routledge.
Johar, N. A., & Abdul, A. A. (2019). Teachers' perceptions on using the *Pulse 2* textbook. *Journal of Educational Research and Indigenous Studies, 2*, 1–15. www.researchgate.net/publication/339458225_Teachers%27_Perceptions_on_Using_the_Pulse_2_textbook
Johns, A. M. (Ed.). (2002). *Genre in the classroom: Multiple perspectives*. Lawrence Erlbaum Associates.
Johnson, K. E. (2006). The sociocultural turn and its challenges for second language teacher education. *TESOL Quarterly, 40*(1), 235–257. https://doi.org/10.2307/40264518
Johnson, K. E. (2009). *Second language teacher education: A sociocultural perspective*. Routledge.
Johnson, K. E. (2022). Mentoring as mediation: Shifting novice teacher instructional stance. *The European Journal of Applied Linguistics and TEFL, 11*(1), 3–22.
Johnson, K. E., & Golombek, P. R. (2002). *Teachers' narrative inquiry as professional development*. Cambridge University Press.
Johnson, K. E., & Golombek, P. R. (2011). *Research on second language teacher education: A sociocultural perspective on professional development*. Routledge.
Johnson, K. E., & Golombek, P. R. (2016). *Mindful L2 teacher education: A sociocultural perspective on cultivating teachers' professional development*. Routledge.
Jolly, D., & Bolitho, R. (2011). A framework for materials writing. In B. Tomlinson (Ed.), *Materials development in language teaching* (pp. 107–134). Cambridge University Press.
Jones, P., & Chen, H. (2012). Teachers' knowledge about language: Issues of pedagogy and expertise. *AJLL, 35*, 147–172. https://doi.org/10.1007/BF03651880
Jones, R. D. (2018). *Developing video game literacy in the EFL classroom: A qualitative analysis of 10th grade classroom game discourse*. Narr.
Jonson, K. E. (2008). *Being an effective mentor: How to help beginning teachers succeed* (2nd ed.). Corwin Press.
Jumani, N. B., & Malik, S. (2017). Promoting teachers' leadership through autonomy and accountability. In I. H. Amzat, & N. P. Valdez (Eds.), *Teacher empowerment toward professional development and practices* (pp. 21–41). Springer.
Kager, K., Mynott, J. P., & Vock, M. (2023). A conceptual model for teachers' continuous professional development through lesson study: Capturing inputs, processes, and outcomes. *International Journal of Educational Research Open, 5*, 100272. https://doi.org/10.1016/j.ijedro.2023.100272

Kaliampos, J. (2022). *EFL learners' task perceptions and agency in blended learning: An exploratory mixed-methods study on the 'U.S. Embassy school election project'*. Narr.

Karaolis, A., & Philippou, G. N. (2019). Teachers' professional identity. In M. S. Hannula, G. C. Leder, F. Morselli, M. Vollstedt, & Q. Zhang (Eds.), *Affect and mathematics education: Fresh perspectives on motivation, engagement, and identity* (pp. 397–417). Springer.

Karimi, M. N., & Nazari, M. (2019): Examining L2 teachers' critical incidents: A complexity theoretic perspective. *Innovation in Language Learning and Teaching*. www.tandfonline.com/doi/pdf/10.1080/17501229.2019.1676755?casa_token=RRBuxX6ve_kAAAAA:fxuniXj4oiQ-LYoyNAh6ovBvNZpvMOHHym-ygBUvZRyjfISS6iDEFtn-B3geDdnx4Uj2Db8Po2bm

Kasemsap, K. (2019). Mastering technology-enhanced language learning, computer-assisted language learning, and mobile-assisted language learning. In D. Tafazoli, & M. Romero (Eds.), *Multiculturalism and technology-enhanced language learning* (pp. 157–180). IGI Global.

Katzenmeyer, M., & Moller, G. (2009). *Awakening the sleeping giant: Helping teachers develop as leaders*. Corwin Press.

Kaufmann, M. (2019). Communities of practice. Forschendes Lernen in Kulturwissenschaften und Ethnologie. [Communities of practice. Learning through research in the humanities]. In M. E. Kaufmann, A. Satilmis, & H. Mieg (Eds.), *Forschendes Lernen in den Geisteswissenschaften: Konzepte, Praktiken und Perspektiven Hermeneutischer Fächer* [*Learning through research in the humanities: Concepts, practices and perspectives of the hermeneutic disciplines*] (pp. 169–190). Springer.

Kayi-Aydar, H., Gao, X., Miller, E. R., Varghese, M., & Vitanova, G. (2019). *Theorizing and analyzing language teacher agency*. Multilingual Matters.

Kearney, E. (2016). *Intercultural learning in modern language education*. Multilingual Matters.

Kelchtermans, G. (2009). Who I am in how I teach is the message: Self-understanding, vulnerability and reflection. *Teachers and Teaching: Theory and Practice, 15*, 257–272. https://doi.org/10.1080/13540600902875332

Kemmis, S., & McTaggart, R. (1988). *The action research reader* (3rd ed.). Deakin University Press.

Kennedy, I. G., Latham, G., & Jacinto, H. (2016). *Education skills for 21st century teachers: Voices from a global online educators' forum*. Springer.

Khalil, B., & Lewis, T. (2019). Understanding language teacher autonomy: A critical realist perspective on EFL settings in Turkey. *International Online Journal of Education and Teaching (IOJET), 6*(4), 749–763.

Khanjani, A., Vahdany, F., & Jafarigohar, M. (2018). Effects of journal writing on EFL teacher trainees' reflective practice. *Research in English Language Pedagogy, 6*(1), 56–77. https://doi.org/10.30486/relp.2018.538761

Khezerlou, E. (2013). Teacher autonomy perceptions of Iranian and Turkish EFL teachers. *Journal of History Culture and Art Research, 2*(2), 199–211. https://doi.org/10.7596/taksad.v2i2.224

Kılıç, M., & Cinkara, E. (2020). Critical incidents in pre-service EFL teachers' identity construction process. *Asia Pacific Journal of Education, 40*(2), 182–196. https://doi.org/10.1080/02188791.2019.1705759

Kim, D., Ruecker, D., & Kim, D.-J. (2019). Mobile assisted language learning experiences. In Information Resources Management Association (Ed.), *Computer-assisted language learning: Concepts, methodologies, tools, and applications* (pp. 1059–1077). IGI Global.

Kıncal, R. Y., Ozan, C., & İleritürk, D. (2019). Increasing students' English language learning levels via lesson study. *English Language Teaching, 12*(9), 88–95. https://doi.org/10.5539/elt.v12n9p88

King, M. B., & Newmann, F. M. (2001). Building school capacity through professional development: Conceptual and empirical considerations. *International Journal of Educational Management, 15*(2), 86–93. https://doi.org/10.1108/09513540110383818

Klafki, W. (2007). *Neue Studien zur Bildungstheorie und Didaktik: Zeitgemäße Allgemeinbildung und kritisch-konstruktive Didaktik [New studies on educational theory and didactics: Modern school education and critical-constructive didactics]*. Beltz.

Klieme, E., Avenarius, H., Blum, W., Döbrich, P., Gruber, H., Prenzel, M., Reiss, K., Riquarts, K., Rost, J., Tenorth, H.-E., & Vollmer, H. J. (2003). *Zur Entwicklung nationaler Bildungsstandards: eine Expertise [Developing national educational standards: A report]*. Bundesministerium für Bildung und Forschung (BMBF).

Klippel, F. (Ed.). (2016). *Teaching languages – Sprachen lehren*. Waxmann.

Koh, S., & Neuman, S. B. (2006). *Exemplary elements of coaching*. University of Michigan.

Kohlmeier, J., & Saye, J. (2017). Developing discussion leaders through scaffolded lesson-study. *The Social Studies, 108*(1), 22–37. https://doi.org/10.1080/00377996.2016.1237466

Kolb, D. A. (1984). *Experiential learning*. Prentice Hall.

Koller, H.-Ch. (2018). *Bildung anders denken: Einführung in die Theorie transformatorischer Bildungsprozesse [A different approach to Bildung: An introduction to transformational education processes]*. Kohlhammer.

Kömür, Ş., & Çepik, H. (2015). Diaries as a reflective tool in pre-service language teacher education. *Educational Research and Reviews, 10*(12), 1593–1598. https://doi.org/10.5897/ERR2015.2207

König, L. (2020). Ethnographisch-exploratives Arbeiten [Ethnographic-explorative work]. In W. Hallet, F. G. Königs, & H. Martinez (Hrsg.), *Handbuch Methoden im Fremdsprachenunterricht [Handbook of methods in language education]* (pp. 517–519). Friedrich-Klett Kallmeyer.

Kong, S. C. (2010). Using a web-enabled video system to support student–teachers' self-reflection in teaching practice. *Computers & Education, 55*(4), 1772–1782. https://doi.org/10.1016/j.compedu.2010.07.026

Korthagen, F. A. J., & Vasalos, A. (2010). Going to the core: Deepening reflection by connecting the person to the profession. In N. Lyons (Ed.), *Handbook of reflection and reflective inquiry: Mapping a way of knowing for professional reflective inquiry* (pp. 529–552). Springer.

Kosnik, C., White, S., Beck, C., Marshall, B., Goodwin, A. L., & Murray, J. (2016). *Building bridges: Rethinking literacy teacher education in a digital era*. Sense Publishers.

Kowalczuk-Walędziak, M., Korzeniecka-Bondar, A., Danilewicz, W., & Lauwers, G. M. L. V. (2019). *Rethinking teacher education for the 21st century: Trends, challenges and new directions*. Verlag Barbara Budrich.

Kowalski, T. J. (2015). *Effective communication for district and school administrators* (2nd ed.). Rowman & Littlefield.

Kramer, J., & Lenz. B. (Eds.). (2020). *How to do cultural studies: Ideas, approaches, scenarios*. Königshausen & Neumann.

Kramer, P. A. (2003). The ABC's of professionalism. *Kappa Delta Pi Record, 40*, 22–25.

Kramsch, C. (1998). *Language and culture*. Oxford University Press.

Kramsch, C. (2009). *The multilingual subject*. Oxford University Press.

Krashen, S. D. (1983). *The natural approach: Language acquisition in the classroom*. Pergamon Press.

Krashen, S. D. (1985). *The input hypothesis: Issues and implications*. Longman.

Kress, G. (2010). *Multimodality: A social semiotic approach to contemporary communication*. Routledge.

Kress, G., & van Leeuwen, T. (2001). *Multimodal discourse: The modes and media of contemporary communication*. Arnold.

Krovetz, M. L., & Arriaza, G. (2006). *Collaborative teacher leadership*. Corwin Press.

Kuhlman, N., & Knežević, B. (n.d.). *The TESOL guidelines for developing EFL professional teaching standards*. www.tesol.org/docs/default-source/papers-and-briefs/tesol-guidelines-for-developing-efl-professional-teaching-standards.pdf?sfvrsn=6

Kumar, R., Chander, S., & Kaushik, B. (2019). *Teacher education in the 21st century*. SAGE Publications.

Kumaravadivelu, B. (2001). Toward a postmethod pedagogy. *TESOL Quarterly, 35*, 537–560. https://doi.org/10.2307/3588427

Kumaravadivelu, B. (2006). *Understanding language teaching: From method to postmethod*. Routledge.

Kurtoğlu-Hooton, N. (2016a). From 'plodder' to 'creative': Feedback in teacher education. *ELT Journal, 70*(1), 39–47. https://doi.org/10.1093/elt/ccv050

Kurtoğlu-Hooton, N. (2016b). *Confirmatory feedback in teacher education: An instigator of student teacher learning*. Palgrave Pivot London.

Kuru Gonen, S. I. (2016). A study on reflective reciprocal peer coaching for pre-service teachers: Change in reflectivity. *Journal of Education and Training Studies, 4*(7), 221–235. https://doi.org/10.11114/jets.v4i7.1452

La Ganza, W. (2008). Learner autonomy – Teacher autonomy: Interrelating and the will to empower. In T. Lamb, & H. Reinders (Eds.), *Learner and teacher autonomy: Concepts, realities and responses* (pp. 63–79). Benjamins.

Ladson-Billings, G. (1995). Toward a theory of culturally relevant pedagogy. *American Educational Research Journal, 32*(3), 465–491.

Lamb, P., & Aldous, D. (2016). Exploring the reflexivity and reflective practice through lesson study within initial teacher education. *International Journal for Lesson and Learning Studies, 5*(2), 99–115. https://ueaeprints.uea.ac.uk/id/eprint/57500/1/IJLLS_11_2015_0040_final_copy_for_PL.pdf

Lamb, T. (2008). *Learner autonomy and teacher autonomy: Synthesising an agenda*. www.researchgate.net/publication/283998700_Learner_autonomy_and_teacher_autonomy_Synthesising_an_agenda/link/57b5932d08aeaab2a104dc97/download

Lamb, T., & Reinders, H. (Eds.). (2008). *Learner and teacher autonomy: Concepts, realities, and responses*. John Benjamins.

Lancee, B. (2010). The economic returns of immigrants' bonding and bridging social capital: The case of the Netherlands. *International Migration Review, 44*(1), 202–226. https://hdl.handle.net/1814/16531

Lantolf, J. (Ed.). (2000). *Sociocultural theory and second language learning*. Oxford University Press.

Lantolf, J. P., & Poehner, M. E. (2014). *Sociocultural theory and the pedagogical imperative in L2 education*. Routledge.

Lantolf, J. P., & Thorne, S. L. (2006). *Sociocultural theory and the genesis of second language development*. Oxford University Press.

Larrivee, B. (2000). Transforming teaching practice: Becoming the critically reflective teacher. *Reflective Practice, 1*, 293–307. https://doi.org/10.1080/713693162

Larsen, C., Walsh, C., Almond, N., & Myers, C. (2017). The 'real value' of field trips in the early weeks of higher education: The student perspective. *Educational Studies, 43*, 110–121. https://doi.org/10.1080/03055698.2016.1245604

Lassonde, C. A., & Israel, S. E. (2010). *Teacher collaboration for professional learning: Facilitating study, research, and inquiry communities*. Jossey-Bass.

Lave, J., & Wenger, E. (1991). *Situated learning: Legitimate peripheral participation*. Cambridge University Press.

Le, V. C., & Renandya, W. A. (2017). Teachers' English proficiency and classroom language use: A conversation analysis study. *RELC Journal, 48*(1), 67–81. https://doi.org/10.1177/0033688217690935

Lee, I. (2008). Fostering preservice reflection through response journal. *Teacher Education Quarterly, 35*(1), 117–139. https://files.eric.ed.gov/fulltext/EJ810661.pdf

Legutke, M. K., Müller-Hartmann, A., & Schocker-von Ditfurth, M. (2009). *Teaching English in the primary school*. Klett.

Legutke, M. K., & Schart, M. (Eds.). (2016). *Fremdsprachendidaktische Professionsforschung: Brennpunkt Lehrerbildung [Researching the profession in foreign language teaching: Focus on teacher education]*. Narr.

Legutke, M. K., & Thomas, H. (1991). *Process and experience in the language classroom*. Longman.

Leont'ev, A. A. (1981). *Psychology and the language learning process*. Pergamon.

Leow, R. P. (Ed.). (2019). *The Routledge handbook of second language research in classroom learning*. Routledge.

Levin, B. B., & Schrum, L. (2017). *Every teacher a leader: Developing the need dispositions, knowledge, and skills for teacher leadership*. Corwin Press.

Li, G., & Edwards, P. A. (2010). *Best practices in ELL instruction*. The Guilford Press.

Li, L. (2017). *Social interaction and teacher cognition*. Edinburgh University Press.

Liddicoat, A. J., & Scarino, A. (2013). *Intercultural language teaching and learning*. Wiley-Blackwell.

Lieberman, A. (2011). Can teachers really be leaders? *Kappa Delta Pi Record, 48*(1), 16–18.

Lim, F. V., & Tan-Chia, L. (2022). *Designing learning for multimodal literacy: Teaching viewing and representing*. Routledge.

Little, D. (1995). Learning as dialogue: The dependence of learner autonomy on teacher autonomy. *System, 23*, 175–182. https://andragogie2012.files.wordpress.com/2012/03/learner-autonomy-little.pdf

Little, D. (1997). Autonomy and self-access in second language learning: Some fundamental issues in theory and practice. In M. Muller-Verweyen (Ed.), *New development in foreign language learning: Self-management – Autonomy* (pp. 33–44). Goethe Institute.

Little, D. (2000). We're all in it together: Exploring the interdependence of teacher and learner autonomy. In L. Karlsson, F. Kjisik, & J. Nordlund (Eds.), *All together now: Papers from the 7th Nordic conference and workshop on autonomous language learning, Helsinki* (pp. 45–56). University of Helsinki Language Centre.

Little, D. (2007). Language learner autonomy: Some fundamental considerations revisited. *Innovation in Language Learning and Teaching, 1*(1), 14–29. https://doi.org/10.2167/illt040.0

Little, D., Ridley, J., & Ushioda, E. (2002). *Towards greater learner autonomy in the foreign language classroom.* Authentik.

Little, J. W. (1990). The persistence of privacy: Autonomy and initiative in teachers' professional relations. *Teachers College Record, 91*(4), 509–536. https://doi.org/10.1177/016146819009100403

Littlejohn, A. (2011). The analysis of language teaching materials: Inside the Trojan Horse. In B. Tomlinson (Ed.), *Materials development in language teaching* (pp. 179–211). Cambridge University Press.

Littlewood, W. (1997). Autonomy in communication and learning in the Asian context. In KMITT (Eds.), *Proceedings of the international conference autonomy 2000* (pp. 124–140). KMITT.

Liu, J., & Berger, C. M. (2015). *TESOL: A guide.* Bloomsbury Academic.

Liu, W., & Wang, Q. (2018). The process of teachers' engagement in action research: An ethnographic study in Beijing. *Educational Action Research, 26*(2), 258–272. https://doi.org/10.1080/09650792.2017.1307128

Lomelino, P. J. (2015). *Community, autonomy, and informed consent: Revisiting the philosophical foundation for informed consent in international research.* Cambridge Scholars Publishing.

Lomos, C., Hofman, R. H., & Bosker, R. J. (2011). Professional communities and student achievement – A meta-analysis. *School Effectiveness and School Improvement, 22*(2), 121–148. https://doi.org/10.1080/09243453.2010.550467

London, M. (Ed.). (2011). *The Oxford handbook of lifelong learning.* Oxford University Press.

Long, M. (2015). *Second language acquisition and task-based language teaching.* John Wiley & Sons.

López-Gopar, M. E. (Ed.). (2019). *International perspectives on critical pedagogies in ELT.* Palgrave Macmillan.

Low, E. L., Chong, S., & Ellis, M. (2014). Teachers' English communication skills: Using IELTS to measure competence of graduates from a Singaporean teacher education program. *Australian Journal of Teacher Education, 38*(10). https://files.eric.ed.gov/fulltext/EJ1041864.pdf

Lu, H.-L. (2007). *Mentor teachers, program supervisors, and peer coaching in the student teaching experience: A phenomenological study of the experiences of mentor teachers, program supervisors, and interns.* Urban Ministries, Inc.

Ludwig, C., & Eisenmann, M. (Eds.). (2018). *Queer beats: Gender and the literature in the EFL classroom.* Peter Lang.

Luke, I., & Gourd, J. (2018). *Thriving as a professional teacher: How to be a principled professional.* Routledge.

Lütge, C. (Ed.). (2022). *Foreign language learning in the digital age: Theory and pedagogy for developing literacies.* Routledge.

References

Lütge, C., Lütge, C., & Faltermeier, M. (Eds.). (2020). *The praxis of diversity*. Palgrave Macmillan.

Lütge, C., & Merse, T. (Eds.). (2021). *Digital teaching and learning: Perspectives for English language education*. Narr.

Lütge, C., Merse, T., & Su, X. (2021). The digital competence of English language educators: Exploring the DigCompEdu framework with an empirical case study. In C. Lütge, & T. Merse (Eds.), *Digital teaching and learning: Perspectives for English language education* (pp. 31–59). Narr.

Lyons, N. (1998). Constructing narratives for understanding: Using portfolio interviews to scaffold teacher reflection. In N. Lyons (Ed.), *With portfolio in hand – Validating the new teacher professionalism* (pp. 103–119). Teachers College Press.

MacDonald, R., Boals, T., Castro, M., Cook, H. G., Lundberg, T., & White, P. (2015). *Formative language assessment for English learners: A four step process*. Heinemann.

Maggin, D. M., & Tejero Hughes, M. (2021). *Developing teacher leaders in special education: An administrator's guide to building inclusive schools*. Routledge.

Malecka, B., Ajjawi, R., Boud, D., & Tai, J. (2021). An empirical study of student action from ipsative design of feedback processes. *Assessment & Evaluation in Higher Education*, 801–815. https://doi.org/10.1080/02602938.2021.1968338

Malecka, B., & Boud, D. (2021). Fostering student motivation and engagement with feedback through ipsative processes. *Teaching in Higher Education, 28*(7), 1761–1776. https://doi.org/10.1080/13562517.2021.1928061

Maley, A. (2011). Squaring the circle – Reconciling materials as a constraint with materials as empowerment. In B. Tomlinson (Ed.), *Materials development in language teaching* (pp. 379–402). Cambridge University Press.

Malone, H. J. (Ed.). (2013). *Leading educational change: Global issues, challenges and lessons on whole-system reform*. Teachers College Press.

Mann, S. (2016). *The research interview: Reflective practice and reflexivity in research processes*. Palgrave Macmillan.

Mann, S., & Hing Tang, E. H. (2012). The role of mentoring in supporting novice English language teachers in Hong Kong. *TESOL Quarterly, 46*(3), 472–495. www.jstor.org/stable/41576064

Mann, S., & Walsh, S. (2017). *Reflective practice in English language teaching: Research-based principles and practices*. Routledge.

Mansfield, G. (2017). Are we digitally literate enough? Some reflections on language pedagogy in a technology enhanced environment. In A. T. Damascelli (Ed.), *Digital resources, creativity and innovative methodologies in language teaching and learning* (pp. 37–60). Cambridge Scholars.

Mansilla, V. B., & Wilson, D. (2020). What is global competence, and what might it look like in Chinese schools? *Journal of Research in International Education, 19*(1), 3–22. https://doi.org/10.1177/1475240920914089

Manzano Vázquez, B. (2018). Teacher development for autonomy: An exploratory review of language teacher education for learner and teacher autonomy. *Innovation in Language Learning and Teaching, 12*(4), 387–398. https://doi.org/10.1080/17501229.2016.1235171

Marques, J., & Dhiman, S. (Eds.). (2022). *Leading with diversity, equity, and inclusion: Approaches, practices and cases for integral leadership strategy*. Springer.

Marsh, B., & Mitchell, N. (2014). The role of video in teacher professional. *Teacher Development, 18*(3), 403–417. https://doi.org/10.1080/13664530.2014.938106

Martins, A. (2009). Making learning journeys through reflective portfolios. In F. Vieira (Ed.), *Struggling for autonomy in language education: Reflecting, acting and being* (pp. 39–62). Peter Lang.

Massey, D. (2012). *Leading the sustainable school: Distributing leadership to inspire school improvement.* Continuum.

Masuhara, H. (2011). What do teachers really want from coursebooks? In B. Tomlinson (Ed.), *Materials development in language teaching* (pp. 236–266). Cambridge University Press.

Mawani, S., & Mukadam, A. A. (Eds.). (2020). *Student empowerment in Higher Education: Reflecting on teaching practice and learner engagement.* Logos Verlag Berlin.

Maxwell, B., & Schwimmer, M. (2016). Professional ethics education for future teachers: A narrative review of the scholarly writings. *Journal of Moral Education, 45*(3), 354–371. https://doi.org/10.1080/03057240.2016.1204271

McConachy, T., Golubeva, I., & Wagner, M. (2022). *Intercultural learning in language education and beyond: Evolving concepts perspectives and practices.* Multilingual Matters.

McDonald, J., & Cater-Steel, A. (2017). *Communities of practice: Facilitating social learning in higher education.* Springer.

McDonough, J., & McDonough, S. (2014). *Research methods for English language teachers.* Routledge.

McDonald, J., & Mercieca, B. M. (2021a). What is a community of practice? In B. M. Mercieca & J. McDonald (Eds.), *Sustaining communities of practice with early career teachers: Supporting early career teachers and secondary schools, and educational social learning spaces* (pp. 1–19). Springer.

McDonald, J., & Mercieca, B.M. (2021b). The value of communities of practice for early career teachers. In B. M. Mercieca & J. McDonald (Eds.), *Sustaining communities of practice with early career teachers: Supporting early career teachers and secondary schools, and educational social learning spaces* (pp. 21–43). Springer.

McGee, C., & Fraser, D. (2012). *The professional practice of teaching* (4th ed.). Cengage Learning.

McGrath, I. (2000). Teacher autonomy. In B. Sinclair, I. McGrath, & T. Lamb (Eds.), *Learner autonomy, teacher autonomy: Future directions* (pp. 100–110). Longman.

McGrath, I. (2013). *Teaching materials and the role of EFL/ESL teachers: Practice and theory.* Bloomsbury Academic.

McGregor, D., & Cartwright, L. (2011). *Developing reflective practice: A guide for beginning teachers.* Open University Press.

McLaughlin, M. W., & Talbert, J. E. (2006). *Building school-based teacher learning communities: Professional strategies to improve student achievement.* Teachers College Press.

McNiff, J., & Whitehead, J. (2011). *All you need to know about action research.* SAGE Publications.

Meissel, K., Parr, J., & Timperley, H. (2016). Can professional development of teachers reduce disparity in student achievement? *Teaching and Teacher Education, 58*, 163–173. www.learntechlib.org/p/202033/

Mello, H., Dutra, D. P., & Jorge, M. (2008). Action research as a tool for teacher autonomy. *DELTA, 24*, 512–528. www.scielo.br/j/delta/a/gTTkm3PtCd8cr8XTZDvyVnh/?format=pdf&lang=en

Meng, J. (2009). The Relationship between linguistics and language teaching. *Asian Social Science, 5*(12), 84–86. https://doi.org/10.5539/ass.v5n12p84

Menna, L. (2016). 'Times are changing, and you've got to keep up': Negotiating multiple literacies within the context of teacher education. In C. Kosnik, S. White, & C. Beck (Eds.), *Building bridges: Rethinking literacy teacher education in a digital era* (pp. 17–30). Sense Publishers.

Mercado, L., & Baecher, L. (2014). Video-based self-observation as a component of developmental teacher evaluation. *Global Education Review, 1*(3), 63–77. https://files.eric.ed.gov/fulltext/EJ1055171.pdf

Mercer, S. (2011). Understanding learner agency as a complex dynamic system. *System, 39*(4), 427–436. https://doi.org/10.1016/j.system.2011.08.001

Mercieca, B. M., & McDonald, J. (Eds.). (2021). *Sustaining communities of practice with early career teachers: Supporting early career teachers in Australian and international primary and secondary schools, and educational social learning spaces.* Springer.

Merse, T. (2021). Task typologies for engaging with cultural diversity: The queer case of LGBTIQ* issues in English language teaching. In D. L. Banegas, G. Beacon, & M. Perez Berbain (Eds.), *International perspectives on diversity in ELT* (pp. 91–109). Palgrave Macmillan.

Mertler, C. A. (2009). *Action research: Teachers as researchers in the classroom* (2nd ed.). SAGE Publications.

Mertler, C. A. (2012). *Action research: Improving schools and empowering educators* (3rd ed.). SAGE Publications.

Meyer, D. (2009). Entering the emotional practices of teaching. In P. A. Schutz, & M. Zembylas (Eds.), *Advances in teacher emotion research* (pp. 73–91). Springer.

Miliander, J. (2008). Portfolios in teacher education. In R. Jimenez, & T. Lamb (Eds.), *Pedagogy for autonomy in language education: Theory, practice and teacher education* (pp. 249–265). Authentik.

Miller, B., Moon, J., & Elko, S. (2000). *Teacher leadership in mathematics and science: Casebook and facilitator's guide.* Heinemann.

Mirzaee, A., & Aliakbari, M. (2017). Ethicality of narrative inquiry as a tool of knowledge production in research. *Journal of Research in Applied Linguistics, 8*(2), 119–135. https://doi.org/10.22055/rals.2017.13094

Mockler, N., & Groundwater-Smith, S. (2015). *Engaging with student voice in research, education and community: Beyond legitimation and guardianship.* Springer.

Moore, A. (2004). *The good teacher: Dominant discourses in teaching and teacher education.* RoutledgeFalmer.

Morettini, B., Luet, K., & Vernon-Dotson, L. (2020). Building beginning teacher resilience: Exploring the relationship between mentoring and contextual acceptance. *The Educational Forum, 84*(1), 48–62. https://doi.org/10.1080/00131725.2020.1679933

Motha, S. (2014). *Race, empire, and English language teaching: Creating responsible and ethical anti-racist practice.* Teachers College Press.

Moyle, K. (2016). *A guide to support coaching and mentoring for school improvement.* Australian Council for Educational Research. https://research.acer.edu.au/professional_dev/12

Muijs, D., & Harris, A. (2006). Teacher led school improvement: Teacher leadership in the UK. *Teachers and Teacher Education, 22*(8), 961–972. https://doi.org/10.1016/j.tate.2006.04.010

Müller-Hartmann, A., & Schocker-v. Ditfurth, M. (2011). *Teaching English: Task-supported language learning*. Schöningh.

Myhill, D. (2005). Ways of knowing: Writing with grammar in mind. *English Teaching: Practice and Critique, 4*(3), 77–96. https://files.eric.ed.gov/fulltext/EJ847265.pdf

Nagai, N., Birch, G. C., Bower, J. V., & Schmidt, M. G. (2020). *CEFR-informed learning, teaching and assessment: A practical guide*. Springer.

Nakata, Y. (2009). Towards learner autonomy and teacher autonomy in the Japanese school context. In F. Kajik, P. Voller, N. Aoki, & Y. Nakata (Eds.), *Mapping the terrain of learner autonomy: Learning environments, learning communities and identities* (pp. 190–213). Tampere University Press.

Nami, F. (Ed.). (2020). *Digital storytelling in second and foreign language teaching*. Peter Lang.

Nascimbeni, F. (2018). Rethinking digital literacy for teachers in open and participatory societies. *International Journal of Digital Literacy and Digital Competence, 9*(3), 1–11. https://doi.org/10.4018/IJDLDC.2018070101

Nashruddin, W., & Nurrachman, D. (2016). The implementation of lesson study in English language learning: A case study. *Dinamika Ilmu, 16*(2), 169–179. https://doi.org/10.21093/di.v16i2.356

Nassaji, H., & Kartchava, E. (Eds.). (2021). *The Cambridge handbook of corrective feedback in second language learning and teaching*. Cambridge University Press.

National Board of Professional Teaching Standards. (2012). *Middle childhood generalist standards for teachers of students aged 7–12* (3rd ed.). NBPTS. www.nbpts.org/wp-content/uploads/2021/09/MC-GEN-1.pdf

Nelson, T. H., & Slavit, D. (2008). Supported teacher collaborative inquiry. *Teacher Education Quarterly, 35*(1), 99–116. Retrieved from www.jstor.org/stable/23479033

Netolicky, D. M. (Ed.). (2022). *Future alternatives for educational leadership: Diversity, inclusion, equity and democracy*. Routledge.

Newby, D., Allan, R., Fenner, A.-B., Jones, B., Komorowska, H., & Soghikyan, K. (2007). *European portfolio for student teachers of languages: A reflection tool for language teacher education*. Council of Europe.

Newton, J., & Nation, P. (2020). *Teaching ESL/EFL listening and speaking*. Routledge.

Nguyen, H. T. M. (2017). *Models of mentoring in language teacher education*. Springer.

Nishizuka, K. (2022). Significance and challenges of formative ipsative assessment in inquiry learning: A case study of writing activities in a 'Contemporary Society' course in a Japanese high school. *SAGE Open, 12*(2). https://doi.org/10.1177/21582440221094599

Nolan, A., & Molla, T. (2017). Teacher confidence and professional capital. *Teaching and Teacher Education: An International Journal of Research and Studies, 62*(1), 10–18. www.learntechlib.org/p/202687/

Norris, J. M., & East, M. (2022). Task-based language assessment. In M. J. Ahmadian, & M. H. Long (Eds.), *The Cambridge handbook of task-based language teaching* (pp. 507–528). Cambridge University Press.

Norton Scott, M. (2008). *Human resources administration for educated leaders*. SAGE Publications.

Nunan, D. (1989). *Designing tasks for the communicative classroom*. Cambridge University Press.

Nunan, D. (2004). *Task-based language teaching*. Cambridge University Press.

Nunan, D. (2013). *Learner-centred English language education: The selected works of David Nunan*. Routledge.

Nurkamto, J., & Sarosa, T. (2020). Engaging EFL teachers in reflective practice as a way to pursue sustained professional development. *International Journal of Pedagogy and Teacher Education, 4*(1), 45–58. https://dx.doi.org/10.20961/ijpte.v4i1.26082

OECD. (2009). *Evaluating and rewarding the quality of teachers: International practices*. OECD Publishing.

OECD. (2016). *Supporting teacher professionalism: Insights from TALIS 2013*. TALIS, OECD Publishing. https://doi.org/10.1787/9789264248601-en

OECD. (2020). *Education at a glance 2020: OECD indicators*. OECD Publishing.

OECD. (2021). *21st-century readers: Developing literacy skills in a digital world*. OECD Publishing.

Osmond-Johnson, P. (2017). Leading professional learning to develop professional capital: The Saskatchewan professional development unit's facilitator community. *International Journal of Teacher Leadership, 8*(1), 26–42. https://files.eric.ed.gov/fulltext/EJ1146799.pdf

Osterman, K. F., & Kottkamp, R. B. (2004). *Reflective practice for educators*. Corwin Press.

Osterwalder, H. (2017). *Teaching contemporary English literature: A task-based approach*. V&R unipress.

Othman, J., & Senom, F. (2020). *Professional development through mentoring: Novice ESL teachers' identity formation and professional practice*. Routledge.

Paradis, A., Lutovac, S., Jokikokko, K., & Kaasila, R. (2019). Towards a relational understanding of teacher autonomy: The role of trust for Canadian and Finnish teachers. *Research in Comparative & International Education, 14*(3), 394–411. https://doi.org/10.1177/1745499919864252

Park-Johnson, S., & Shin, S. (2020). *Linguistics for language teachers: Lessons for classroom practice*. Routledge.

Parsons, R. D., & Brown, K. S. (2002). *Teacher as reflective practitioner and action researcher*. Wadsworth/Thomson Learning.

Pastore, S., & Andrade, H. L. (2019). Teacher assessment literacy: A three-dimensional model. *Teaching and Teacher Education, 84*, 128–138. https://doi.org/10.1016/j.tate.2019.05.003

Patton, K., Parker, W., & Tannehill, D. (2015). Helping teachers help themselves: Professional development that makes a difference. *NASSP Bulletin, 99*(1), 26–42. https://doi.org/10.1177/0192636515576040

Pawlak, M. (2016). *Classroom-oriented research: Reconciling theory and practice*. Springer.

Pearson, L. C., & Moomaw, W. (2006). Continuing validation of the teacher autonomy scale. *Journal of Educational Research, 100*, 44–51. https://doi.org/10.3200/JOER.100.1.44-51

Penn, P. R., & Wells, I. G. (2018). Making assessment promote effective learning practices: An example of ipsative assessment from the School of Psychology at UEL. *Psychology Teaching Review, 24*(2), 70–74. https://doi.org/10.1177/1475725718814315

Pennington, M. C., & Richards, J. C. (2016). Teacher identity in language teaching: Integrating personal, contextual, and professional factors. *RELC Journal, 47*(1), 5–23. https://doi.org/10.1177/0033688216631219

Peterson, B. R. (2016). The development of a disposition for reflective practice. In A. G. Welch, & S. Areepattamannil (Eds.), *Dispositions in teacher education: A global perspective* (pp. 3–30). Sense Publishers.

Petko, D., Egger N., & Cantieni, A. (2017). Weblogs in teacher education internships: Promoting reflection and self-efficacy while reducing stress. *Journal of Digital Learning in Teacher Education, 33*(2), 78–87. https://doi.org/10.1080/21532974.2017.1280434

Petrie, H. G. (Ed.). (1995). *Professionalization, partnership, and power: Building professional development schools*. State University of New York Press.

Piccardo, E., Berchoud, M., Cignatta, T., Mentz, O., & Pamula, M. (2011). *Pathways through assessing, learning and teaching in the CEFR*. Council of Europe.

Pole, C., & Morrison, M. (2003). *Ethnography for education*. Open University Press.

Pollard, A. (Ed.). (2014). *Readings for reflective teaching in schools*. Bloomsbury Academic.

Porras, N. I., Smith Díaz, L., & Nieves, M. M. (2018). Reverse mentoring and peer coaching as professional development strategies. *Colombian Applied Linguistics Journal, 20*(2), 169–183. https://doi.org/10.14483/22487085.12422

Posner, R. (2004). Basic tasks of cultural semiotics. In G. Withalm, & J. Wallmannsberger (Eds.), *Signs of power – Power of signs: Essays in honor of Jeff Bernard* (pp. 56–89). INST.

Priestley, M., Biesta, G. J. J., & Robinson, S. (2015). *Teacher agency: An ecological approach*. Bloomsbury Academic.

Pu, C., & Wright, W. E. (2022). *Innovating the TESOL practicum in teacher education*. Routledge.

Punie, Y., & Redecker, C. (Eds.). (2017). *European framework for the digital competence of educators: DigCompEdu*. Publications Office of the European Union.

Purpura, J. E. (2016). Assessing meaning. In E. Shohamy, & N. H. Hornberger (Eds.), *Language testing and assessment, Encyclopedia of language and education, vol. 7* (pp. 1–29). Springer.

Quetz, J., & Vogt, K. (2009). Bildungsstandards für die Erste Fremdsprache: Sprachenpolitik auf unsicherer Basis. Antwort auf das Positionspapier der DGFF [Educational standards for the first foreign language: Language policy on an uncertain basis. A response to the statement of the German Association for Foreign Language Research]. *Zeitschrift für Fremdsprachenforschung, 20*(1), 63–89.

Raffone, A. (2020). Digital storytelling in education and second language acquisition: Towards a theoretical framework. In F. Nami (Ed.), *Digital storytelling in second and foreign language teaching* (pp. 3–26). Peter Lang.

Rai, A. K. (2021). *School education and national education policy, 2020*. www.researchgate.net/publication/352178558_School_Education_and_National_Education_Policy_2020

Rattray, J. (2018). Affect and ipsative approaches as a counter to pedagogic frailty: The guardian of traditional models of student success. *Higher Education Research & Development, 37*(7), 1489–1500. https://doi.org/10.1080/07294360.2018.1494141

Raven, B. H., & Kruglanski, A. W. (1970). Conflict and power. In P. G. Swingle (Ed.), *The structure of conflict* (pp. 69–109). Academic Press.

Raz, J. (1986). *The morality of freedom*. Oxford University Press.

Rein, V. (2017). Towards the compatibility of professional and scientific learning outcomes: Insights and options in the context of competence orientation. *International

Journal for Research in Vocational Education and Training, 4, 325–345. https://doi.org/10.13152/IJRVET.4.4.2

Reis Monteiro, A. (2015). *The teaching profession: Present and future.* Springer.

Richards, G., & Armstrong, F. (Eds.). (2016). *Key issues for teaching assistants: Working in diverse and inclusive classrooms.* Routledge.

Richards, H., Conway, C., Roskvist, A., & Harvey, S. (2013). Foreign language teachers' language proficiency and their language teaching practice. *The Language Learning Journal, 41*(2), 231–246. www.tandfonline.com/doi/abs/10.1080/09571736.2012.707676

Richards, J. C. (2010). Competence and performance in language teaching. *RELC Journal, 41*(2), 101–122. https://doi.org/10.1177/0033688210372953

Richards, J. C. (2012). Competence and performance in language teaching. In A. Burns, & J. C. Richards (Eds.), *The Cambridge guide to pedagogy and practice in second language teaching* (pp. 46–59). Cambridge University Press.

Richards, J. C. (2015). *Key issues in language teaching.* Cambridge University Press.

Richards, J. C., & Farrell, T. S. C. (2005). *Professional development for language teachers.* Cambridge University Press.

Richards, J. C., & Farrell, T. S. C. (2011). *Practice teaching: A reflective approach.* Cambridge University Press.

Rizvi, M., & Elliot, B. (2005). Teachers' perceptions of their professionalism in government primary schools in Karachi, Pakistan. *Asia-Pacific Journal of Teacher Education, 33*(1), 35–52. https://doi.org/10.1080/1359866052000341115

Robbins, P. (2015). *Peer coaching to enrich professional practice school culture, and student learning.* ASCD Publications.

Robnett, R. D., Nelson, P. A., Zurbriggen, E. L., Crosby, F. J., & Chemers, M. M. (2018). Research mentoring and scientist identity: Insights from undergraduates and their mentors. *International Journal of STEM Education, 5*(1), 41. https://doi.org/10.1186/s40594-018-0139-y

Roe, B., Smith, S. H., & Kolodziej, N. J. (2019). *Teaching reading in today's elementary schools* (12th ed.). Cengage Learning.

Rogers, C. (1969). *Freedom to learn: A view of what education might become.* Charles E. Merrill.

Rose, H., Syrbe, M., Montakantiwong, A., & Funada, N. (2020). *Global TESOL for the 21st century: Teaching English in a changing world.* Multilingual Matters.

Russell, C. (2018). *Linguistics for teachers of English.* New Prairie Press.

Sachs, J. (2005). Teacher education and the development of professional identity: Learning to be a teacher. In P. Denicolo, & M. Kompf (Eds.), *Connecting policy and practice: Challenges for teaching and learning in schools and universities* (pp. 5–21). Routledge.

Sachs, J. (2016). Teacher professionalism: Why are we still talking about it? *Teachers and Teaching: Theory and Practice, 22*(4), 413–425. https://doi.org/10.1080/13540602.2015.1082732

Sadler, D. R. (2010). Beyond feedback: Developing student capability in complex appraisal. *Assessment & Evaluation in Higher Education, 35*(5), 535–550. https://doi.org/10.1080/02602930903541015

Salisbury, D., & Lartigue, C., Jr. (Eds.). (2004). *Educational freedom in urban America: Brown v. Board after half a century.* Cato Institute.

Sammons, L. A., & Smith, N. M. (2017). *A handbook for unstoppable learning: Make the complexities of unit and lesson design manageable.* Solution Tree.

Samuda, V., & Bygate, M. (2008). *Tasks in second language learning*. Palgrave Macmillan.

Sato, M., & Loewen, S. (2019). Do teachers care about research? The research-pedagogy dialogue. *ELT Journal, 73*(1), 1–10. https://doi.org/10.1093/elt/ccy048

Savage, T. V., & Savage, M. K. (2010). *Successful classroom management and discipline: Teaching self-control and responsibility* (3rd ed.). SAGE Publications.

Schipper, T., Goei, S. L., de Vries, S., & van Veen, K. (2017). Professional growth in adaptive teaching competence as a result of Lesson Study. *Teaching and Teacher Education, 68*, 289–303. https://doi.org/10.1016/j.tate.2017.09.015

Schleicher, A. (2019). *PISA 2018: Insights and interpretations*. OECD Publishing.

Schön, D. A. (1983). *The reflective practitioner: How professionals think in action*. Ashgate.

Schön, D. A. (1987). *Educating the reflective practitioner: Toward a new design for teaching and learning in the professions*. Jossey-Bass.

Schön, D. A. (1991). *The reflective turn: Case studies in and on educational practice*. Teachers Press, Columbia University.

Schuck, S., & Russell, T. (2005). Self-study, critical friendship, and the complexities of teacher education. *Studying Teacher Education, 1*(2), 107–121. https://doi.org/10.1080/17425960500288291

Scrivener, J. (2011). *Learning teaching: The essential guide to English language teaching*. Macmillan Education.

Scrivener, J. (2017). *Learning teaching* (4th ed.). Macmillan Education.

Searle, M., & Swartz, M. (2015). *Teacher teamwork: How do we make it work?* Association for Supervision & Curriculum Development.

Seery, A. (2008). Ethics and professionalism in teaching. *Studies: An Irish Quarterly Review, 97*(386), 183–192. www.jstor.org/stable/25660559

Sehlaoui, A. S. (2018). *Teaching ESL and STEM content through CALL: A research-based interdisciplinary critical pedagogical approach*. Rowman & Littlefield.

Sercu, L., & Bandura, E. (2005). *Foreign language teachers and intercultural competence: An international investigation*. Multilingual Matters.

Serna-Gutiérrez, J. I. O., & Mora-Pablo, I. (2018). Critical incidents of transnational student-teachers in Central Mexico. *Profile: Issues in Teachers' Professional Development, 20*(1), 137–150. https://doi.org/10.15446/profile.v20n1.62860

Sert, N. (2006). EFL student teachers' learning autonomy. *The Asian EFL Journal, 8*(2), 180–201. www.asian-efl-journal.com/June_2006_EBook_editions.pdf

Shapira-Lishchinsky, O. (2012). Teachers' withdrawal behaviors: Integrating theory and findings. *Journal of Educational Administration, 50*(3), 307–326. https://doi.org/10.1108/09578231211223329

Shapiro, S., Farrelly, R., & Curry, M. J. (2018). *Educating refugee-background students: Critical issues and dynamic contexts*. Multilingual Matters.

Shaw, J. (2002). Team-teaching as negotiating autonomy and shared understandings of what we are doing. http://lc.ust.hk/%7Eailasc/symposium/Responses08Shaw.pdf

Showers, B. (1984). *Peer coaching: A strategy for facilitating transfer of training*. Center for Educational Policy and Mana.

Shulman, L. S. (1987). Knowledge and teaching. *Harvard Educational Review, 57*(1), 1–23. https://doi.org/10.17763/haer.57.1.j463w79r56455411

Siljander, P., Kivela, A., & Sutinen, A. (Eds.). (2012). *Theories of Bildung and growth: Connections and controversies between continental educational thinking and American pragmatism*. Sense Publishers.

Sipman, G., Thölke, J., Martens, R., & McKenney, S. (2019). The role of intuition in pedagogical tact: Educator views. *British Educational Research Journal, 45*(6), 1186–1202. https://doi.org/10.1002/berj.3557

Skaalvik, E. M., & Skaalvik, S. (2014). Teacher self-efficacy and perceived autonomy: Relations with teacher engagement, job satisfaction, and emotional exhaustion. *Psychological Reports, 114*(1), 68–77. https://doi.org/10.2466/14.02.PR0.114k14w0

Slembrouck, S. (2010). Discourse, critique and ethnography: Class-oriented coding in accounts of child protection. In C. Coffin, T. Lillis, & K. O'Halloran (Eds.), *Applied linguistics methods: A reader* (pp. 251–266). Routledge.

Slimani-Rolls, A., & Kiely, R. (2019). *Exploratory practice for continuing professional development: An innovative approach for language teachers.* Palgrave Macmillan.

Smith, R., & Erdoğan, S. (2008). Teacher-learner autonomy: Programme goals and student-teacher constructs. In T. Lamb, & H. Reinders (Eds.), *Learner and teacher autonomy: Concepts, realities, and response* (pp. 83–103). John Benjamins.

Sockett, H. (2012). *Knowledge and virtue in teaching and learning: The primacy of dispositions.* Routledge.

Soisangwarn, A., & Wongwanich, S. (2014). Promoting reflective teacher through peer coaching for improve teaching skills. *Procedia-Social and Behavioral Sciences, 116*, 2504–2511. https://doi.org/10.1016/j.sbspro.2014.01.601

Soto Gómez, E., Serván Núñez, M. J., & Caparros-Vida, R. (2016). Learning to teach with lesson study: The practicum and the degree essay as the scenario for reflective and cooperative creation. *International Journal for Lesson and Learning Studies, 5*(2), 116–129. https://doi.org/10.1108/IJLLS-12-2015-0042

Spiro, J. (2013). *Changing methodologies in TESOL.* Edinburgh University Press.

Spreitzer, G. (1995). Psychological empowerment in the workplace: Dimensions, measurement, and validation. *The Academy of Management Journal, 38*(5), 1442–1465. https://doi.org/10.5465/256865

Sprod, T. (2003). *Philosophical discussion in moral education: The community of ethical inquiry.* Routledge.

Stalder, F. (2016). *Kultur der Digitalität [The culture of digitality].* Suhrkamp.

Stanford, L. (2019). *Tactical influence: A practical approach to increase your influence and leadership skills.* Instafo.

State of Victoria Department of Education and Training. (2014). *A teacher's guide to effective mentoring.* State of Victoria Department of Education and Training.

Steinberg, S. R. (2015). Employing the bricolage as critical research in teaching English as a foreign language. In M. Vicars, S. R. Steinberg, T. McKenna, & M. Cacciattolo (Eds.), *The praxis of English language teaching and learning (PELT): Beyond the binaries: Researching critically in EFL classrooms* (pp. 1–20). Sense Publishers.

Stevens, D., & Cooper, J. (2009). *Journal keeping: How to use reflective writing for learning, teaching, professional insight and positive change.* Stylus Publishing, LLC.

Stevens, D. D., & Levi, A. (2013). *Introduction to rubrics: An assessment tool to save grading time, convey effective feedback, and promote student learning* (2nd ed.). Stylus Publishing, LLC.

Stockwell, G. (2021). *Mobile assisted language learning: Concepts, contexts and challenges.* Cambridge University Press.

Stoll, L., Bolam, R., McMahon, A., Wallace, M., & Thomas, S. (2006). Professional learning communities: A review of the literature. *Journal of Educational Change, 7*(4), 221–258. https://doi.org/10.1007/s10833-006-0001-8

Strasser, T. (2021). AI in the EFL classroom: Clarifications, potentials and limitations. In C. Lütge, & T. Mere (Eds.), *Digital teaching and learning: Perspectives for English language education* (pp. 85–102). Narr.

Street, B. V. (2010). Adopting an ethnographic perspective in research and pedagogy. In C. Coffin, T. Lillis, & K. O'Halloran (Eds.), *Applied linguistics methods: A reader* (pp. 201–215). Routledge.

Strike, K. T., Fitzsimmons, J. C., & Meyer, D. K. (2019). *The impact of teacher leaders: Case studies from the field.* Rowman & Littlefield.

Stronge, J. H. (2018). *Qualities of effective teachers.* ASCD Publications.

Taggart, G., & Wilson, A. (2005). *Promoting reflective thinking in teachers: 44 action strategies.* Corwin Press.

Tajeddin, Z., & Aghababazadeh, Y. (2018). Blog-mediated reflection for professional development: Exploring themes and criticality of L2 teachers' reflective practice. *TESL Canada Journal, 35*(2), 26–50. https://doi.org/10.18806/tesl.v35i2.1289

Tajeddin, Z., & Watanabe, A. (Eds.). (2022). *Teacher reflection: Policies, practices and impacts.* Multilingual Matters.

Tajino, A., Stewart, T., & Dalsky, D. (Eds.). (2016). *Team teaching and team learning in the language classroom: Collaboration for innovation in ELT.* Routledge.

Talbert, J. E., & McLaughlin, M. W. (1994). Teacher professionalism in local school context. *American Journal of Education, 102*, 123–153. https://doi.org/10.1086/444062

Tang, E. (2009). Introduction and development of a blog-based teaching portfolio: A case study in a pre-service teacher education programme. *The International Journal of Learning, 16*(8), 89–100. https://doi.org/10.18848/1447-9494/CGP/v16i08/46520

Tateo, L. (2012). What do you mean by 'teacher'? Psychological research on teacher professional identity. *Psicologia e Sociedade, 24*(2), 344–353. www.scielo.br/j/psoc/a/TCnPYMyrBhdhXbVRKbvCnhn/?format=pdf&lang=en

Taylor, E. W. (2009a). Fostering transformative learning. In J. Mezirow, E. W. Taylor, & Associates (Eds.), *Transformative learning in practice* (pp. 3–17). Jossey-Bass.

Taylor, E. W. (2009b). *The handbook of transformative learning.* Jossey-Bass.

Teacher Leadership Exploratory Consortium. (2011). Teacher leader model standards. www.nea.org/resource-library/teacher-leader-model-standards

Tedick, D. (Ed.). (2005). *Second language teacher education: International perspectives.* Lawrence Erlbaum Associates.

Teng, F. (2019). Understanding teacher autonomy, teacher agency, and teacher identity: Voices from four EFL student teachers. *English Teaching & Learning, 43*, 189–212. https://doi.org/10.1007/s42321-019-00024-3

Teng, F. (2020). Understanding TEFL teacher identity: Agency, authority, and vulnerability. *TESOL Journal, 11*(3), e00511. https://doi.org/10.1002/tesj.511

Teranishi, M., Saitō, Y., & Wales, K. (2015). *Literature and language learning in the EFL classroom.* Palgrave Macmillan.

Thavenius, C. (1999). Teacher autonomy for learner autonomy. In S. Cotterall, & D. Crabbe (Eds.), *Learner autonomy in language learning: Defining the field and effecting change* (pp. 159–163). Peter Lang.

The New London Group. (2000). A pedagogy of multiliteracies: Designing social futures. In B. Cope, & M. Kalantzis (Eds.), *Multiliteracies: Literacy learning and the design of social futures* (pp. 9–37). Routledge.

The Teaching Council. (2012). *Code of professional conduct for teachers* (2nd ed.). www.hereteach.org.uk/uploads/1541411125-Code%20of%20Conduct.pdf

The Teaching Council. (2016). *Code of professional conduct for teachers. Updated 2nd Edition 2016*. www.teachingcouncil.ie/en/Publications/Fitness-to-Teach/Code-of-Professional-Conduct-for-Teachers1.pdf

Thiel, T. (1999). Reflections on critical incidents. *Prospect, 14*, 44–52.

Thomson, K. (2022). *Classroom discourse competence: Current issues in language teaching and teacher education*. Narr Francke Attempto Verlag.

Thornbury, S. (1997). *About language: Tasks for teachers of English*. Cambridge University Press.

Tichnor-Wagner, A., Parkhouse, H., Glazier, J., & Cain, J. M. (2019). *Becoming a globally competent teacher*. ASCD Publications.

Timperley, H. (2011). *Realising the power of professional learning*. McGraw-Hill.

Tirri, K., & Kuusisto, E. (2022). *Teachers' professional ethics theoretical frameworks and empirical research from Finland*. Brill.

Tomlinson, B. (2001). Materials development. In R. Carter, & D. Nunan (Eds.), *The Cambridge guide to teaching English to speakers of other languages* (pp. 66–71). Cambridge University Press.

Tomlinson, B. (Ed.). (2011). *Materials development in language teaching*. Cambridge University Press.

Tomlinson, B. (Ed.). (2013a). Introduction: Are materials developing? In B. Tomlinson (Ed.), *Developing materials for language teaching* (2nd ed., pp. 1–17). Bloomsbury Academic.

Tomlinson, B. (Ed.). (2013b). Materials evaluation. In B. Tomlinson (Ed.), *Developing materials for language teaching* (2nd ed., pp. 21–48). Bloomsbury Academic.

Tomlinson, B. (Ed.). (2013c). Developing principled frameworks for materials development. In B. Tomlinson (Ed.), *Developing materials for language teaching* (2nd ed., pp. 95–11). Bloomsbury Academic.

Tomlinson, B. (Ed.). (2013d). Humanizing the coursebook. In B. Tomlinson (Ed.), *Developing materials for language teaching* (2nd ed., pp. 139–156). Bloomsbury Academic.

Tomlinson, B. (Ed.). (2016). *SLA research and materials development for language learning*. Routledge.

Too, W. K. (2013). Facilitating the development of pre-service teachers as reflective learners: A Malaysian experience. *The Language Learning Journal, 41*(2), 161–174. https://doi.org/10.1080/09571736.2013.790131

Toom, A., Pyhältö, K., & Rust, F. O. C. (2015). Teachers' professional agency in contradictory times. *Teachers and Teaching, 21*(6), 615–623. https://doi.org/10.1080/13540602.2015.1044334

Tort-Moloney, D. (1997). *Teacher autonomy: A Vygotskian theoretical framework*. CLCS Occasional Paper No. 48. Trinity College, CLCS.

Tsagari, D., & Banerjee, J. (Eds.). (2016). *Handbook of second language assessment* (vol. 12). DeGruyter Mouton.

Twadell, E., Onuscheck, M., Reibel, A. R., & Gobble, T. (2019). *Proficiency-based instruction: Rethinking lesson design and delivery*. Solution Tree.

UCLES. (2018). *Cambridge English teaching framework*. www.cambridgeenglish.org/images/172992-full-level-descriptors-cambridge-english-teaching-framework.pdf

University of York. (n.d.). *Research methods for language education I: Researching questions – EDU00108M.* www.york.ac.uk/students/studying/manage/programmes/module-catalogue/module/EDU00108M/latest

University of York. (n.d.b). *Research methods for education II: Answering questions – EDU00109M.* www.york.ac.uk/students/studying/manage/programmes/module-catalogue/module/EDU00109M/latest

Ur, P. (2012). *A course in English language teaching.* Cambridge University Press.

Ur, P. (2015). Using the coursebook: A teacher's perspective. *The European Journal of Applied Linguistics and TEFL, 4*(2), 5–17. www.itdi.pro/itdihome/wp-content/downloads/advanced_courses_readings/urmaterials.pdf

Usma Wilches, J. (2007). Teacher autonomy: A critical review of the research and concept beyond applied linguistics. *Íkala, Revista de Lenguaje y Cultura, 12*(8), 245–275. https://doi.org/10.17533/udea.ikala.2720

Vacilotto, S., & Cummings, R. (2007). Peer coaching in TEFL/TESL programmes. *ELT Journal, 61*(2), 153–160. https://doi.org/10.1093/elt/ccm008

van Compernolle, R. A. (2014). *Sociocultural theory and L2 instructional pragmatics.* Multilingual Matters.

van den Branden, K. (Ed.). (2006). *Task-based language education: From theory to practice.* Cambridge University Press.

van den Branden, K., van Gorp, K., & Verhelst, M. (2007). Introduction: Tasks in action: Language-based education from a classroom-based perspective. In K. van den Branden, K. van Gorp, & M. Verhelst (Eds.), *Tasks in action: Language-based education from a classroom-based perspective* (pp. 1–6). Cambridge Scholars Publishing.

van Halem, N., Goei, S. L., & Akkerman, S. F. (2016). Formative assessment in teacher talk during lesson studies. *International Journal for Lesson and Learning Studies, 5*(4), 313–328. https://doi.org/10.1108/IJLLS-11-2015-0041

van Leeuwen, T. (2005). *Introducing social semiotics.* Routledge.

van Lier, L. (1988). *The classroom and the language learner.* Longman.

van Maele, D., & van Houtte, M. (2011). The quality of school life: Teacher-student trust relationships and the organizational school context. *Social Indicators Research, 100*(1), 85–100. https://doi.org/10.1007/s11205-010-9605-8

van Velzen, C. P., Volman, M. L. L., Brekelmans, M., & White, S. H. (2012). Guided work-based learning: Sharing practical teaching knowledge with student teachers. *Teaching and Teacher Education, 28*, 229–239. https://doi.org/10.1016/j.tate.2011.09.011

Varghese, M. M., & Snyder, R. (2018). Critically examining the agency and professional identity development of novice dual language teachers through figured worlds. *International Multilingual Research Journal, 12*(3), 145–159. https://doi.org/10.1080/19313152.2018.1474060

Varkøy, Ø. (2010). The concept of 'Bildung'. *Philosophy of Music Education Review, 18*(1), 85–96. https://doi.org/10.2979/pme.2010.18.1.85

Vassiliou, S., Papadima-Sophocleous, S., & Giannikas, C. N. (2022). *Formative assessment in second language learning: A systematic review and an annotated bibliography.* Research-publishing.net.

Verdonk, P. (2002). *Stylistics.* Oxford University Press.

Vescio, V., Ross, D., & Adams, A. (2008). A review of research on the impact of professional learning communities on teaching practices and student learning. *Teaching and Teacher Education, 24*, 80–91. https://doi.org/10.1016/j.tate.2007.01.004

Vidmar, D. J. (2006). Reflective peer coaching: Crafting collaborative self-assessment in teaching. *Research Strategies, 20*, 135–148. https://doi.org/10.1016/j.resstr.2006.06.002

Vieira, F. (2003). Addressing constraints on autonomy in school contexts – Lessons from working with teachers. In R. Smith, & D. Palfreyman (Eds.), *Learner autonomy across cultures – Language education perspectives* (pp. 220–239). Palgrave.

Vieira, F. (2006). Developing professional autonomy as ... writing with a broken pencil. *Independence, 38*, 23–25.

Vieira, F., Barbosa, I., Paiva, M., & Fernandes, I. S. (2002). Teacher education towards teacher (and learner) autonomy: What can be learnt from teacher development practices? In T. Lamb, & H. Reinders (Eds.), *Learner and teacher autonomy: Concepts, realities and responses* (pp. 217–235). John Benjamins.

Vinogradova, P., & Shin, J. K. (Eds.). (2020). *Contemporary foundations for teaching English as an additional language: Pedagogical approaches and classroom applications*. Routledge.

Vogt, K. (2011). *Fremdsprachliche Kompetenzprofile: Entwicklung und Abgleichung von GeR-Deskriptoren für Fremdsprachenlernen mit einer beruflichen Anwendungsorientierung* [Foreign language competence profiles: Developing and aligning CEFR descriptors with an orientation on vocational application]. Narr.

Vrikki, M., Warwick, P., Vermunt, J. D., Mercer, N., & van Halem, N. (2017). Teacher learning in the context of lesson study: A video-based analysis of teacher discussions. *Teaching and Teacher Education, 61*, 211–224. https://doi.org/10.17863/CAM.7057

Vygotsky, L. S. (1978). *Mind in society: The development of higher psychological processes*. Harvard University Press.

Walker, A., & White, G. (2013). *Technology enhanced language learning: Connecting theory and practice*. Oxford University Press.

Wallace, M. J. (1991). *Training foreign language teachers: A reflective approach*. Cambridge University Press.

Walsh, S. (2011). *Exploring classroom discourse: Language in action*. Routledge.

Walsh, S. (2013). *Classroom discourse and teacher development*. Edinburgh University Press.

Wang, J., & Hartley, K. (2003). Video technology as a support for teacher education reform. *Journal of Technology and Teacher Education, 11*(1), 105–138. www.learntechlib.org/primary/p/17791

Wang, Q., & Zhang, H. (2013). Promoting teacher autonomy through university–school collaborative action research. *Language Teaching Research, 18*(2), 222–241. https://doi.org/10.1177/1362168813505942

Warfield, J., Wood, T., & Lehman, J. D. (2005). Autonomy, beliefs and the learning of elementary mathematics teachers. *Teaching and Teacher Education, 21*(4), 439–456. https://doi.org/10.1016/j.tate.2005.01.011

Wedell, M., & Malderez, A. (2013). *Understanding language classroom contexts: The starting point for change*. Bloomsbury Academic.

Weinert, F. E. (Ed.). (2001). *Leistungsmessung in Schulen* [*Assessment in schools*]. Beltz.

Welsch, W. (1999). Transculturality – The puzzling form of cultures today. In M. Featherstone, & S. Lash (Eds.), *Spaces of culture: City, nation, world* (pp. 94–213). SAGE Publications.

Wenger, E. (1998). *Communities of practice: Learning, meaning, and identity*. Cambridge University Press.

Wenner, J. A., & Campbell, T. (2017). The theoretical and empirical basis of teacher leadership: A review of the literature. *Review of Educational Research, 87*(1), 134–171. https://doi.org/10.3102/0034654316653478

Wermke, W., & Höstfält, G. (2014). Contextualising teacher autonomy in time and space: A model for comparing various forms of governing the teaching profession. *Journal of Curriculum Studies, 46*(1), 58–80. https://doi.org/10.1080/00220272.2013.812681

Wermke, W., Olason Rick, S., & Salokangas, M. (2018): Decision-making and control: Perceived autonomy of teachers in Germany and Sweden. *Journal of Curriculum Studies, 51*(3), 306–325. https://doi.org/10.1080/00220272.2018.1482960

Widodo, H. P. (2015). *The development of vocational English materials from a social semiotic perspective: Participatory action research* [Unpublished PhD thesis]. University of Adelaide.

Widodo, H. P., Perfecto, M. R., Canh, L. V., & Buripakdi, A. (2018). *Situating moral and cultural values in ELT materials: The Southeast Asian context*. Springer.

Wiland, S. M. (2016). *Reading and teaching English literature: How to bridge the gaps between teacher education and the English classroom*. Cappelen Damm Akademisk.

Willis, D., & Willis, J. (2007). *Doing task-based teaching*. Oxford University Press.

Willis, J. (1996). *A framework for task-based learning*. Longman.

Wise, A. (1989). Professional teaching: A new paradigm for the management of education. In T. J. Sergiovanni, & J. H. Moore (Eds.), *Schooling for tomorrow* (pp. 301–310). Allyn & Bacon.

Wood, D., Bruner, J., & Ross, G. (1976). The role of tutoring in problem solving. *Journal of Child Psychology and Child Psychiatry, 17*, 89–100. http://doi.org/10.1111/j.1469-7610.1976.tb00381.x

Woods, G. (2020). *How to influence people and get what you want now*. Native Publisher.

Woolcock, M., & Sweetser, A. T. (2002). Bright ideas: Social capital – The bonds that connect. *ADB Review, 34*(2), 26–27.

Wu, S., & Ware, P. (2022). Supporting novice TESOL teachers' learning: Integration of mediated mentoring into community-based teacher learning. *The European Journal of Applied Linguistics and TEFL, 11*(1), 77–94.

Wyatt, M., & Dikilitaş, K. (2016). English language teachers becoming more efficacious through research engagement at their Turkish University. *Educational Action Research, 24*(4), 550–570. https://doi.org/10.1080/09650792.2015.1076731

Xu, H. (2015). The development of teacher autonomy in collaborative lesson preparation: A multiple-case study of EFL teachers in China. *System, 52*, 139–148. https://doi.org/10.1016/j.system.2015.05.007

Yaccob, N. S., Yunus, M. M., & Hashim, H. (2022). Globally competent teachers: English as a second language teachers' perceptions on global competence in English lessons. *Frontiers in Psychology*, 13. https://doi.org/10.3389/fpsyg.2022.925160

Yacek, D. (2021). *The transformative classroom: Philosophical foundations and practical applications*. Routledge.

Yadav, P. K. (2011). Blogging as a means of professional development for ELT professionals. *Journal of NELTA, 16*(1–2), 123–132. https://doi.org/10.3126/nelta.v16i1-2.6136

Yan, Z. (2023). *Student self-assessment as a process for learning*. Routledge.

Yandell, J. (2013). *The social construction of meaning: Reading literature in urban English classrooms*. Routledge.

Yang, S.-H. (2009). Using blogs to enhance critical reflection and community of practice. *Educational Technology & Society, 12*(2), 11–21. www.jstor.org/stable/jeductechsoci.12.2.11

Yazan, B., & Lindahl, K. (2020). *Language teacher identity in TESOL: Teacher education and practice as identity work*. Routledge.

Yee, B. C., Abdullah, T., & Nawi, A. M. (2022). Exploring preservice teachers' reflective practice through an analysis of six-stage framework in reflective journals. *Reflective Practice, 23*(5), 552–564. https://doi.org/10.1080/14623943.2022.2071246

Yildirim, R. (2013). The portfolio effect: Enhancing Turkish ELT student-teachers' autonomy. *Australian Journal of Teacher Education, 38*(8), 92–110. https://doi.org/10.14221/ajte.2013v38n8.8

York-Barr, J., & Duke, K. (2004). What do we know about teacher leadership? Findings from two decades of scholarship. *Review of Educational Research, 74*(3), 255–316. https://doi.org/10.3102/00346543074003255

Young, J. W., Freeman, D., Hauck, M., Garcia Gomez, P., & Papageorgiou. S. (2014). *A design framework for the ELTeach Program assessments*. Educational Testing Service.

Young, R. (1986). *Personal autonomy: Beyond negative and positive liberty*. Croom Helm.

Yuan, R., & Burns, A. (2017). Teacher identity development through action research: A Chinese experience. *Teachers and Teaching, 23*(6), 729–749. https://doi.org/10.1080/13540602.2016.1219713

Yuan, R., Sun, P., & Teng, L. (2016). Understanding language teachers' motivations towards research. *TESOL Quarterly, 50*(1), 220–234. https://doi.org/10.1002/tesq.279

Yukselir, C., & Ozer, O. (2022). Investigating the interplay between English language teachers' autonomy, well-being and efficacy. *Issues in Educational Research, 32*(4), 1643–1657. www.iier.org.au/iier32/yukselir.pdf

Zapf, H. (2016). *Literature as cultural ecology: Sustainable texts*. Bloomsbury Academic.

Zeichner, K. (2010). Rethinking the connections between campus courses and field experiences in college and university-based teacher education. *Journal of Teacher Education, 61*(1–2), 89–99. https://doi.org/10.1177/0022487109347671

Zepeda, S. J., Stewart Mayers, R., & Benson, B. N. (2003). *The call to teacher leadership*. Eye On Education.

Zheng, H., Zhao, L., & Ruan, S. (2020). How does mentoring affect protégés' adaptive performance in the workplace: Roles of thriving at work promotion focus. *Frontiers in Psychology, 11*, 546152. https://doi.org/10.3389/fpsyg.2020.546152

Zwozdiak-Myers, P. (2012). *The teacher's reflective practice handbook: Becoming an extended professional through capturing evidence-informed practice*. Routledge.

Index

abilities, 11, 100, 102
   decision-making, 107
   professional, 54
activities, 48, 54, 117
   collaborative, 199
   online, 176
agency, 104, 129
   cultural, 137
   professional, 27
   sociocultural, 9
   teacher, 104
agents
   of change, 202
   cultural, 47, 160
algorithmicity, 161
anglophone cultures, 136–137
approaches
   communicative, 46
   outcome-oriented, 49
Artificial Intelligence, 157, 182
assessment, 19, 62–63, 197
   formative, 34, 63
   ipsative, 64
   professional, 63
   rubrics, 66
   scales, 66
   strategies, 20
   summative, 34, 64
   task, 65
   task-based language, 153
   tools for, 20
attitudes, 2, 3
autonomy, 10, 99, 104–106, 118, 138
   collective, 111
   collegial professional, 102
   individual, 102
   moral, 99
   personal, 99
   political, 99
   professional, 3, 100, 102, 107, 118, 123
   relational, 105
   teacher, 100–106, 108–111, 114, 128–129, 198

awareness
   language, 18
   self-, 84
   target language, 32

backward planning, 49
beliefs, 3
Bildung, 1, 9–11, 46, 133, 234

citizens, 10, 14, 45
citizenship, 9, 14
classroom
   communicative, 139
   discourse, 22
   ethnographers, 233
   ethnography, 234
   inquiry, 108
   interaction, 19
   physical, 169
   procedures, 19
   teacher-led, 91
   technologies, 167
   virtual, 169
classrooms
   diverse, 19
   learner-oriented, 19
code of ethics, 38
collaboration, 107, 114–115, 194, 202, 212–214, 224
   digital, 176
   productive, 211
   professional, 212, 225
   teacher, 29, 128
collaborative blogs, 82
collaborative culture, 211
collective responsibility, 214
collegiality, 198
communality, 160
communication, 9
   cultural, 165
   digital, 158, 162, 175
   digital forms of, 158

Index

digital modes of, 180
effective, 199, 225
modes of, 163
online, 168
real-life, 46
communities
epistemic, 2
institutional, 220
learning, 206
online and offline, 21
of practice, 215
professional, 206
professional learning, 213
teacher, 4
competences, 3, 10–11, 29, 47
communicative, 48, 139
digital, 167, 171, 178–179
discursive, 11, 43
ELT, 44
intertextual, 134
language, 5
leadership, 185
linguistic, 43
literary, 62
orientation, 44, 49
pedagogical, 7, 52–53
professional, 16, 47
procedural, 179
professional, 19, 49, 61, 70
social, 21
socio-digital, 179
teacher, 18
teacher competences, 1
computer assisted language learning, 158
connections, 132
text-to-self, 132
text-to-text, 132
text-to-world, 132
connectivity, 132
coursebook limitations, 120
coursebooks, 15, 58, 60, 118–120
creative imagination, 74
criteria, 121
age-specific, 121
content-specific, 121
local, 121
media-specific, 121
critical incident focus groups, 81, 83
critical incidents, 83–85
critical memory, 74
critical reason, 74
curricula, 15
development of, 47
curricular content, 44
curricular objectives, 13

decision-making, 101
decisions, 101–102, 198
administrative, 101
developmental, 101
educational, 101
independent, 110
social, 101
democratic societies, 9–11
descriptors, 14
can-do, 14, 44, 49–50
CEFR, 15
developmental psychology, 99
diagnosis, 19
digital age, 157, 164
digital content creation, 171, 175, 234
digital language learning, 168
digital resources, 52, 173–174
digitality, 159, 179, 182
digitisation, 11, 157, 159, 162, 165, 167, 170
of the classroom, 169
dimensions
iterational, 104
practical-evaluative, 104
projective, 104
discourse competence, 43, 45–46, 48, 143
digital, 159, 167, 179
learner's, 44, 49, 55, 178
professional, 55–56
discourses, 45–46
classroom, 18, 55–56, 169
cultural, 22, 56, 134, 136, 142, 164
global, 60
in a globalised world, 12
political, 10, 22, 46
professional, 56, 86
public, 22, 44
real-life, 46
social, 22
diversity, 8, 46, 199
cultural, 5, 136

education, 11
digital, 165, 167, 177
school, 10
theories of, 5
educational change, 203
empowerment, 9–10
learner's, 173, 178
symbolic, 10
teacher, 29, 105, 177
environments
digital, 138
pedagogical, 117
textual and medial, 117
equity, 199

ethnographic observation, 95
ethnographic tools, 96, 222, 234
ethnography, 60, 94–95, 233
evaluation, 16, 20, 62
   critical, 123
   materials, 122
   self-, 84
exercises, 117
experiential learning theory, 99
exploitability, 132

framework, 16, 43, 52–53
   CEFR, 15
   for the digital competence of educators, 171
   for materials writing, 125
frameworks, 6, 13
   curricular, 13
   teacher education, 13–14
freedom, 100

genres, 12, 180
   digital, 166, 180
goals
   educational, 8, 11
   pedagogical, 44

inclusion, 199
inclusive membership, 215
influence, 201
   strategic, 201
   tactical, 202
inquiry, 222
   collaborative, 83
   reflective professional, 214
interactions, 46
   cultural, 21
   social, 10, 209–210
intercultural communicative competence, 61

job motivation, 37

knowledge, 11
   cultural, 18, 46, 60, 95
   disciplinary, 3, 22, 32–33, 54, 69, 72–75, 97
   domain-specific, 48
   language, 57
   linguistic, 58
   literary-aesthetic, 18
   pedagogical content, 32–33, 73
   professional, 3, 13, 18, 32–33, 36, 54, 198
   subject matter, 57

language
   education, 9
   education policies, 15
   teacher education, 1

language awareness, professional, 59
language learning
   digital, 168
   software, 168
leaders
   educational, 234
   principled, 200
   teacher, 184, 196, 198, 200–203, 234
leadership, 191, 200–201, 204
   association, 191–192
   collaborative, 197
   formal, 191
   hybrid, 191
   informal, 191
   instructional, 191
   policy, 191–192
   teacher, 24, 29, 184, 189–190, 193, 202, 204
learner orientation, 61
learning
   cultural, 95, 141
   diversity, 143
   experiential, 40
   lifelong, 4, 102
   task-based language, 144
   task-supported language, 144
   transformative, 202
lesson design, 67
lesson study, 81, 89–90
lifelong learners, 4, 34, 106, 200, 233
lifeworld, 11, 24, 45, 60, 161
literacies, 164, 166
   digital, 180
literature, 61–62

managers, classroom, 7
materials, 49, 118, 130–136
   collaboratively developed, 125
   development, 124
   evaluation of, 120, 126
   teacher-made, 123
   teaching, 15
mentoring, 204–205
   teacher, 205
mentors, 208
modes, 45
   of communication, 12
   semiotic, 10, 135–136
multiliteracies, 164, 166
multimodality, 133–134, 163–164, 167, 175
multiperspectivity, 132–134
multitextuality, 133–134

outcome, 14, 49, 152
   orientation, 50
outcome-oriented approaches, 49

Index

participation, 9–11, 45
pedagogical environment, 117
pedagogical transformation, 212
peer coaching, 81, 86–88
personalisation, 132
personality development, 9
personality traits, 38
portfolios, 109, 114
post-observation conferences, 81, 88–89
power, 192
  connection, 192
  expert, 192
  informational, 192
  legitimate, 193
  referent, 192
  reward, 193
practices
  beyond, 80
  classroom, 13, 46
  communicative, 11–12
  exploratory, 76–77
  digital, 165–166
  media, 11
  professional, 32–33, 81
  reflective, 31, 35, 72–73, 75–77, 80, 82, 86, 89, 91, 108
  reflective classroom, 129
  social, 21
practicum, 69
practitioners
  autonomous, 35
  classroom, 2, 5
  ethical, 28
  language, 4
  reflective, 30, 73, 75
professional communities, 10, 35, 41, 212, 216, 218, 225
  of inquiry, 213
  of practice, 213
professional community, 220, 223–224
professional development, 34–35, 37, 40, 82, 87, 97, 100, 110–111, 114–115
  communities, 24, 218
professional engagement, 34, 41
professional ethics, 38
professional identity, 36–37, 41, 105
professional language awareness, 59
professional learning, 37, 40, 82, 89, 105, 107, 214
  job-embedded, 194
professional organisations, 97
professional skills, 31, 102
professionalisation, 4, 13, 213
  of ELT teachers, 17
  of English teacher education, 8

  of learning, 215
  of teaching, 1, 215
professionalism, 4, 30–31, 38
  occupational, 30
  organisational, 30
  teacher, 1, 24, 26, 41, 184
professionals
  educational, 28
  ethical, 38
proficiency, 14, 18, 48
  language, 14, 20, 22
  teacher language, 56–57

qualifications, 3
  professional, 14
  teacher, 6

referentiality, 160
reflection, 74
  -for-action, 76–77
  -in-action, 74, 76–77
  -on-action, 76–77
  -after-lesson, 78
  -before-lesson, 78
  -beyond-lesson, 78
  collective, 84
  critical, 73–74, 76, 81, 88–89, 91, 97, 100, 118, 202, 208
  -during-lesson, 78
reflective cycle model, 75
reflective diaries, 87
reflective journals, 81–82
reflective processes, 73
reflexivity, 74–76, 87
research
  action, 84, 90, 92, 103, 108, 114
  classroom-based, 40, 69, 72, 76, 92, 96
  ethnographic, 92, 96, 174
  methods, 70
  online, 166
  proposal, 70
  skills, 69
  teacher-led, 72, 81, 222
researchers
  classroom, 28
  teacher-, 92
resources, digital, 174
reverse psychology, 202

scaffolding, 152, 209
  graphic, 209
  interactive, 209
  linguistic, 209
  procedural, 209
  sensory, 209
self-determination, 10, 29, 45–46

self-esteem, 37
self-image, 37
self-observation, 84
self-reflective narratives, 84
semiotic modes, 163–164
skills, 10–11
  descriptors, 16, 47
  digital, 178
  language, 14
  pedagogical, 52
  productive, 14
  professional, 54
  receptive, 14
social capital, 210–211
  bonding, 211
  bridging, 211
  linking, 211
sociocultural process, 208
sociocultural theory, 99, 209
standards
  educational, 6, 14
  ethical, 29
  for teacher education, 1, 7, 50
  professional, 16, 31–32
  professional teaching, 50
suitability for personalisation, 132
summative assessments, 20, 64
syllabus design, 66

talents, 9
task perception, 37
tasks, 48, 117
  approach, 145
  closed, 141
  collaborative, 197
  communicative, 46, 142
  complex, 127, 143, 150–153
  complex competence, 150, 152
  convergent, 141
  design, 146, 148
  pedagogical, 145
  process, 145, 153

target, 145
typologies of, 140
teacher, professional, 208
teacher development stages, 51
teacher education, 2–3, 5–8, 13, 43, 59, 62
  English language, 5, 7
  programmes, 5, 7, 12, 22, 44, 67–68, 100, 110, 115
teacher educators, 5, 10, 52
teacher efficacy, 29
teacher identity, 37
teacher journals, 81
teacher mentors, 204–205
teacher professionalism, 1–4, 27–31, 34, 36, 40–41
  attitudinal, 27
  behavioural, 27
  intellectual, 27
teacher training, 43
teacherpreneurs, 190, 202
teachers
  autonomous, 105
  professional, 29, 33–35, 80, 233–234
teaching
  co-, 35, 86, 114
  peer, 114
  profession, 2, 5
technology enhanced language
    learning, 158
texts, 12, 130–136
  selection of, 12
theories, subjective, 7

values, 3
  ethical, 2
  shared, 2
variety, 132–133
  target language, 59

willingness, 100, 102

zone of proximal development, 131, 209

For EU product safety concerns, contact us at Calle de José Abascal, 56–1°,
28003 Madrid, Spain or eugpsr@cambridge.org.